空
知

Hideaki Sorachi (signature)

Man...I wish I could, you know, write something more...cool.

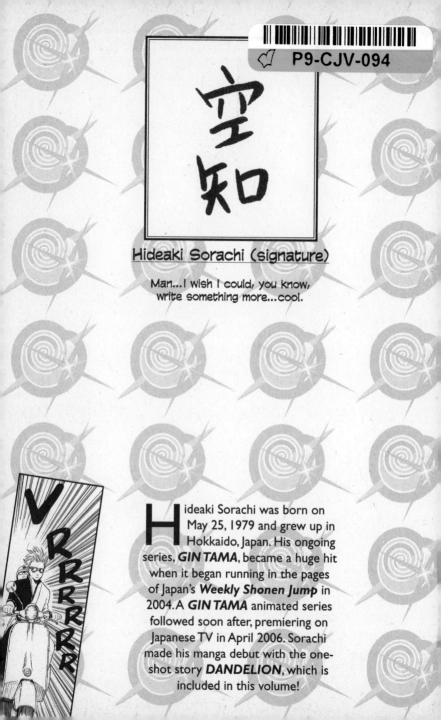

Hideaki Sorachi was born on May 25, 1979 and grew up in Hokkaido, Japan. His ongoing series, *GIN TAMA*, became a huge hit when it began running in the pages of Japan's *Weekly Shonen Jump* in 2004. A *GIN TAMA* animated series followed soon after, premiering on Japanese TV in April 2006. Sorachi made his manga debut with the one-shot story *DANDELION*, which is included in this volume!

P9-CJV-094

GIN TAMA VOL. 6
The SHONEN JUMP ADVANCED Manga Edition

STORY & ART BY HIDEAKI SORACHI

Translation/Matthew Rosin, Honyaku Center Inc.
English Adaptation/Gerard Jones
Touch-up Art & Lettering/Avril Averill
Cover Design/Sean Lee
Interior Design/Aaron Cruse
Editor/Mike Montesa

Editor in Chief, Books/Alvin Lu
Editor in Chief, Magazines/Marc Weidenbaum
VP of Publishing Licensing/Rika Inouye
VP of Sales/Gonzalo Ferreyra
Sr. VP of Marketing/Liza Coppola
Publisher/Hyoe Narita

GINTAMA © 2003 by Hideaki Sorachi. All rights reserved. First published in Japan in 2003 by SHUEISHA Inc., Tokyo. English translation rights arranged by SHUEISHA Inc. The stories, characters and incidents mentioned in this publication are entirely fictional.

No portion of this book may be reproduced or transmitted in any form or by any means without written permission from the copyright holders.

Printed in the U.S.A.

Published by VIZ Media, LLC
P.O. Box 77010
San Francisco, CA 94107

SHONEN JUMP ADVANCED Manga Edition
10 9 8 7 6 5 4 3 2 1
First printing, May 2008

PARENTAL ADVISORY
GIN TAMA is rated T+ for Older Teen and is recommended for ages 16 and up. It contains suggestive situations.
ratings.viz.com

www.viz.com

THE WORLD'S MOST CUTTING-EDGE MANGA
SHONEN JUMP ADVANCED
www.shonenjump.com

STORY & ART BY
HIDEAKI SORACHI

GIN TAMA

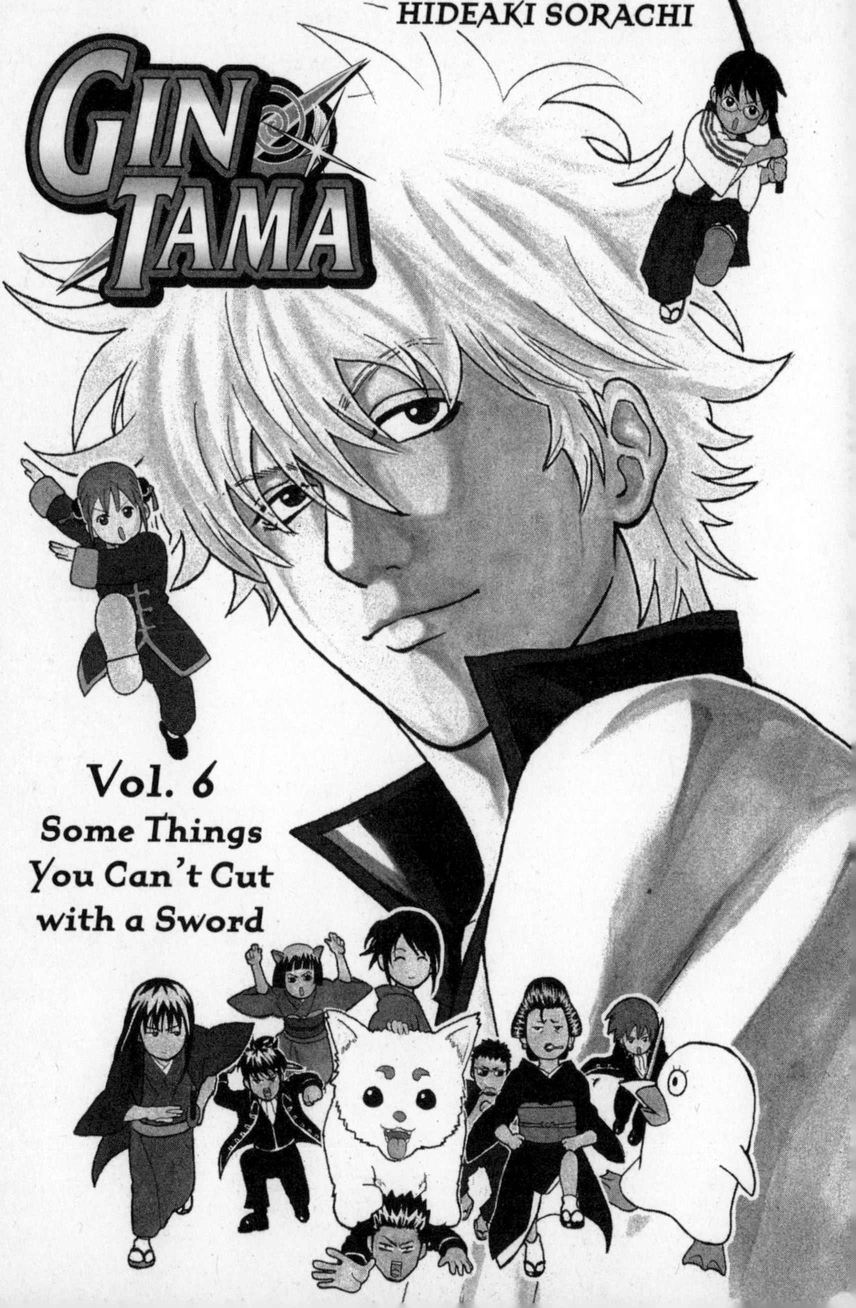

Vol. 6
Some Things You Can't Cut with a Sword

Cast of Characters

Yorozuya Members

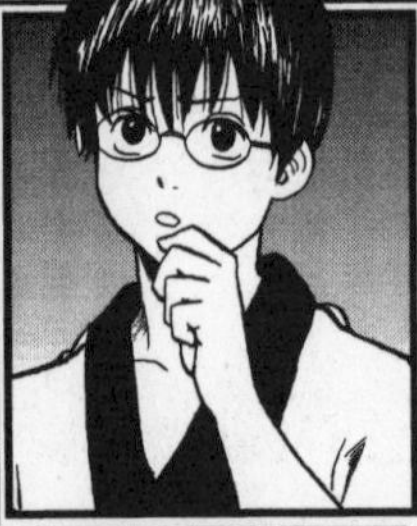

Shinpachi Shimura

Works under Gintoki in an attempt to learn about the samurai spirit, but has been regretting his decision recently. Also president of idol singer Tsu Terakado's fan club.

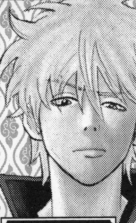

Gintoki Sakata

The hero of our story. He needs to eat something sweet periodically or he gets cranky. He commands a powerful sword arm but is one step away from diabetes. A former member of the exclusionist faction which seeks to eliminate the space aliens and protect the nation.

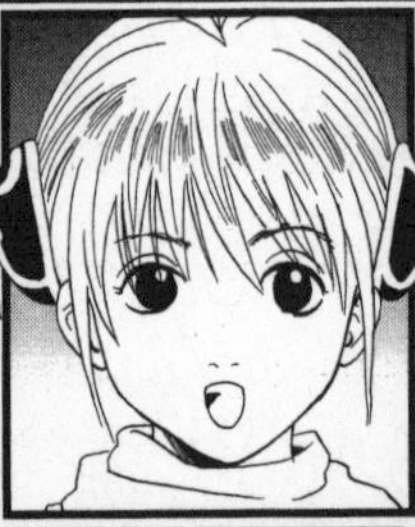

Kagura

A member of the "Yato Clan," the most powerful warrior race in the universe. Her voracious appetite and often inadvertent comic timing are unrivalled.

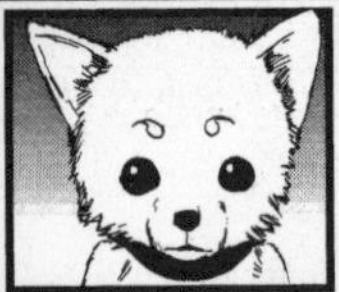

Sadaharu/animal

A giant space creature kept as a pet in the Yorozuya office. Likes to bite people (especially Gintoki).

Shinsengumi Soldiers

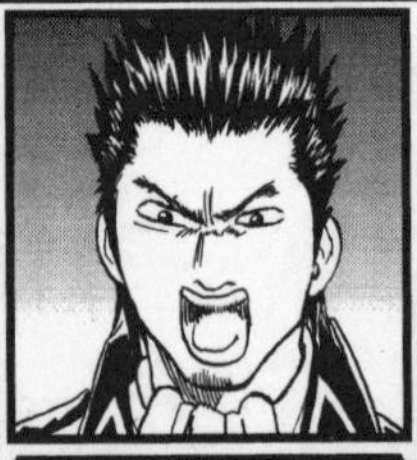

Kondo

Chief of the Shinsengumi, and trusted by all its soldiers. Also stalking Shinpachi's elder sister Otae.

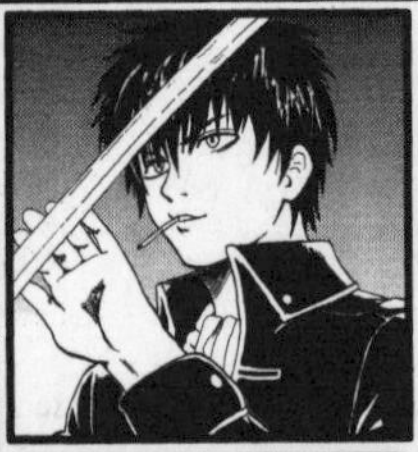

Hijikata

Vice-Chief of the Shinsengumi, Edo's elite Delta Force police unit. His cool demeanor turns to rage the moment he draws his sword. The pupils of his eyes always seem a bit dilated.

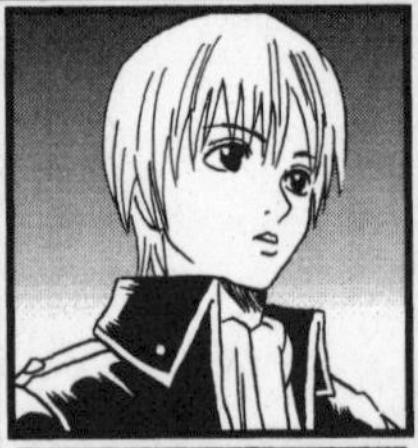

Okita

The most formidable swordsman in the Shinsengumi. His jovial attitude hides an utterly black heart. He wants to take over as the Vice-Chief.

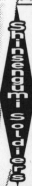

Other Characters

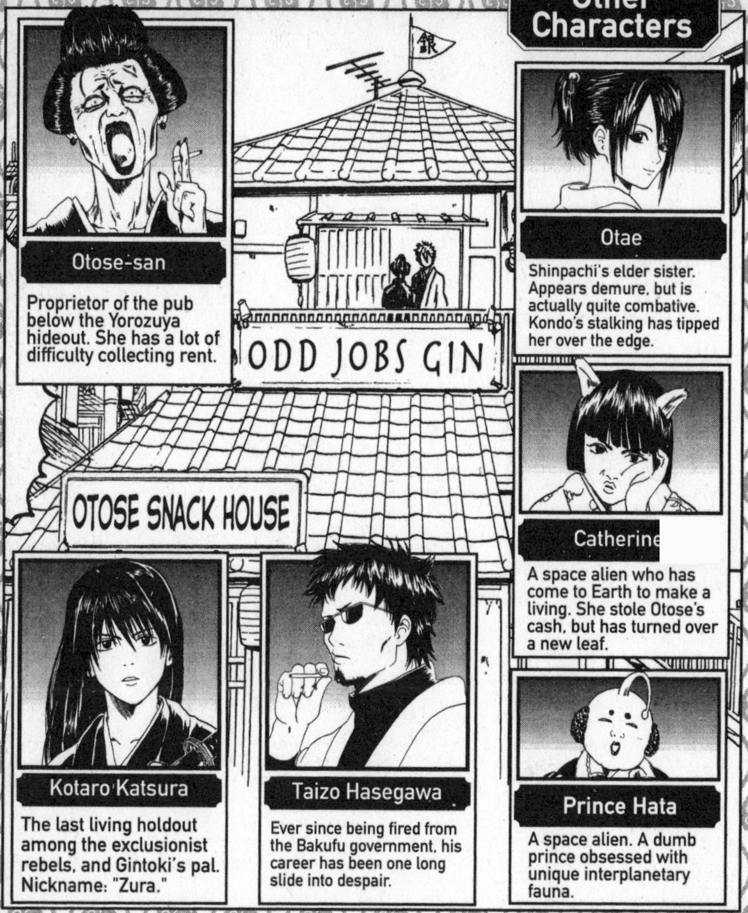

ODD JOBS GIN
OTOSE SNACK HOUSE

Otose-san

Proprietor of the pub below the Yorozuya hideout. She has a lot of difficulty collecting rent.

Otae

Shinpachi's elder sister. Appears demure, but is actually quite combative. Kondo's stalking has tipped her over the edge.

Catherine

A space alien who has come to Earth to make a living. She stole Otose's cash, but has turned over a new leaf.

Kotaro Katsura

The last living holdout among the exclusionist rebels, and Gintoki's pal. Nickname: "Zura."

Taizo Hasegawa

Ever since being fired from the Bakufu government, his career has been one long slide into despair.

Prince Hata

A space alien. A dumb prince obsessed with unique interplanetary fauna.

The

In an alternate-universe Edo (Tokyo), extraterrestrials land in Japan and the new government issues an order outlawing swords. The samurai, who have reached the pinnacle of power and prosperity, fall into rapid decline.

Twenty years hence, only one samurai has managed to hold onto his fighting spirit: a somewhat eccentric fellow named Gintoki "Odd Jobs Gin" Sakata. A lover of sweets and near diabetic, our hero sets up shop as a *yorozuya*—an expert at managing trouble and handling the oddest jobs.

Joining "Gin" in his business is Shinpachi Shimura, whose sister Gin saved from the clutches of nefarious debt collectors. After a series of unexpected circumstances, the trio meet a powerful alien named Kagura, who becomes—after some arm-twisting—a part-time team member.

Lured by the promise of a reward for ridding the beach of a sea monster, the Yorozuya get more than they bargained for as they find themselves mixed up in a real ghost story at Shinsengumi Headquarters. Later, Gin and his pals are chased by a sword-collecting Amanto and fight it out with a biker gang—before somehow getting forced to work at a drag queen cabaret! What else can go wrong?!

WHAT THIS MANGA'S FULL OF
vol. 6

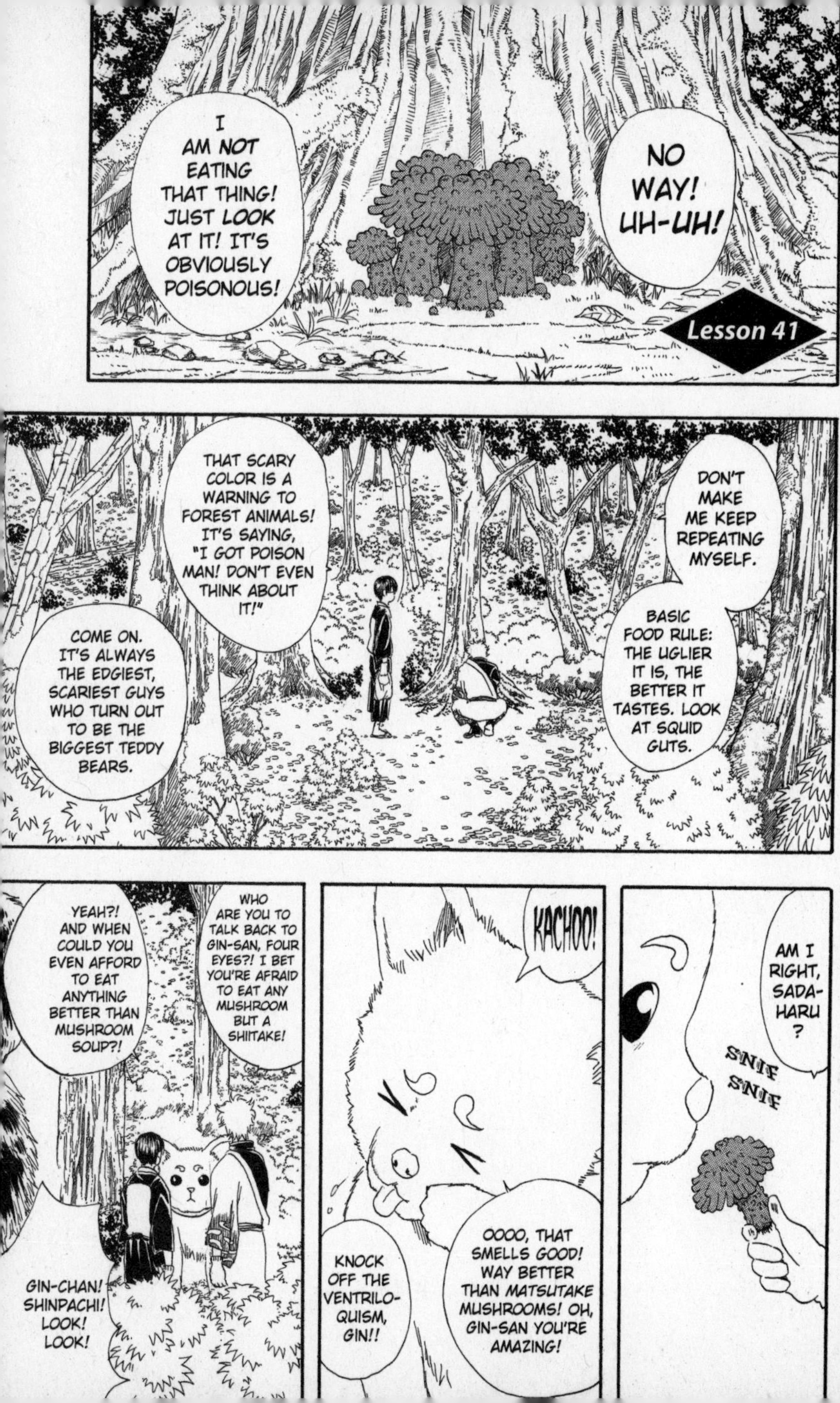
NO WAY! UH-UH!
I AM NOT EATING THAT THING! JUST LOOK AT IT! IT'S OBVIOUSLY POISONOUS!
Lesson 41
DON'T MAKE ME KEEP REPEATING MYSELF.
BASIC FOOD RULE: THE UGLIER IT IS, THE BETTER IT TASTES. LOOK AT SQUID GUTS.
THAT SCARY COLOR IS A WARNING TO FOREST ANIMALS! IT'S SAYING, "I GOT POISON MAN! DON'T EVEN THINK ABOUT IT!"
COME ON. IT'S ALWAYS THE EDGIEST, SCARIEST GUYS WHO TURN OUT TO BE THE BIGGEST TEDDY BEARS.
AM I RIGHT, SADAHARU?
SNIF SNIF
KACHOO!
OOOO, THAT SMELLS GOOD! WAY BETTER THAN MATSUTAKE MUSHROOMS! OH, GIN-SAN YOU'RE AMAZING!
KNOCK OFF THE VENTRILOQUISM, GIN!!
WHO ARE YOU TO TALK BACK TO GIN-SAN, FOUR EYES?! I BET YOU'RE AFRAID TO EAT ANY MUSHROOM BUT A SHIITAKE!
YEAH?! AND WHEN COULD YOU EVEN AFFORD TO EAT ANYTHING BETTER THAN MUSHROOM SOUP?!
GIN-CHAN! SHINPACHI! LOOK! LOOK!

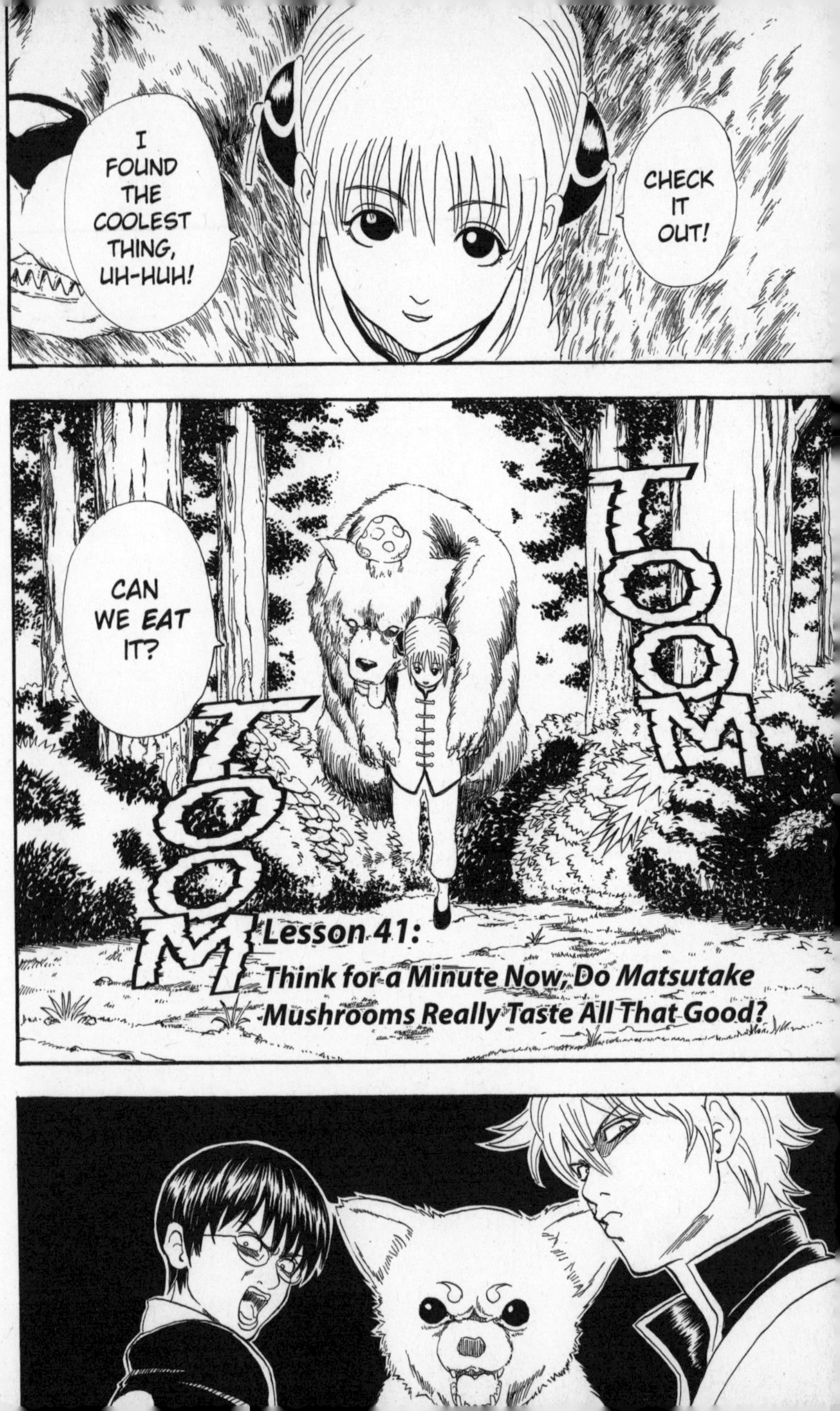
CHECK IT OUT!
I FOUND THE COOLEST THING, UH-HUH!
TOOOM
CAN WE EAT IT?
TOOOM
Lesson 41:
Think for a Minute Now, Do Matsutake Mushrooms Really Taste All That Good?

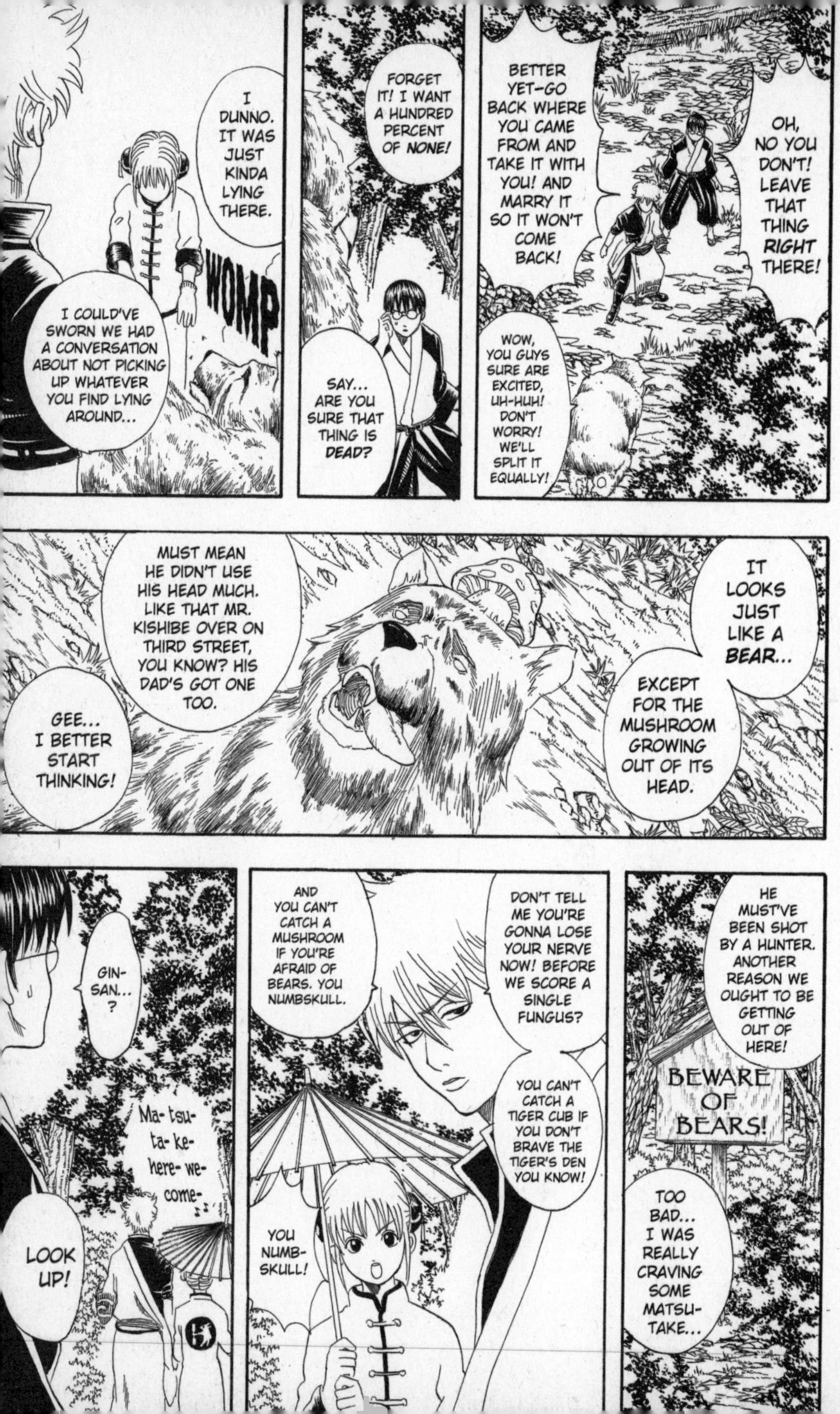

OH, NO YOU DON'T! LEAVE THAT THING RIGHT THERE!
BETTER YET–GO BACK WHERE YOU CAME FROM AND TAKE IT WITH YOU! AND MARRY IT SO IT WON'T COME BACK!
WOW, YOU GUYS SURE ARE EXCITED, UH-HUH! DON'T WORRY! WE'LL SPLIT IT EQUALLY!
FORGET IT! I WANT A HUNDRED PERCENT OF NONE!
SAY... ARE YOU SURE THAT THING IS DEAD?
I DUNNO. IT WAS JUST KINDA LYING THERE.
WOMP
I COULD'VE SWORN WE HAD A CONVERSATION ABOUT NOT PICKING UP WHATEVER YOU FIND LYING AROUND...
IT LOOKS JUST LIKE A BEAR...
EXCEPT FOR THE MUSHROOM GROWING OUT OF ITS HEAD.
MUST MEAN HE DIDN'T USE HIS HEAD MUCH. LIKE THAT MR. KISHIBE OVER ON THIRD STREET, YOU KNOW? HIS DAD'S GOT ONE TOO.
GEE... I BETTER START THINKING!
HE MUST'VE BEEN SHOT BY A HUNTER. ANOTHER REASON WE OUGHT TO BE GETTING OUT OF HERE!
BEWARE OF BEARS!
TOO BAD... I WAS REALLY CRAVING SOME MATSU-TAKE...
DON'T TELL ME YOU'RE GONNA LOSE YOUR NERVE NOW! BEFORE WE SCORE A SINGLE FUNGUS?
YOU CAN'T CATCH A TIGER CUB IF YOU DON'T BRAVE THE TIGER'S DEN YOU KNOW!
AND YOU CAN'T CATCH A MUSHROOM IF YOU'RE AFRAID OF BEARS. YOU NUMBSKULL.
YOU NUMB-SKULL!
GIN-SAN...?
Ma-tsu-ta-ke-here-we-come-♪
LOOK UP!

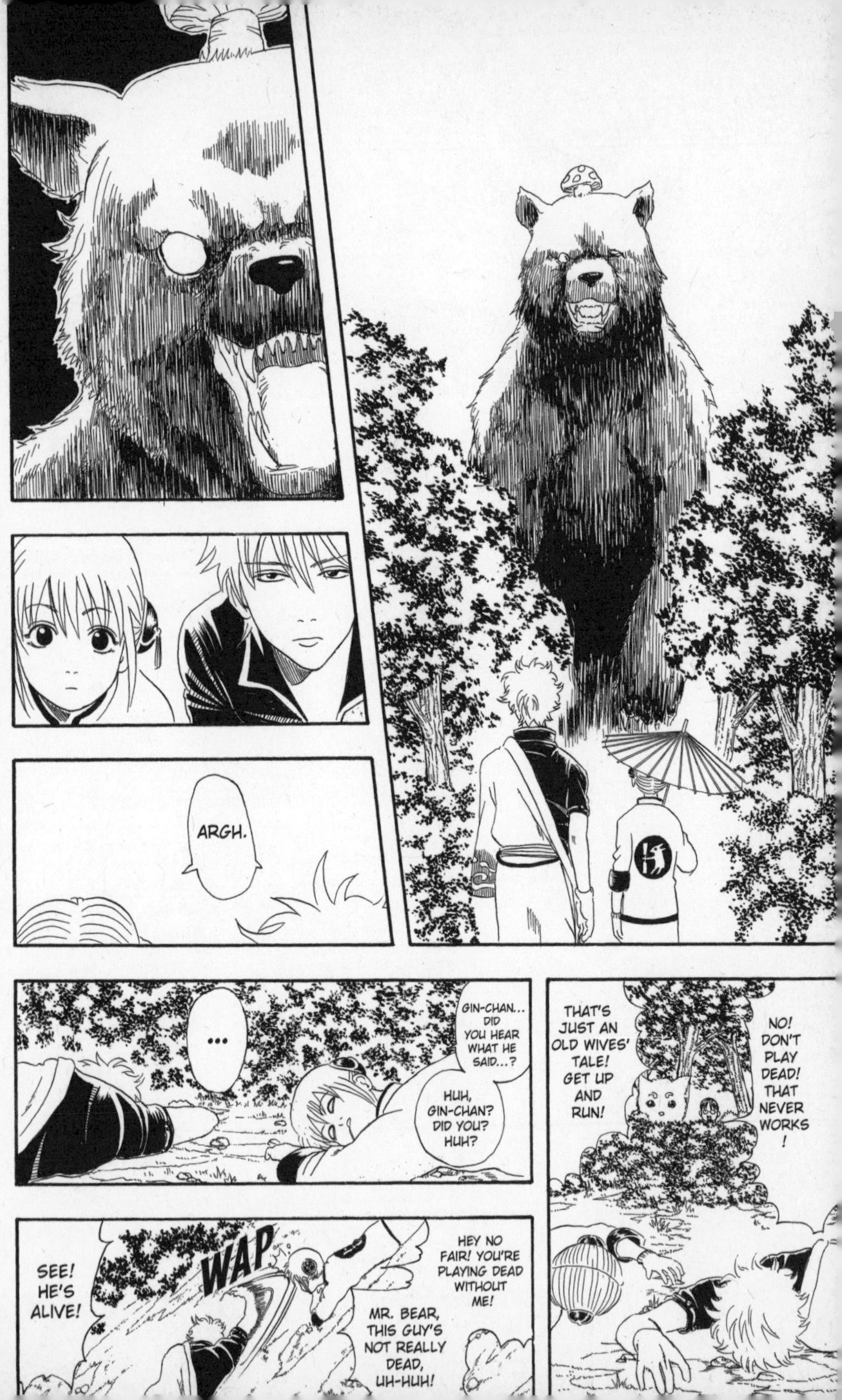
ARGH.
NO! DON'T PLAY DEAD! THAT NEVER WORKS!
THAT'S JUST AN OLD WIVES' TALE! GET UP AND RUN!
GIN-CHAN... DID YOU HEAR WHAT HE SAID...?
...
HUH, GIN-CHAN? DID YOU? HUH?
HEY NO FAIR! YOU'RE PLAYING DEAD WITHOUT ME!
MR. BEAR, THIS GUY'S NOT REALLY DEAD, UH-HUH!
WAP
SEE! HE'S ALIVE!

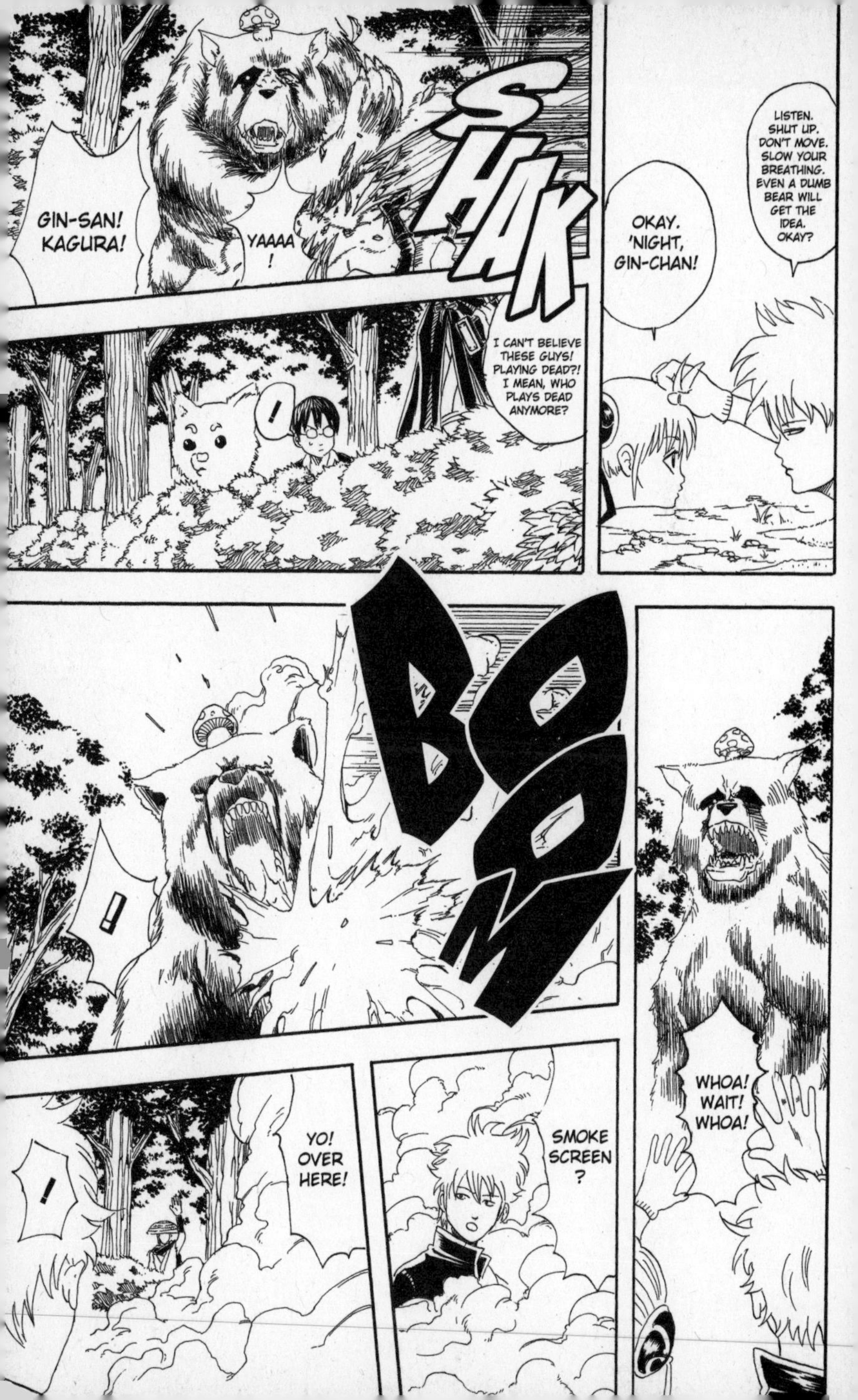
LISTEN. SHUT UP. DON'T MOVE. SLOW YOUR BREATHING. EVEN A DUMB BEAR WILL GET THE IDEA. OKAY?
OKAY. 'NIGHT, GIN-CHAN!
SHAK
YAAAA!
GIN-SAN! KAGURA!
I CAN'T BELIEVE THESE GUYS! PLAYING DEAD?! I MEAN, WHO PLAYS DEAD ANYMORE?
!
WHOA! WAIT! WHOA!
BOOM
!
SMOKE SCREEN?
YO! OVER HERE!
!

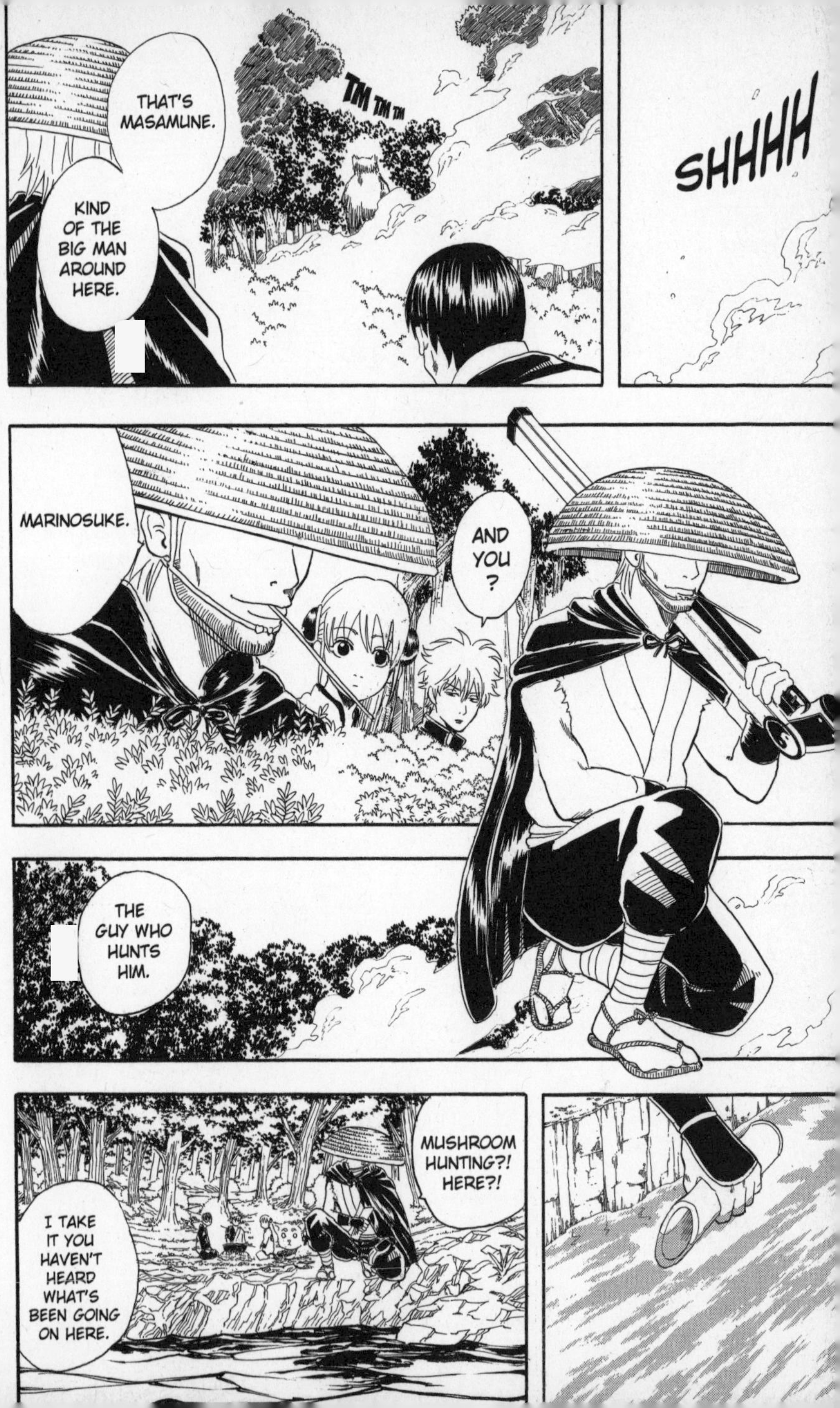
SHHHH
TM TM TM
THAT'S MASAMUNE.
KIND OF THE BIG MAN AROUND HERE.
AND YOU?
MARINOSUKE.
THE GUY WHO HUNTS HIM.
MUSHROOM HUNTING?! HERE?!
I TAKE IT YOU HAVEN'T HEARD WHAT'S BEEN GOING ON HERE.

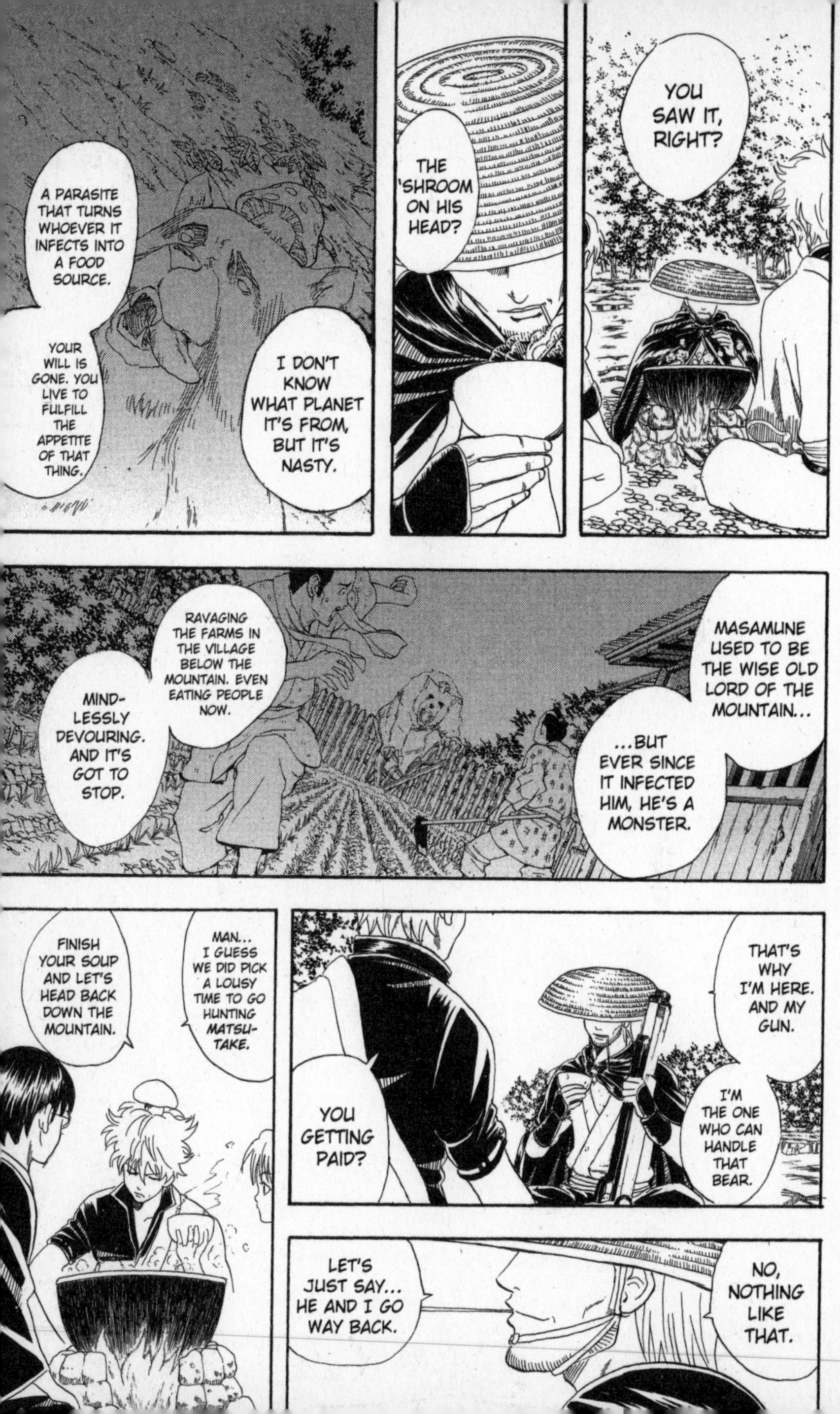
YOU SAW IT, RIGHT?
THE 'SHROOM ON HIS HEAD?
I DON'T KNOW WHAT PLANET IT'S FROM, BUT IT'S NASTY.
A PARASITE THAT TURNS WHOEVER IT INFECTS INTO A FOOD SOURCE.
YOUR WILL IS GONE. YOU LIVE TO FULFILL THE APPETITE OF THAT THING.
MASAMUNE USED TO BE THE WISE OLD LORD OF THE MOUNTAIN...
...BUT EVER SINCE IT INFECTED HIM, HE'S A MONSTER.
RAVAGING THE FARMS IN THE VILLAGE BELOW THE MOUNTAIN. EVEN EATING PEOPLE NOW.
MIND-LESSLY DEVOURING. AND IT'S GOT TO STOP.
THAT'S WHY I'M HERE. AND MY GUN.
I'M THE ONE WHO CAN HANDLE THAT BEAR.
YOU GETTING PAID?
NO, NOTHING LIKE THAT.
LET'S JUST SAY... HE AND I GO WAY BACK.
MAN... I GUESS WE DID PICK A LOUSY TIME TO GO HUNTING MATSU-TAKE.
FINISH YOUR SOUP AND LET'S HEAD BACK DOWN THE MOUNTAIN.

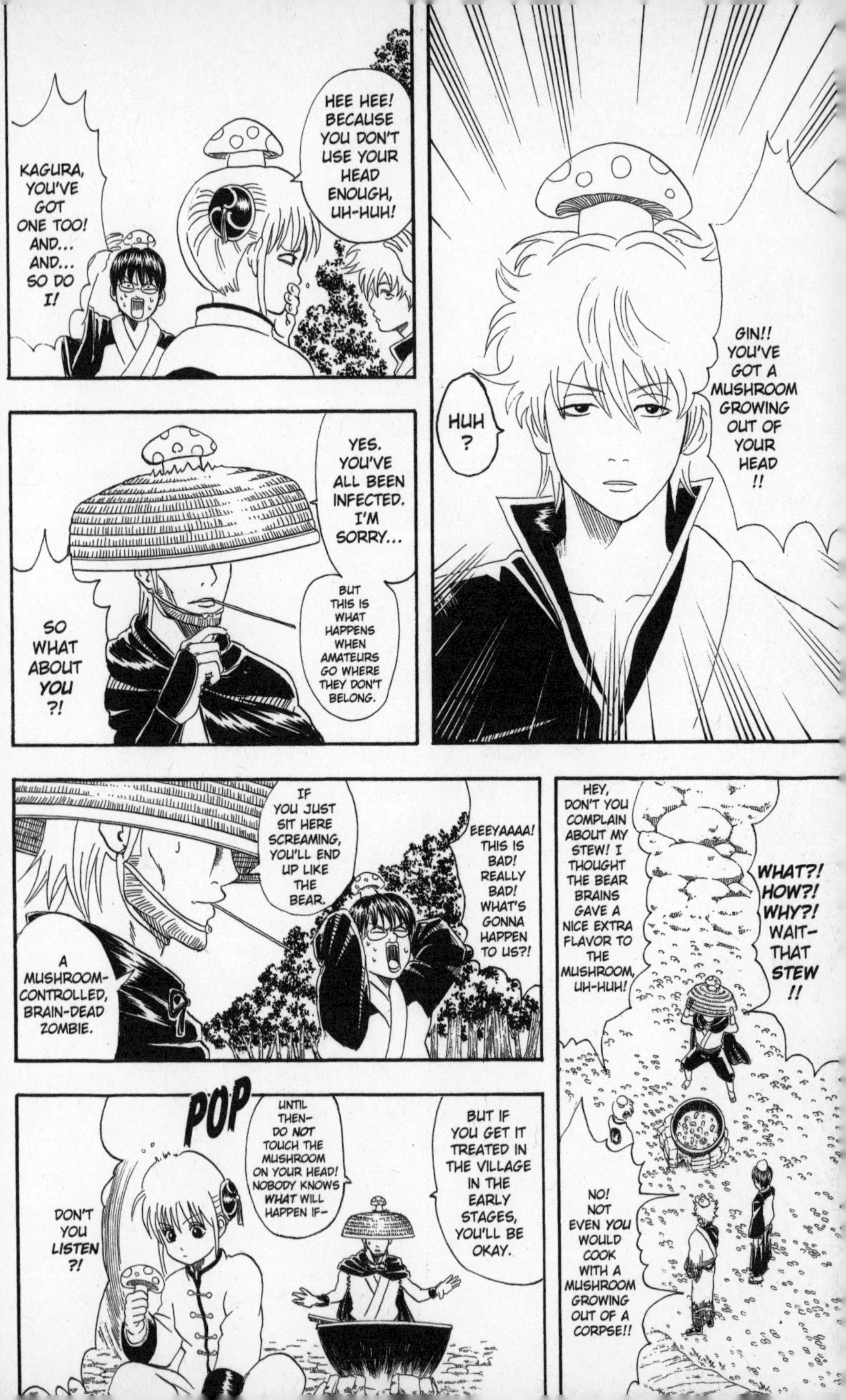
GIN!! YOU'VE GOT A MUSHROOM GROWING OUT OF YOUR HEAD!!
HUH?
HEE HEE! BECAUSE YOU DON'T USE YOUR HEAD ENOUGH, UH-HUH!
KAGURA, YOU'VE GOT ONE TOO! AND... AND... SO DO I!
YES. YOU'VE ALL BEEN INFECTED. I'M SORRY...
BUT THIS IS WHAT HAPPENS WHEN AMATEURS GO WHERE THEY DON'T BELONG.
SO WHAT ABOUT YOU?!
WHAT?! HOW?! WHY?! WAIT— THAT STEW!!
HEY, DON'T YOU COMPLAIN ABOUT MY STEW! I THOUGHT THE BEAR BRAINS GAVE A NICE EXTRA FLAVOR TO THE MUSHROOM, UH-HUH!
NO! NOT EVEN YOU WOULD COOK WITH A MUSHROOM GROWING OUT OF A CORPSE!!
EEEYAAAA! THIS IS BAD! REALLY BAD! WHAT'S GONNA HAPPEN TO US?!
IF YOU JUST SIT HERE SCREAMING, YOU'LL END UP LIKE THE BEAR.
A MUSHROOM-CONTROLLED, BRAIN-DEAD ZOMBIE.
BUT IF YOU GET IT TREATED IN THE VILLAGE IN THE EARLY STAGES, YOU'LL BE OKAY.
UNTIL THEN— DO NOT TOUCH THE MUSHROOM ON YOUR HEAD! NOBODY KNOWS WHAT WILL HAPPEN IF—
POP
DON'T YOU LISTEN?!

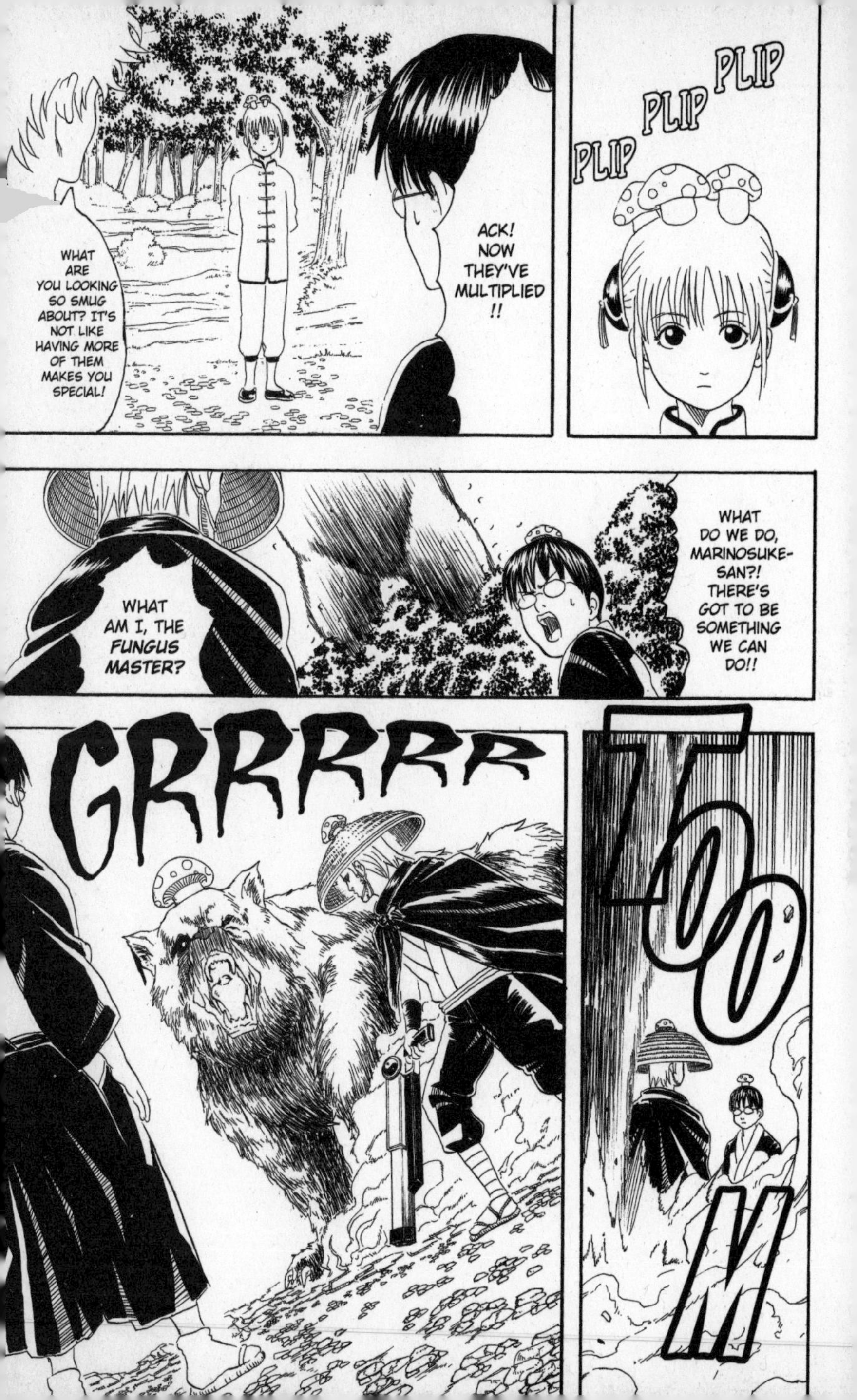
PLIP
PLIP
PLIP
ACK! NOW THEY'VE MULTIPLIED !!
WHAT ARE YOU LOOKING SO SMUG ABOUT? IT'S NOT LIKE HAVING MORE OF THEM MAKES YOU SPECIAL!
WHAT DO WE DO, MARINOSUKE-SAN?! THERE'S GOT TO BE SOMETHING WE CAN DO!!
WHAT AM I, THE FUNGUS MASTER?
TOOOM
GRRRRRR

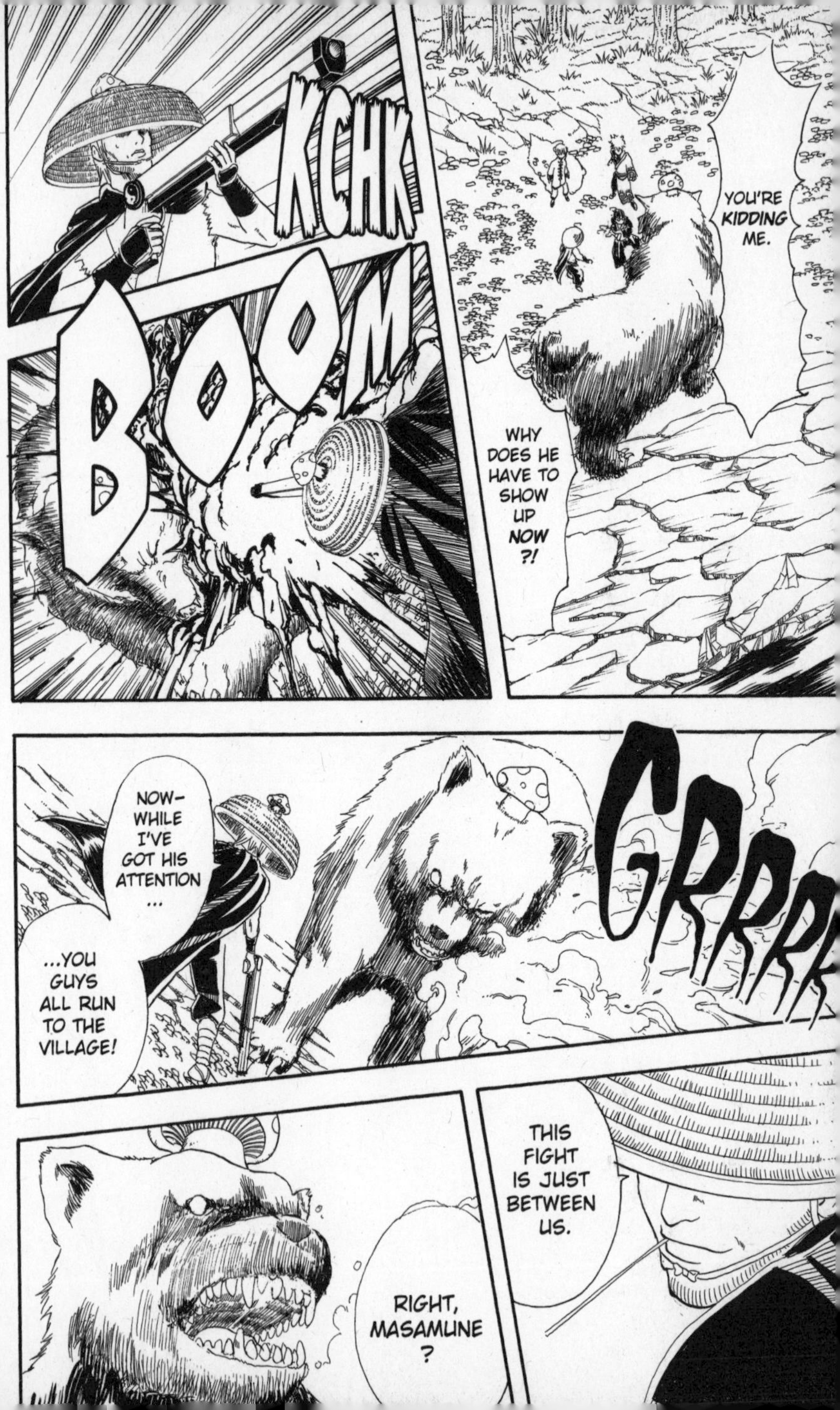
YOU'RE KIDDING ME.
WHY DOES HE HAVE TO SHOW UP NOW?!
KCHK
BOOM
GRRRR
NOW-WHILE I'VE GOT HIS ATTENTION...
...YOU GUYS ALL RUN TO THE VILLAGE!
THIS FIGHT IS JUST BETWEEN US.
RIGHT, MASAMUNE?

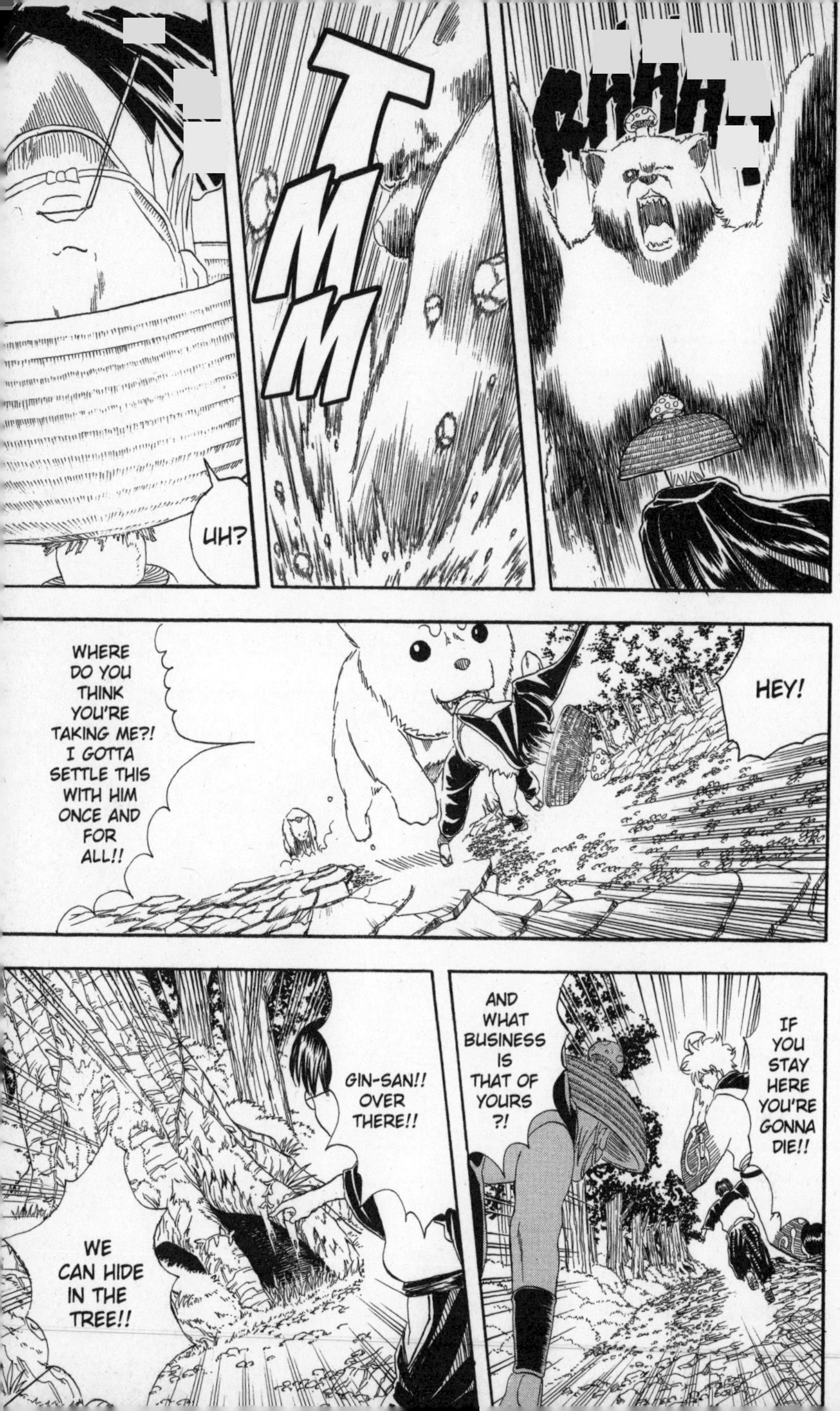
TMM
UH?
HEY!
WHERE DO YOU THINK YOU'RE TAKING ME?! I GOTTA SETTLE THIS WITH HIM ONCE AND FOR ALL!!
IF YOU STAY HERE YOU'RE GONNA DIE!!
AND WHAT BUSINESS IS THAT OF YOURS?!
GIN-SAN!! OVER THERE!!
WE CAN HIDE IN THE TREE!!

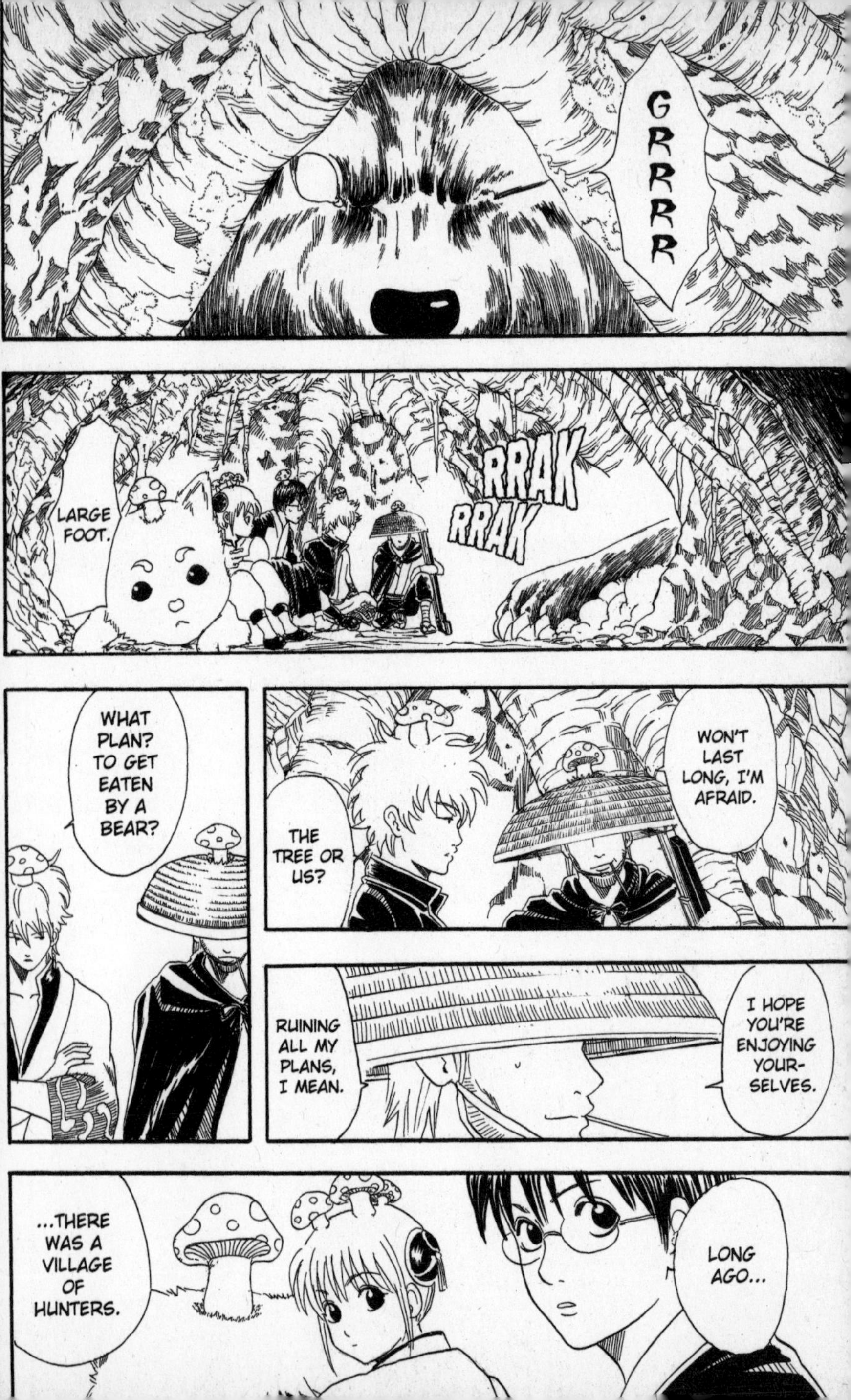
GRRRR
RRAK RRAK
LARGE FOOT.
WON'T LAST LONG, I'M AFRAID.
THE TREE OR US?
I HOPE YOU'RE ENJOYING YOUR-SELVES.
RUINING ALL MY PLANS, I MEAN.
WHAT PLAN? TO GET EATEN BY A BEAR?
LONG AGO...
...THERE WAS A VILLAGE OF HUNTERS.

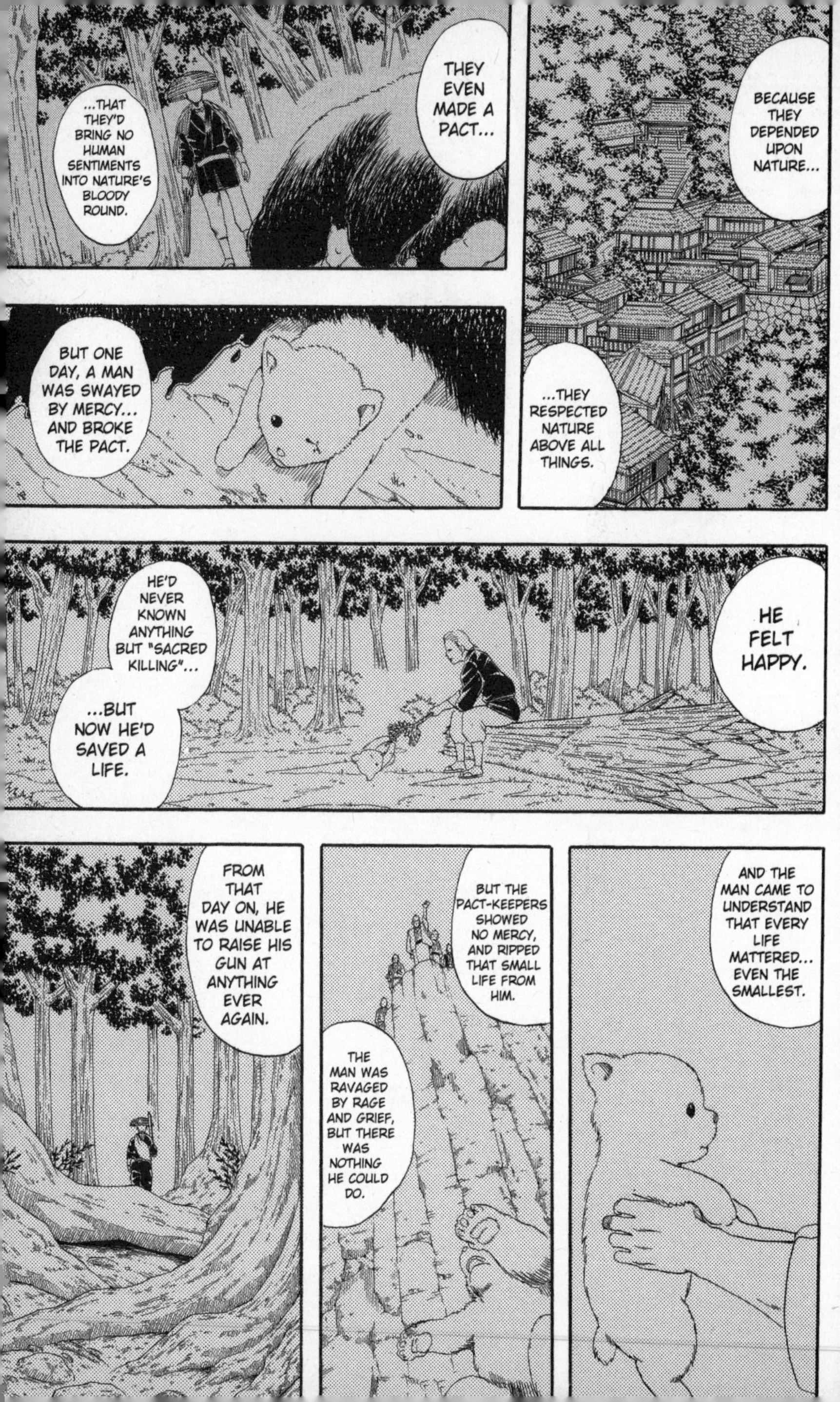
BECAUSE THEY DEPENDED UPON NATURE...
...THEY RESPECTED NATURE ABOVE ALL THINGS.
THEY EVEN MADE A PACT...
...THAT THEY'D BRING NO HUMAN SENTIMENTS INTO NATURE'S BLOODY ROUND.
BUT ONE DAY, A MAN WAS SWAYED BY MERCY... AND BROKE THE PACT.
HE'D NEVER KNOWN ANYTHING BUT "SACRED KILLING"...
...BUT NOW HE'D SAVED A LIFE.
HE FELT HAPPY.
AND THE MAN CAME TO UNDERSTAND THAT EVERY LIFE MATTERED... EVEN THE SMALLEST.
BUT THE PACT-KEEPERS SHOWED NO MERCY, AND RIPPED THAT SMALL LIFE FROM HIM.
THE MAN WAS RAVAGED BY RAGE AND GRIEF, BUT THERE WAS NOTHING HE COULD DO.
FROM THAT DAY ON, HE WAS UNABLE TO RAISE HIS GUN AT ANYTHING EVER AGAIN.

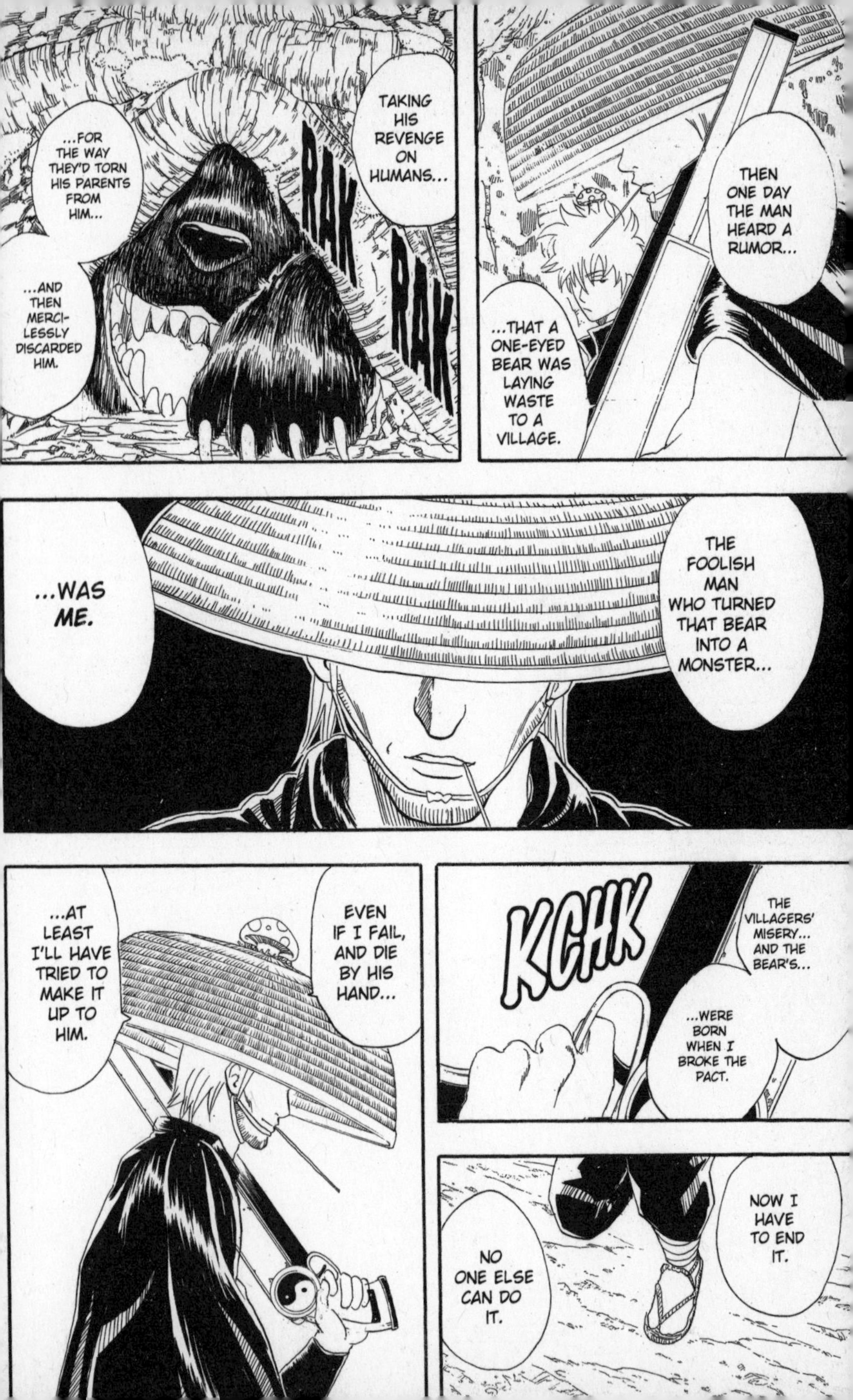
THEN ONE DAY THE MAN HEARD A RUMOR...
...THAT A ONE-EYED BEAR WAS LAYING WASTE TO A VILLAGE.
TAKING HIS REVENGE ON HUMANS...
RAK RAK
...FOR THE WAY THEY'D TORN HIS PARENTS FROM HIM...
...AND THEN MERCILESSLY DISCARDED HIM.
THE FOOLISH MAN WHO TURNED THAT BEAR INTO A MONSTER...
...WAS ME.
THE VILLAGERS' MISERY... AND THE BEAR'S...
...WERE BORN WHEN I BROKE THE PACT.
KCHK
NOW I HAVE TO END IT.
NO ONE ELSE CAN DO IT.
EVEN IF I FAIL, AND DIE BY HIS HAND...
...AT LEAST I'LL HAVE TRIED TO MAKE IT UP TO HIM.

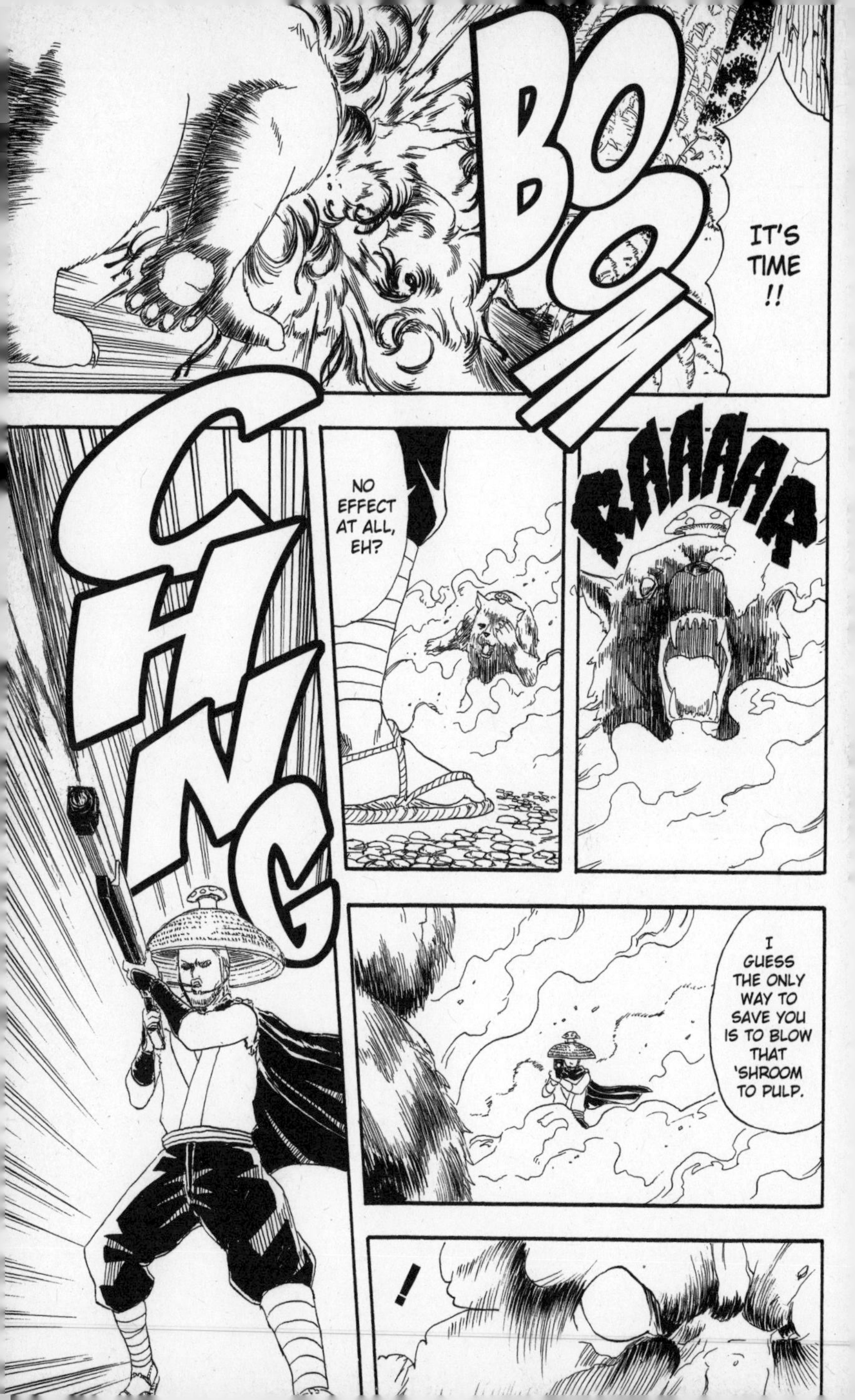
BOOM
IT'S TIME!!
RAAAAR
NO EFFECT AT ALL, EH?
I GUESS THE ONLY WAY TO SAVE YOU IS TO BLOW THAT 'SHROOM TO PULP.
!
CHING

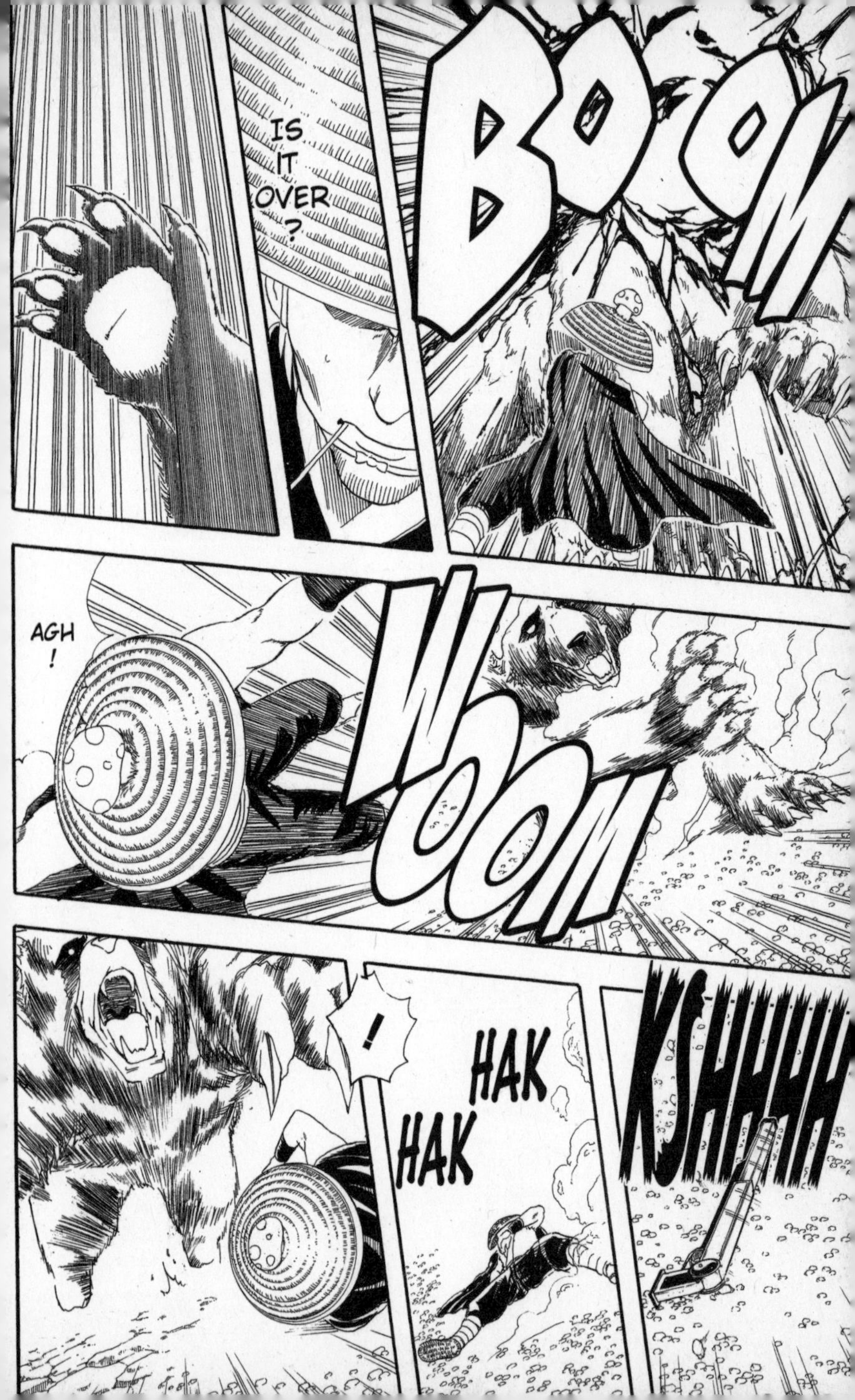
BOOM
IS IT OVER?
WHOOM
AGH!
KSHHHH
HAK HAK
!

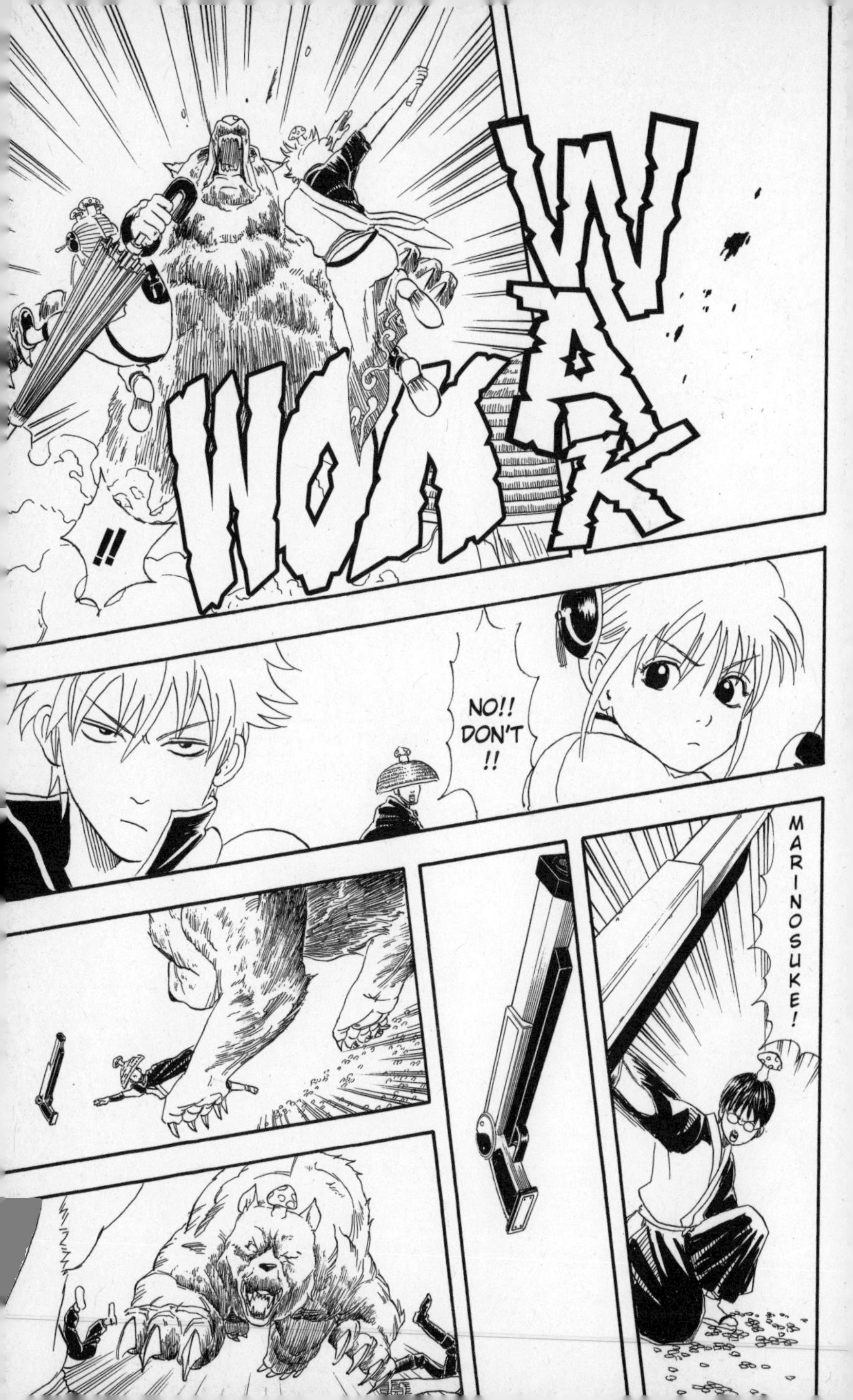
WARK
WO
!!
NO!! DON'T !!
MARINOSUKE!

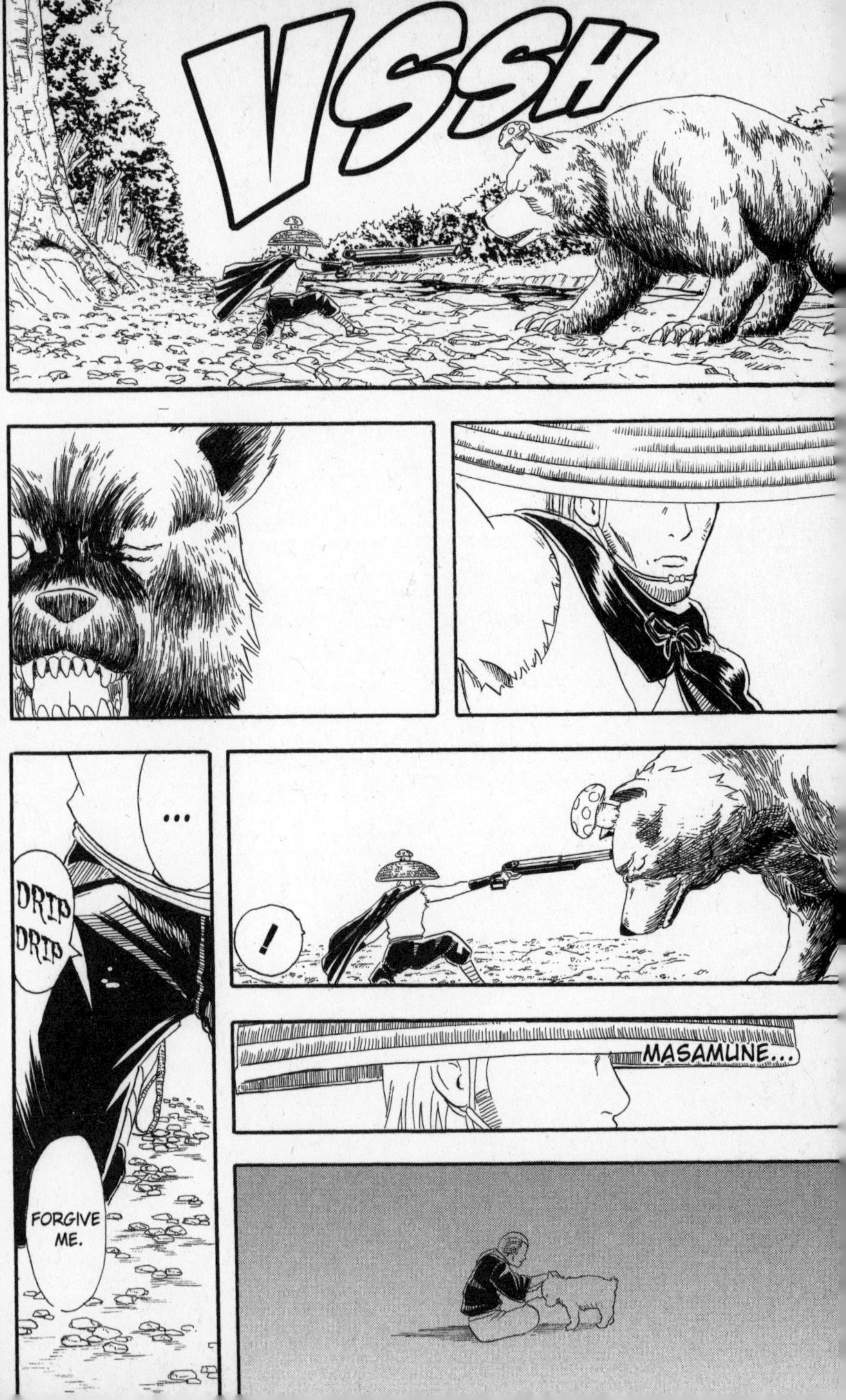
VSSH
!
MASAMUNE...
...
DRIP DRIP
FORGIVE ME.

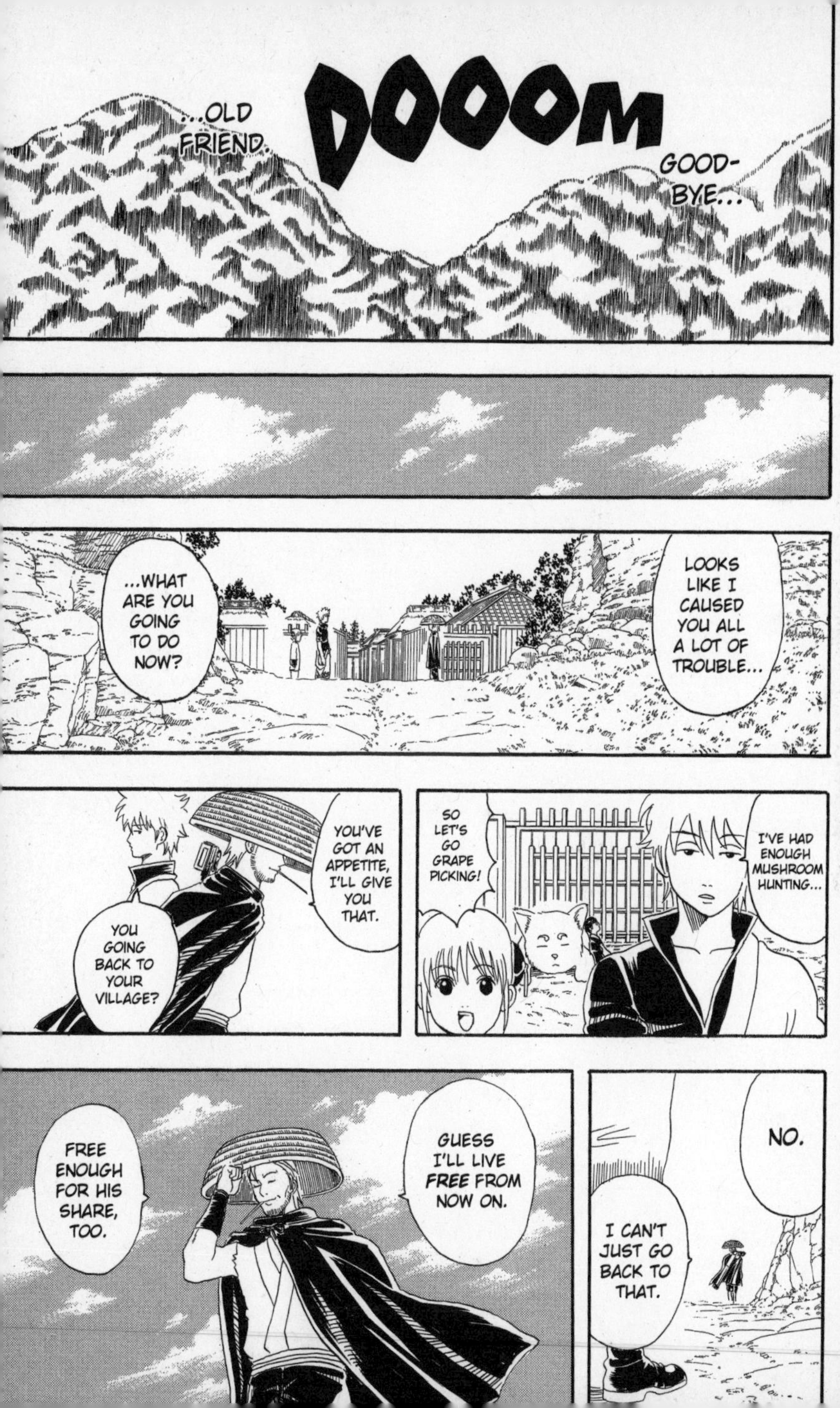
GOOD-BYE...
DOOOM
...OLD FRIEND.
LOOKS LIKE I CAUSED YOU ALL A LOT OF TROUBLE...
...WHAT ARE YOU GOING TO DO NOW?
I'VE HAD ENOUGH MUSHROOM HUNTING...
SO LET'S GO GRAPE PICKING!
YOU'VE GOT AN APPETITE, I'LL GIVE YOU THAT.
YOU GOING BACK TO YOUR VILLAGE?
NO.
I CAN'T JUST GO BACK TO THAT.
GUESS I'LL LIVE FREE FROM NOW ON.
FREE ENOUGH FOR HIS SHARE, TOO.

Yo! Sorachi here! Thanks a load for reading Gin Tama volume 6 and supporting this project for a whole year! I originally got into this project just when the Shinsengumi *Taiga* series was booming, but now I hear it's about to end—so I'm going to have to stand on my own feet now. I've always been obsessed with the Shinsengumi, so it's gonna be a blow to lose it, both professionally and personally. Thanks for everything, Shinsengumi!

But honestly, I'm so sick of riding on somebody else's success, it'll be good to start the year off fresh. Kinda like, I'm gonna do it my way, see how far I can go or how bad I fall, you know?

My editor? Who's that? Oh, you mean that little monkey lying dead on the side of the road? It just jumped out into the middle of the road and I hit it. That's kind of the way I feel about this first year...I want to do something new, something...how to explain it...kind of elegant, you know? Kind of Heian Period. Or Kamakura. Something like...Benkei! Or Ushiwakamaru! Or...damn. Suddenly I'm back to the hit *Taiga* series...

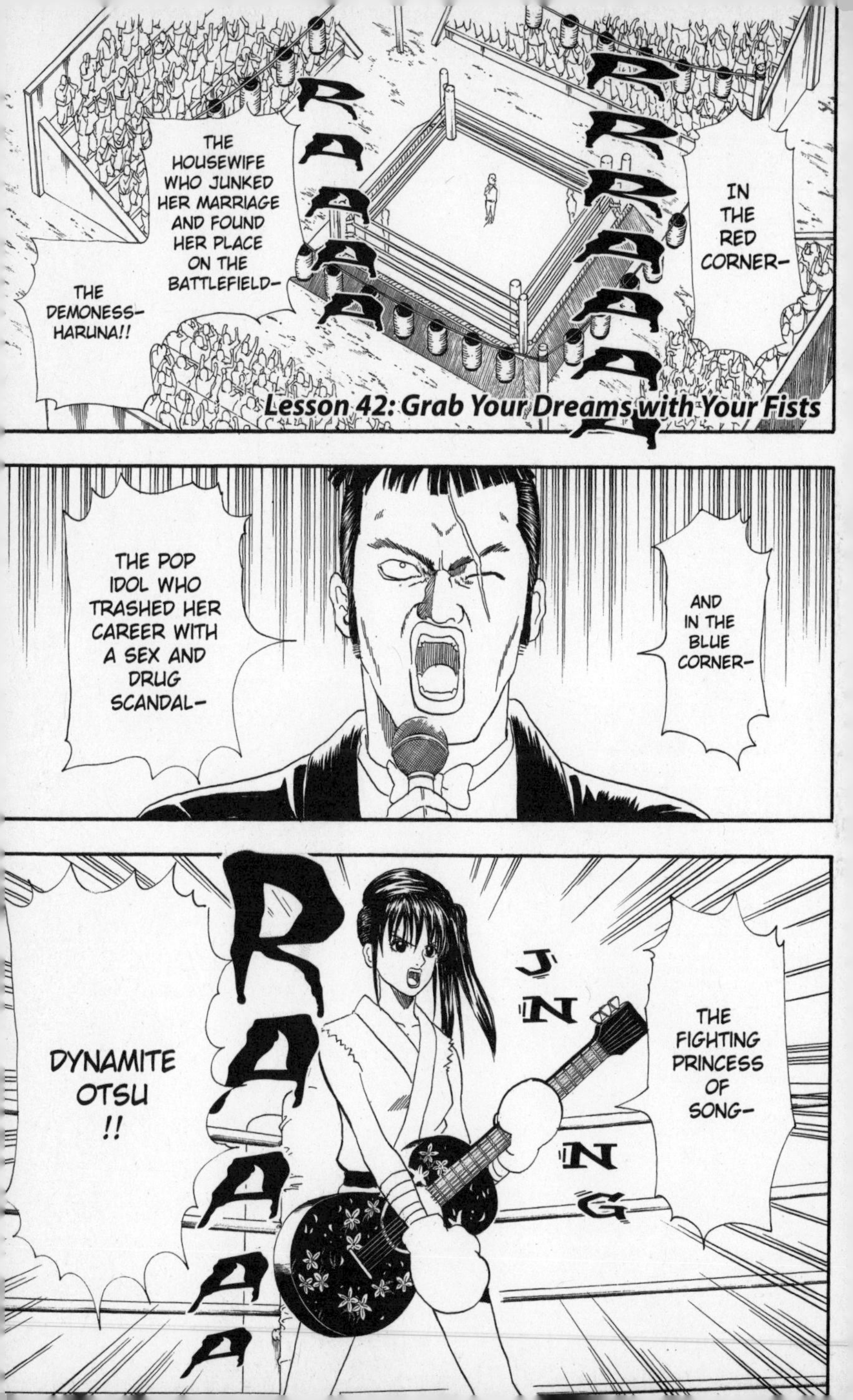
RRAAAA
IN THE RED CORNER-
THE HOUSEWIFE WHO JUNKED HER MARRIAGE AND FOUND HER PLACE ON THE BATTLEFIELD-
THE DEMONESS-HARUNA!!
RAAAA
Lesson 42: Grab Your Dreams with Your Fists
AND IN THE BLUE CORNER-
THE POP IDOL WHO TRASHED HER CAREER WITH A SEX AND DRUG SCANDAL-
THE FIGHTING PRINCESS OF SONG-
JN
NG
DYNAMITE OTSU !!
RAAAAA

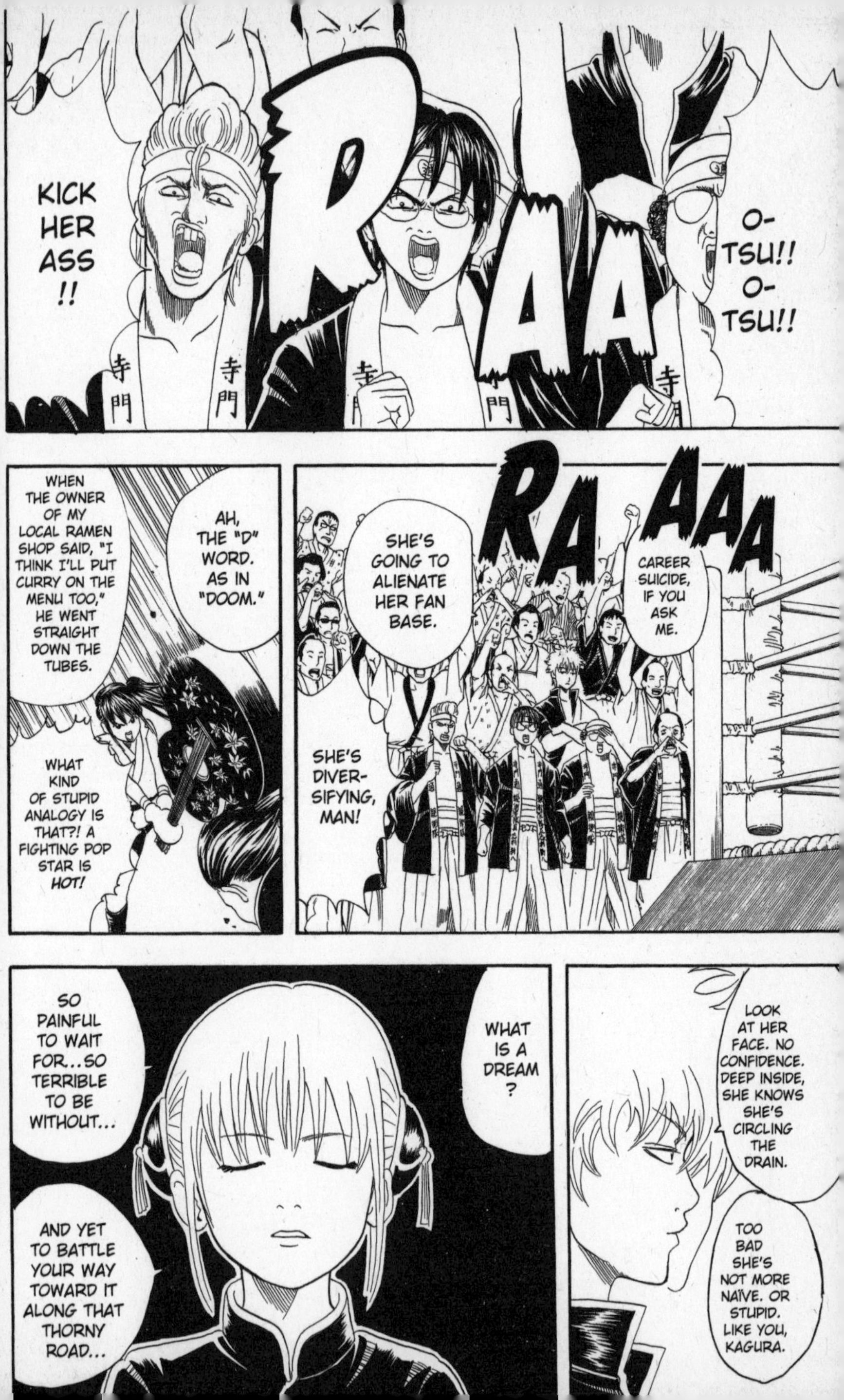
O-TSU!! O-TSU!!
RAA
KICK HER ASS!!
RAAAA
CAREER SUICIDE, IF YOU ASK ME.
SHE'S GOING TO ALIENATE HER FAN BASE.
SHE'S DIVERSIFYING, MAN!
AH, THE "D" WORD. AS IN "DOOM."
WHEN THE OWNER OF MY LOCAL RAMEN SHOP SAID, "I THINK I'LL PUT CURRY ON THE MENU TOO," HE WENT STRAIGHT DOWN THE TUBES.
WHAT KIND OF STUPID ANALOGY IS THAT?! A FIGHTING POP STAR IS HOT!
LOOK AT HER FACE. NO CONFIDENCE. DEEP INSIDE, SHE KNOWS SHE'S CIRCLING THE DRAIN.
TOO BAD SHE'S NOT MORE NAÏVE. OR STUPID. LIKE YOU, KAGURA.
WHAT IS A DREAM?
SO PAINFUL TO WAIT FOR...SO TERRIBLE TO BE WITHOUT...
AND YET TO BATTLE YOUR WAY TOWARD IT ALONG THAT THORNY ROAD...

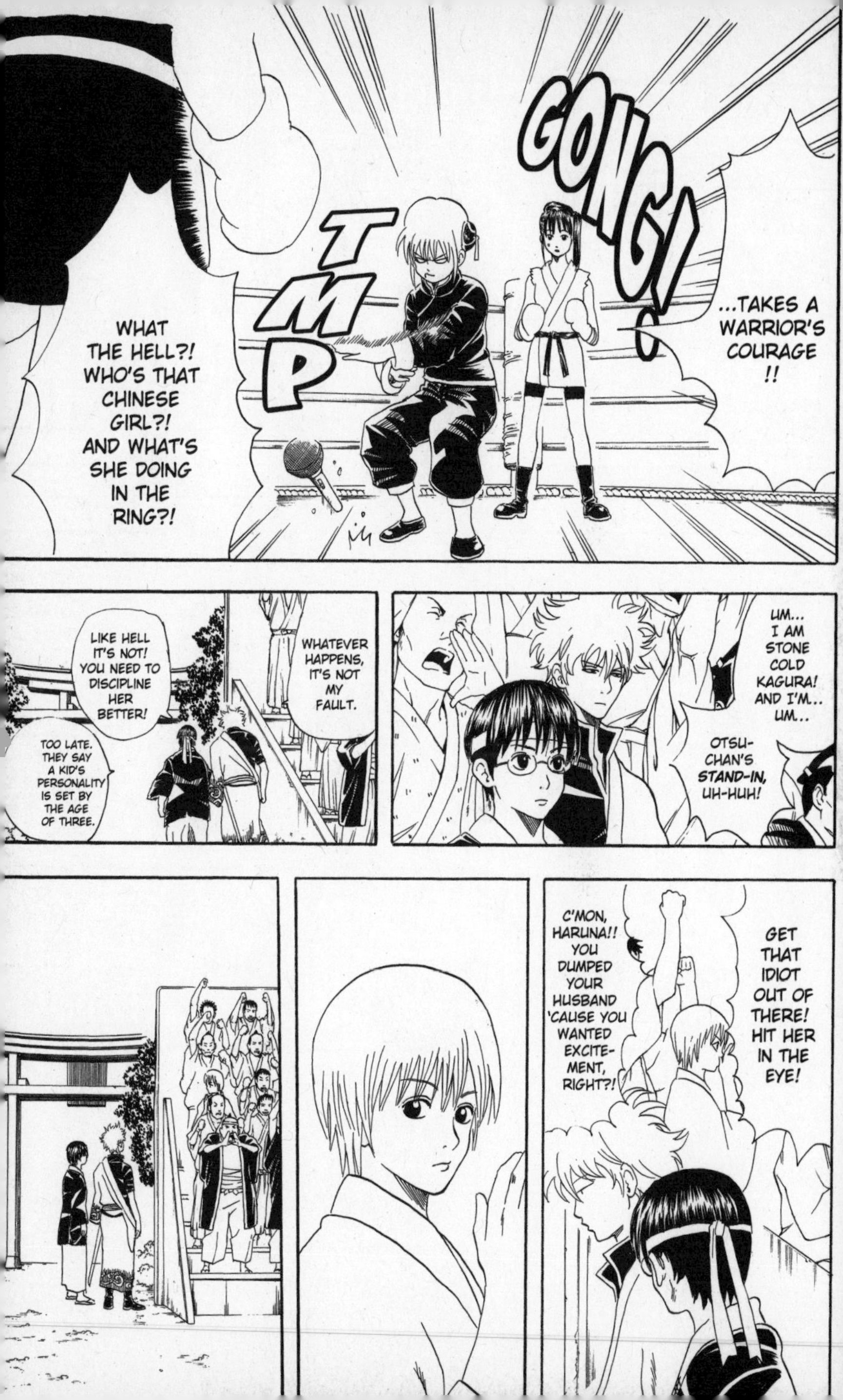
...TAKES A WARRIOR'S COURAGE!!
GONG!
TMP
WHAT THE HELL?! WHO'S THAT CHINESE GIRL?! AND WHAT'S SHE DOING IN THE RING?!
UM... I AM STONE COLD KAGURA! AND I'M.. UM..
OTSU-CHAN'S STAND-IN, UH-HUH!
WHATEVER HAPPENS, IT'S NOT MY FAULT.
LIKE HELL IT'S NOT! YOU NEED TO DISCIPLINE HER BETTER!
TOO LATE. THEY SAY A KID'S PERSONALITY IS SET BY THE AGE OF THREE.
GET THAT IDIOT OUT OF THERE! HIT HER IN THE EYE!
C'MON, HARUNA!! YOU DUMPED YOUR HUSBAND 'CAUSE YOU WANTED EXCITE-MENT, RIGHT?!

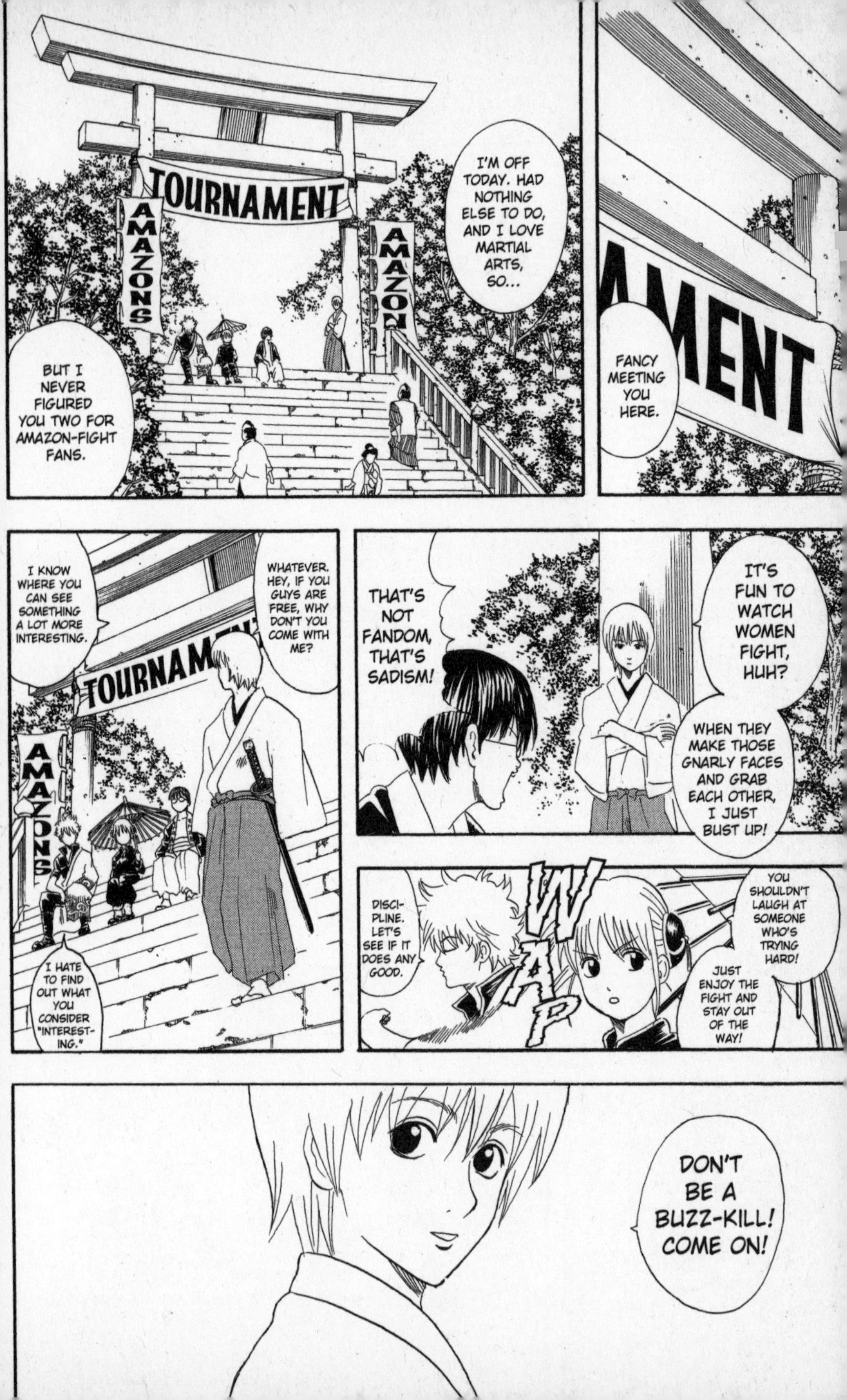

AMENT
FANCY MEETING YOU HERE.
TOURNAMENT
AMAZONS
AMAZON
I'M OFF TODAY. HAD NOTHING ELSE TO DO, AND I LOVE MARTIAL ARTS, SO...
BUT I NEVER FIGURED YOU TWO FOR AMAZON-FIGHT FANS.
IT'S FUN TO WATCH WOMEN FIGHT, HUH?
WHEN THEY MAKE THOSE GNARLY FACES AND GRAB EACH OTHER, I JUST BUST UP!
THAT'S NOT FANDOM, THAT'S SADISM!
YOU SHOULDN'T LAUGH AT SOMEONE WHO'S TRYING HARD!
JUST ENJOY THE FIGHT AND STAY OUT OF THE WAY!
WAP
DISCI-PLINE. LET'S SEE IF IT DOES ANY GOOD.
WHATEVER. HEY, IF YOU GUYS ARE FREE, WHY DON'T YOU COME WITH ME?
I KNOW WHERE YOU CAN SEE SOMETHING A LOT MORE INTERESTING.
TOURNAMENT
AMAZONS
I HATE TO FIND OUT WHAT YOU CONSIDER "INTEREST-ING."
DON'T BE A BUZZ-KILL! COME ON!

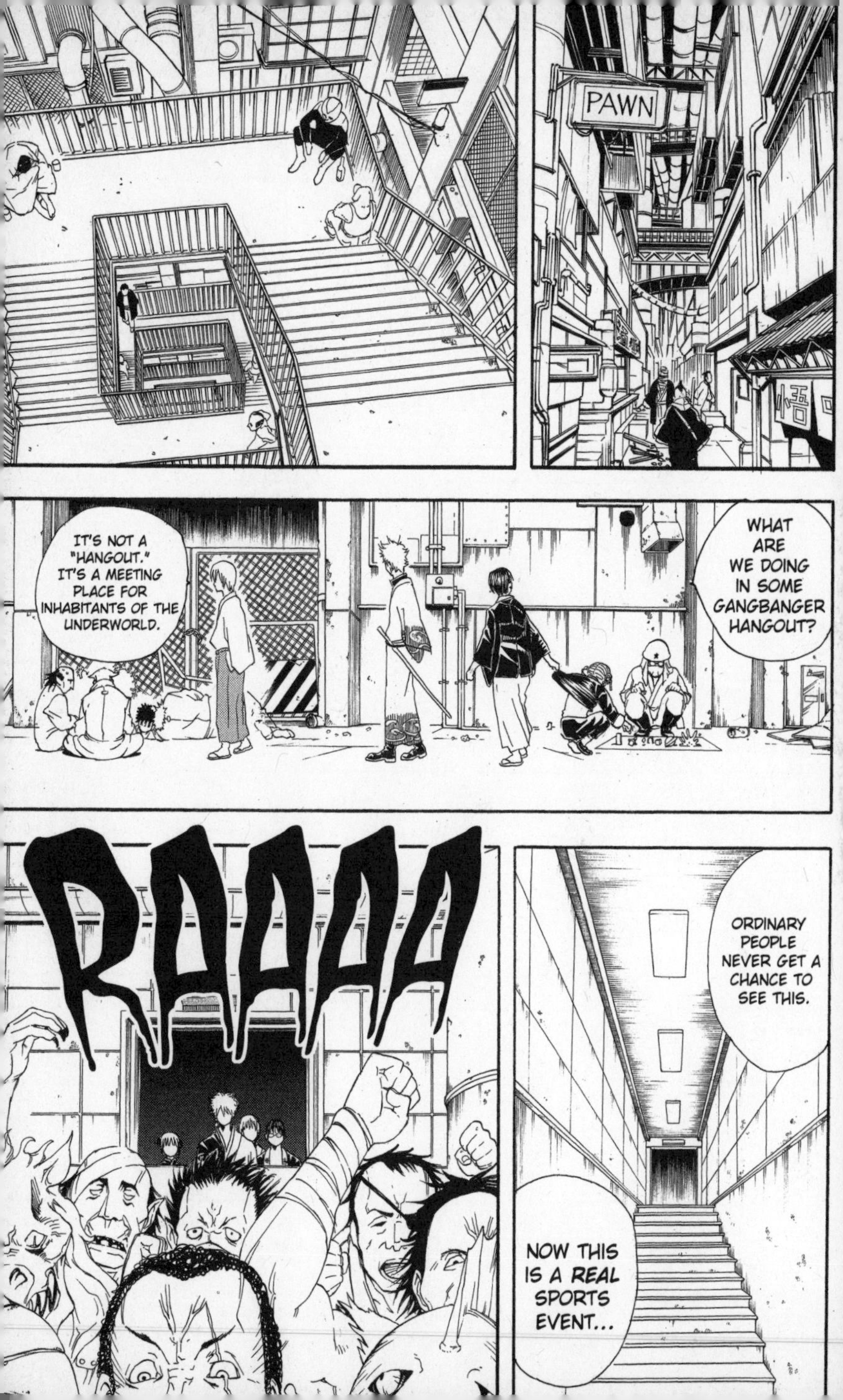
PAWN
WHAT ARE WE DOING IN SOME GANGBANGER HANGOUT?
IT'S NOT A "HANGOUT." IT'S A MEETING PLACE FOR INHABITANTS OF THE UNDERWORLD.
ORDINARY PEOPLE NEVER GET A CHANCE TO SEE THIS.
NOW THIS IS A *REAL* SPORTS EVENT...
RAAAA

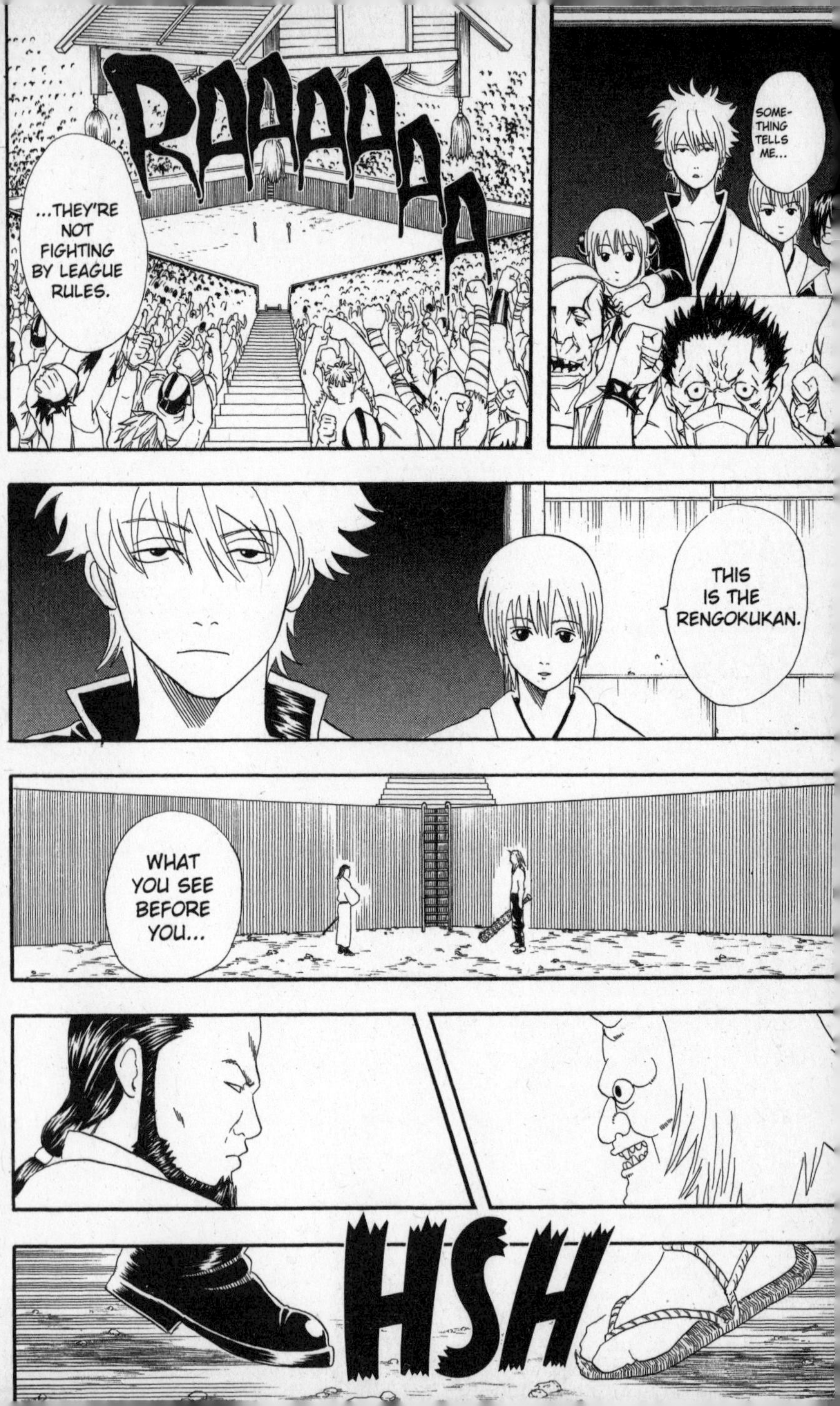
SOME-THING TELLS ME...
RAAAAAA
...THEY'RE NOT FIGHTING BY LEAGUE RULES.
THIS IS THE RENGOKUKAN.
WHAT YOU SEE BEFORE YOU...
HSH

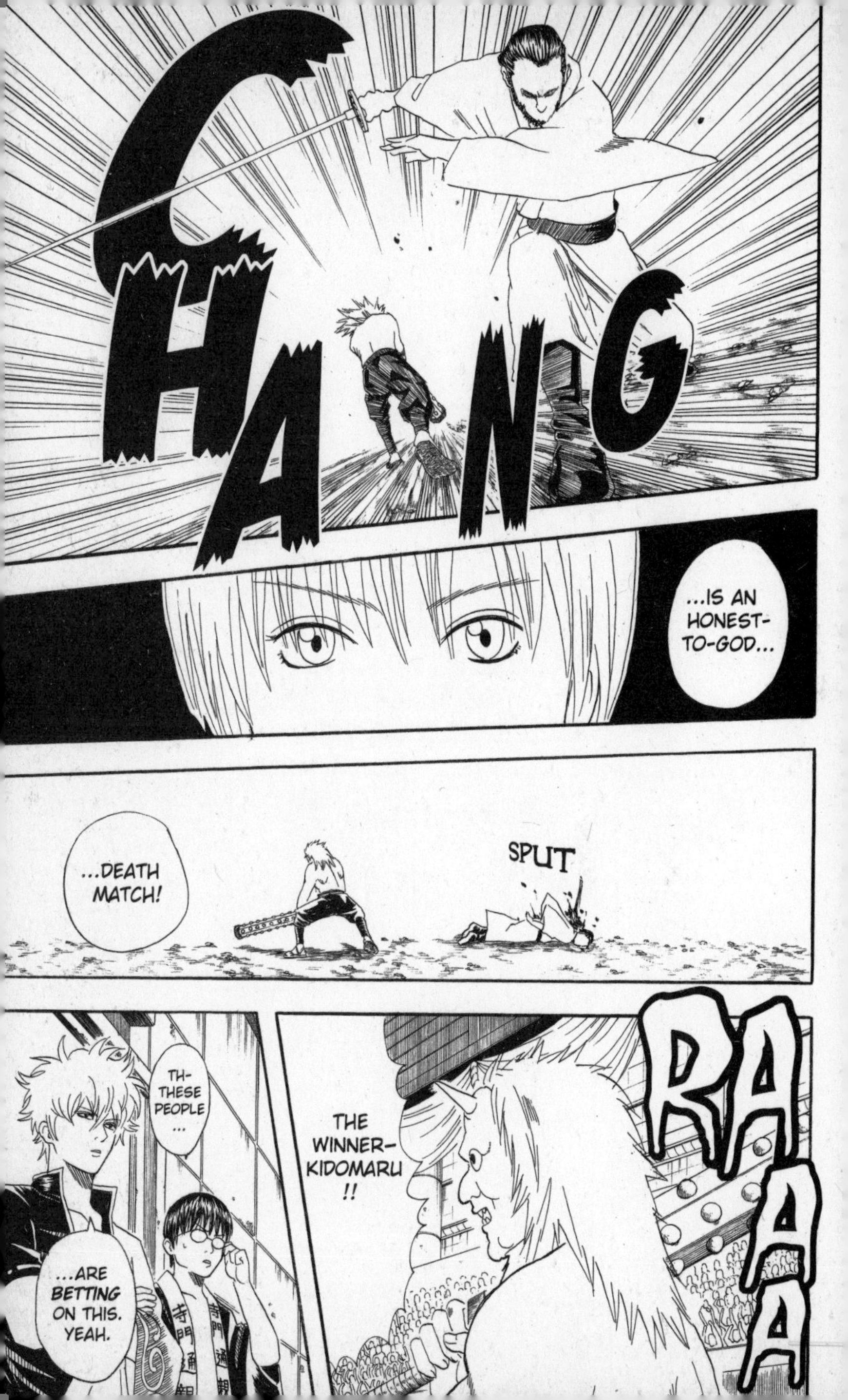
HANG
...IS AN HONEST-TO-GOD...
SPUT
...DEATH MATCH!
RAAA
THE WINNER-KIDOMARU!!
TH-THESE PEOPLE...
...ARE BETTING ON THIS. YEAH.

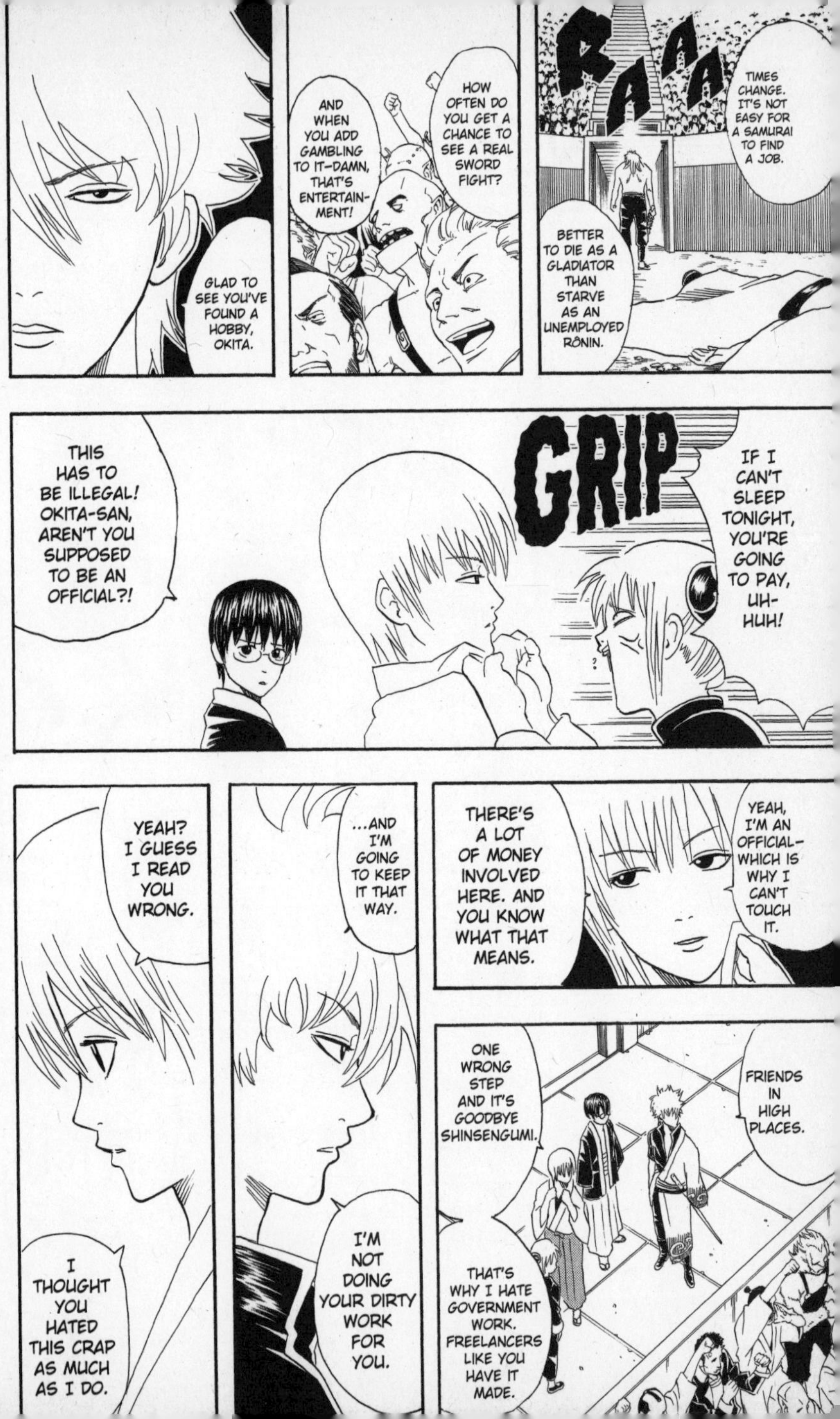

TIMES CHANGE. IT'S NOT EASY FOR A SAMURAI TO FIND A JOB.
RAAA
BETTER TO DIE AS A GLADIATOR THAN STARVE AS AN UNEMPLOYED RÕNIN.
HOW OFTEN DO YOU GET A CHANCE TO SEE A REAL SWORD FIGHT?
AND WHEN YOU ADD GAMBLING TO IT—DAMN, THAT'S ENTERTAIN-MENT!
GLAD TO SEE YOU'VE FOUND A HOBBY, OKITA.
IF I CAN'T SLEEP TONIGHT, YOU'RE GOING TO PAY, UH-HUH!
GRIP
THIS HAS TO BE ILLEGAL! OKITA-SAN, AREN'T YOU SUPPOSED TO BE AN OFFICIAL?!
YEAH, I'M AN OFFICIAL—WHICH IS WHY I CAN'T TOUCH IT.
THERE'S A LOT OF MONEY INVOLVED HERE. AND YOU KNOW WHAT THAT MEANS.
FRIENDS IN HIGH PLACES.
ONE WRONG STEP AND IT'S GOODBYE SHINSENGUMI.
THAT'S WHY I HATE GOVERNMENT WORK. FREELANCERS LIKE YOU HAVE IT MADE.
...AND I'M GOING TO KEEP IT THAT WAY.
I'M NOT DOING YOUR DIRTY WORK FOR YOU.
YEAH? I GUESS I READ YOU WRONG.
I THOUGHT YOU HATED THIS CRAP AS MUCH AS I DO.

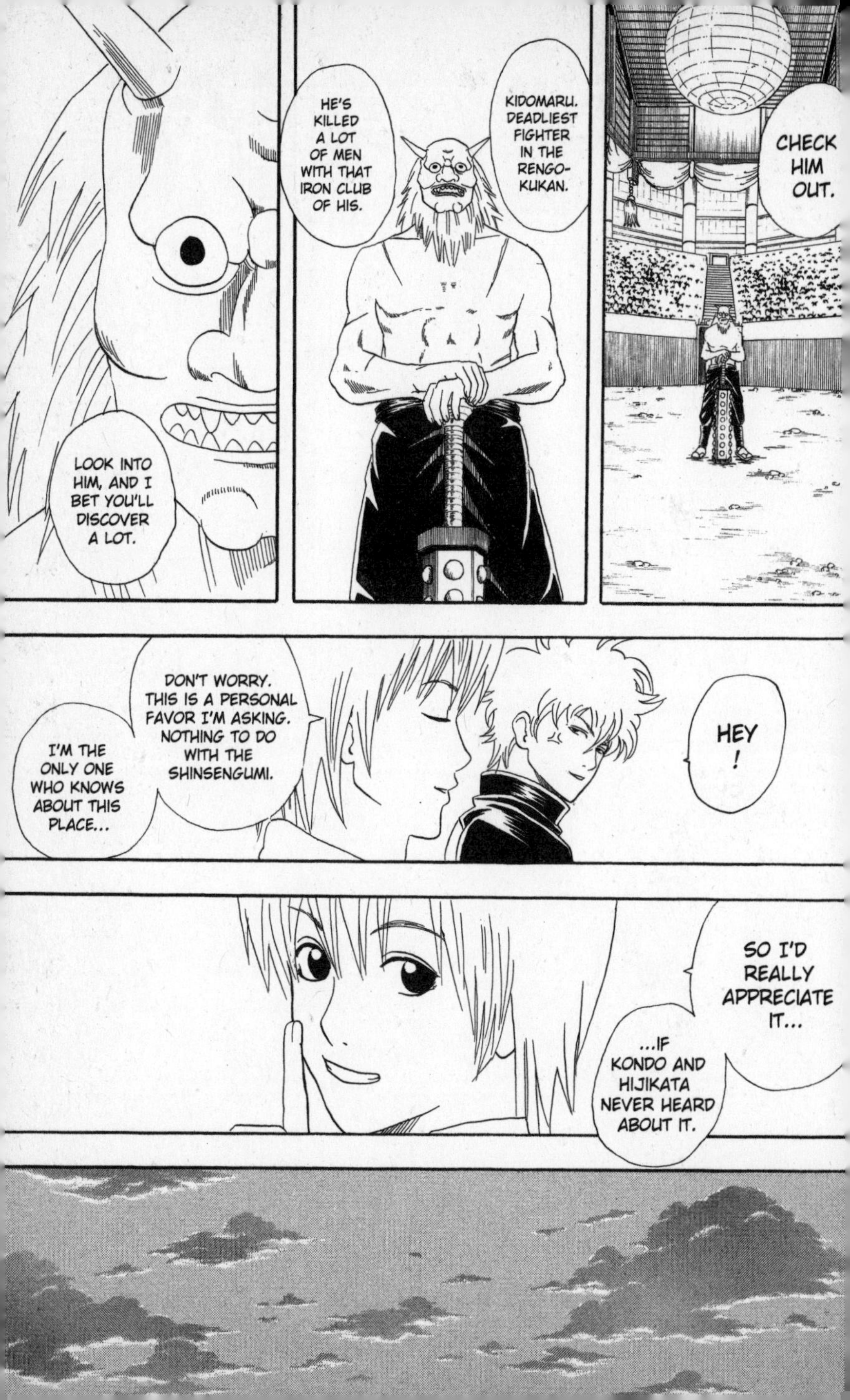
CHECK HIM OUT.
KIDOMARU. DEADLIEST FIGHTER IN THE RENGO-KUKAN.
HE'S KILLED A LOT OF MEN WITH THAT IRON CLUB OF HIS.
LOOK INTO HIM, AND I BET YOU'LL DISCOVER A LOT.
HEY!
DON'T WORRY. THIS IS A PERSONAL FAVOR I'M ASKING. NOTHING TO DO WITH THE SHINSENGUMI.
I'M THE ONLY ONE WHO KNOWS ABOUT THIS PLACE...
SO I'D REALLY APPRECIATE IT...
...IF KONDO AND HIJIKATA NEVER HEARD ABOUT IT.

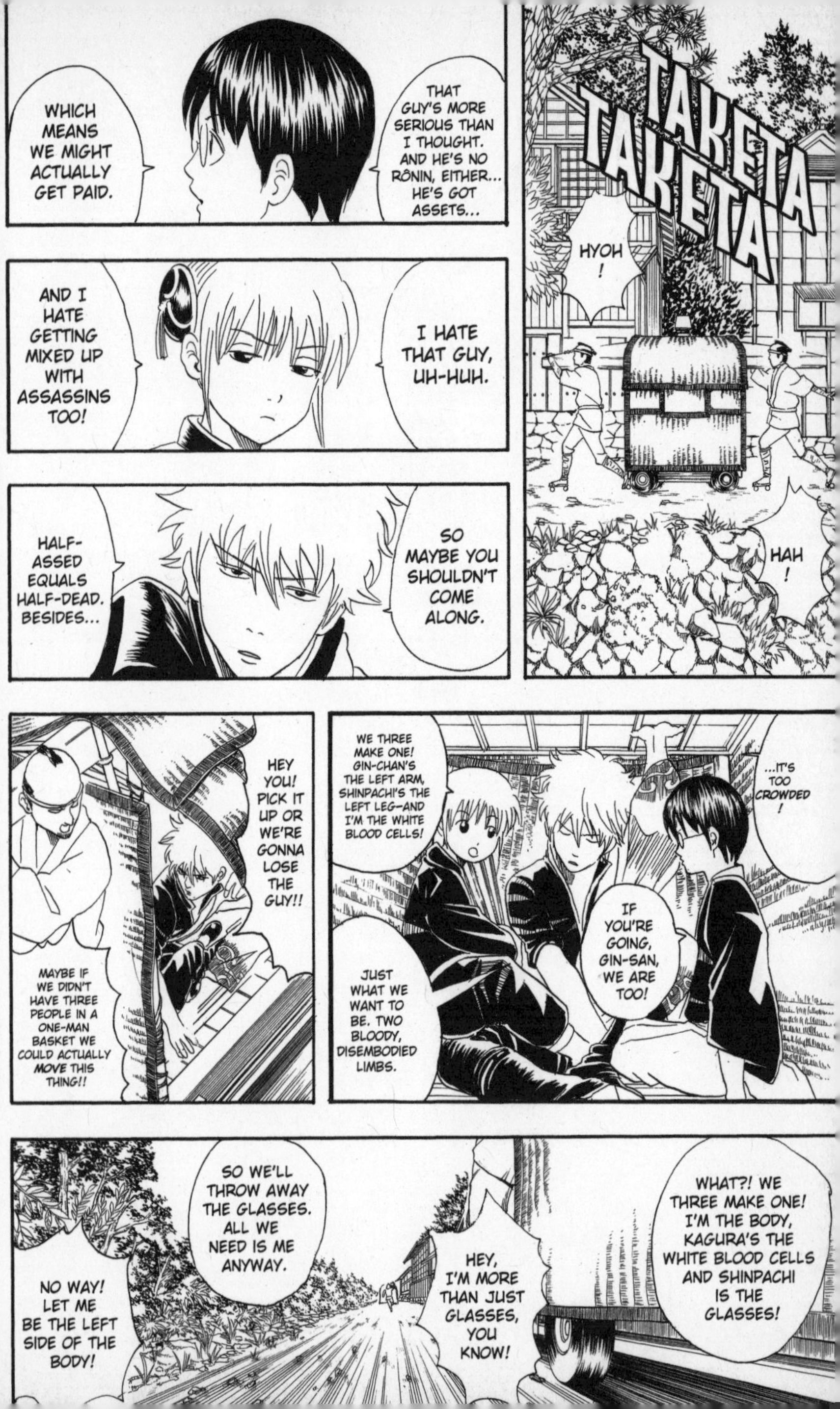
TAKETA TAKETA
HYOH!
HAH!
THAT GUY'S MORE SERIOUS THAN I THOUGHT. AND HE'S NO RÔNIN, EITHER... HE'S GOT ASSETS...
WHICH MEANS WE MIGHT ACTUALLY GET PAID.
I HATE THAT GUY, UH-HUH.
AND I HATE GETTING MIXED UP WITH ASSASSINS TOO!
SO MAYBE YOU SHOULDN'T COME ALONG.
HALF-ASSED EQUALS HALF-DEAD. BESIDES...
...IT'S TOO CROWDED!
WE THREE MAKE ONE! GIN-CHAN'S THE LEFT ARM, SHINPACHI'S THE LEFT LEG—AND I'M THE WHITE BLOOD CELLS!
IF YOU'RE GOING, GIN-SAN, WE ARE TOO!
JUST WHAT WE WANT TO BE. TWO BLOODY, DISEMBODIED LIMBS.
HEY YOU! PICK IT UP OR WE'RE GONNA LOSE THE GUY!!
MAYBE IF WE DIDN'T HAVE THREE PEOPLE IN A ONE-MAN BASKET WE COULD ACTUALLY MOVE THIS THING!!
WHAT?! WE THREE MAKE ONE! I'M THE BODY, KAGURA'S THE WHITE BLOOD CELLS AND SHINPACHI IS THE GLASSES!
HEY, I'M MORE THAN JUST GLASSES, YOU KNOW!
SO WE'LL THROW AWAY THE GLASSES. ALL WE NEED IS ME ANYWAY.
NO WAY! LET ME BE THE LEFT SIDE OF THE BODY!

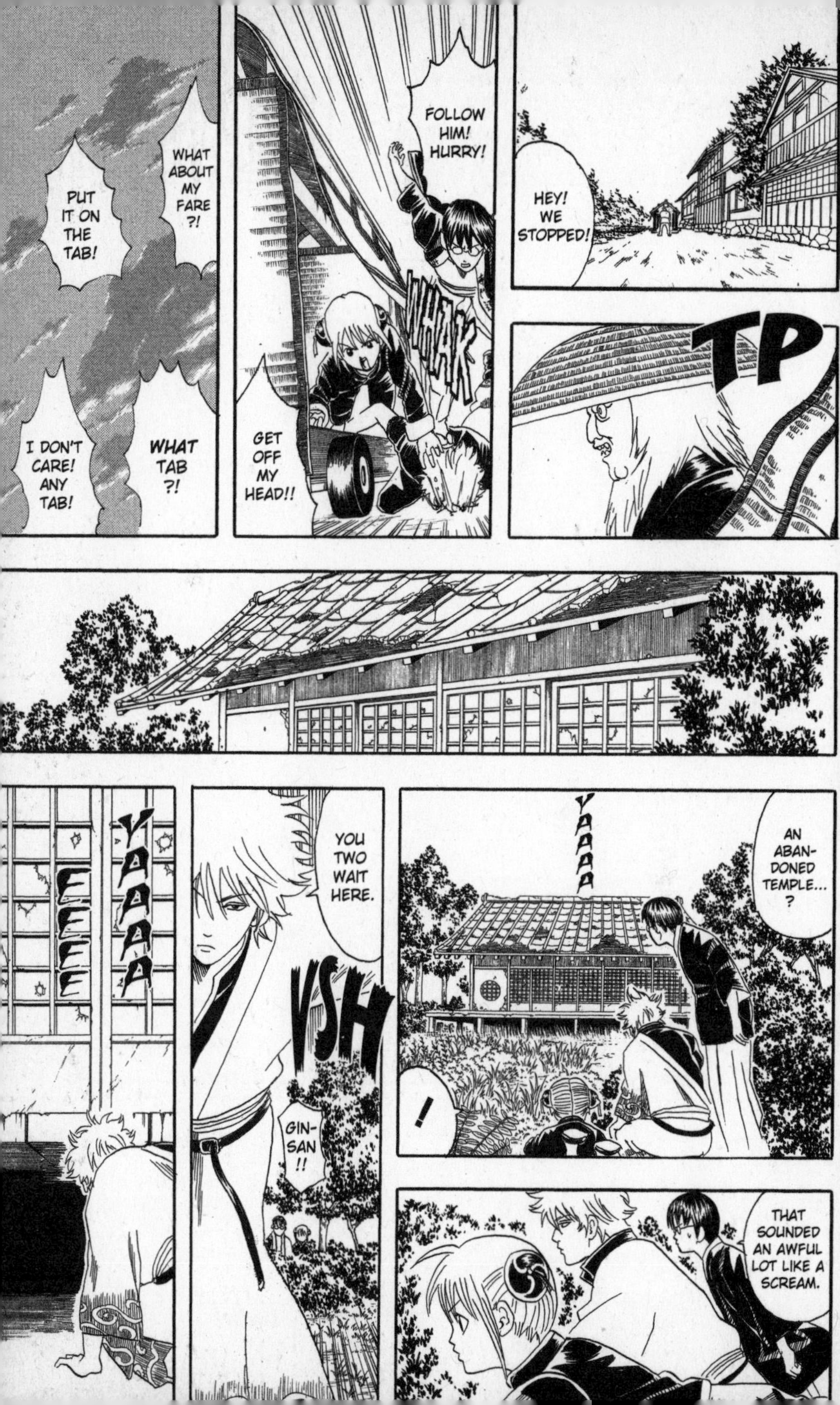
HEY! WE STOPPED!
TP
FOLLOW HIM! HURRY!
WHAK
GET OFF MY HEAD!!
WHAT ABOUT MY FARE?!
PUT IT ON THE TAB!
WHAT TAB?!
I DON'T CARE! ANY TAB!
AN ABANDONED TEMPLE...?
!
THAT SOUNDED AN AWFUL LOT LIKE A SCREAM.
YOU TWO WAIT HERE.
VSH
GIN-SAN!!

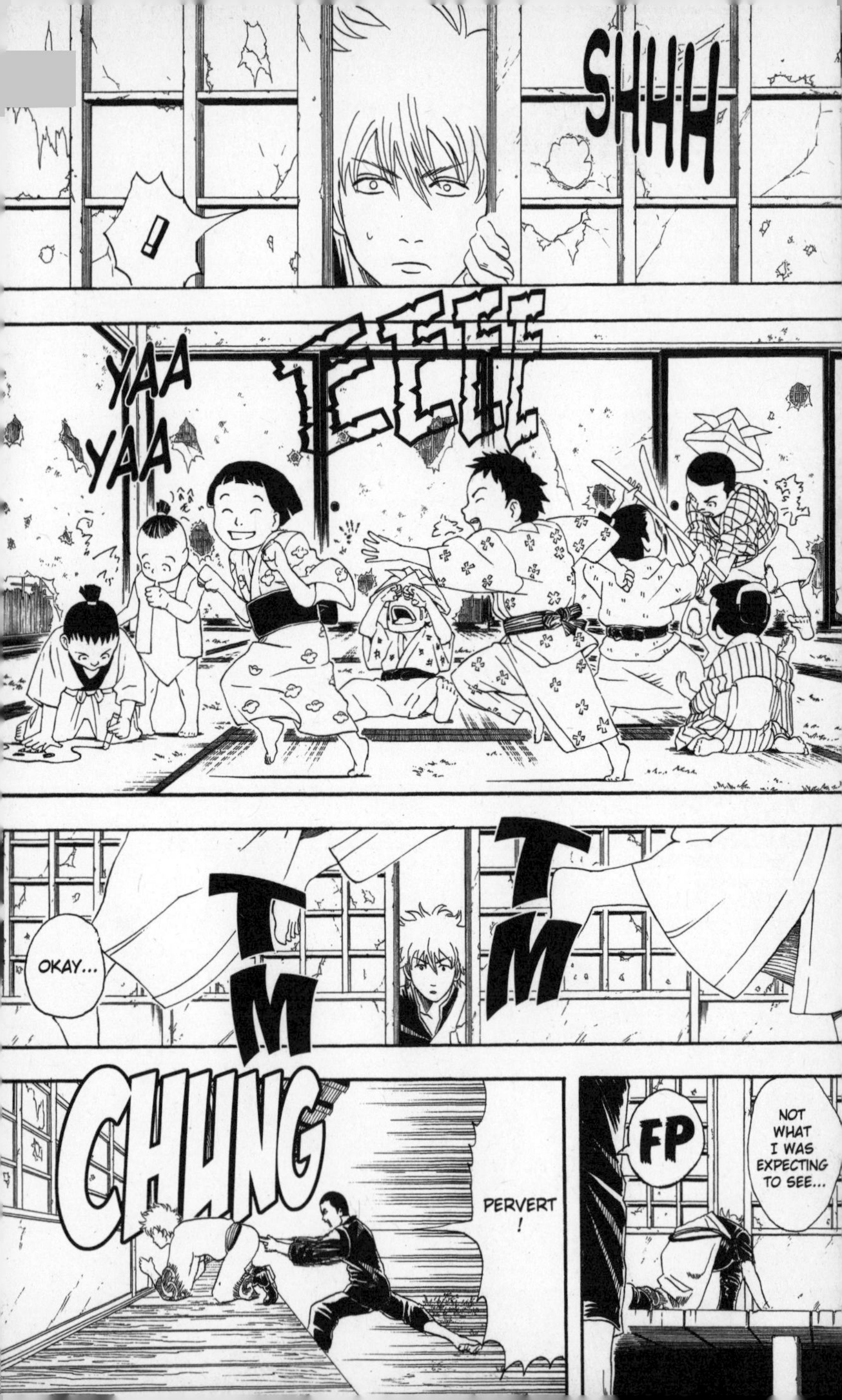
SHHH
!
TEEEE
YAA YAA
TM
TM
OKAY...
NOT WHAT I WAS EXPECTING TO SEE...
FP
CHUNG
PERVERT!

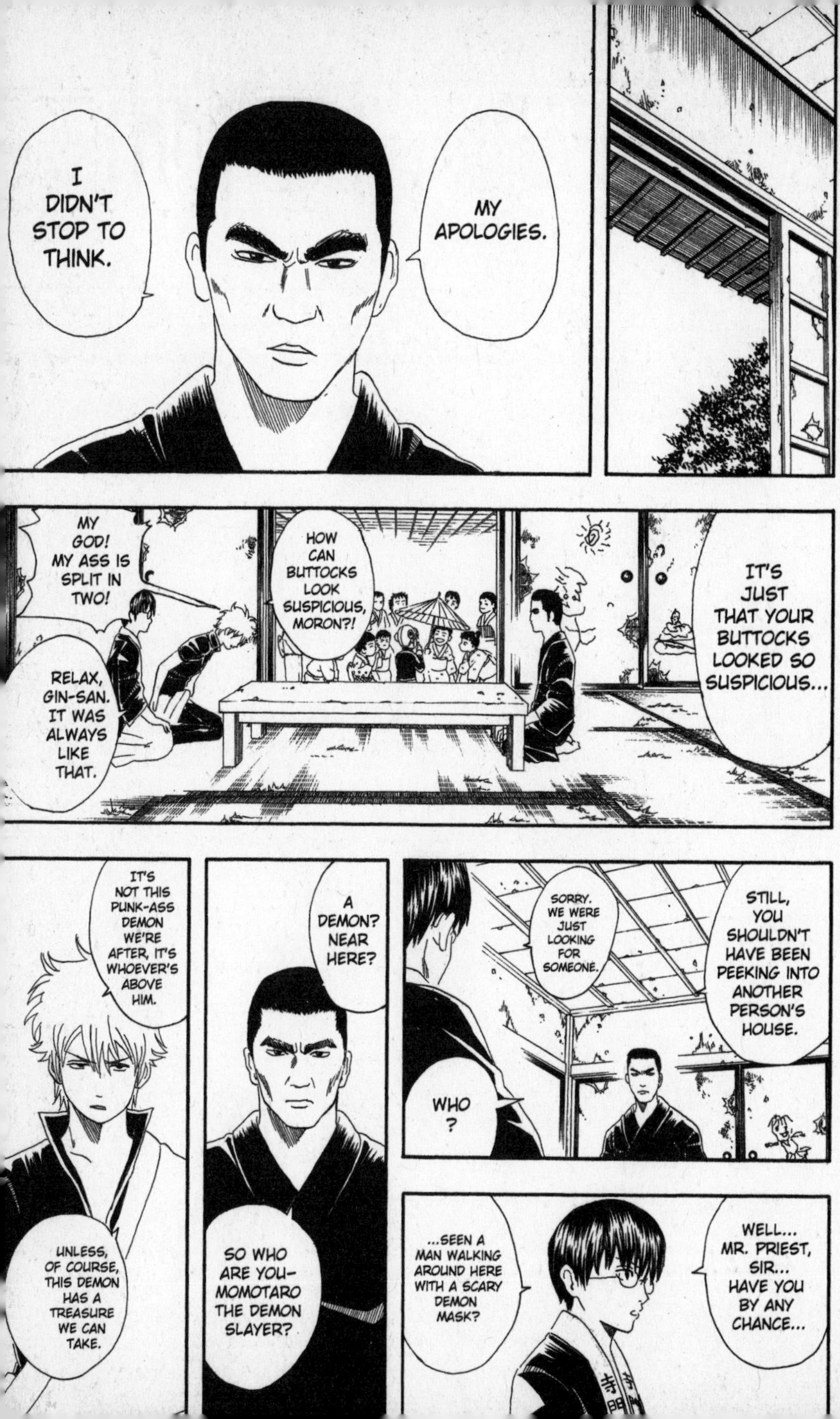
MY APOLOGIES.
I DIDN'T STOP TO THINK.
IT'S JUST THAT YOUR BUTTOCKS LOOKED SO SUSPICIOUS...
HOW CAN BUTTOCKS LOOK SUSPICIOUS, MORON?!
MY GOD! MY ASS IS SPLIT IN TWO!
RELAX, GIN-SAN. IT WAS ALWAYS LIKE THAT.
STILL, YOU SHOULDN'T HAVE BEEN PEEKING INTO ANOTHER PERSON'S HOUSE.
SORRY. WE WERE JUST LOOKING FOR SOMEONE.
WHO?
WELL... MR. PRIEST, SIR... HAVE YOU BY ANY CHANCE...
...SEEN A MAN WALKING AROUND HERE WITH A SCARY DEMON MASK?
A DEMON? NEAR HERE?
SO WHO ARE YOU—MOMOTARO THE DEMON SLAYER?
IT'S NOT THIS PUNK-ASS DEMON WE'RE AFTER, IT'S WHOEVER'S ABOVE HIM.
UNLESS, OF COURSE, THIS DEMON HAS A TREASURE WE CAN TAKE.

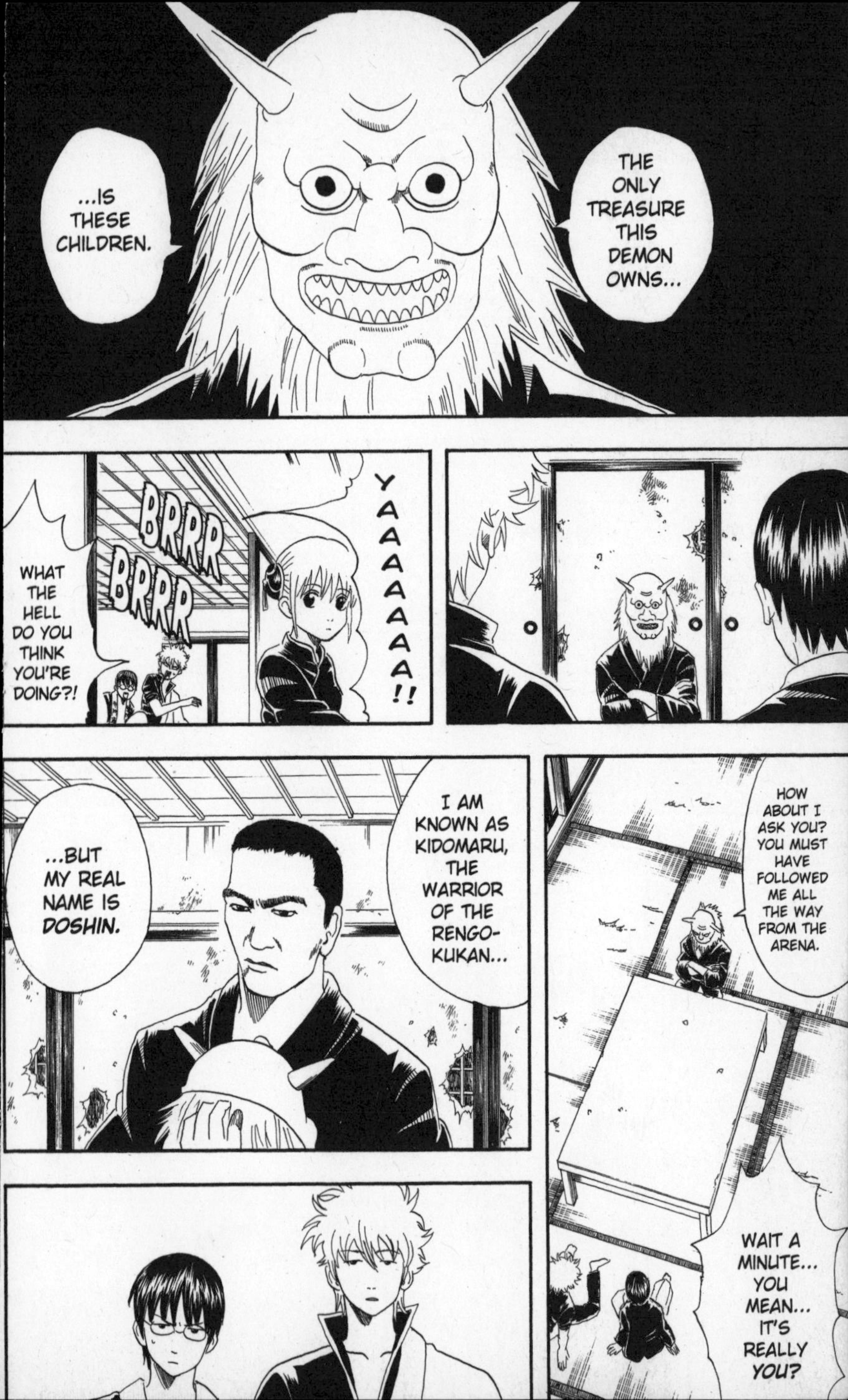
THE ONLY TREASURE THIS DEMON OWNS...
...IS THESE CHILDREN.
YAAAAAAA!!
BRRR BRRR
WHAT THE HELL DO YOU THINK YOU'RE DOING?!
HOW ABOUT I ASK YOU? YOU MUST HAVE FOLLOWED ME ALL THE WAY FROM THE ARENA.
WAIT A MINUTE... YOU MEAN... IT'S REALLY *YOU*?
I AM KNOWN AS KIDOMARU, THE WARRIOR OF THE RENGO-KUKAN...
...BUT MY REAL NAME IS *DOSHIN*.

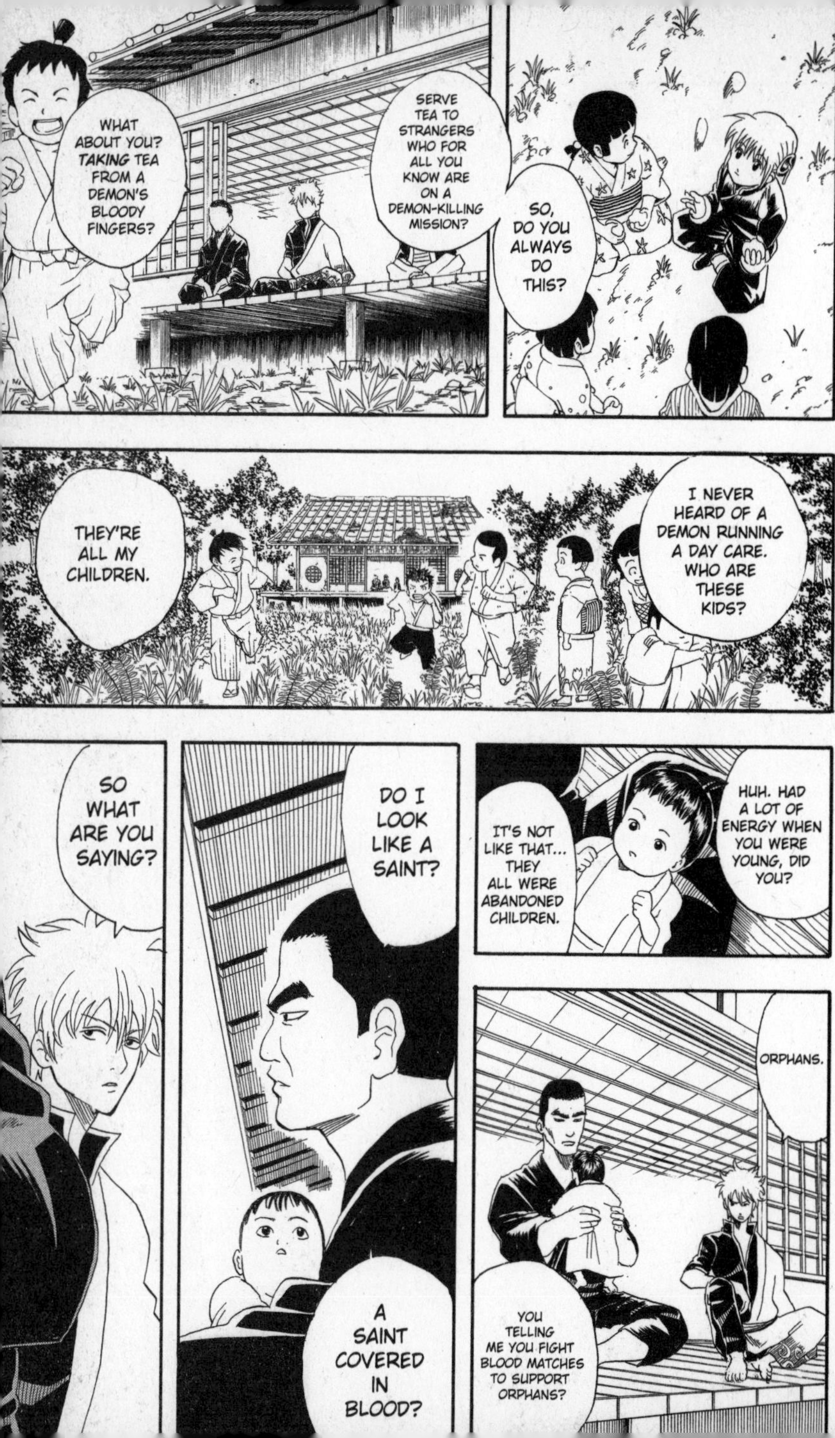
SO, DO YOU ALWAYS DO THIS?
SERVE TEA TO STRANGERS WHO FOR ALL YOU KNOW ARE ON A DEMON-KILLING MISSION?
WHAT ABOUT YOU? *TAKING* TEA FROM A DEMON'S BLOODY FINGERS?
I NEVER HEARD OF A DEMON RUNNING A DAY CARE. WHO ARE THESE KIDS?
THEY'RE ALL MY CHILDREN.
HUH. HAD A LOT OF ENERGY WHEN YOU WERE YOUNG, DID YOU?
IT'S NOT LIKE THAT... THEY ALL WERE ABANDONED CHILDREN.
ORPHANS.
YOU TELLING ME YOU FIGHT BLOOD MATCHES TO SUPPORT ORPHANS?
DO I LOOK LIKE A SAINT?
A SAINT COVERED IN BLOOD?
SO WHAT ARE YOU SAYING?

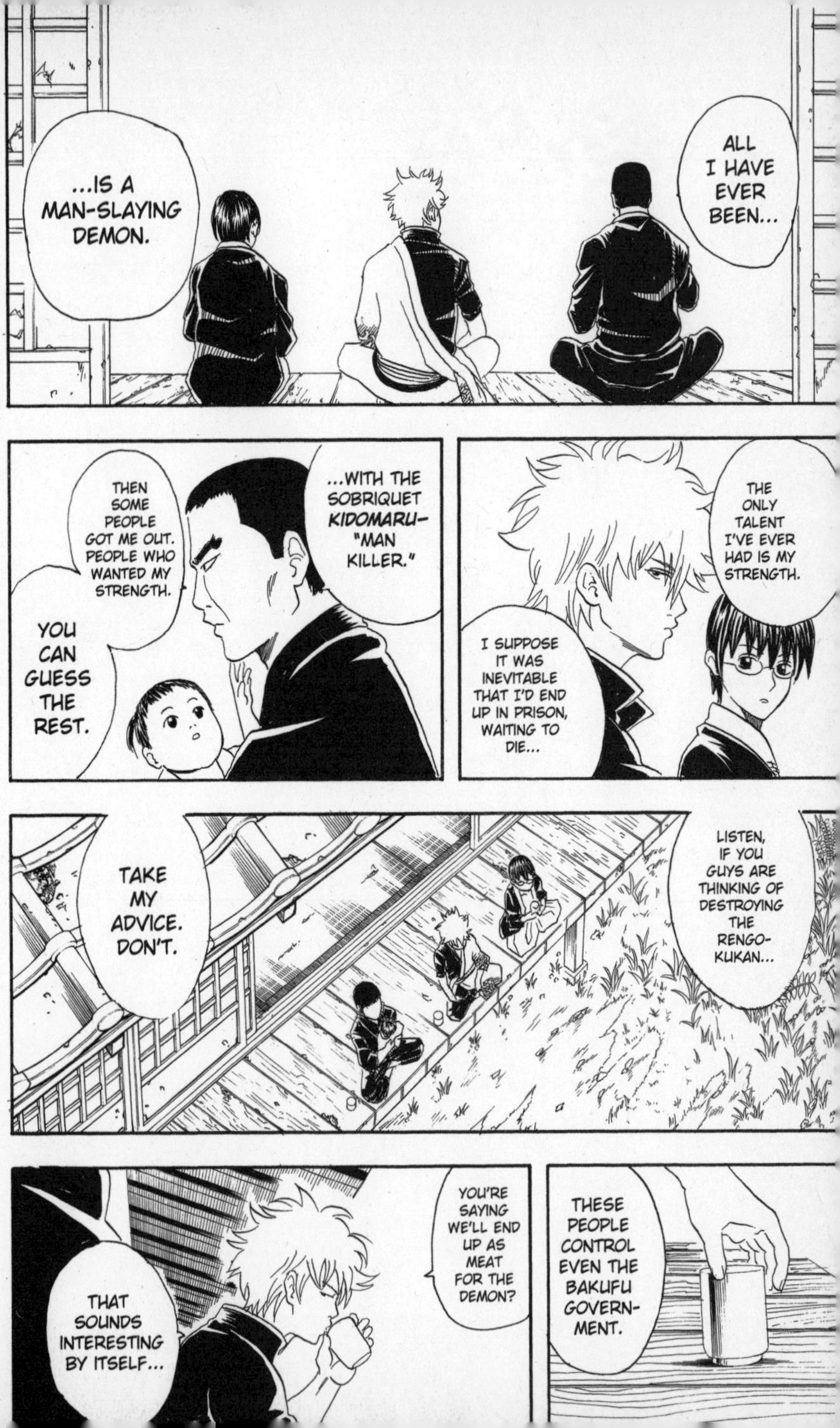
ALL I HAVE EVER BEEN...
...IS A MAN-SLAYING DEMON.
THE ONLY TALENT I'VE EVER HAD IS MY STRENGTH.
I SUPPOSE IT WAS INEVITABLE THAT I'D END UP IN PRISON, WAITING TO DIE...
...WITH THE SOBRIQUET *KIDOMARU*-"MAN KILLER."
THEN SOME PEOPLE GOT ME OUT. PEOPLE WHO WANTED MY STRENGTH.
YOU CAN GUESS THE REST.
LISTEN, IF YOU GUYS ARE THINKING OF DESTROYING THE RENGO-KUKAN...
TAKE MY ADVICE. DON'T.
THESE PEOPLE CONTROL EVEN THE BAKUFU GOVERNMENT.
YOU'RE SAYING WE'LL END UP AS MEAT FOR THE DEMON?
THAT SOUNDS INTERESTING BY ITSELF...

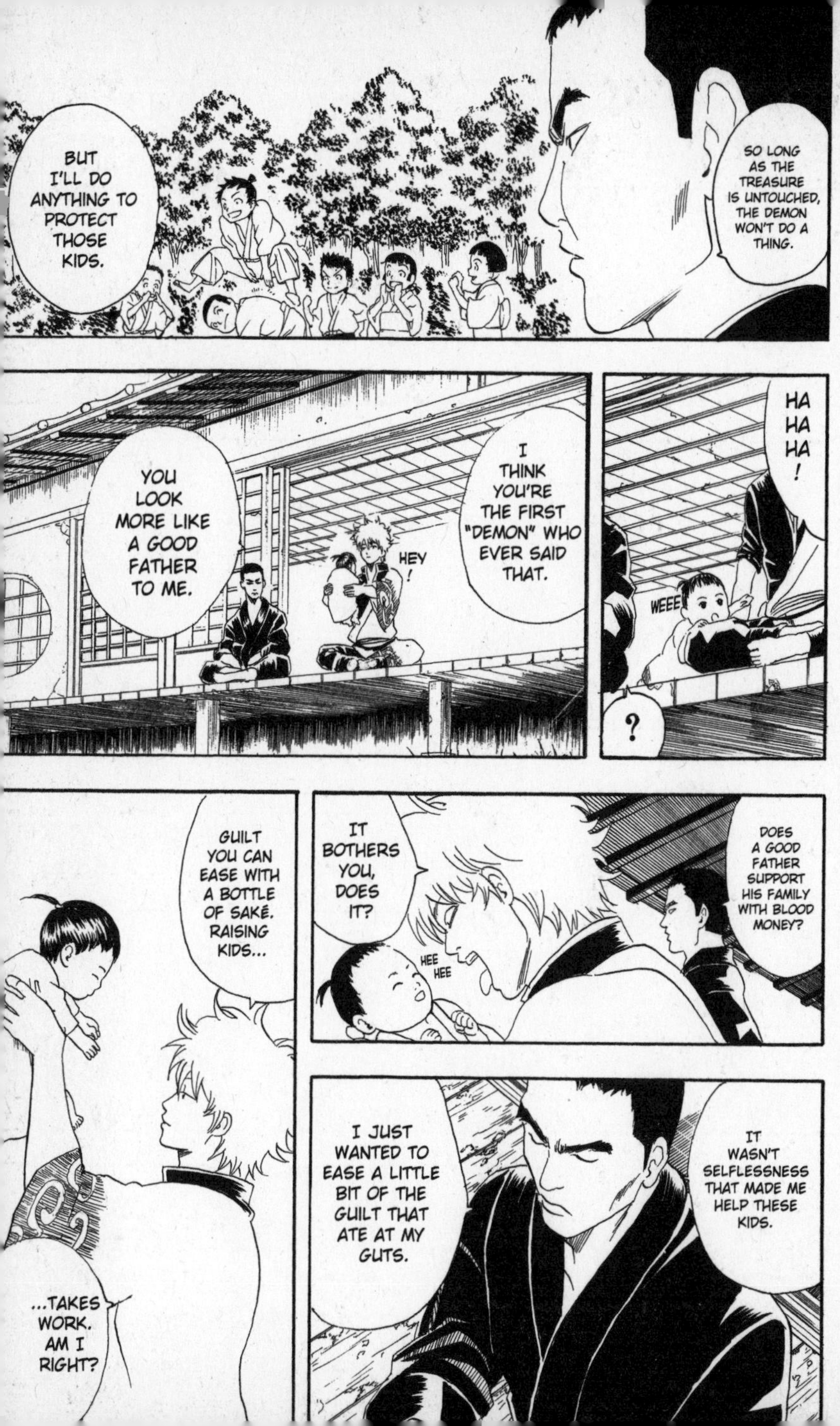
SO LONG AS THE TREASURE IS UNTOUCHED, THE DEMON WON'T DO A THING.
BUT I'LL DO ANYTHING TO PROTECT THOSE KIDS.
HA HA HA!
WEEE
?
I THINK YOU'RE THE FIRST "DEMON" WHO EVER SAID THAT.
HEY!
YOU LOOK MORE LIKE A GOOD FATHER TO ME.
DOES A GOOD FATHER SUPPORT HIS FAMILY WITH BLOOD MONEY?
IT BOTHERS YOU, DOES IT?
HEE HEE
IT WASN'T SELFLESSNESS THAT MADE ME HELP THESE KIDS.
I JUST WANTED TO EASE A LITTLE BIT OF THE GUILT THAT ATE AT MY GUTS.
GUILT YOU CAN EASE WITH A BOTTLE OF SAKÉ. RAISING KIDS...
...TAKES WORK. AM I RIGHT?

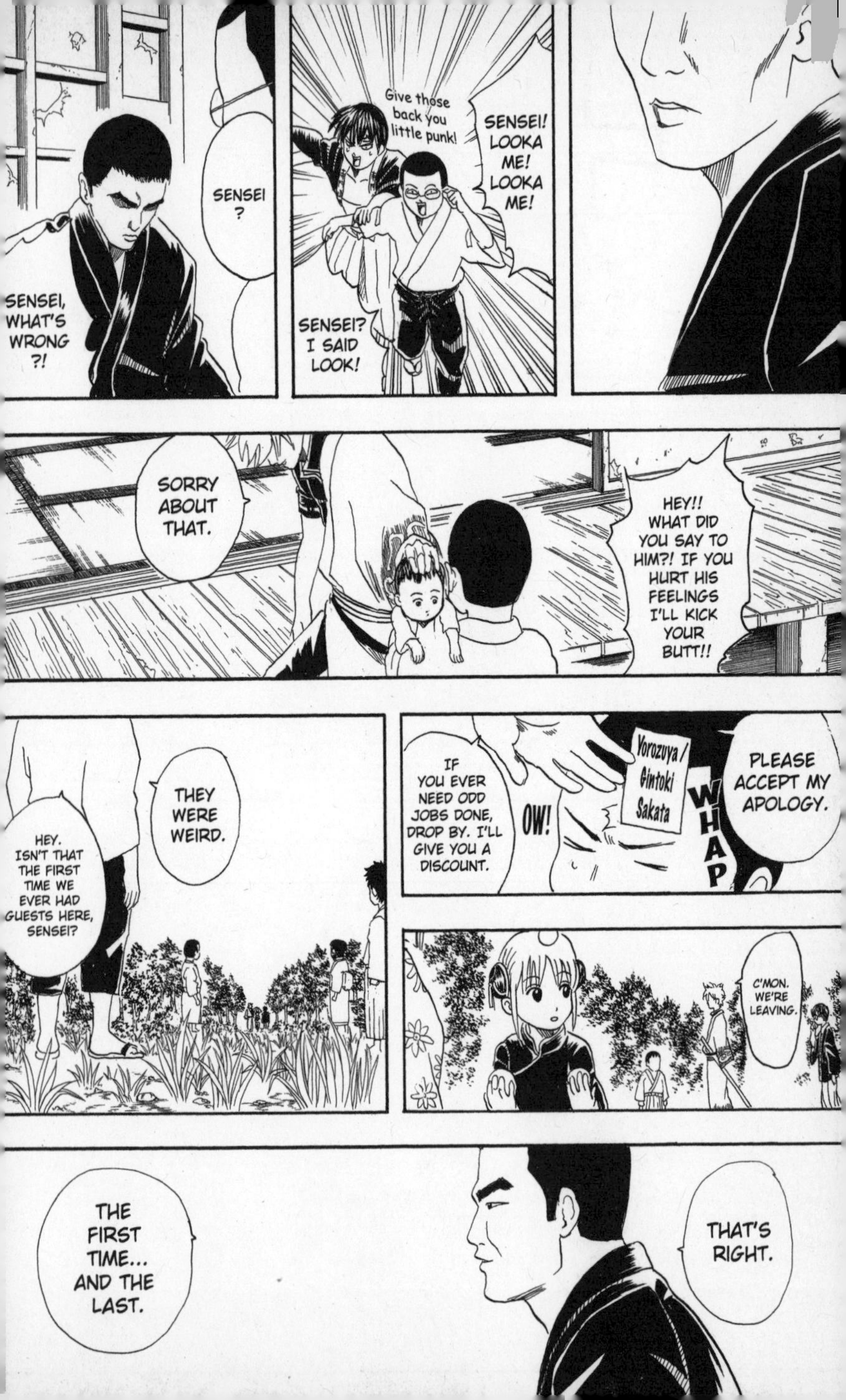
SENSEI! LOOKA ME! LOOKA ME!
Give those back you little punk!
SENSEI? I SAID LOOK!
SENSEI ?
SENSEI, WHAT'S WRONG ?!
HEY!! WHAT DID YOU SAY TO HIM?! IF YOU HURT HIS FEELINGS I'LL KICK YOUR BUTT!!
SORRY ABOUT THAT.
PLEASE ACCEPT MY APOLOGY.
WHAP
Yorozuya / Gintoki Sakata
OW!
IF YOU EVER NEED ODD JOBS DONE, DROP BY. I'LL GIVE YOU A DISCOUNT.
C'MON. WE'RE LEAVING.
THEY WERE WEIRD.
HEY. ISN'T THAT THE FIRST TIME WE EVER HAD GUESTS HERE, SENSEI?
THAT'S RIGHT.
THE FIRST TIME... AND THE LAST.

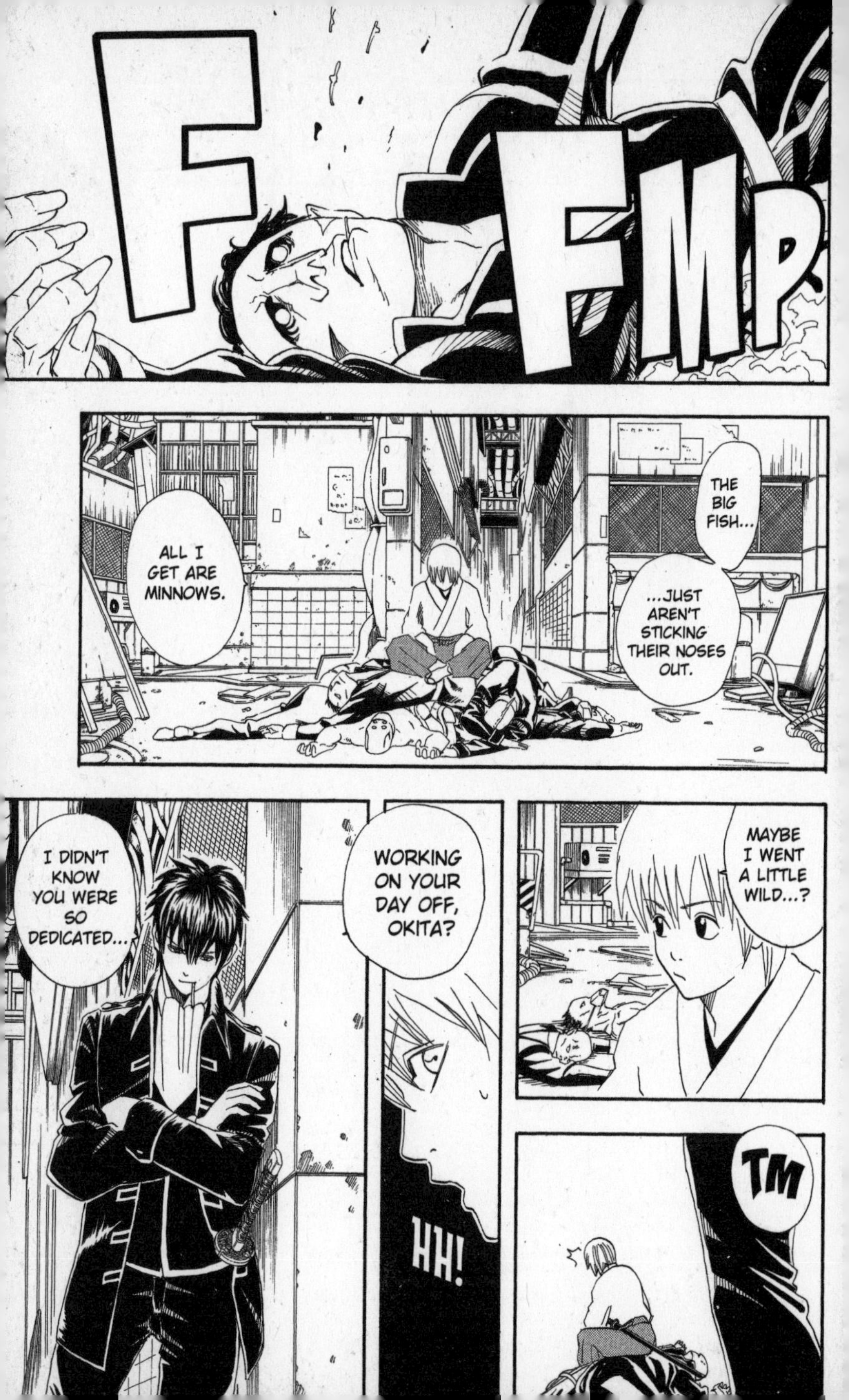
F
FMP
THE BIG FISH...
...JUST AREN'T STICKING THEIR NOSES OUT.
ALL I GET ARE MINNOWS.
MAYBE I WENT A LITTLE WILD...?
TM
WORKING ON YOUR DAY OFF, OKITA?
HH!
I DIDN'T KNOW YOU WERE SO DEDICATED...

NAKED SORACHI

Hello everybody! The feature you all love is back again—I'm gonna take off my clothes! I was cleaning my room and found a dirty old pair of underwear, and I thought, "Hey, I can strip on the freebie page with these!" So I put them on, and I've been waiting for this chance since Volume 5. Like I said earlier, in the early going of *Gin Tama* the heroes were the Shinsengumi and their opponents were the Amanto, so this manga was totally riding on the coattails of the *TAIGA* series. But then, I dug up part of the character chart and discovered a shocking secret! And that shocking secret is...

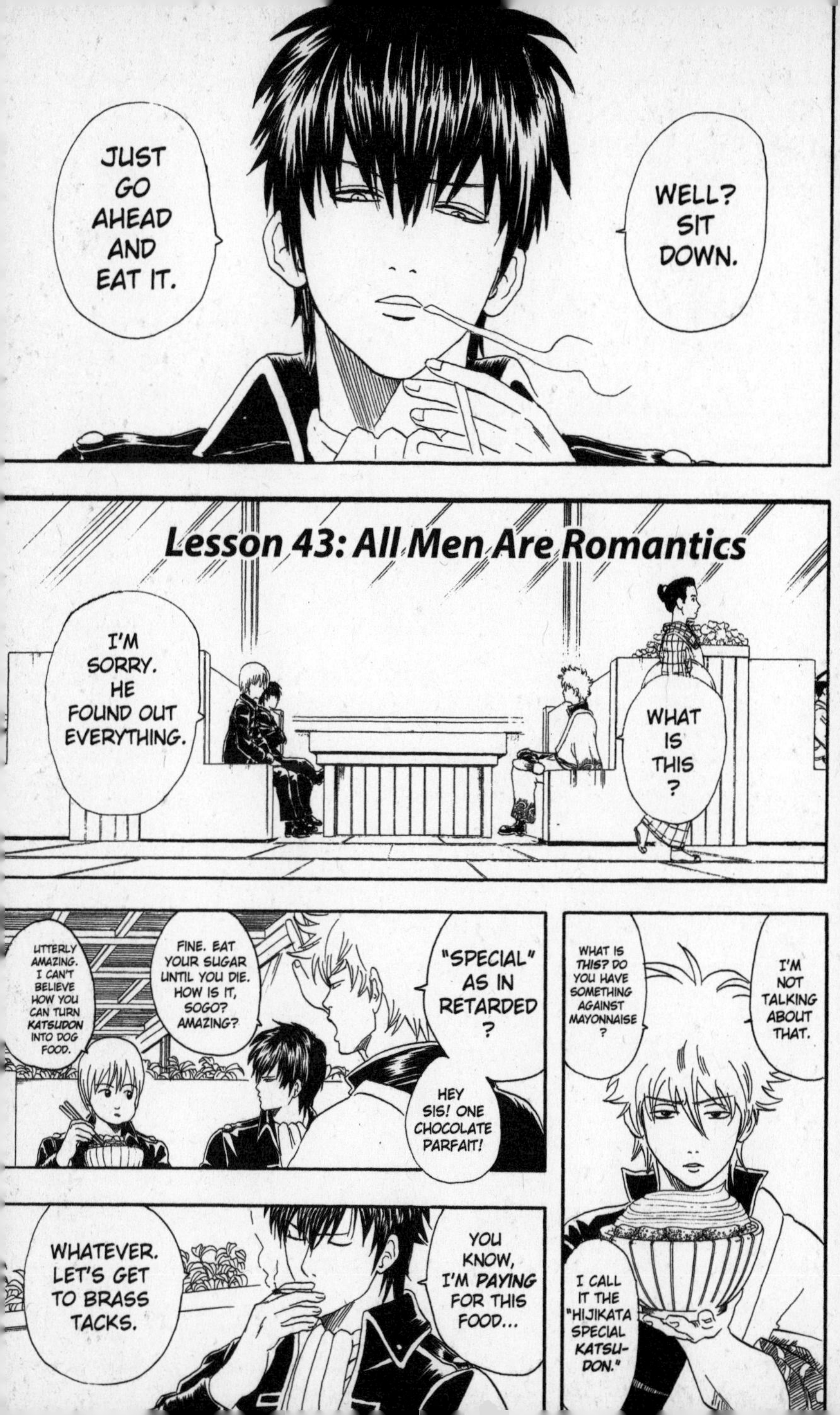
WELL? SIT DOWN.
JUST GO AHEAD AND EAT IT.
Lesson 43: All Men Are Romantics
WHAT IS THIS?
I'M SORRY. HE FOUND OUT EVERYTHING.
I'M NOT TALKING ABOUT THAT.
WHAT IS THIS? DO YOU HAVE SOMETHING AGAINST MAYONNAISE?
I CALL IT THE "HIJIKATA SPECIAL KATSUDON."
"SPECIAL" AS IN RETARDED?
HEY SIS! ONE CHOCOLATE PARFAIT!
FINE. EAT YOUR SUGAR UNTIL YOU DIE. HOW IS IT, SOGO? AMAZING?
UTTERLY AMAZING. I CAN'T BELIEVE HOW YOU CAN TURN KATSUDON INTO DOG FOOD.
YOU KNOW, I'M PAYING FOR THIS FOOD...
WHATEVER. LET'S GET TO BRASS TACKS.

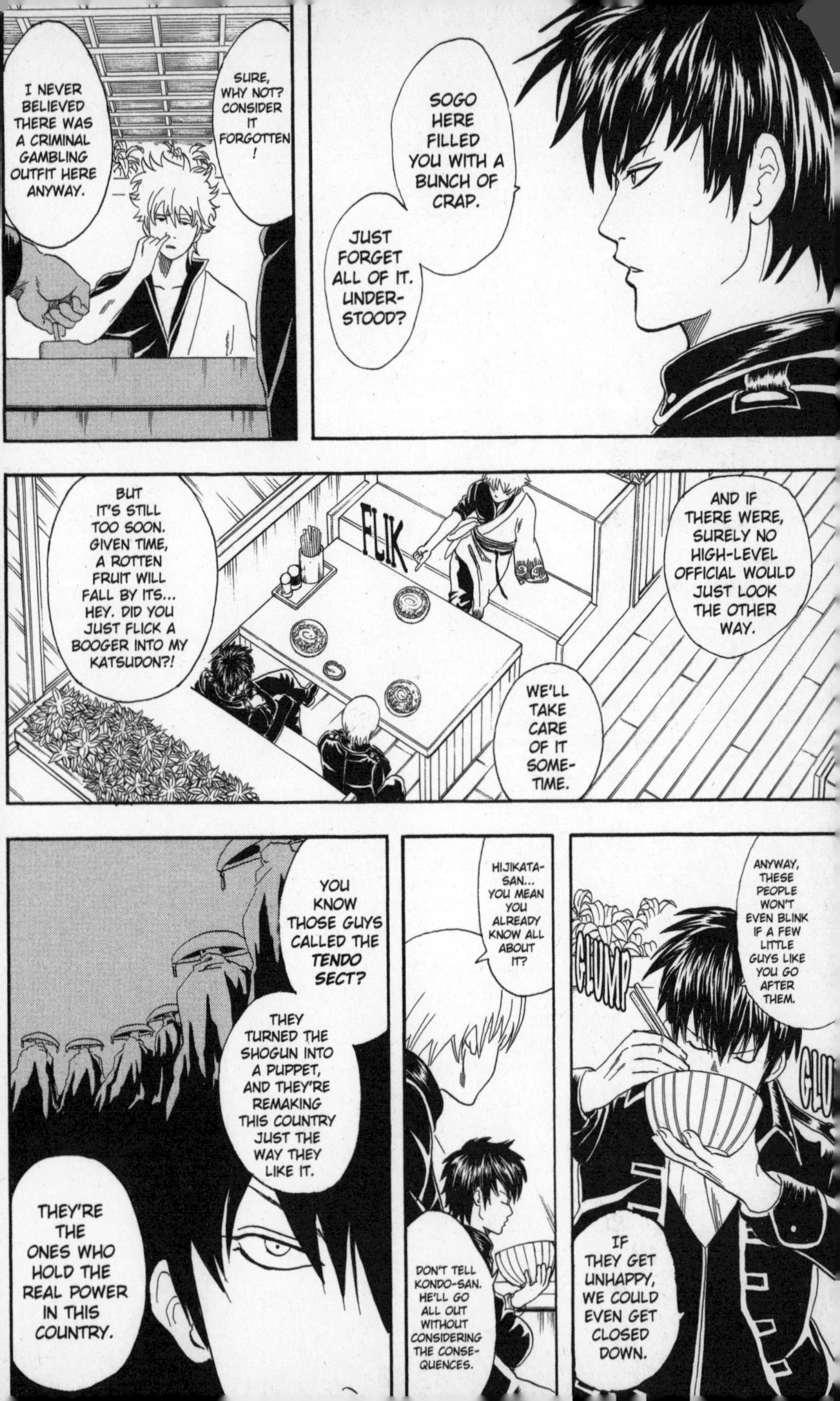
SOGO HERE FILLED YOU WITH A BUNCH OF CRAP.
JUST FORGET ALL OF IT. UNDER-STOOD?
SURE, WHY NOT? CONSIDER IT FORGOTTEN!
I NEVER BELIEVED THERE WAS A CRIMINAL GAMBLING OUTFIT HERE ANYWAY.
AND IF THERE WERE, SURELY NO HIGH-LEVEL OFFICIAL WOULD JUST LOOK THE OTHER WAY.
WE'LL TAKE CARE OF IT SOME-TIME.
FLIK
BUT IT'S STILL TOO SOON. GIVEN TIME, A ROTTEN FRUIT WILL FALL BY ITS... HEY. DID YOU JUST FLICK A BOOGER INTO MY KATSUDON?!
ANYWAY, THESE PEOPLE WON'T EVEN BLINK IF A FEW LITTLE GUYS LIKE YOU GO AFTER THEM.
CLUMP
CLU
IF THEY GET UNHAPPY, WE COULD EVEN GET CLOSED DOWN.
HIJIKATA-SAN... YOU MEAN YOU ALREADY KNOW ALL ABOUT IT?
DON'T TELL KONDO-SAN. HE'LL GO ALL OUT WITHOUT CONSIDERING THE CONSE-QUENCES.
YOU KNOW THOSE GUYS CALLED THE *TENDO SECT*?
THEY TURNED THE SHOGUN INTO A PUPPET, AND THEY'RE REMAKING THIS COUNTRY JUST THE WAY THEY LIKE IT.
THEY'RE THE ONES WHO HOLD THE REAL POWER IN THIS COUNTRY.

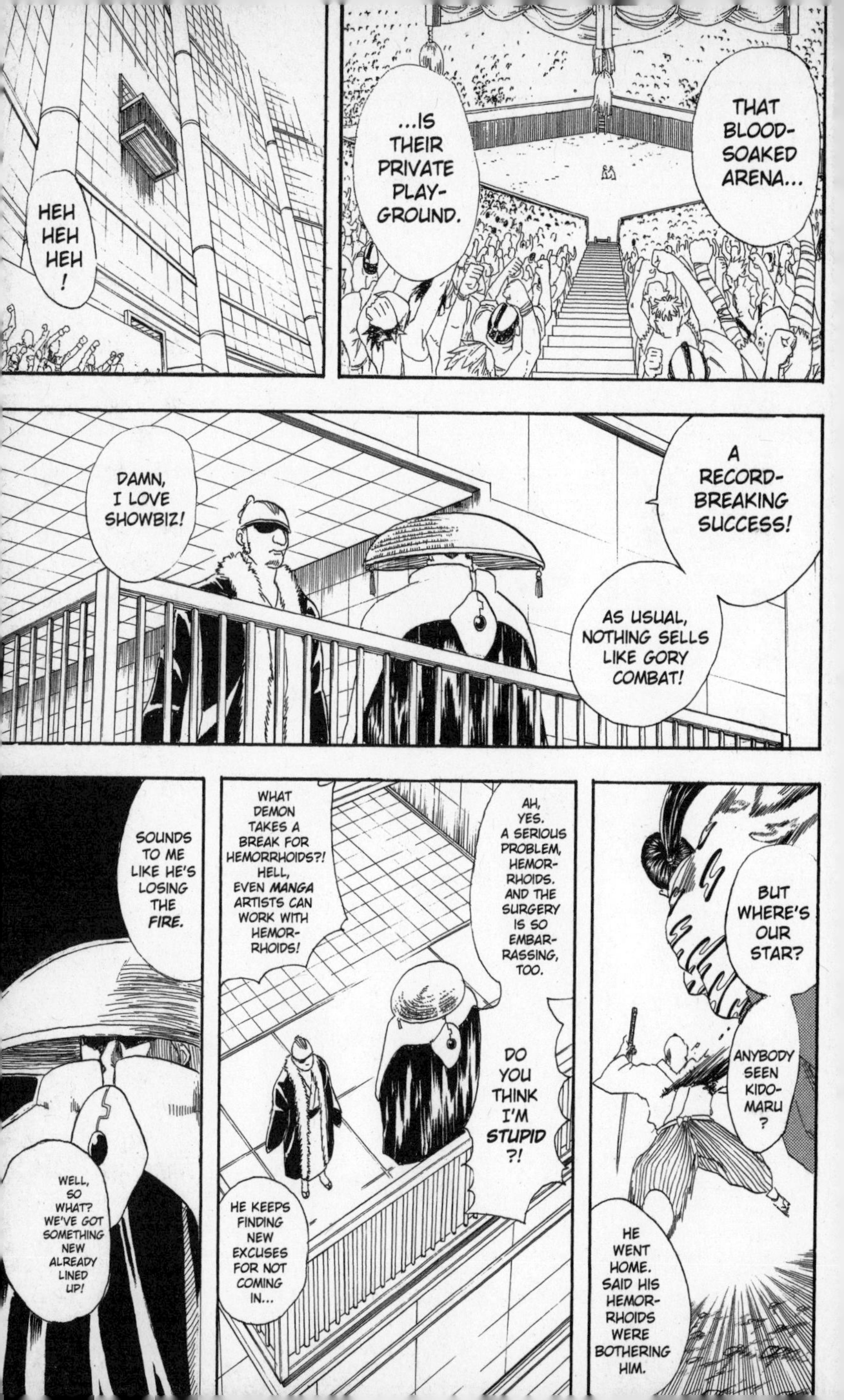
THAT BLOOD-SOAKED ARENA...
...IS THEIR PRIVATE PLAY-GROUND.
HEH HEH HEH!
A RECORD-BREAKING SUCCESS!
AS USUAL, NOTHING SELLS LIKE GORY COMBAT!
DAMN, I LOVE SHOWBIZ!
BUT WHERE'S OUR STAR?
ANYBODY SEEN KIDO-MARU?
HE WENT HOME. SAID HIS HEMOR-RHOIDS WERE BOTHERING HIM.
AH, YES. A SERIOUS PROBLEM, HEMOR-RHOIDS. AND THE SURGERY IS SO EMBAR-RASSING, TOO.
DO YOU THINK I'M *STUPID*?!
WHAT DEMON TAKES A BREAK FOR HEMORRHOIDS?! HELL, EVEN *MANGA* ARTISTS CAN WORK WITH HEMOR-RHOIDS!
HE KEEPS FINDING NEW EXCUSES FOR NOT COMING IN...
SOUNDS TO ME LIKE HE'S LOSING THE *FIRE*.
WELL, SO WHAT? WE'VE GOT SOMETHING NEW ALREADY LINED UP!

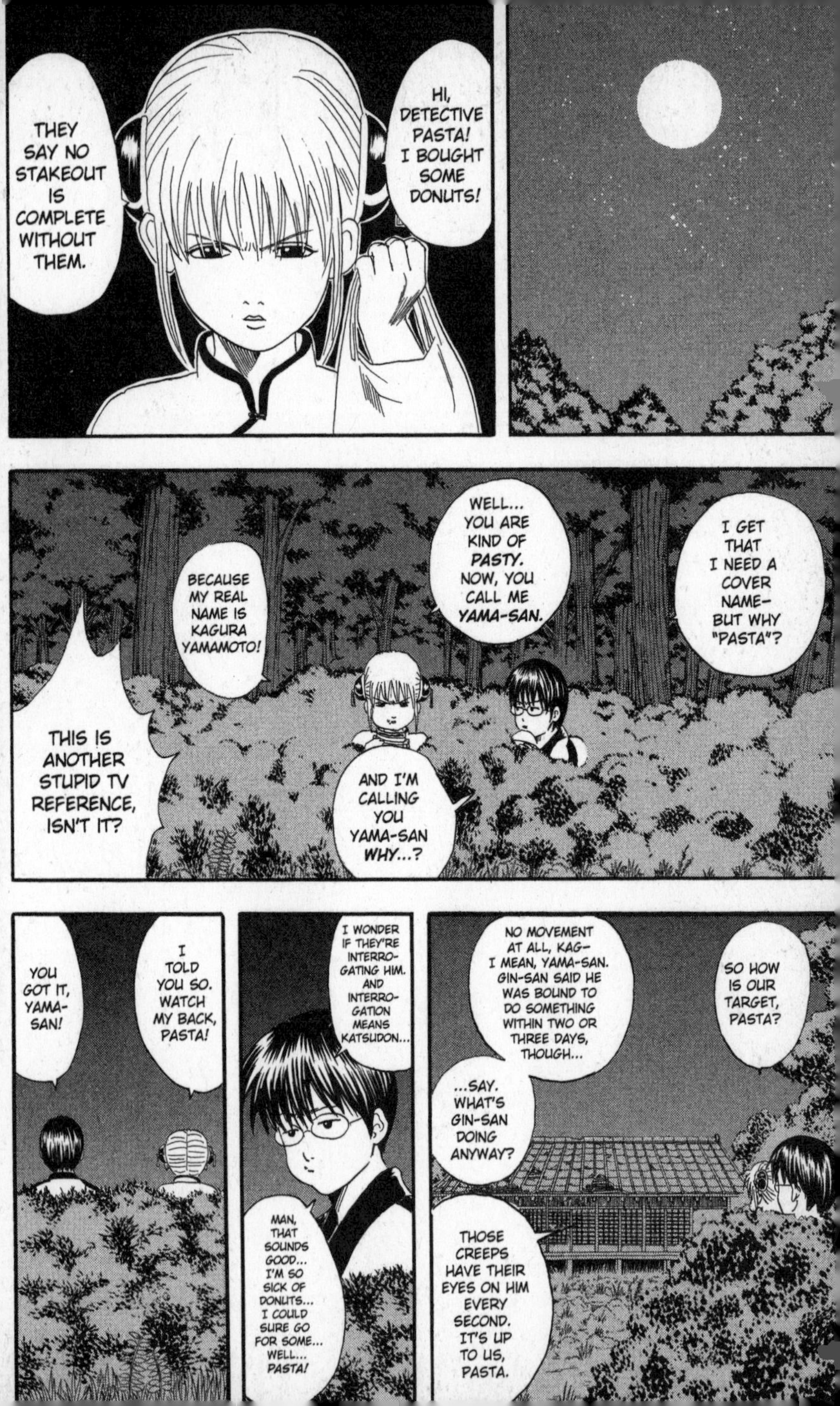
HI, DETECTIVE PASTA! I BOUGHT SOME DONUTS!
THEY SAY NO STAKEOUT IS COMPLETE WITHOUT THEM.
I GET THAT I NEED A COVER NAME-BUT WHY "PASTA"?
WELL... YOU ARE KIND OF *PASTY.* NOW, YOU CALL ME *YAMA-SAN.*
BECAUSE MY REAL NAME IS KAGURA YAMAMOTO!
AND I'M CALLING YOU YAMA-SAN *WHY...?*
THIS IS ANOTHER STUPID TV REFERENCE, ISN'T IT?
SO HOW IS OUR TARGET, PASTA?
NO MOVEMENT AT ALL, KAG- I MEAN, YAMA-SAN. GIN-SAN SAID HE WAS BOUND TO DO SOMETHING WITHIN TWO OR THREE DAYS, THOUGH...
...SAY. WHAT'S GIN-SAN DOING ANYWAY?
THOSE CREEPS HAVE THEIR EYES ON HIM EVERY SECOND. IT'S UP TO US, PASTA.
I WONDER IF THEY'RE INTERROGATING HIM. AND INTERROGATION MEANS KATSUDON...
MAN, THAT SOUNDS GOOD... I'M SO SICK OF DONUTS... I COULD SURE GO FOR SOME... WELL... *PASTA!*
I TOLD YOU SO. WATCH MY BACK, PASTA!
YOU GOT IT, YAMA-SAN!

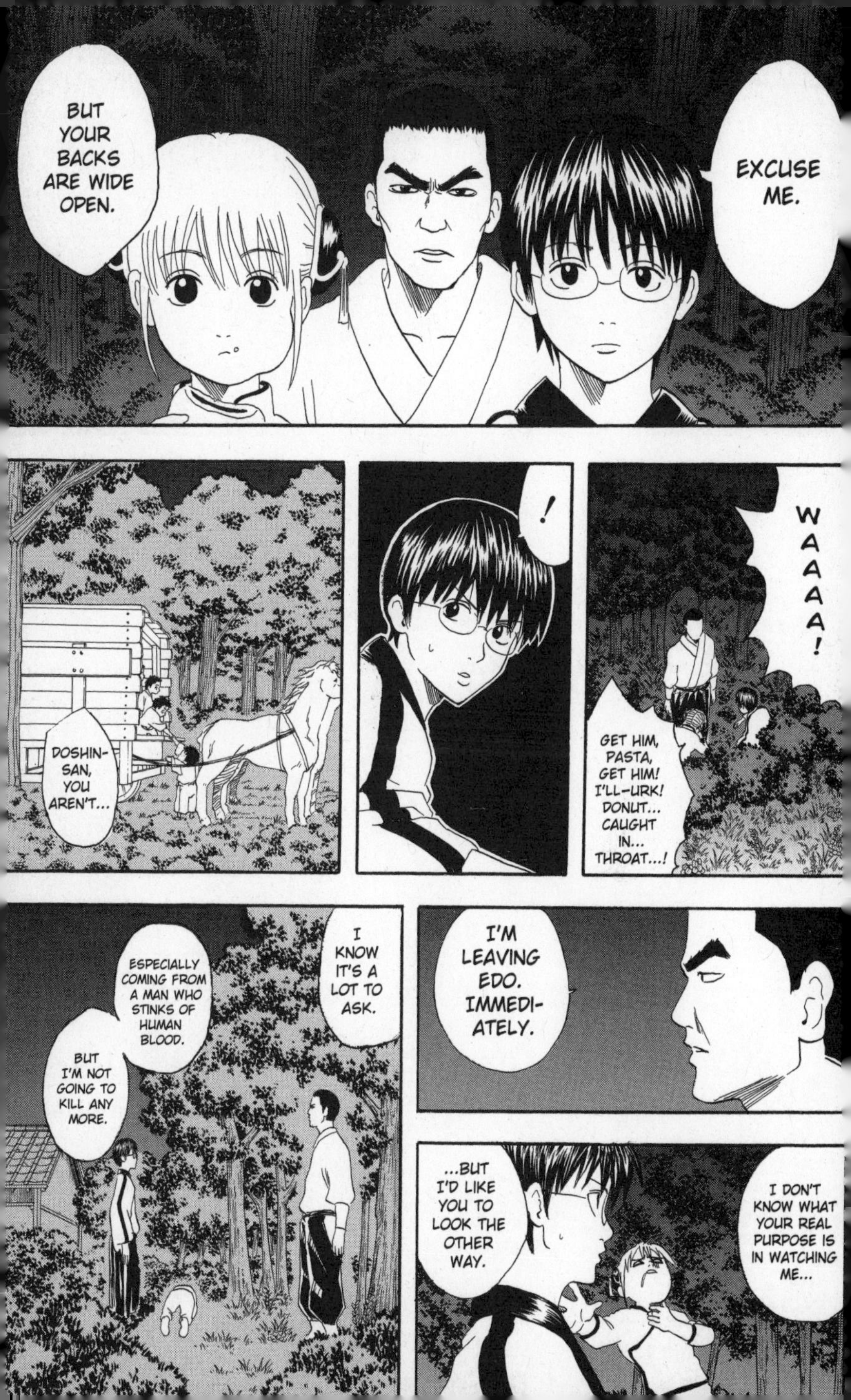
EXCUSE ME.
BUT YOUR BACKS ARE WIDE OPEN.
WAAAAA!
GET HIM, PASTA, GET HIM! I'LL–URK! DONUT... CAUGHT IN... THROAT...!
!
DOSHIN-SAN, YOU AREN'T...
I'M LEAVING EDO. IMMEDIATELY.
I DON'T KNOW WHAT YOUR REAL PURPOSE IS IN WATCHING ME...
...BUT I'D LIKE YOU TO LOOK THE OTHER WAY.
I KNOW IT'S A LOT TO ASK.
ESPECIALLY COMING FROM A MAN WHO STINKS OF HUMAN BLOOD.
BUT I'M NOT GOING TO KILL ANY MORE.

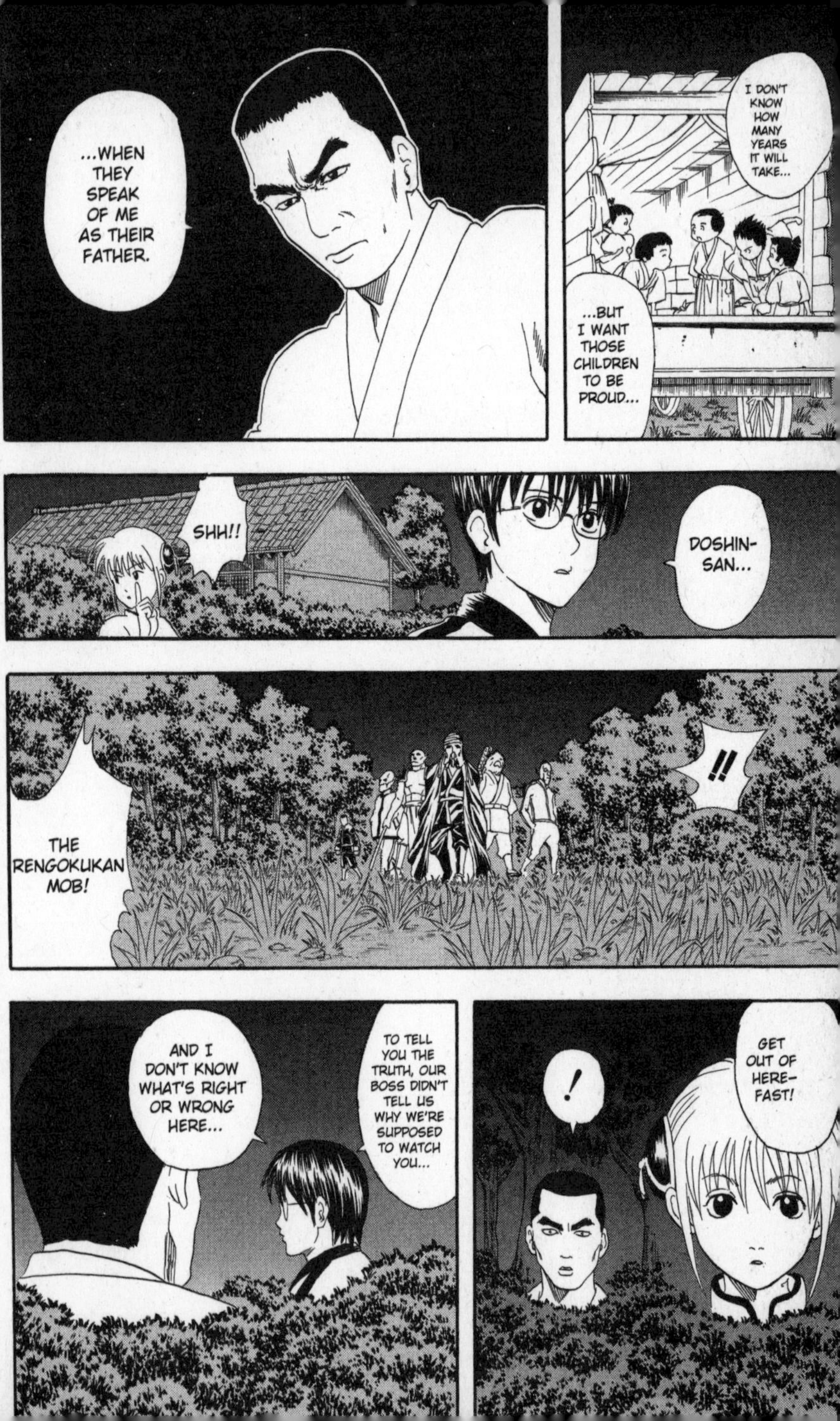
I DON'T KNOW HOW MANY YEARS IT WILL TAKE...
...BUT I WANT THOSE CHILDREN TO BE PROUD...
...WHEN THEY SPEAK OF ME AS THEIR FATHER.
DOSHIN-SAN...
SHH!!
!!
THE RENGOKUKAN MOB!
TO TELL YOU THE TRUTH, OUR BOSS DIDN'T TELL US WHY WE'RE SUPPOSED TO WATCH YOU...
AND I DON'T KNOW WHAT'S RIGHT OR WRONG HERE...
GET OUT OF HERE-FAST!
!

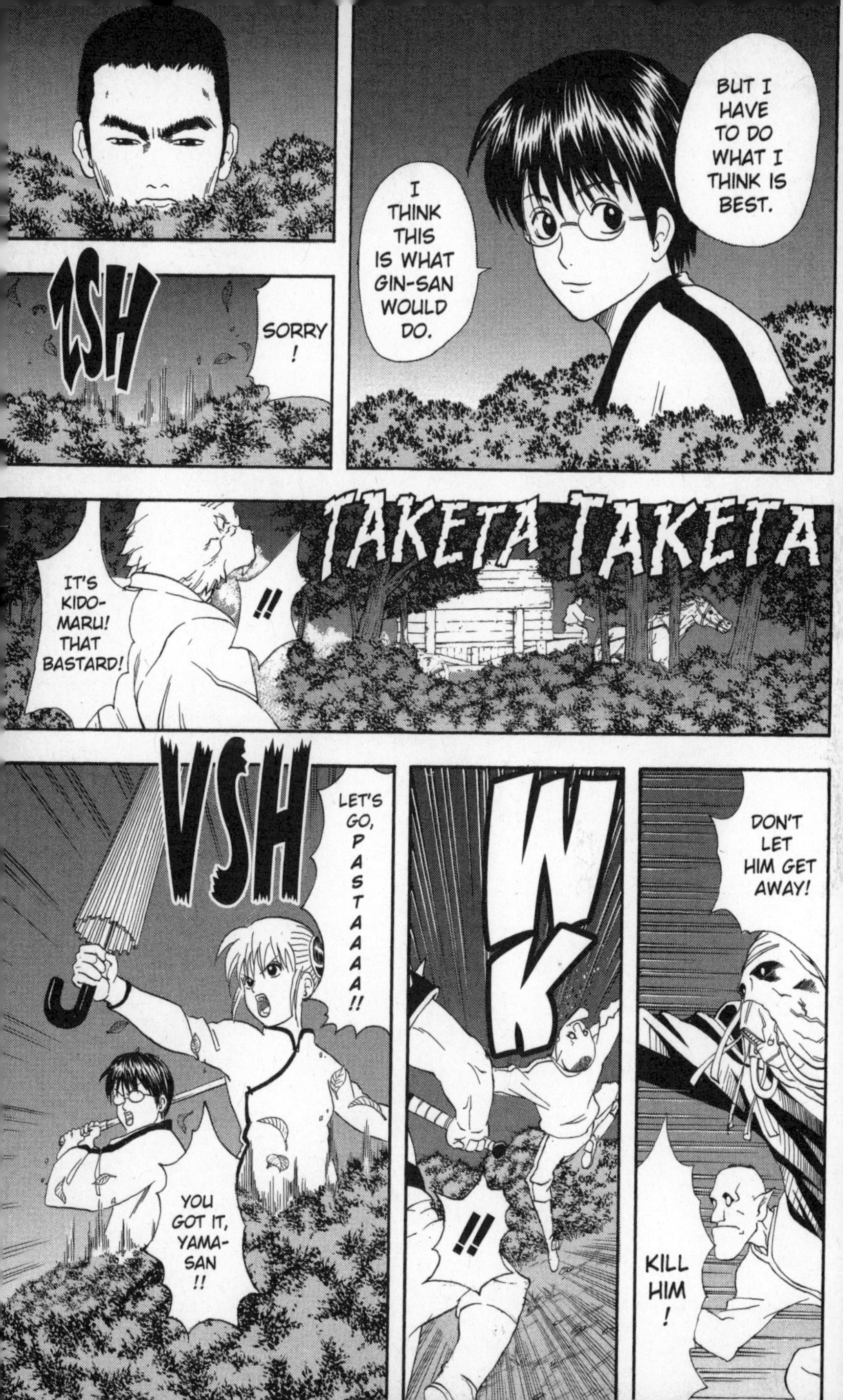
BUT I HAVE TO DO WHAT I THINK IS BEST.
I THINK THIS IS WHAT GIN-SAN WOULD DO.
SORRY!
ZSH
TAKETA TAKETA
!!
IT'S KIDO-MARU! THAT BASTARD!
DON'T LET HIM GET AWAY!
KILL HIM!
WK
!!
LET'S GO, PASTAAAAAA!!
VSH
YOU GOT IT, YAMA-SAN!!

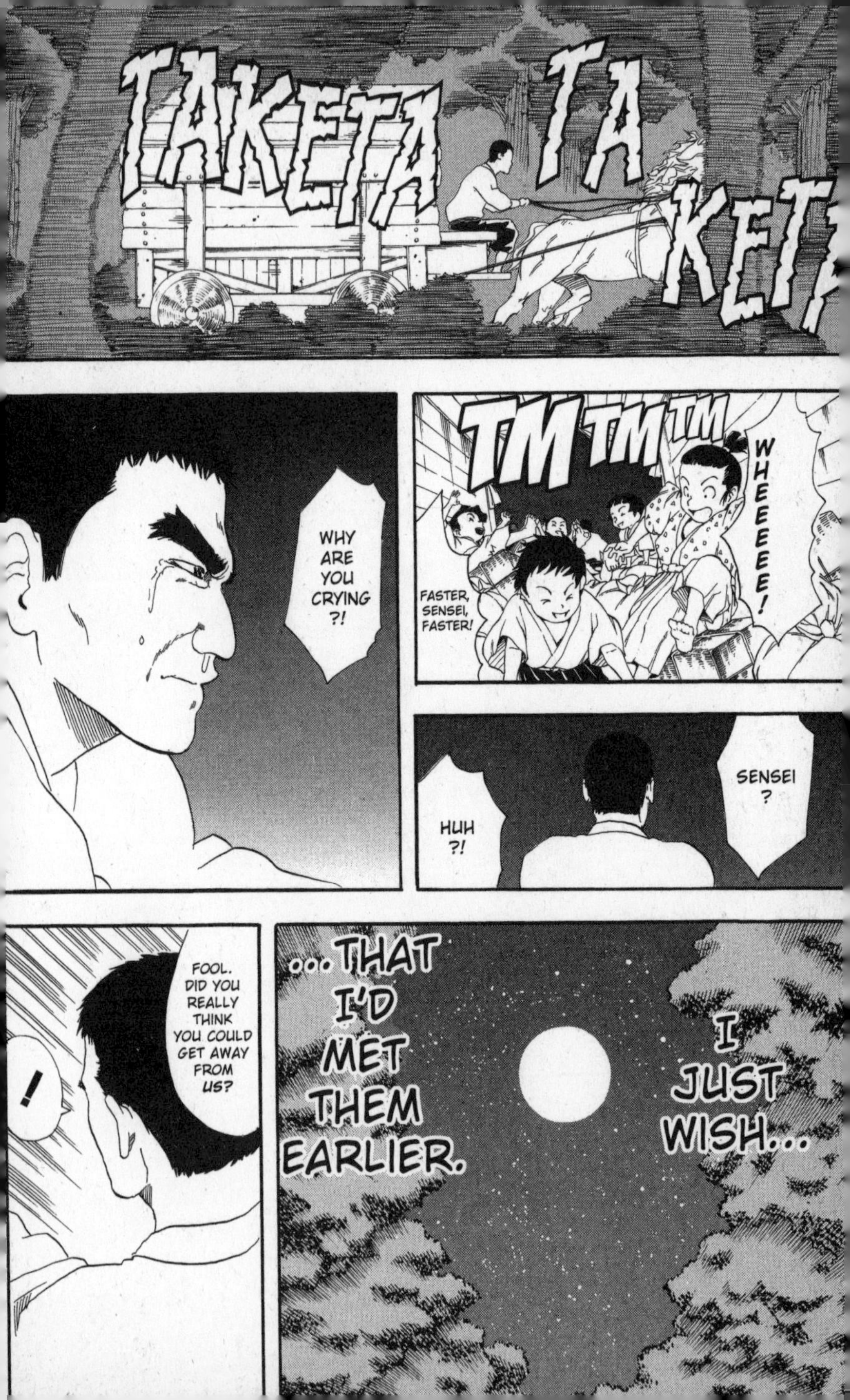
TAKETA TA KETA
WHEEEEEE!
TM TM TM
FASTER, SENSEI, FASTER!
SENSEI?
HUH?!
WHY ARE YOU CRYING?!
I JUST WISH...
...THAT I'D MET THEM EARLIER.
FOOL. DID YOU REALLY THINK YOU COULD GET AWAY FROM US?
!

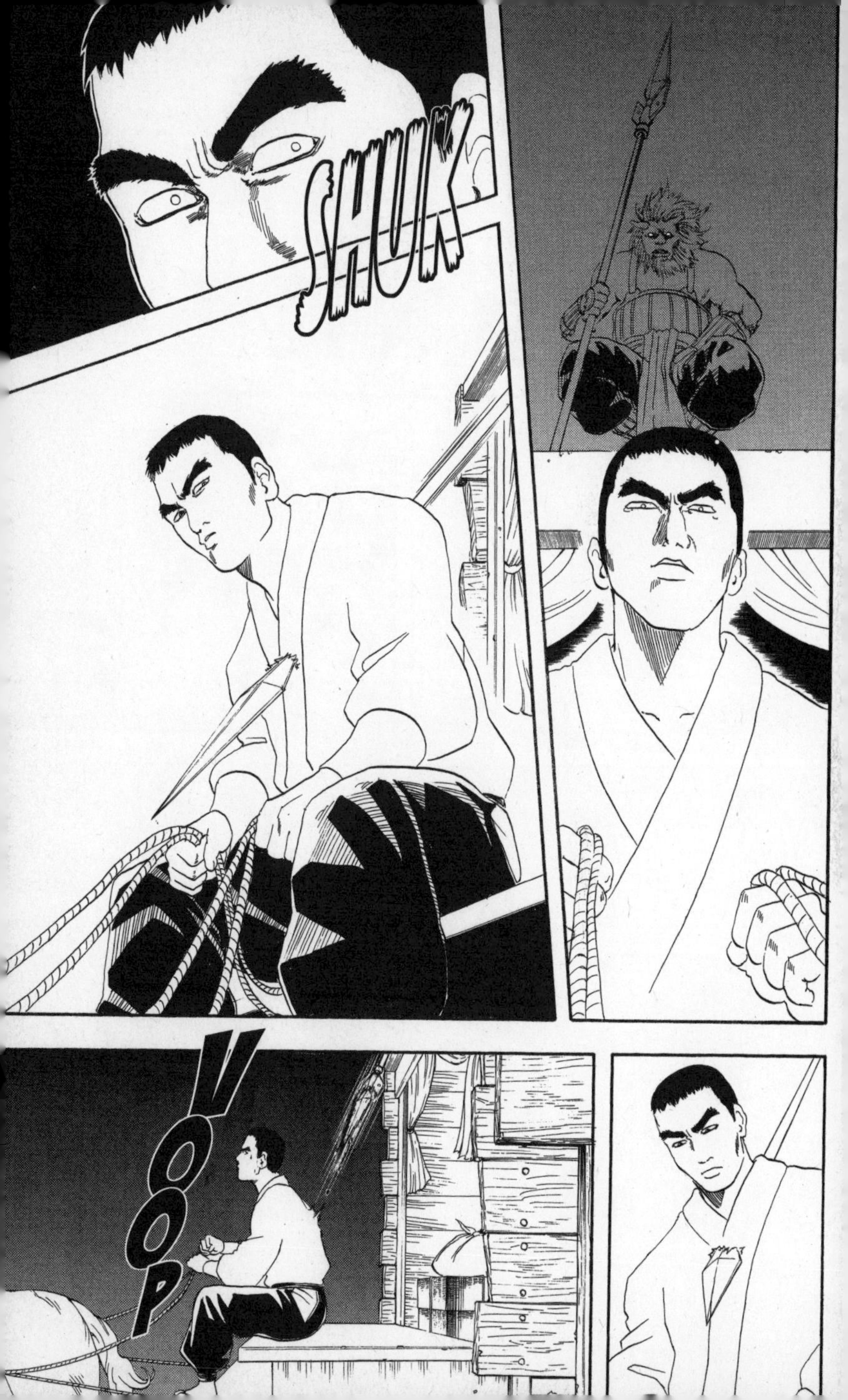
SHUK
VOOOP

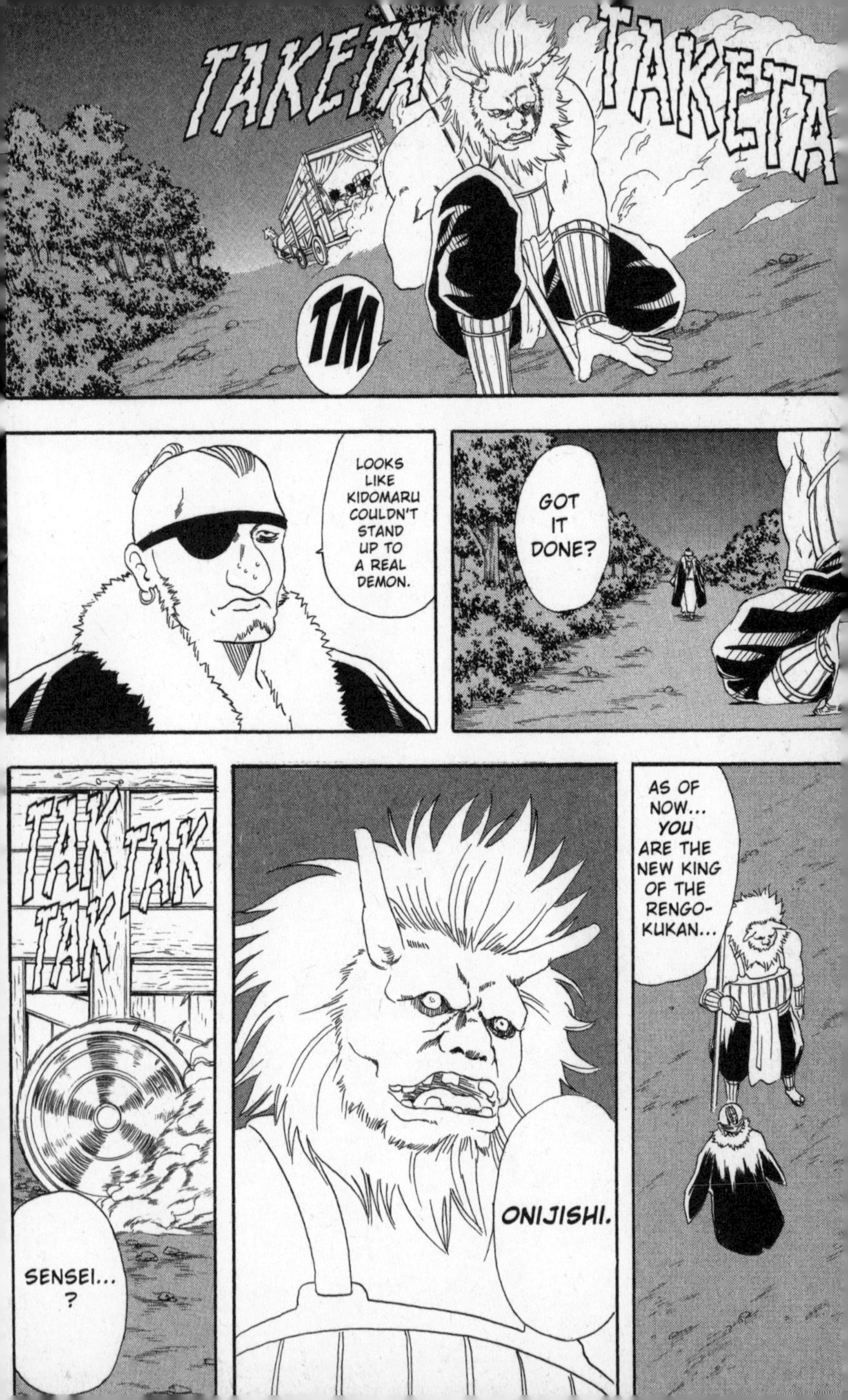
TAKETA
TAKETA
TM
GOT IT DONE?
LOOKS LIKE KIDOMARU COULDN'T STAND UP TO A REAL DEMON.
AS OF NOW... *YOU* ARE THE NEW KING OF THE RENGO-KUKAN...
ONIJISHI.
TAK TAK TAK TAK
SENSEI... ?

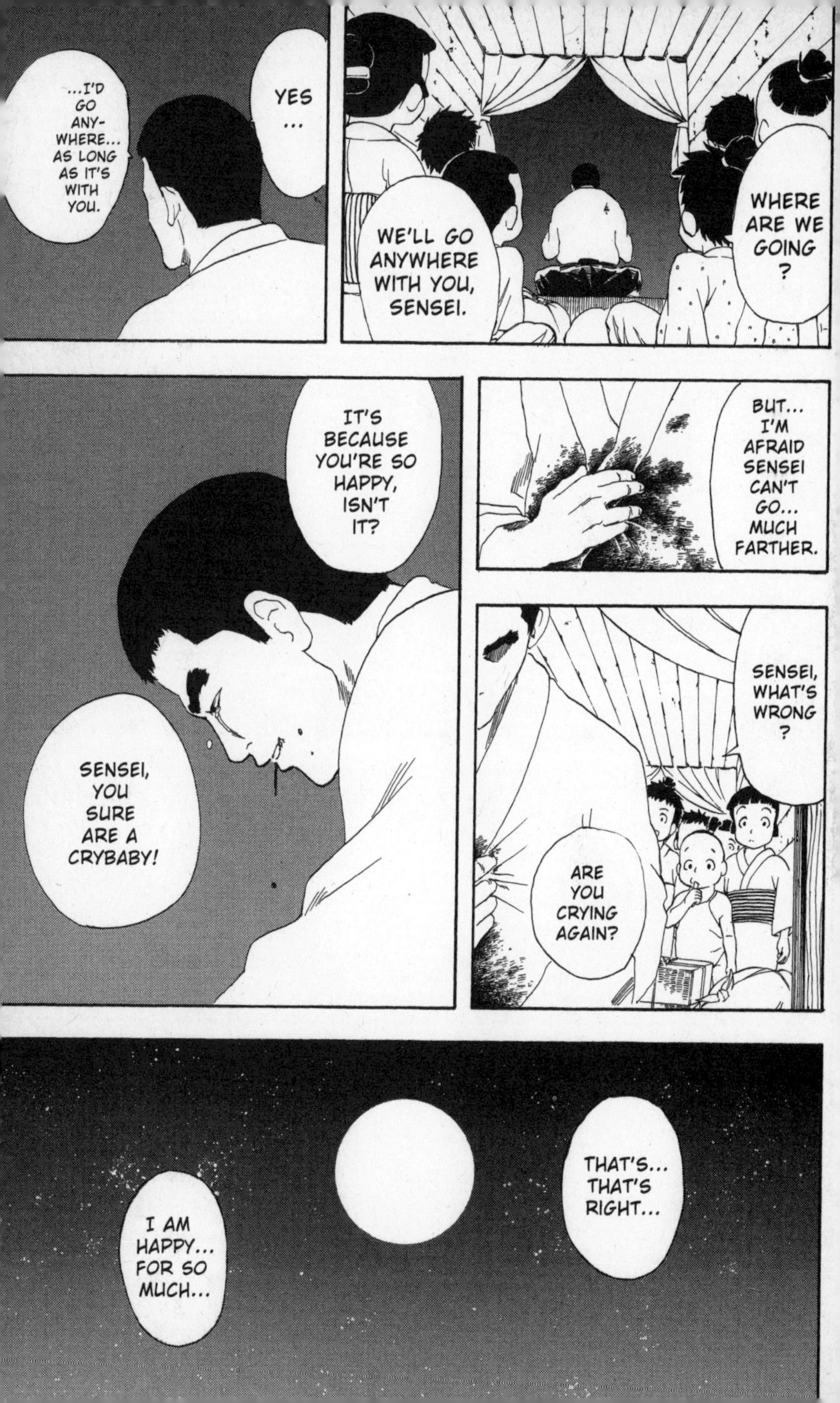
WHERE ARE WE GOING?
WE'LL GO ANYWHERE WITH YOU, SENSEI.
YES...
...I'D GO ANYWHERE... AS LONG AS IT'S WITH YOU.
BUT... I'M AFRAID SENSEI CAN'T GO... MUCH FARTHER.
SENSEI, WHAT'S WRONG?
ARE YOU CRYING AGAIN?
IT'S BECAUSE YOU'RE SO HAPPY, ISN'T IT?
SENSEI, YOU SURE ARE A CRYBABY!
THAT'S... THAT'S RIGHT...
I AM HAPPY... FOR SO MUCH...

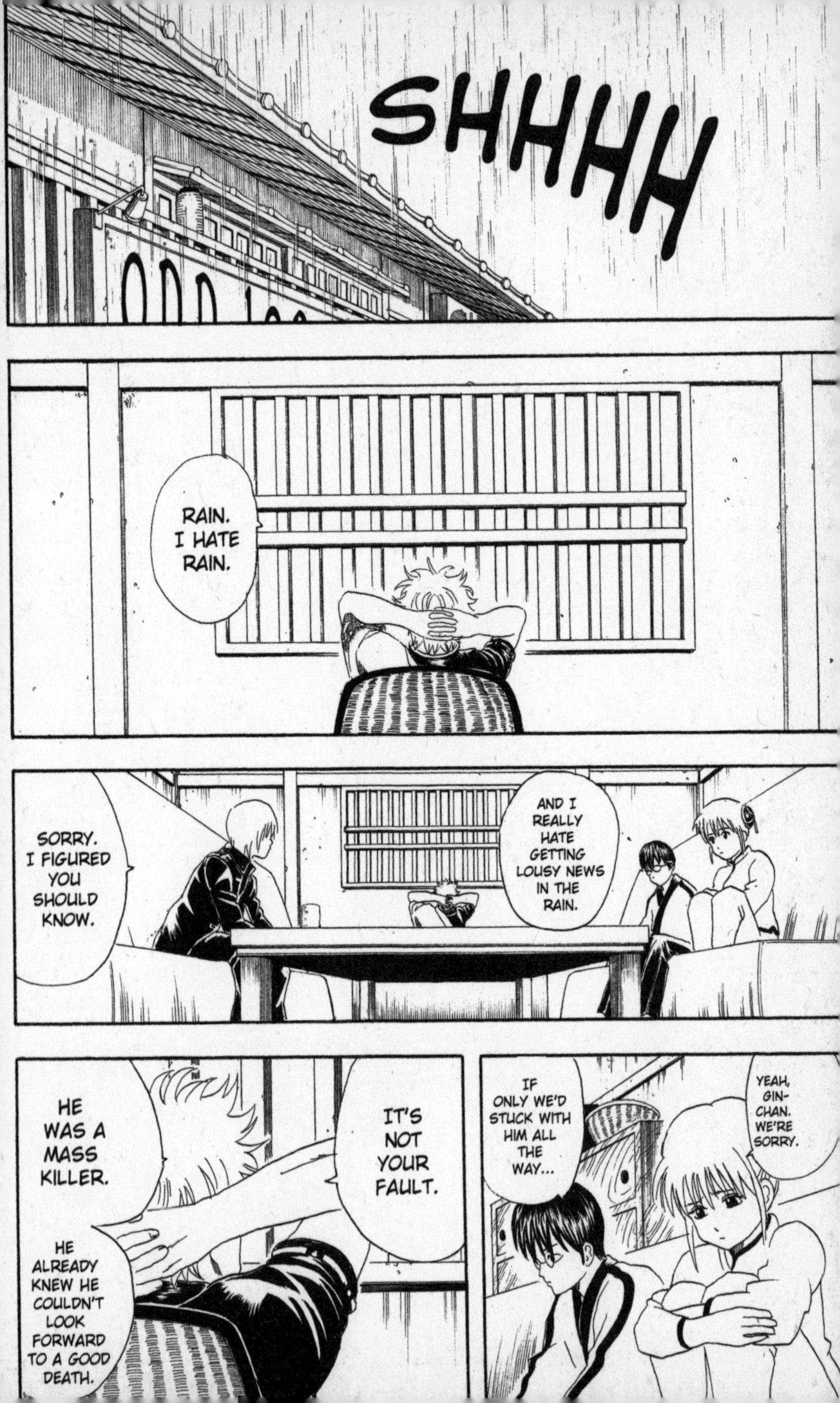
SHHHH
RAIN. I HATE RAIN.
AND I REALLY HATE GETTING LOUSY NEWS IN THE RAIN.
SORRY. I FIGURED YOU SHOULD KNOW.
YEAH, GIN-CHAN. WE'RE SORRY.
IF ONLY WE'D STUCK WITH HIM ALL THE WAY...
IT'S NOT YOUR FAULT.
HE WAS A MASS KILLER.
HE ALREADY KNEW HE COULDN'T LOOK FORWARD TO A GOOD DEATH.

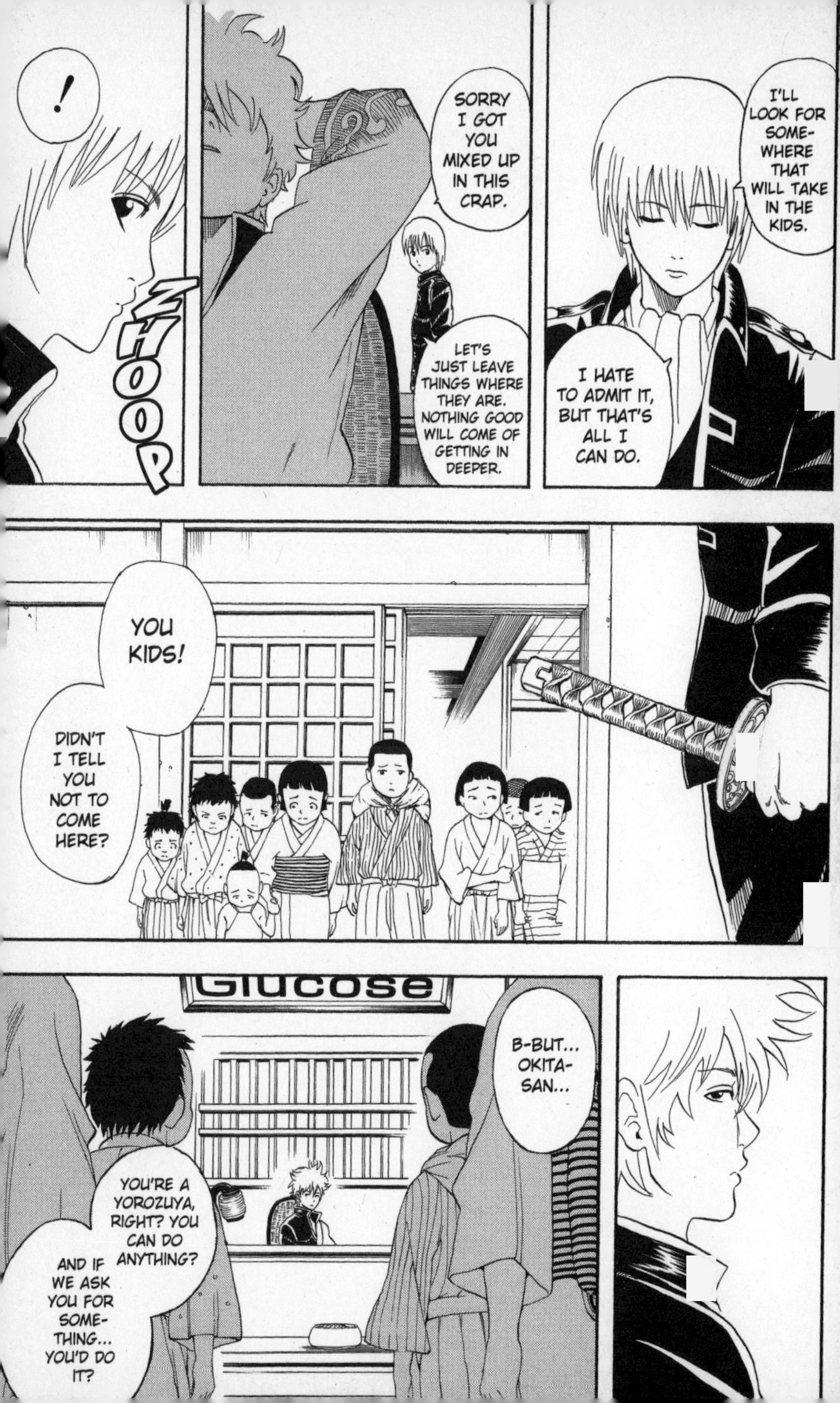
I'LL LOOK FOR SOME-WHERE THAT WILL TAKE IN THE KIDS.
I HATE TO ADMIT IT, BUT THAT'S ALL I CAN DO.
SORRY I GOT YOU MIXED UP IN THIS CRAP.
LET'S JUST LEAVE THINGS WHERE THEY ARE. NOTHING GOOD WILL COME OF GETTING IN DEEPER.
!
ZHOOP
YOU KIDS!
DIDN'T I TELL YOU NOT TO COME HERE?
B-BUT... OKITA-SAN...
Glucose
YOU'RE A YOROZUYA, RIGHT? YOU CAN DO ANYTHING?
AND IF WE ASK YOU FOR SOME-THING... YOU'D DO IT?

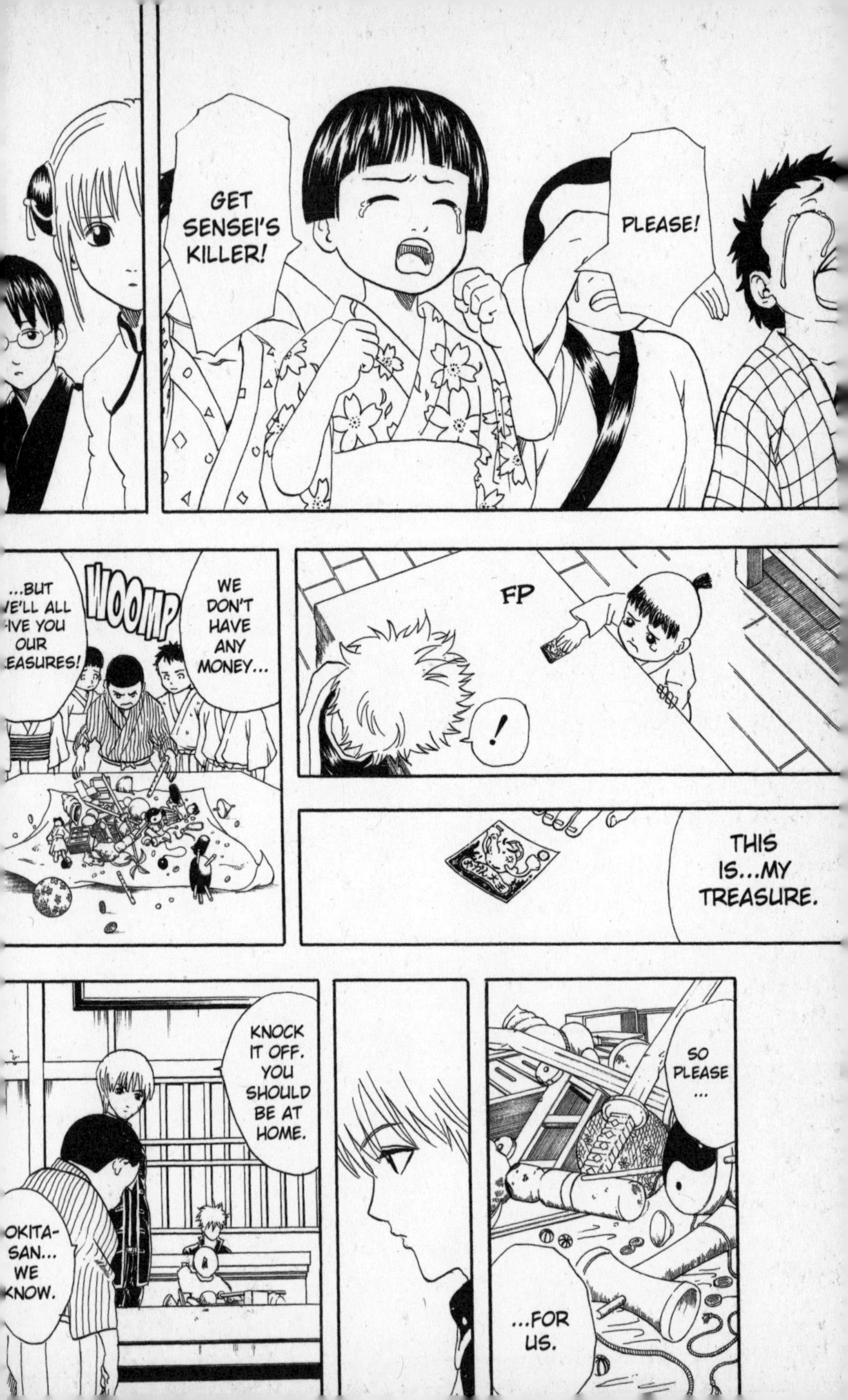
PLEASE!
GET SENSEI'S KILLER!
FP
!
THIS IS...MY TREASURE.
WE DON'T HAVE ANY MONEY...
WOOMP
...BUT E'LL ALL IVE YOU OUR EASURES!
SO PLEASE ...
...FOR US.
KNOCK IT OFF. YOU SHOULD BE AT HOME.
OKITA-SAN... WE KNOW.

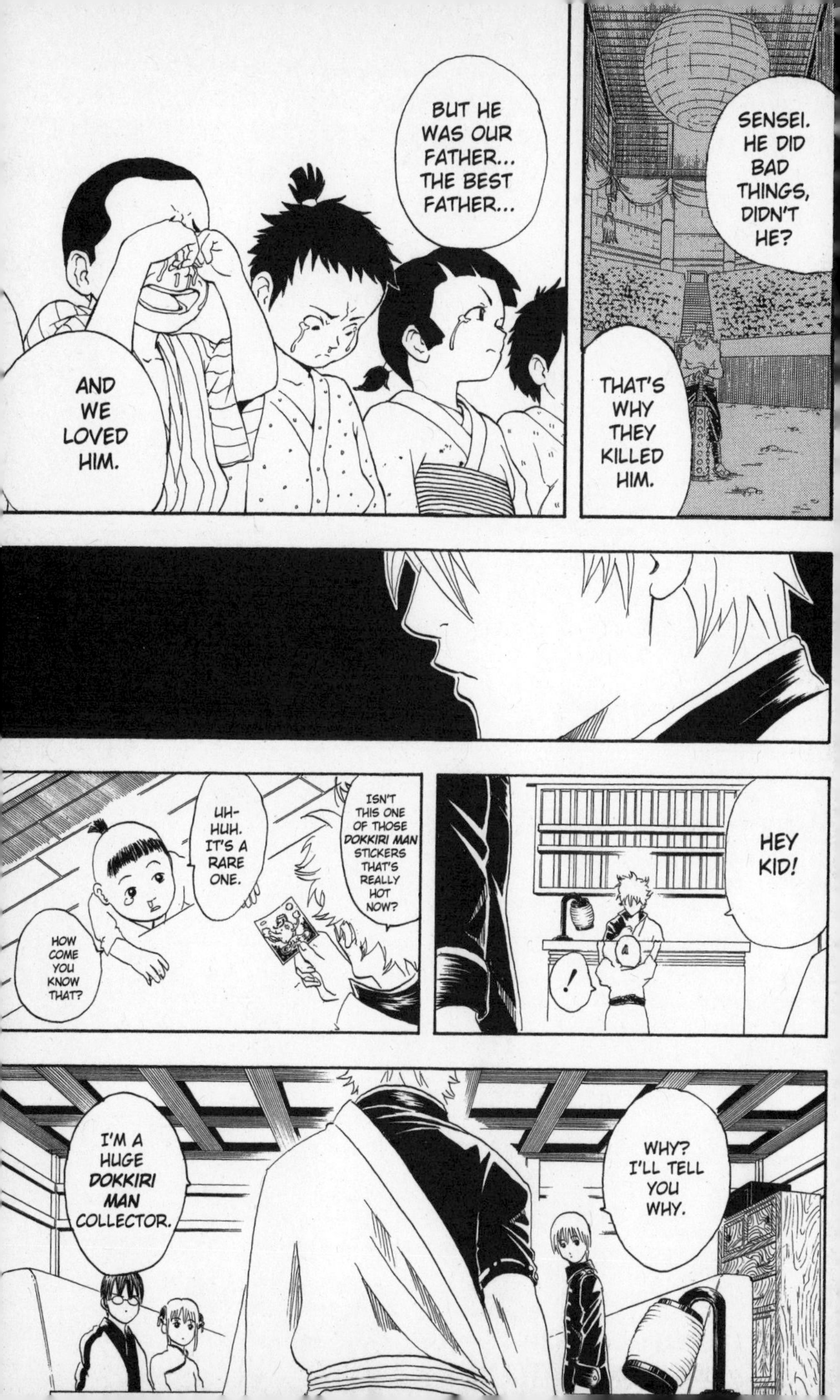
SENSEI. HE DID BAD THINGS, DIDN'T HE?
THAT'S WHY THEY KILLED HIM.
BUT HE WAS OUR FATHER... THE BEST FATHER...
AND WE LOVED HIM.
HEY KID!
!
ISN'T THIS ONE OF THOSE *DOKKIRI MAN* STICKERS THAT'S REALLY HOT NOW?
UH-HUH. IT'S A RARE ONE.
HOW COME YOU KNOW THAT?
WHY? I'LL TELL YOU WHY.
I'M A HUGE *DOKKIRI MAN* COLLECTOR.

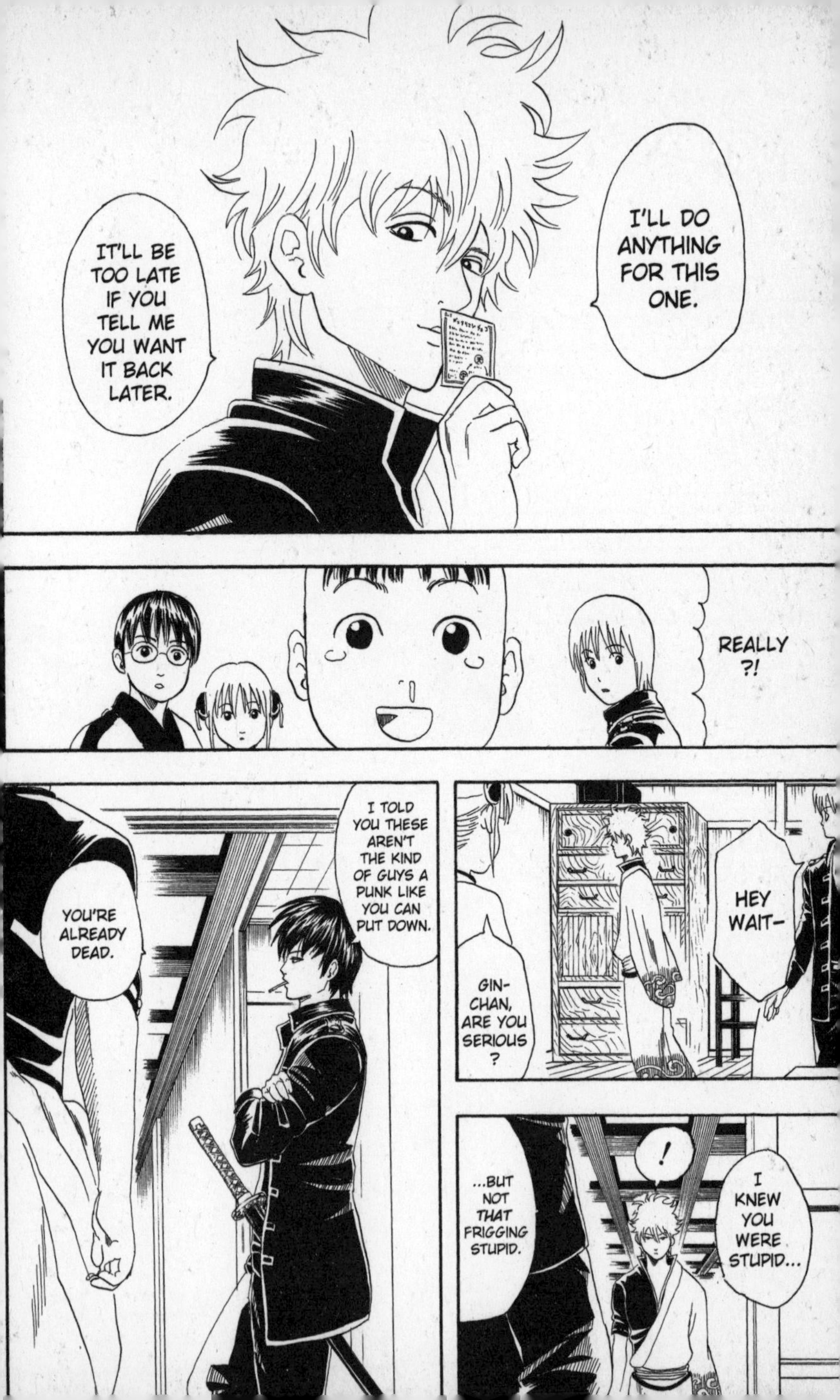
I'LL DO ANYTHING FOR THIS ONE.
IT'LL BE TOO LATE IF YOU TELL ME YOU WANT IT BACK LATER.
REALLY ?!
HEY WAIT-
GIN-CHAN, ARE YOU SERIOUS ?
!
I KNEW YOU WERE STUPID...
...BUT NOT THAT FRIGGING STUPID.
I TOLD YOU THESE AREN'T THE KIND OF GUYS A PUNK LIKE YOU CAN PUT DOWN.
YOU'RE ALREADY DEAD.

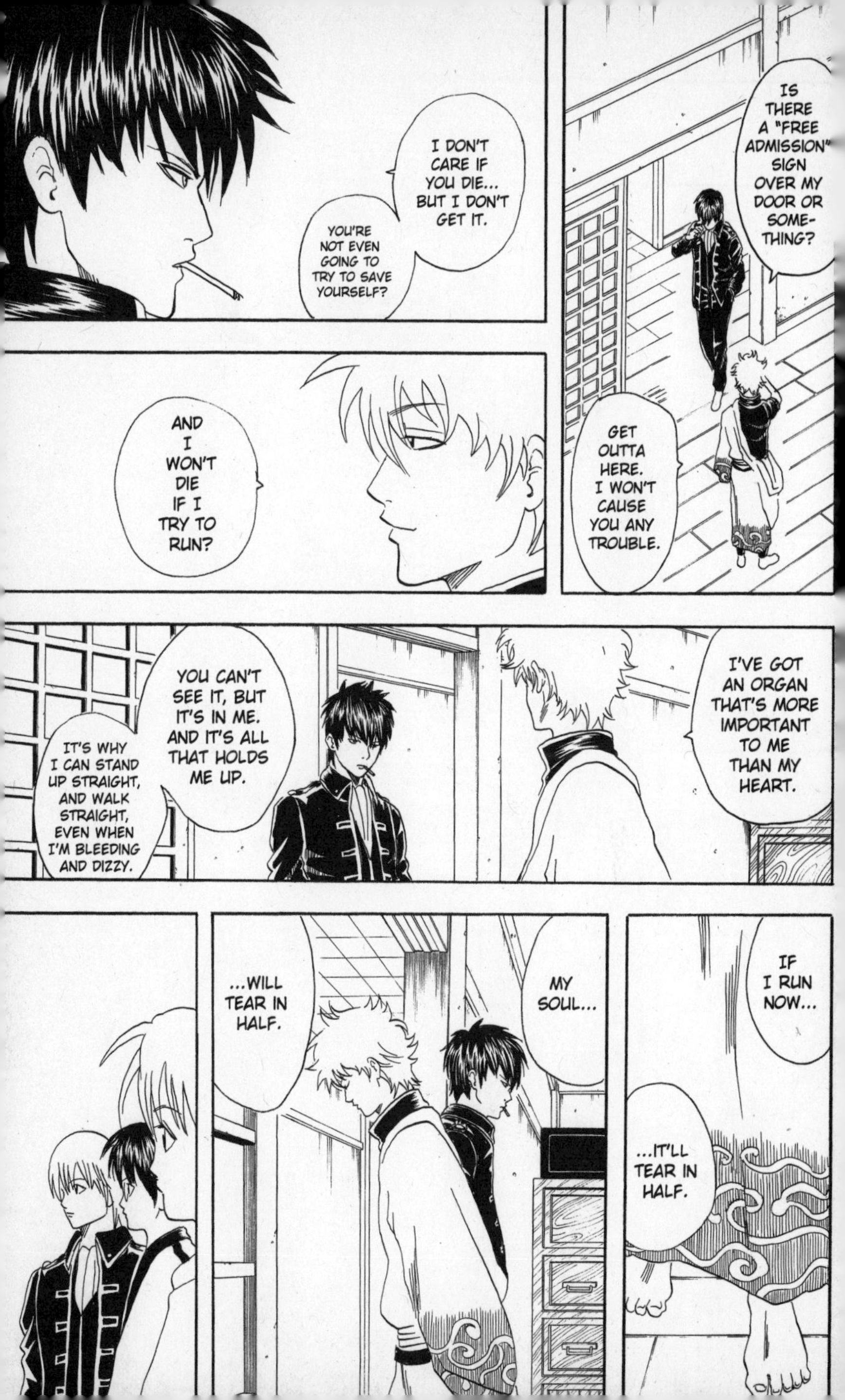

IS THERE A "FREE ADMISSION" SIGN OVER MY DOOR OR SOME-THING?
GET OUTTA HERE. I WON'T CAUSE YOU ANY TROUBLE.
I DON'T CARE IF YOU DIE... BUT I DON'T GET IT.
YOU'RE NOT EVEN GOING TO TRY TO SAVE YOURSELF?
AND I WON'T DIE IF I TRY TO RUN?
I'VE GOT AN ORGAN THAT'S MORE IMPORTANT TO ME THAN MY HEART.
YOU CAN'T SEE IT, BUT IT'S IN ME. AND IT'S ALL THAT HOLDS ME UP.
IT'S WHY I CAN STAND UP STRAIGHT, AND WALK STRAIGHT, EVEN WHEN I'M BLEEDING AND DIZZY.
IF I RUN NOW...
...IT'LL TEAR IN HALF.
MY SOUL...
...WILL TEAR IN HALF.

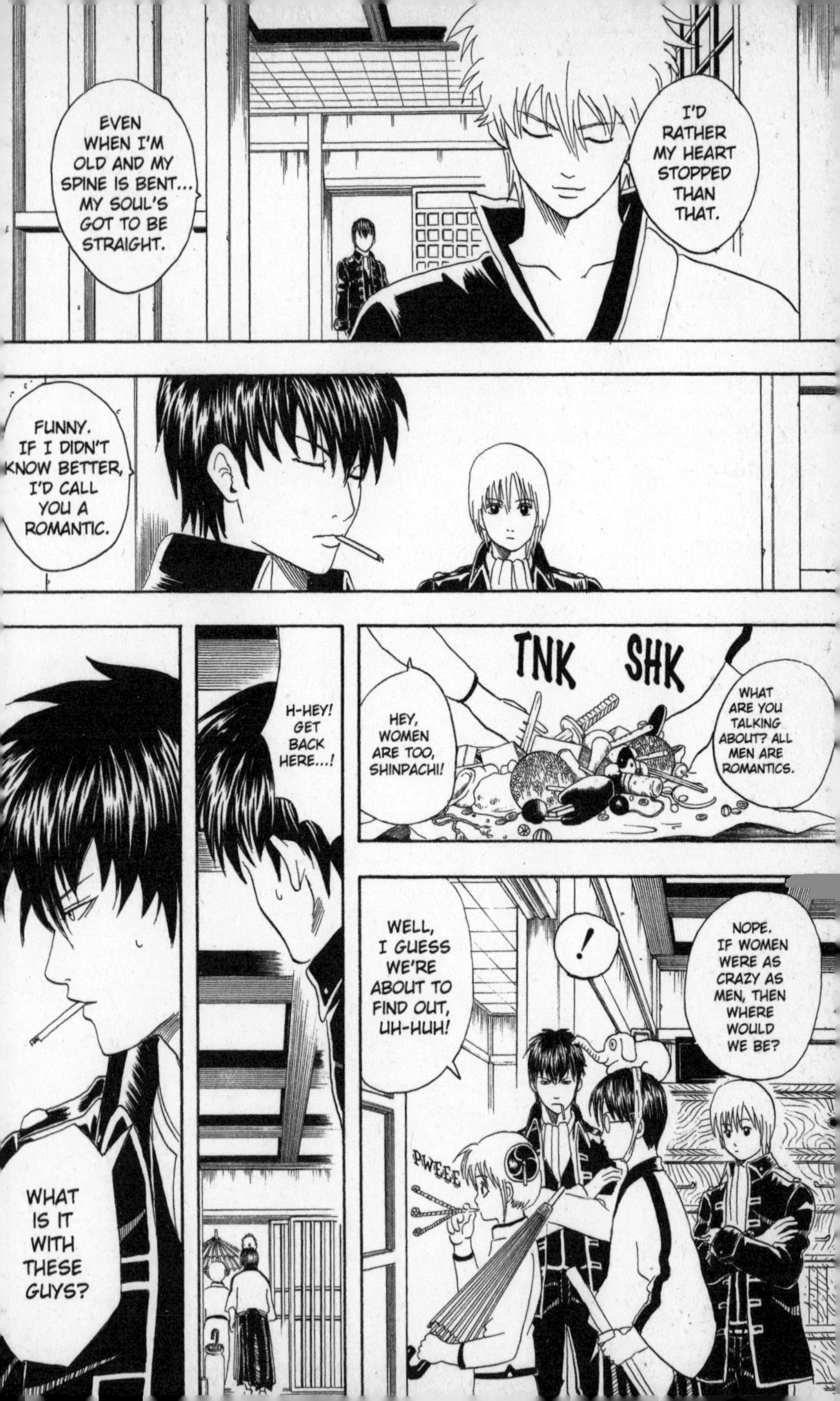
I'D RATHER MY HEART STOPPED THAN THAT.
EVEN WHEN I'M OLD AND MY SPINE IS BENT... MY SOUL'S GOT TO BE STRAIGHT.
FUNNY. IF I DIDN'T KNOW BETTER, I'D CALL YOU A ROMANTIC.
SHK
WHAT ARE YOU TALKING ABOUT? ALL MEN ARE ROMANTICS.
TNK
HEY, WOMEN ARE TOO, SHINPACHI!
NOPE. IF WOMEN WERE AS CRAZY AS MEN, THEN WHERE WOULD WE BE?
!
WELL, I GUESS WE'RE ABOUT TO FIND OUT, UH-HUH!
PWEEE
H-HEY! GET BACK HERE...!
WHAT IS IT WITH THESE GUYS?

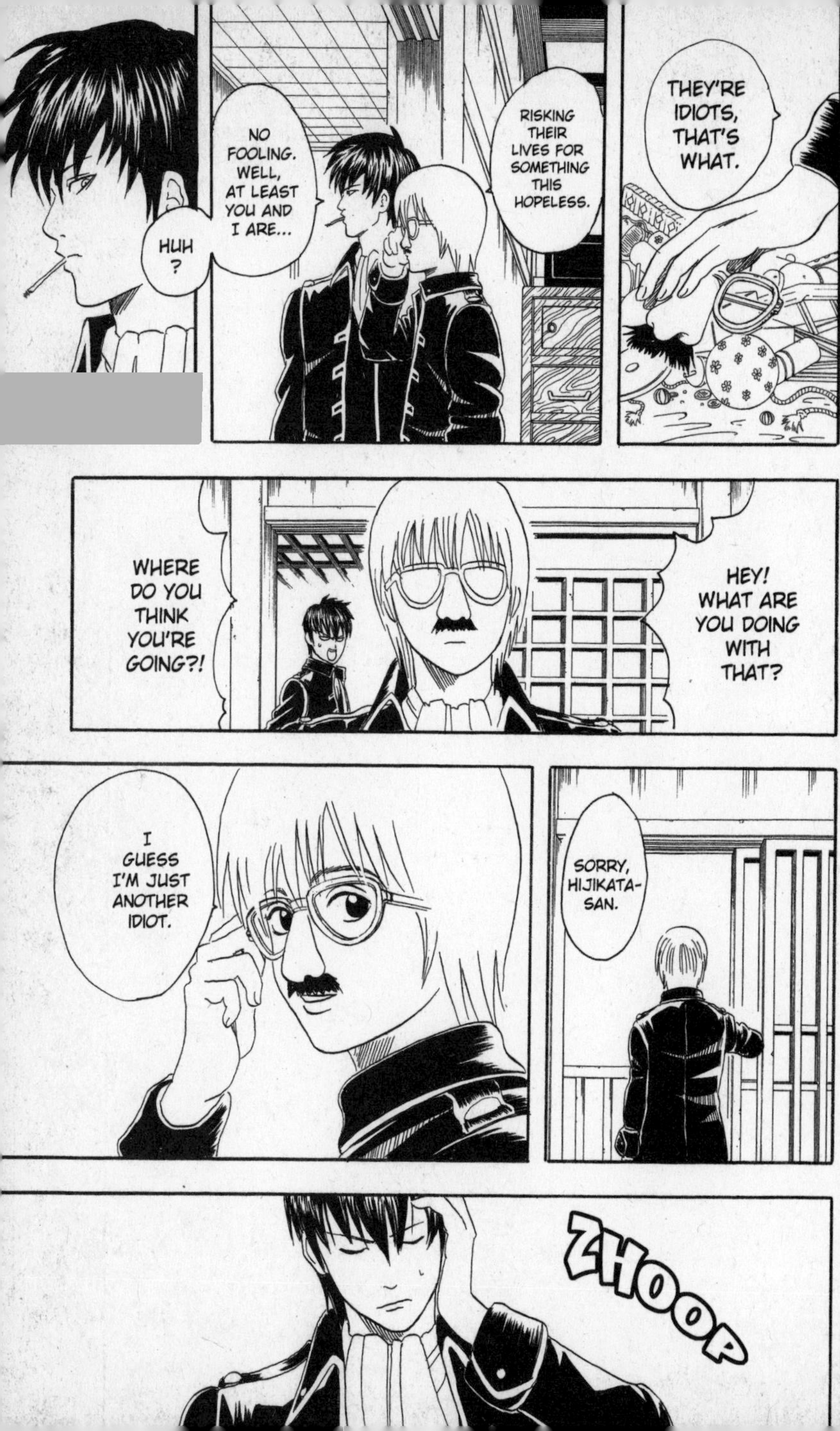
THEY'RE IDIOTS, THAT'S WHAT.
RISKING THEIR LIVES FOR SOMETHING THIS HOPELESS.
NO FOOLING. WELL, AT LEAST YOU AND I ARE...
HUH?
HEY! WHAT ARE YOU DOING WITH THAT?
WHERE DO YOU THINK YOU'RE GOING?!
SORRY, HIJIKATA-SAN.
I GUESS I'M JUST ANOTHER IDIOT.
ZHOOP

This is an early version of Chief Kondo. He's just Hasegawa! Seriously—I based my final Hasegawa on this Kondo design. Hasegawa was really the chief of the Shinsengumi. This Chief Kondo is sort of best described as what you'd get if you mix the current Kondo and Hasegawa, divide by 2 and get 3 left over. He's just an old creep, basically, always angling for an arranged marriage. Incidentally, Hasegawa is consistently my favorite or second-favorite character in **Gin Tama**. I'm always tempted to get him into the story—if I can come up with an excuse!

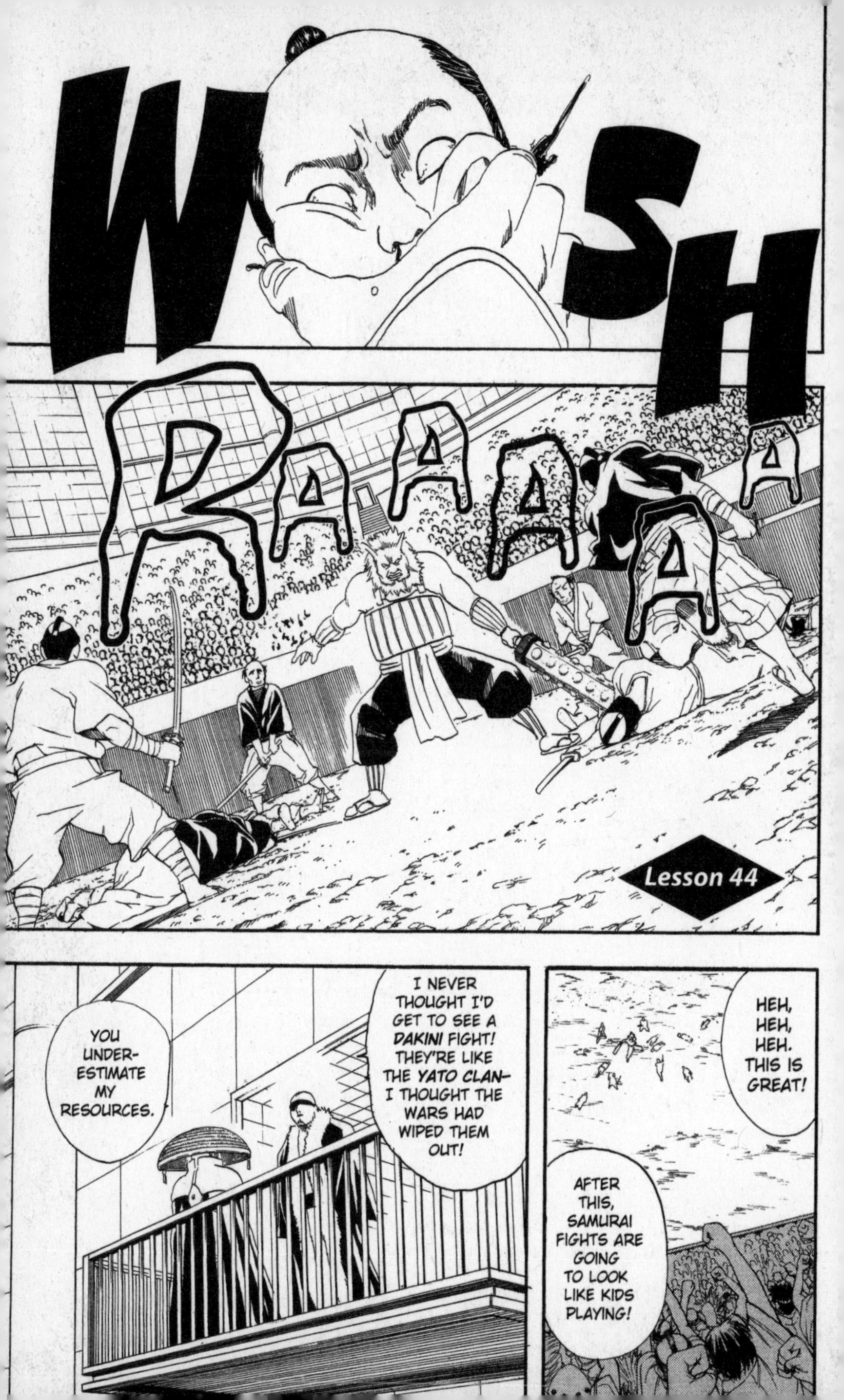
WHSH
RAAAAAA
Lesson 44
HEH, HEH, HEH. THIS IS GREAT!
AFTER THIS, SAMURAI FIGHTS ARE GOING TO LOOK LIKE KIDS PLAYING!
I NEVER THOUGHT I'D GET TO SEE A DAKINI FIGHT! THEY'RE LIKE THE YATO CLAN— I THOUGHT THE WARS HAD WIPED THEM OUT!
YOU UNDER-ESTIMATE MY RESOURCES.

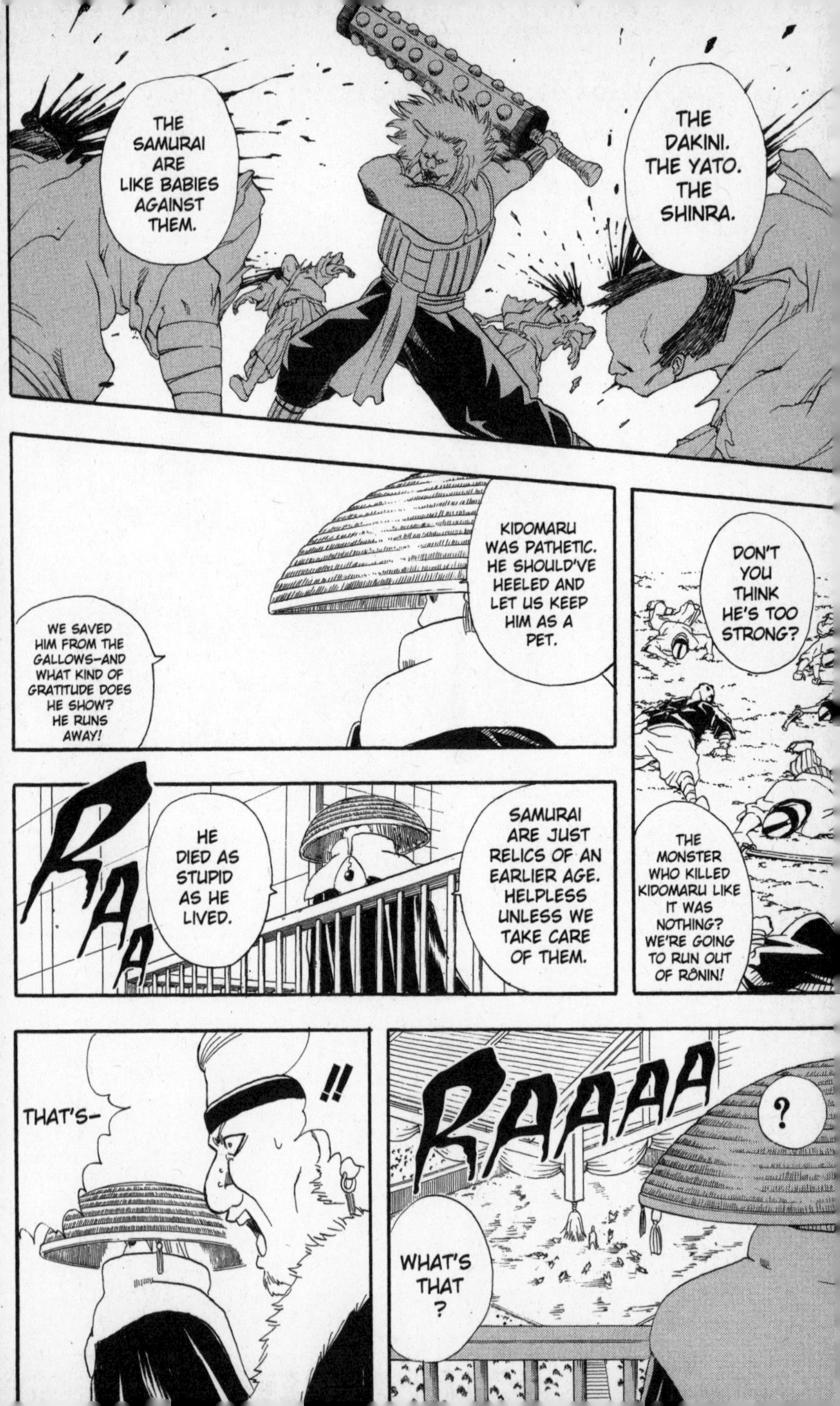
THE DAKINI. THE YATO. THE SHINRA.
THE SAMURAI ARE LIKE BABIES AGAINST THEM.
DON'T YOU THINK HE'S TOO STRONG?
THE MONSTER WHO KILLED KIDOMARU LIKE IT WAS NOTHING? WE'RE GOING TO RUN OUT OF RŌNIN!
KIDOMARU WAS PATHETIC. HE SHOULD'VE HEELED AND LET US KEEP HIM AS A PET.
WE SAVED HIM FROM THE GALLOWS—AND WHAT KIND OF GRATITUDE DOES HE SHOW? HE RUNS AWAY!
SAMURAI ARE JUST RELICS OF AN EARLIER AGE. HELPLESS UNLESS WE TAKE CARE OF THEM.
HE DIED AS STUPID AS HE LIVED.
RAAA
RAAAAA
?
WHAT'S THAT?
!!
THAT'S—

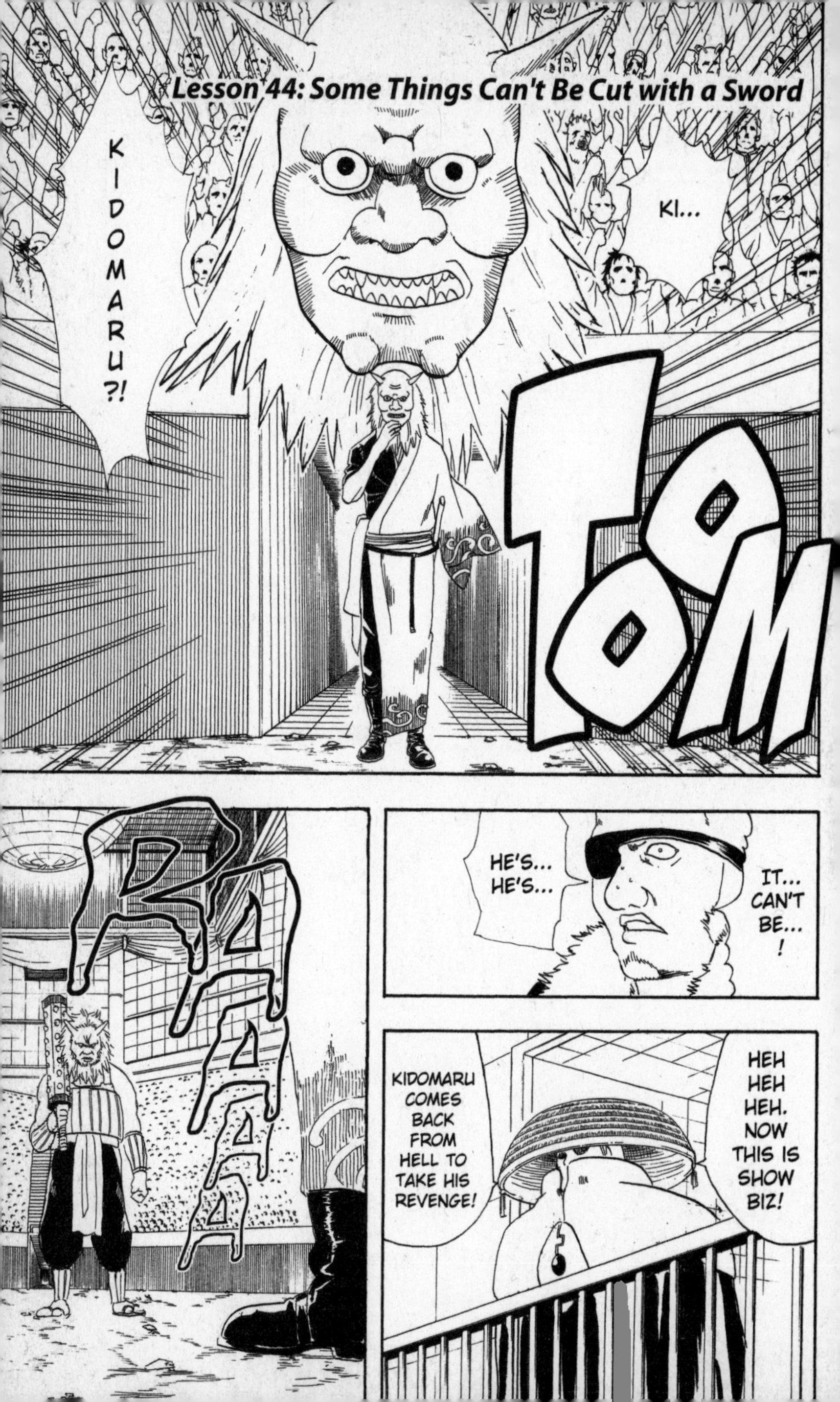
Lesson 44: Some Things Can't Be Cut with a Sword
KI...
KIDOMARU?!
TOTOM
IT... CAN'T BE...!
HE'S... HE'S...
HEH HEH HEH. NOW THIS IS SHOW BIZ!
KIDOMARU COMES BACK FROM HELL TO TAKE HIS REVENGE!

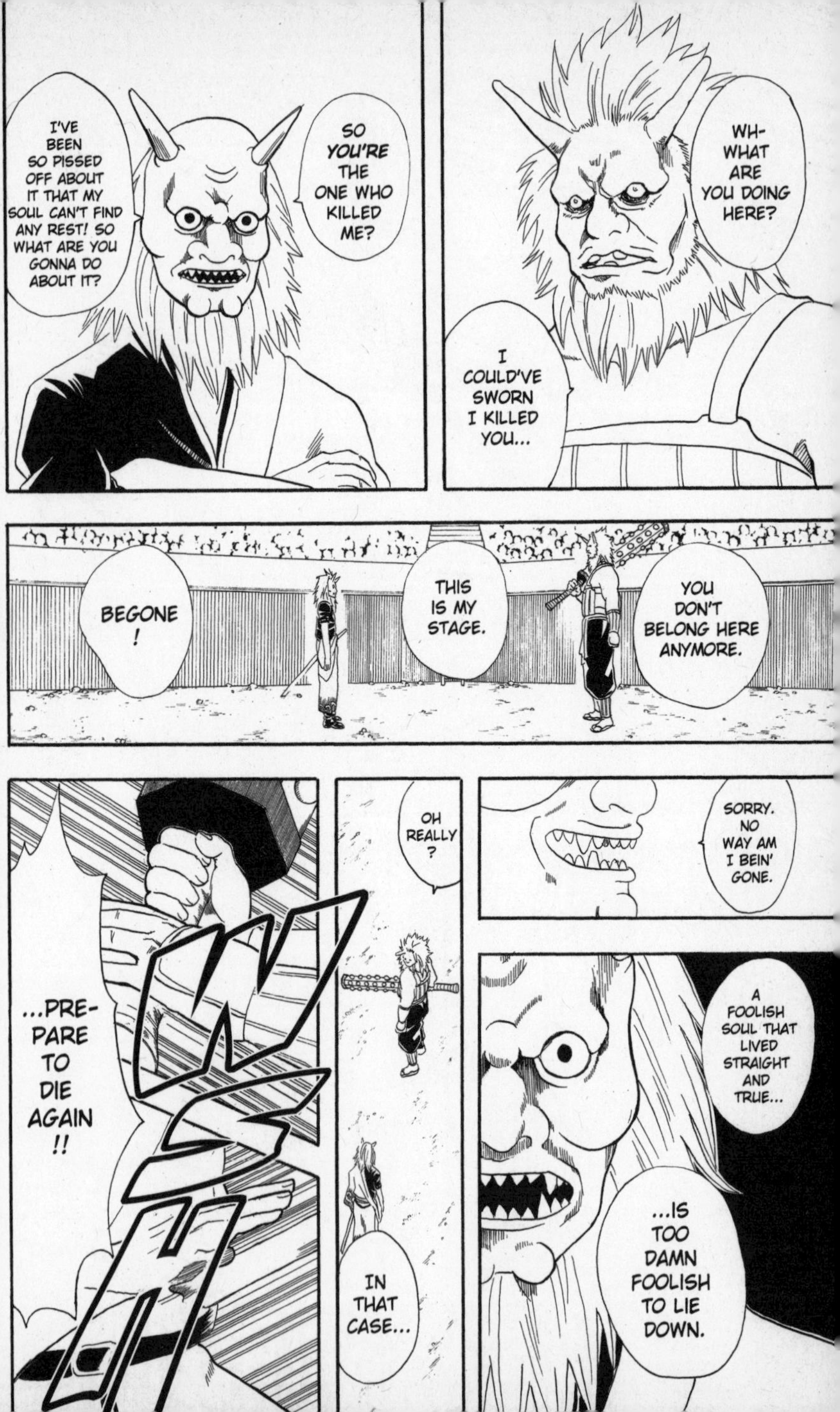
WH- WHAT ARE YOU DOING HERE?
I COULD'VE SWORN I KILLED YOU...
SO YOU'RE THE ONE WHO KILLED ME?
I'VE BEEN SO PISSED OFF ABOUT IT THAT MY SOUL CAN'T FIND ANY REST! SO WHAT ARE YOU GONNA DO ABOUT IT?
YOU DON'T BELONG HERE ANYMORE.
THIS IS MY STAGE.
BEGONE!
SORRY. NO WAY AM I BEIN' GONE.
A FOOLISH SOUL THAT LIVED STRAIGHT AND TRUE...
...IS TOO DAMN FOOLISH TO LIE DOWN.
OH REALLY?
IN THAT CASE...
...PRE-PARE TO DIE AGAIN!!

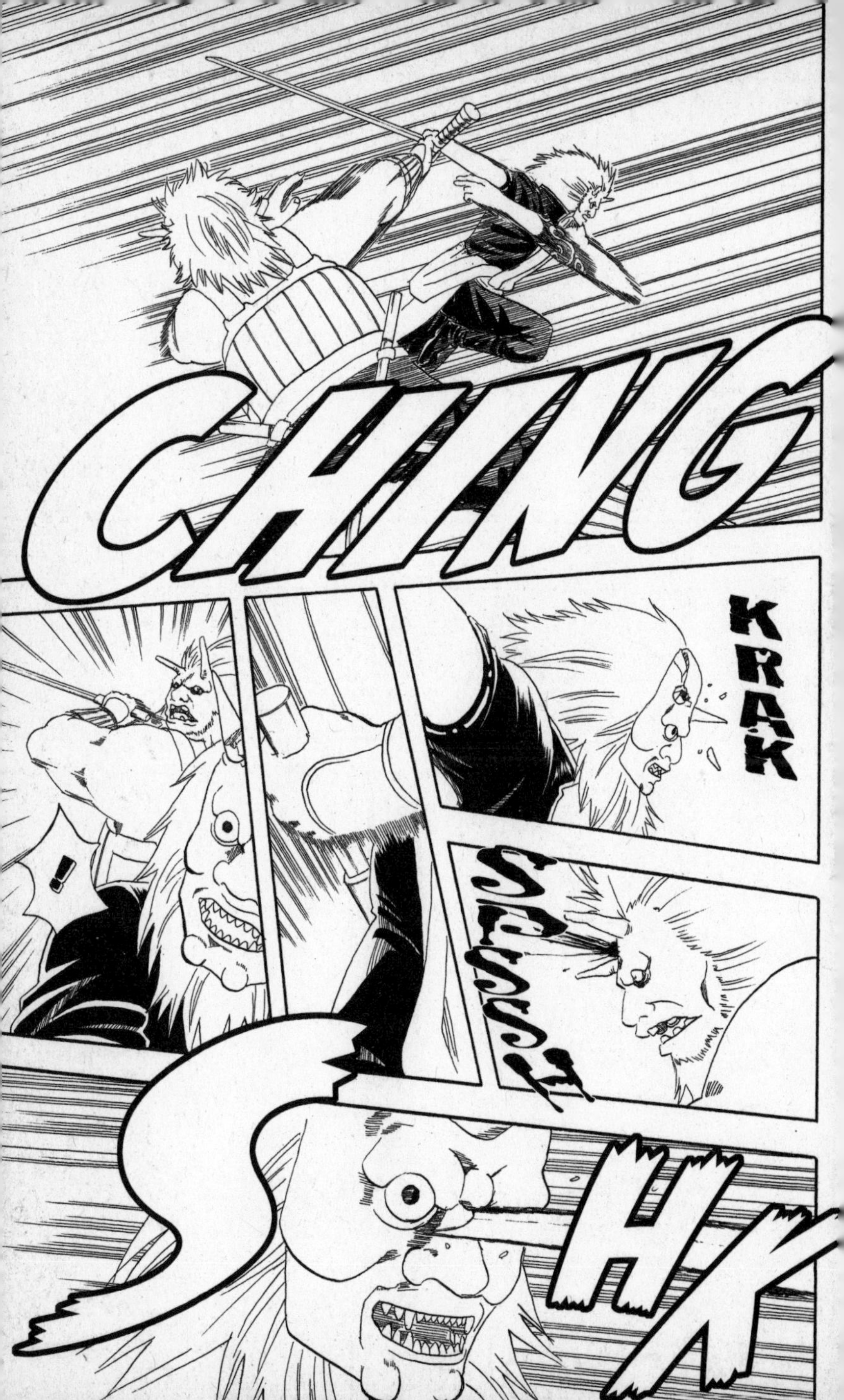
CHING
KRAK
SFSSST
!
SHK

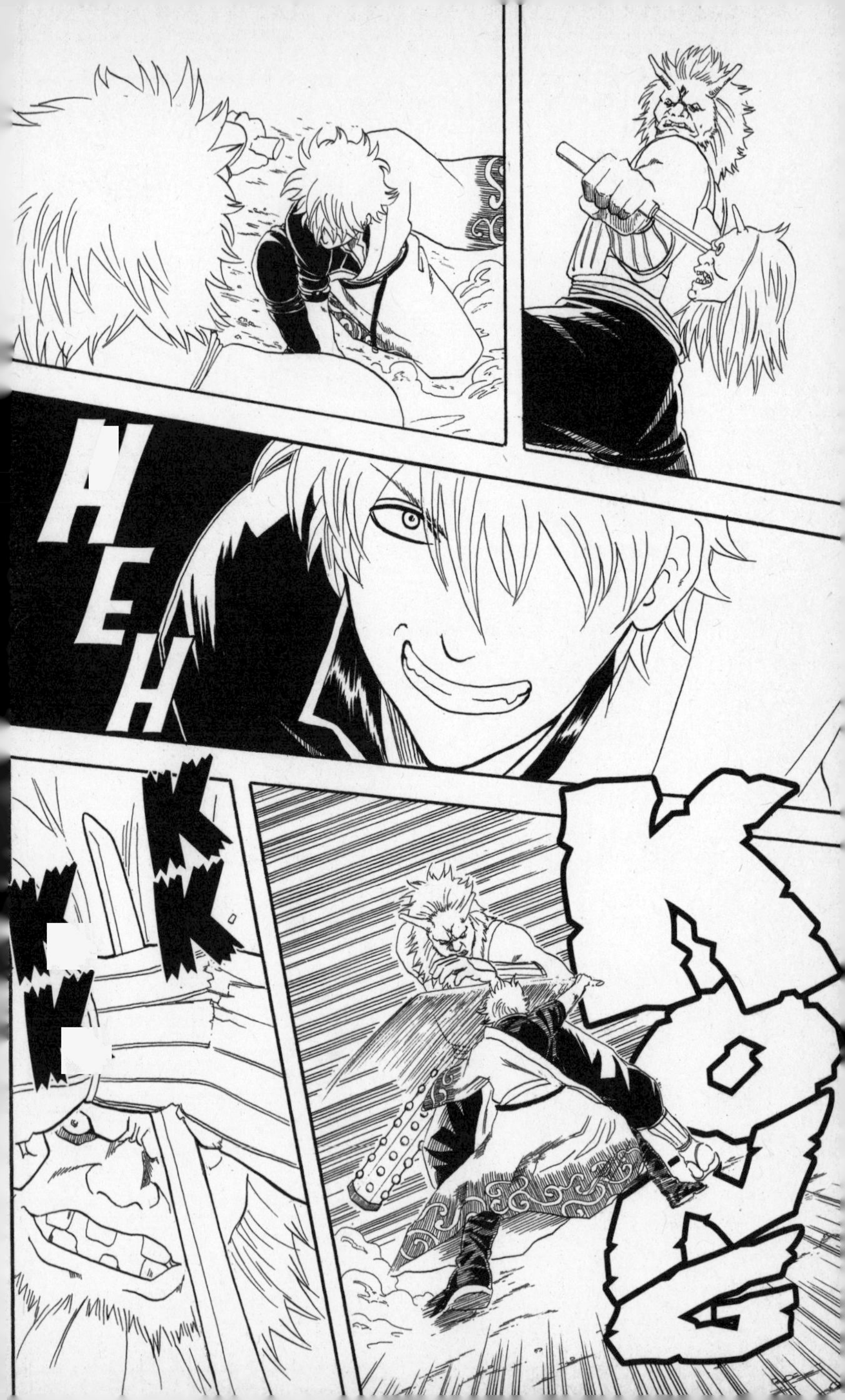
HEH

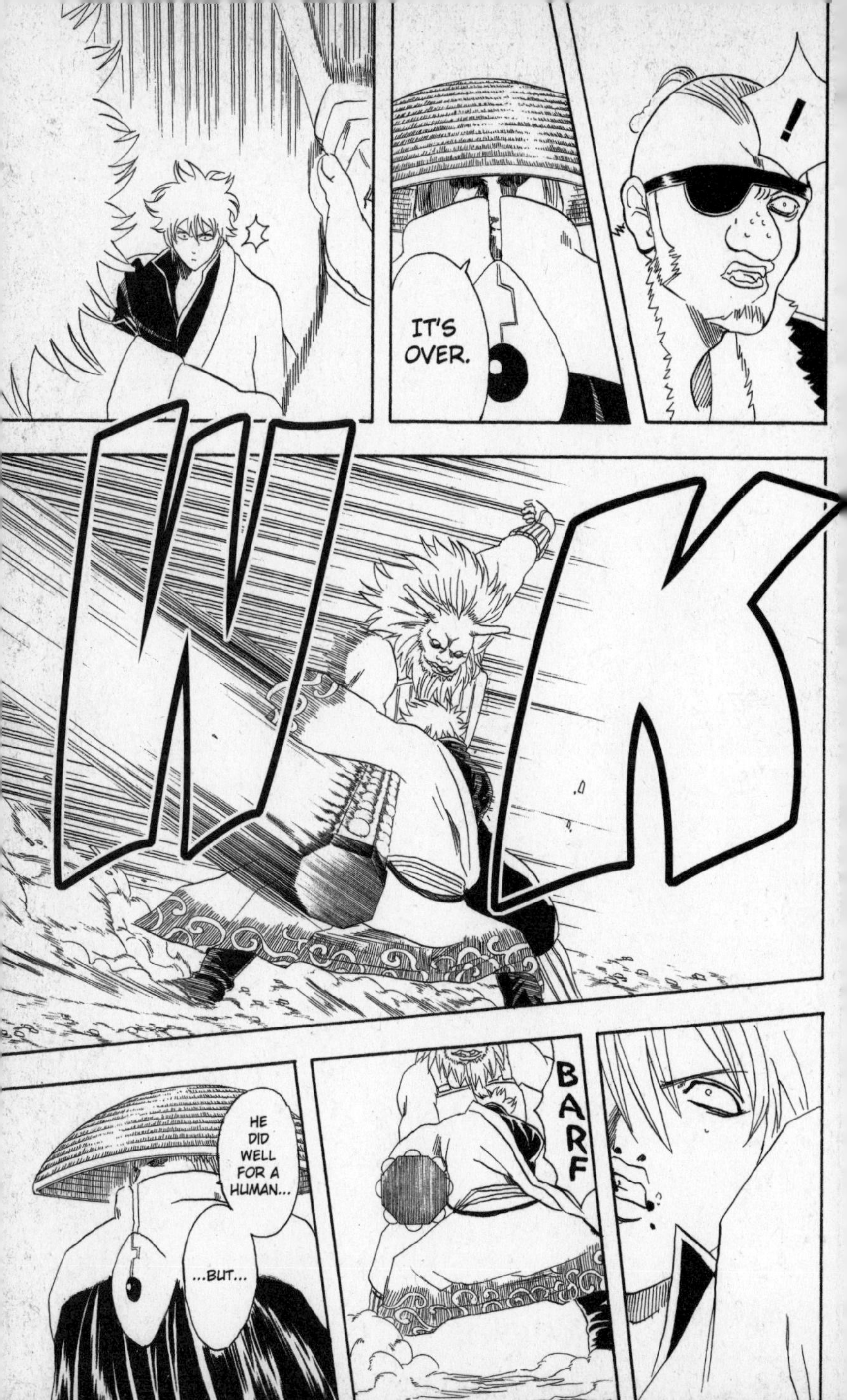
!
IT'S OVER.
BARF
HE DID WELL FOR A HUMAN...
...BUT...

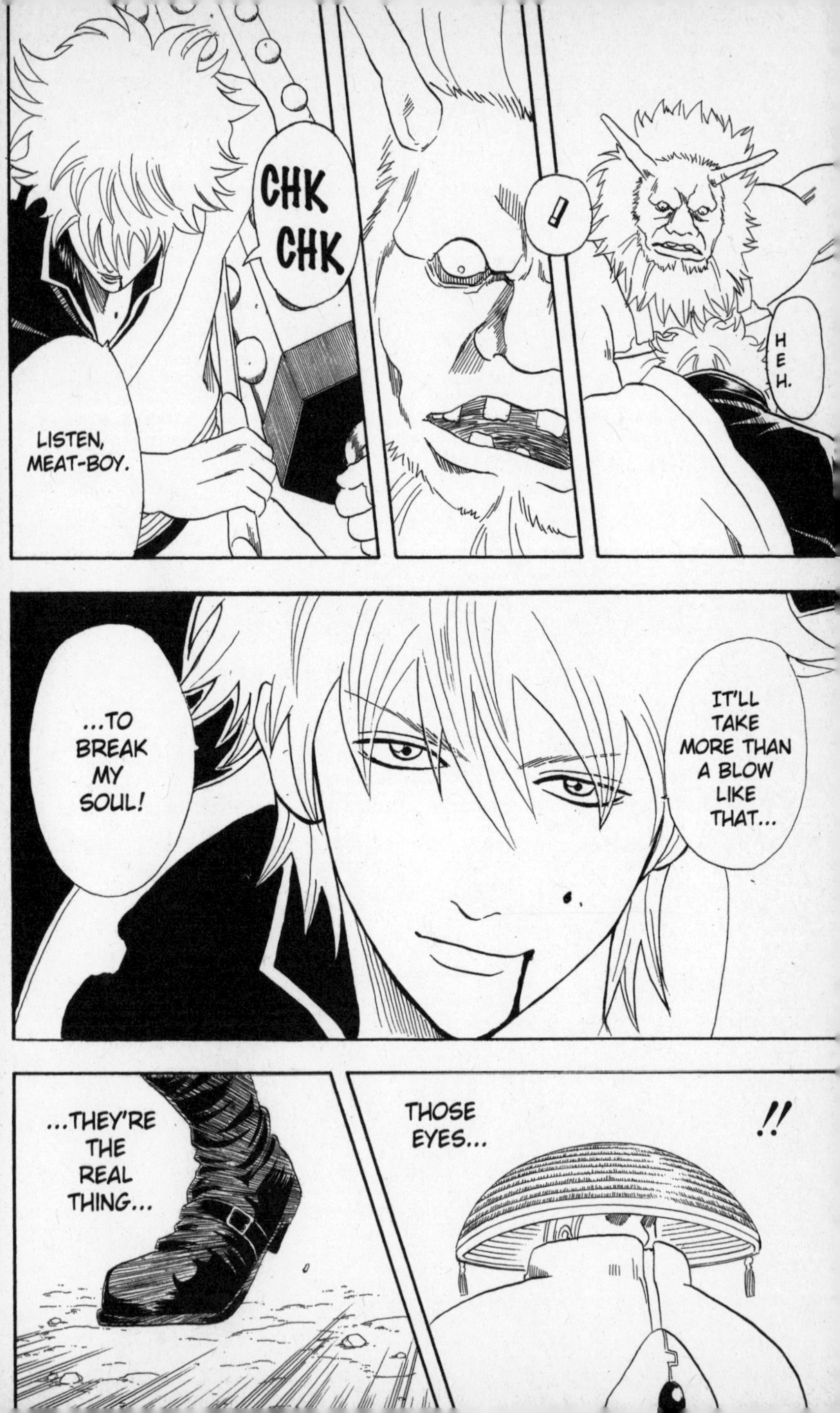
HEH.
!
CHK CHK
LISTEN, MEAT-BOY.
IT'LL TAKE MORE THAN A BLOW LIKE THAT...
...TO BREAK MY SOUL!
!!
THOSE EYES...
...THEY'RE THE REAL THING...

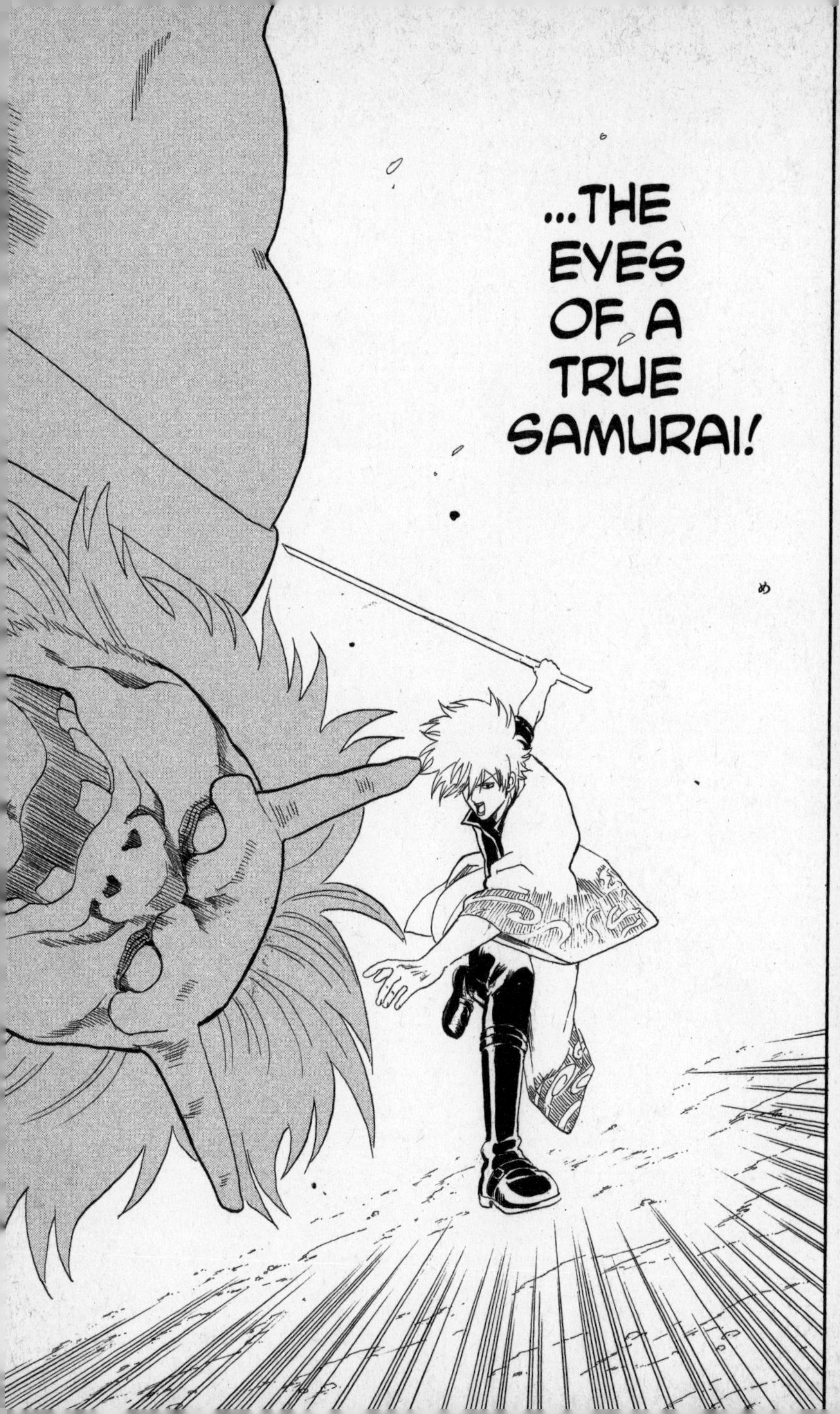
...THE EYES OF A TRUE SAMURAI!

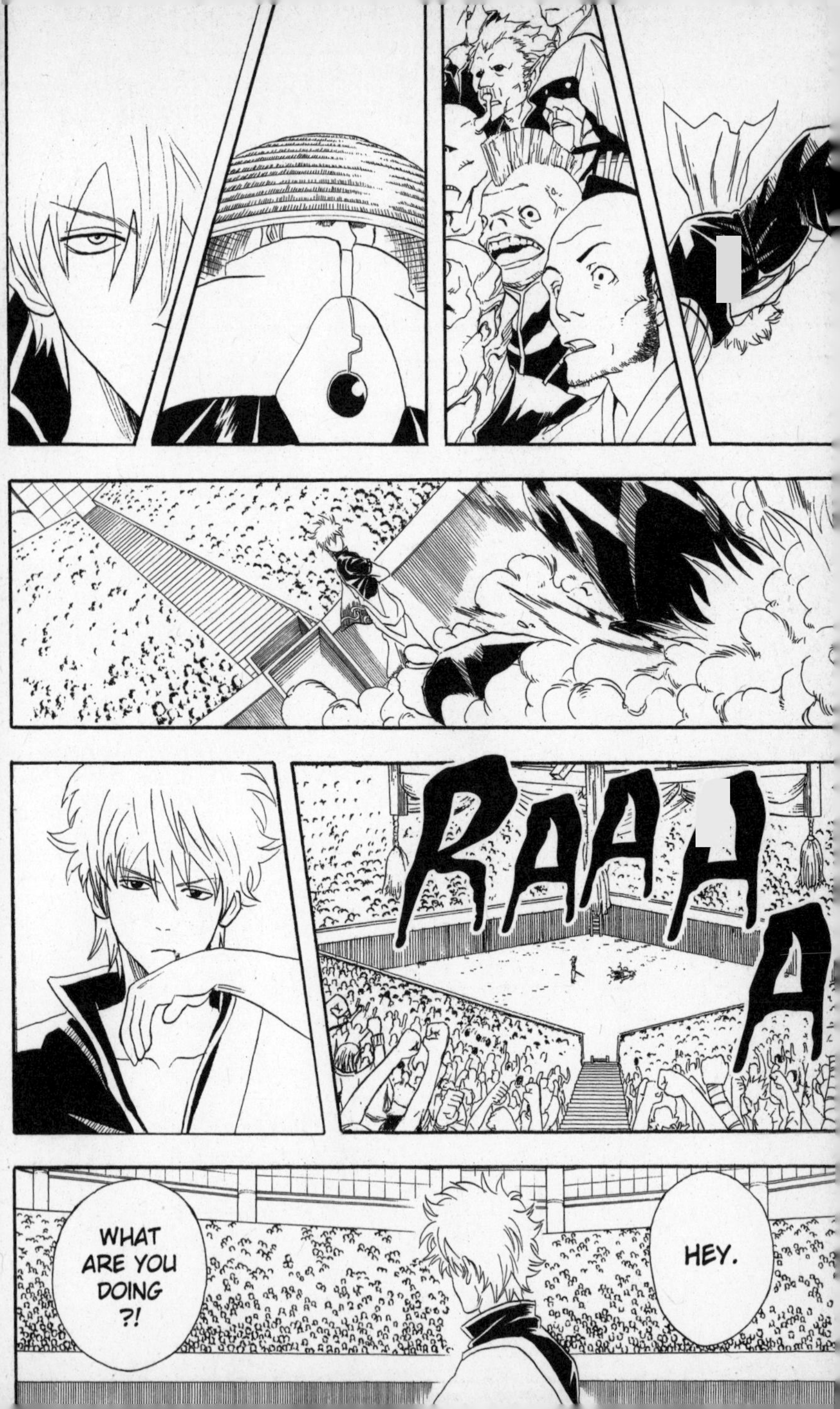
RAAAA
HEY.
WHAT ARE YOU DOING?!

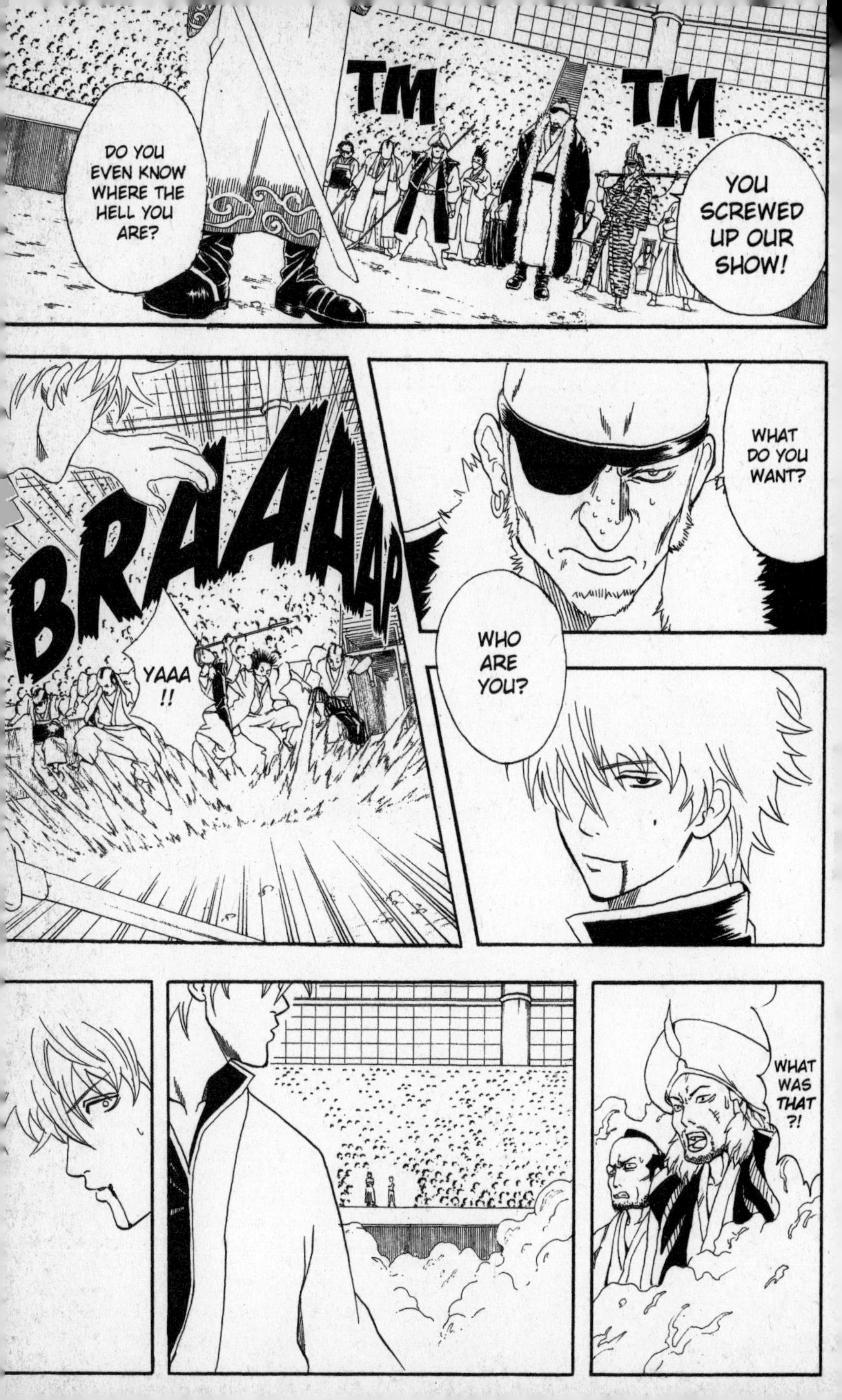
TM TM
YOU SCREWED UP OUR SHOW!
DO YOU EVEN KNOW WHERE THE HELL YOU ARE?
WHAT DO YOU WANT?
WHO ARE YOU?
BRAAAAP
YAAA !!
WHAT WAS THAT ?!

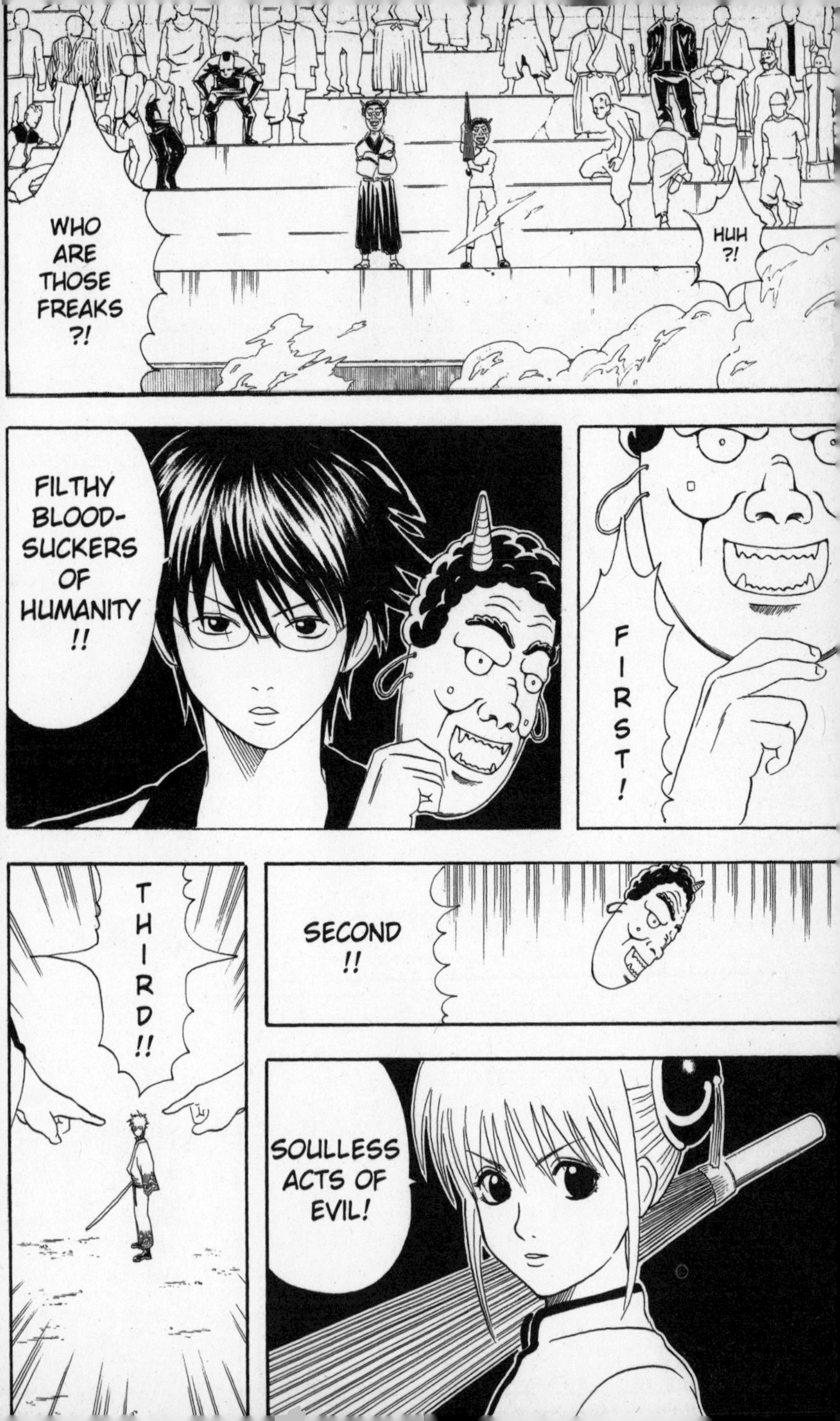
HUH ?!
WHO ARE THOSE FREAKS ?!
FIRST!
FILTHY BLOOD-SUCKERS OF HUMANITY !!
SECOND !!
SOULLESS ACTS OF EVIL!
THIRD!!

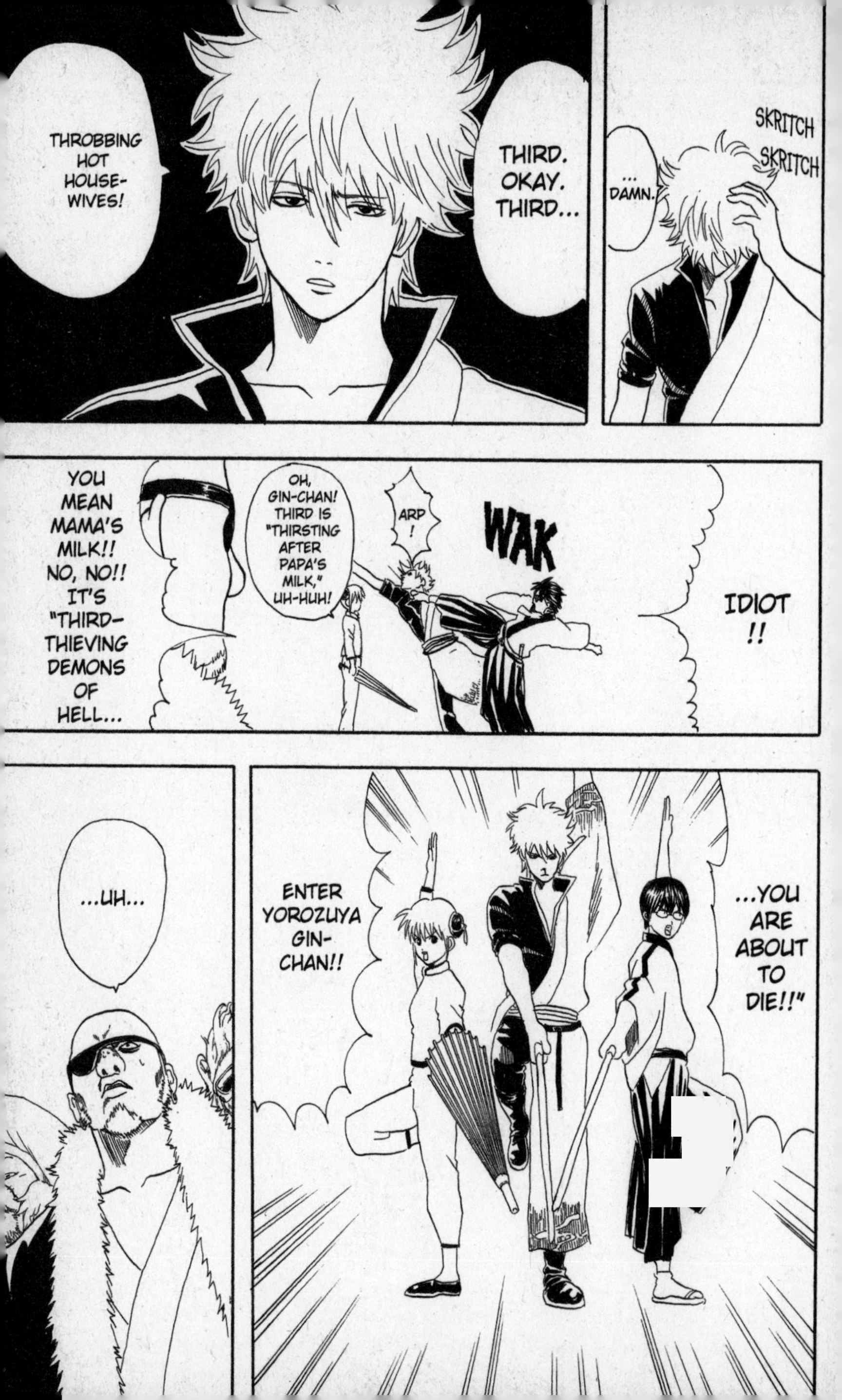
SKRITCH
SKRITCH
... DAMN.
THIRD. OKAY. THIRD...
THROBBING HOT HOUSE-WIVES!
IDIOT !!
WAK
ARP !
OH, GIN-CHAN! THIRD IS "THIRSTING AFTER PAPA'S MILK," UH-HUH!
YOU MEAN MAMA'S MILK!! NO, NO!! IT'S "THIRD-THIEVING DEMONS OF HELL...
...YOU ARE ABOUT TO DIE!!"
ENTER YOROZUYA GIN-CHAN!!
...UH...

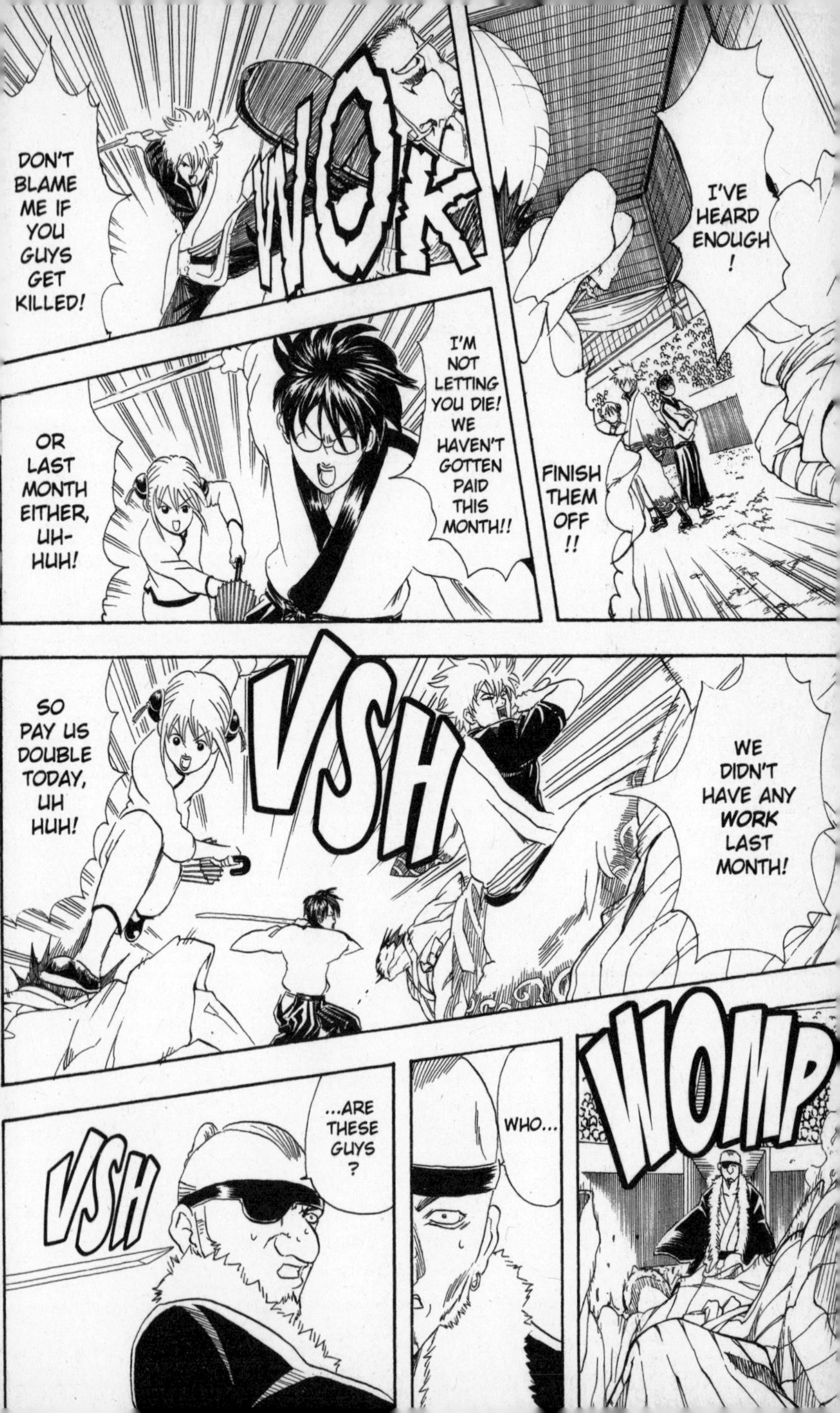
I'VE HEARD ENOUGH!
FINISH THEM OFF!!
WOK
DON'T BLAME ME IF YOU GUYS GET KILLED!
I'M NOT LETTING YOU DIE! WE HAVEN'T GOTTEN PAID THIS MONTH!!
OR LAST MONTH EITHER, UH-HUH!
VSH
WE DIDN'T HAVE ANY WORK LAST MONTH!
SO PAY US DOUBLE TODAY, UH HUH!
WOMP
WHO...
...ARE THESE GUYS?
VSH

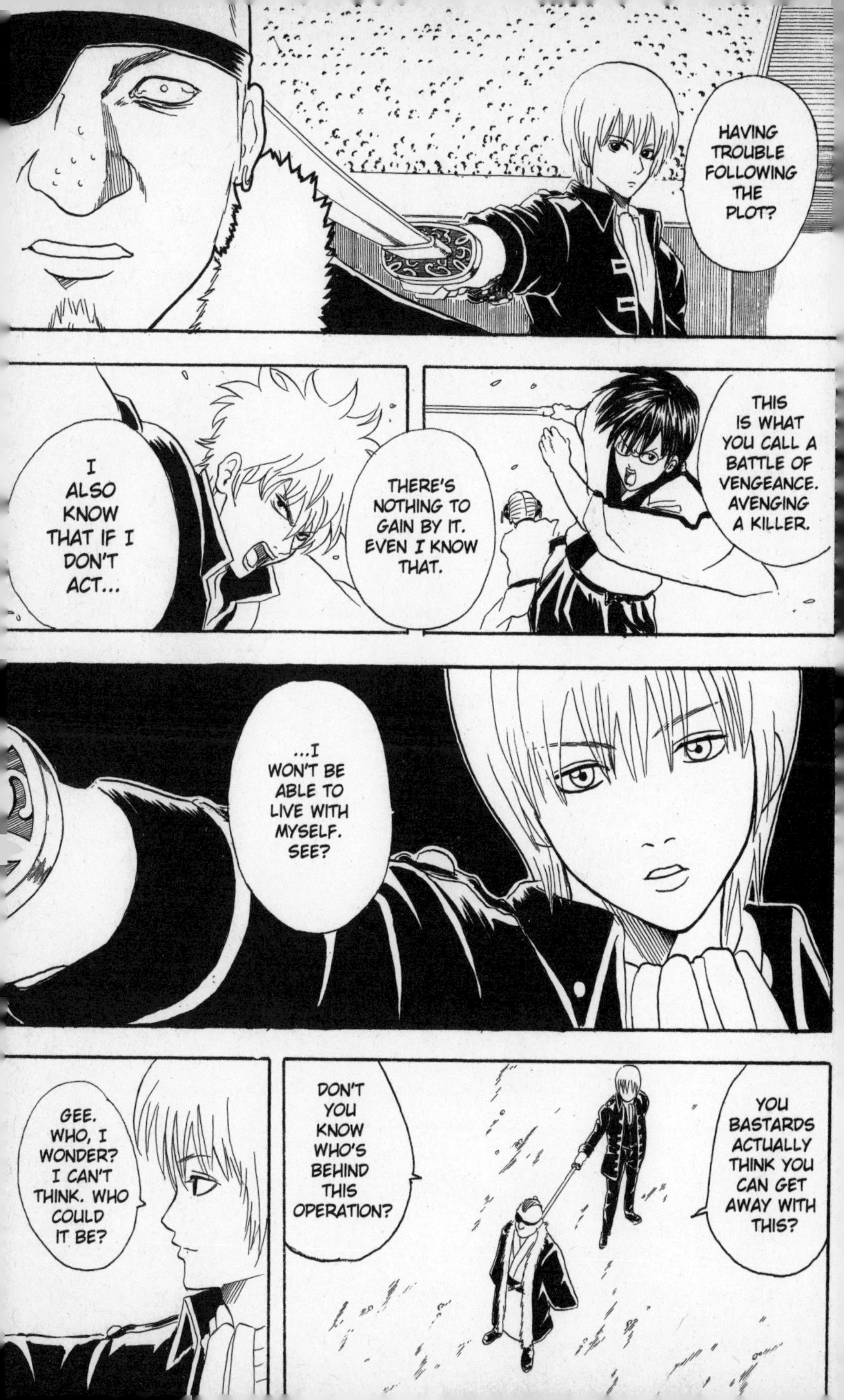
HAVING TROUBLE FOLLOWING THE PLOT?
THIS IS WHAT YOU CALL A BATTLE OF VENGEANCE. AVENGING A KILLER.
THERE'S NOTHING TO GAIN BY IT. EVEN I KNOW THAT.
I ALSO KNOW THAT IF I DON'T ACT...
...I WON'T BE ABLE TO LIVE WITH MYSELF. SEE?
YOU BASTARDS ACTUALLY THINK YOU CAN GET AWAY WITH THIS?
DON'T YOU KNOW WHO'S BEHIND THIS OPERATION?
GEE. WHO, I WONDER? I CAN'T THINK. WHO COULD IT BE?

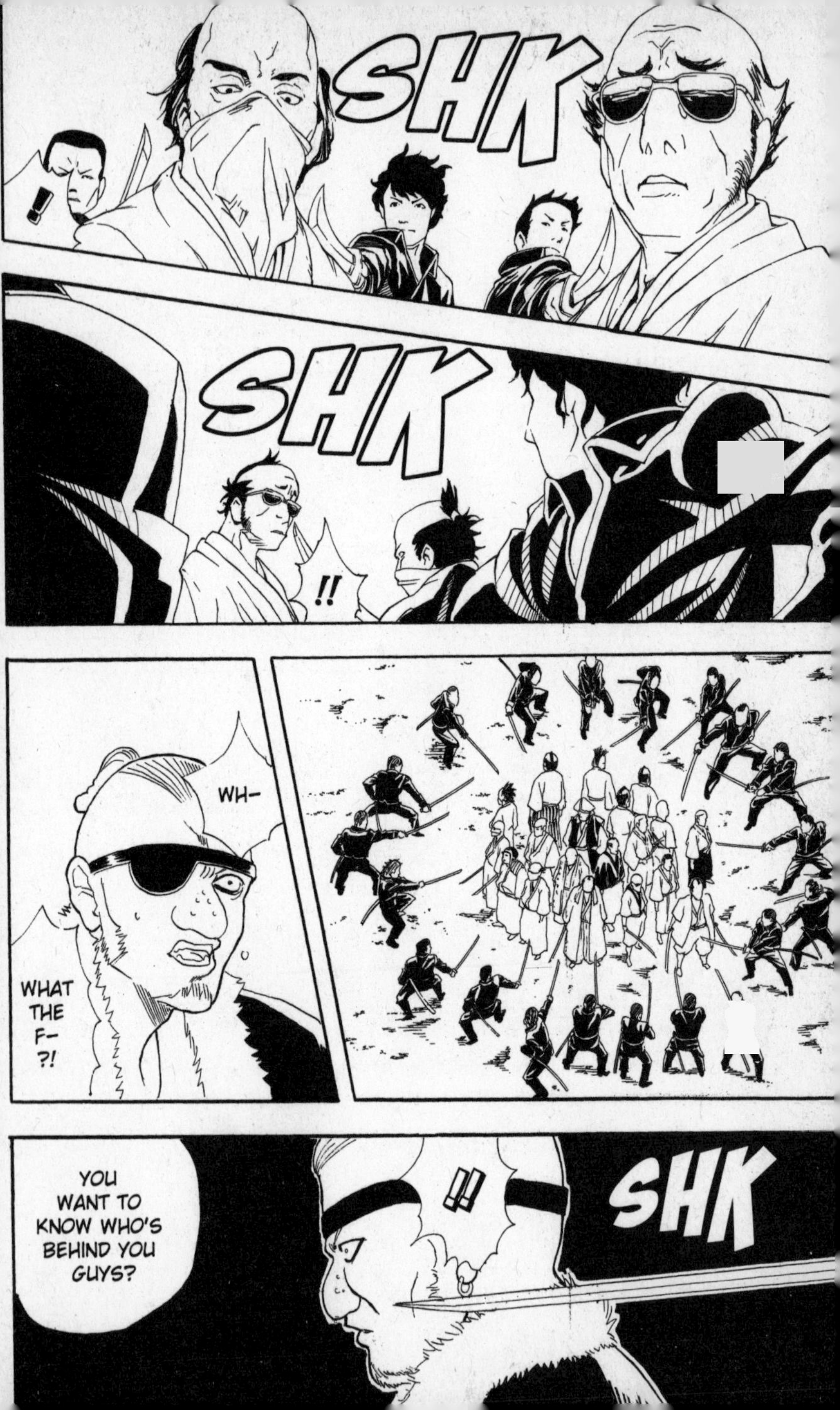
SHK
!
SHK
!!
WH-
WHAT THE F-?!
SHK
!!
YOU WANT TO KNOW WHO'S BEHIND YOU GUYS?

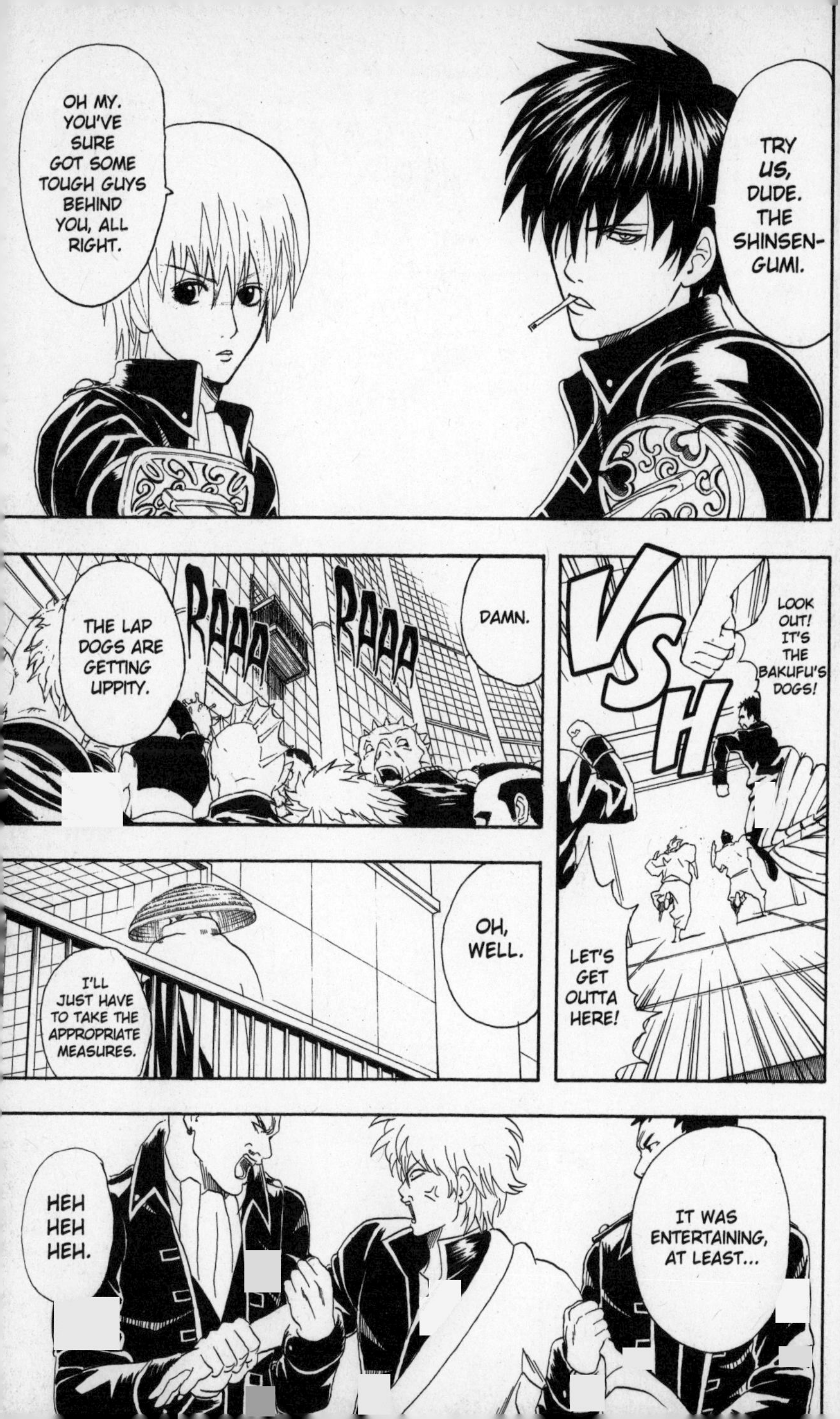
TRY US, DUDE. THE SHINSEN-GUMI.
OH MY. YOU'VE SURE GOT SOME TOUGH GUYS BEHIND YOU, ALL RIGHT.
VSH
LOOK OUT! IT'S THE BAKUFU'S DOGS!
LET'S GET OUTTA HERE!
DAMN.
RAAA
RAAA
THE LAP DOGS ARE GETTING UPPITY.
OH, WELL.
I'LL JUST HAVE TO TAKE THE APPROPRIATE MEASURES.
IT WAS ENTERTAINING, AT LEAST...
HEH HEH HEH.

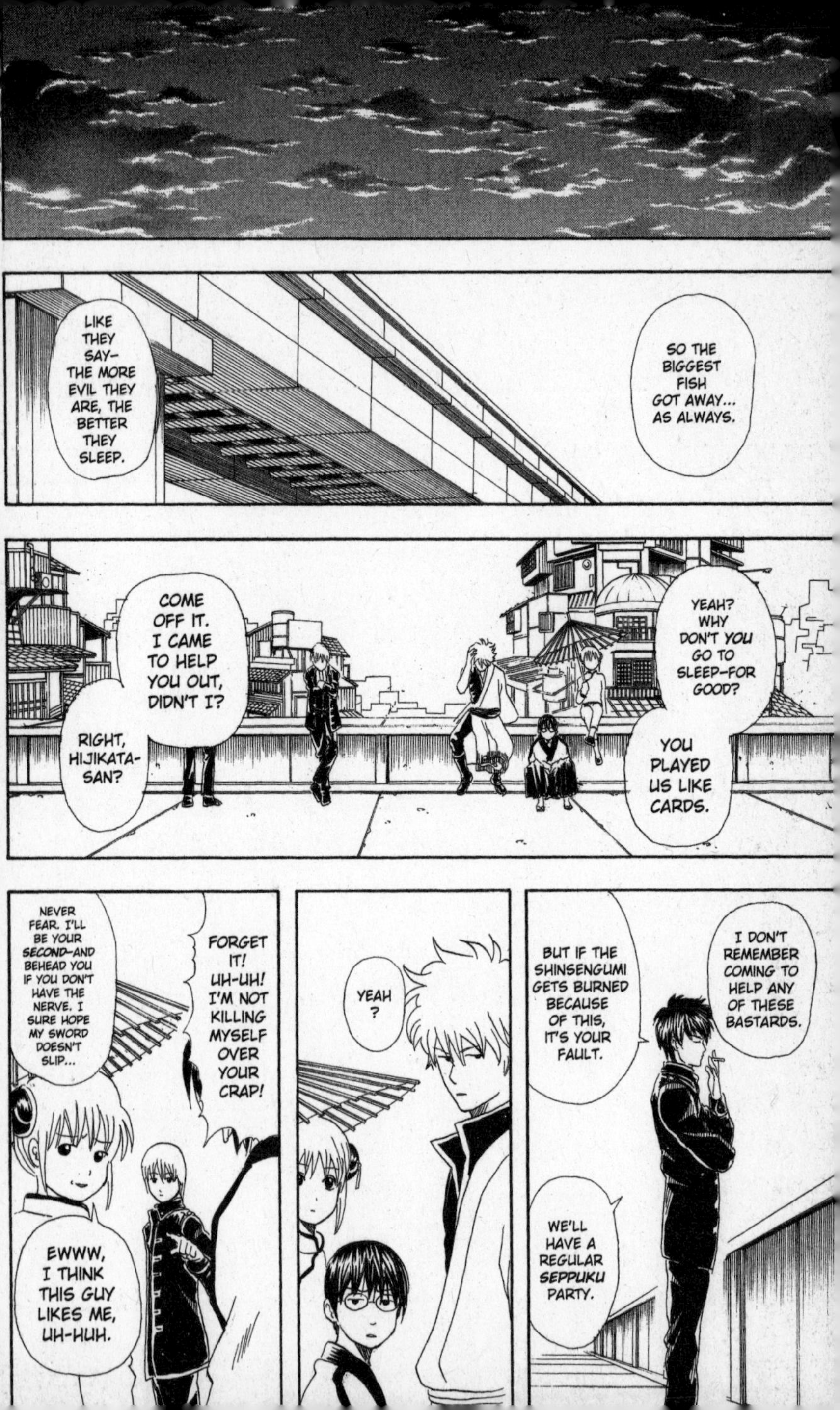
SO THE BIGGEST FISH GOT AWAY... AS ALWAYS.
LIKE THEY SAY— THE MORE EVIL THEY ARE, THE BETTER THEY SLEEP.
YEAH? WHY DON'T *YOU* GO TO SLEEP—FOR GOOD?
YOU PLAYED US LIKE CARDS.
COME OFF IT. I CAME TO HELP YOU OUT, DIDN'T I?
RIGHT, HIJIKATA-SAN?
I DON'T REMEMBER COMING TO HELP ANY OF THESE BASTARDS.
BUT IF THE SHINSENGUMI GETS BURNED BECAUSE OF THIS, IT'S YOUR FAULT.
WE'LL HAVE A REGULAR *SEPPUKU* PARTY.
YEAH?
FORGET IT! UH-UH! I'M NOT KILLING MYSELF OVER YOUR CRAP!
NEVER FEAR. I'LL BE YOUR *SECOND*—AND BEHEAD YOU IF YOU DON'T HAVE THE NERVE. I SURE HOPE MY SWORD DOESN'T SLIP...
EWWW, I THINK THIS GUY LIKES ME, UH-HUH.

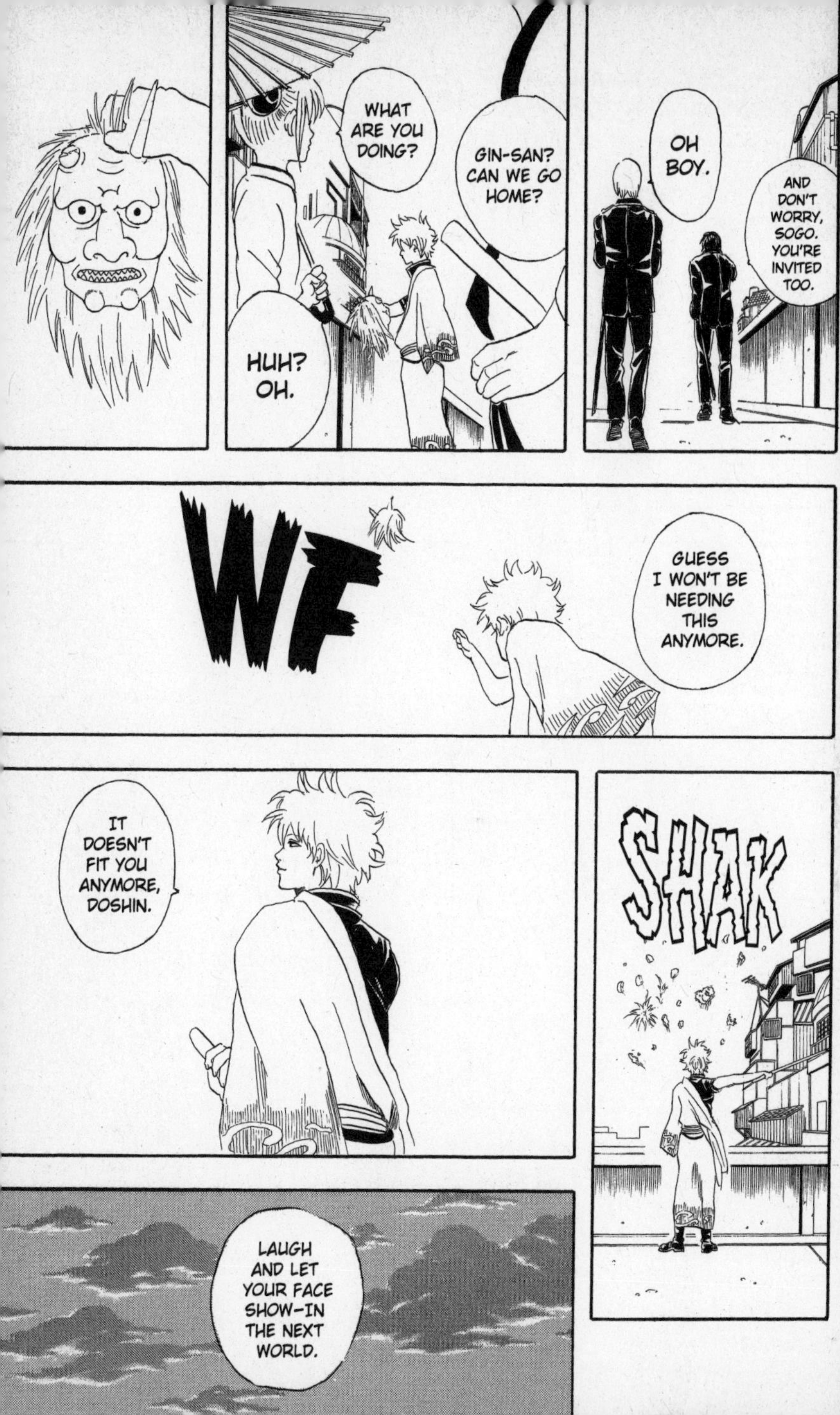
OH BOY.
AND DON'T WORRY, SOGO. YOU'RE INVITED TOO.
GIN-SAN? CAN WE GO HOME?
WHAT ARE YOU DOING?
HUH? OH.
GUESS I WON'T BE NEEDING THIS ANYMORE.
WF
SHAK
IT DOESN'T FIT YOU ANYMORE, DOSHIN.
LAUGH AND LET YOUR FACE SHOW—IN THE NEXT WORLD.

I'm sure you're asking, "Who's that?" But this, in fact, is the original model for Shinpachi. My original story was built around this Shinpachi Nakagura, who travels from his home in the country to the city to learn the art of the sword. He meets Kondo and friends, who are still trying to run a swordsman's school in Edo, where the samurai have been destroyed by the Amanto invasion, and he joins the Shinsengumi. After this design I tried making him bald and giving him a topknot, among other things. I couldn't come to a decision. In the end I gave him glasses because he's sort of like Nobita from *Doraemon*.

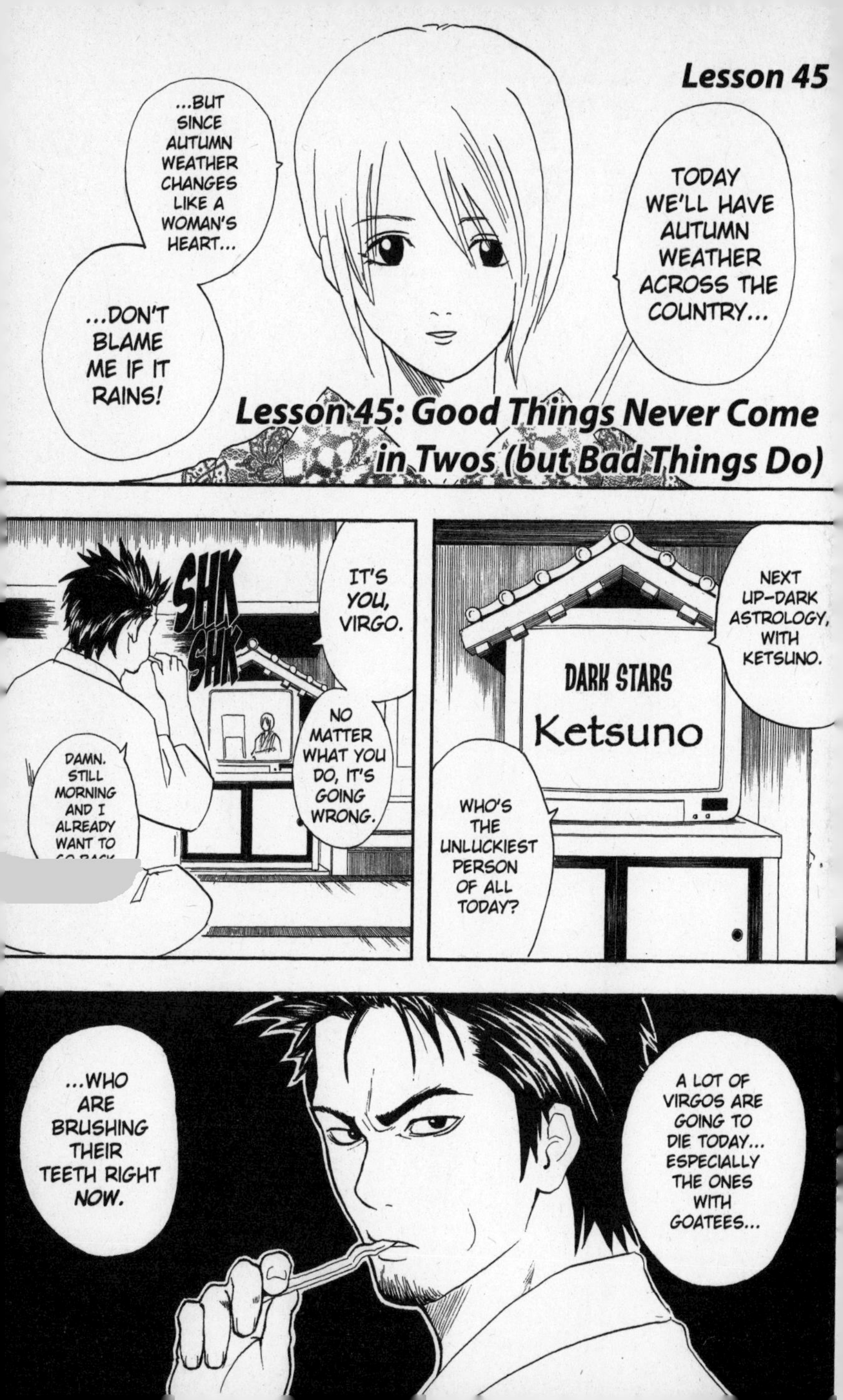
Lesson 45
TODAY WE'LL HAVE AUTUMN WEATHER ACROSS THE COUNTRY...
Lesson 45: Good Things Never Come in Twos (but Bad Things Do)
...BUT SINCE AUTUMN WEATHER CHANGES LIKE A WOMAN'S HEART...
...DON'T BLAME ME IF IT RAINS!
NEXT UP—DARK ASTROLOGY, WITH KETSUNO.
DARK STARS
Ketsuno
WHO'S THE UNLUCKIEST PERSON OF ALL TODAY?
IT'S YOU, VIRGO.
SHK SHK
NO MATTER WHAT YOU DO, IT'S GOING WRONG.
DAMN. STILL MORNING AND I ALREADY WANT TO
A LOT OF VIRGOS ARE GOING TO DIE TODAY... ESPECIALLY THE ONES WITH GOATEES...
...WHO ARE BRUSHING THEIR TEETH RIGHT NOW.

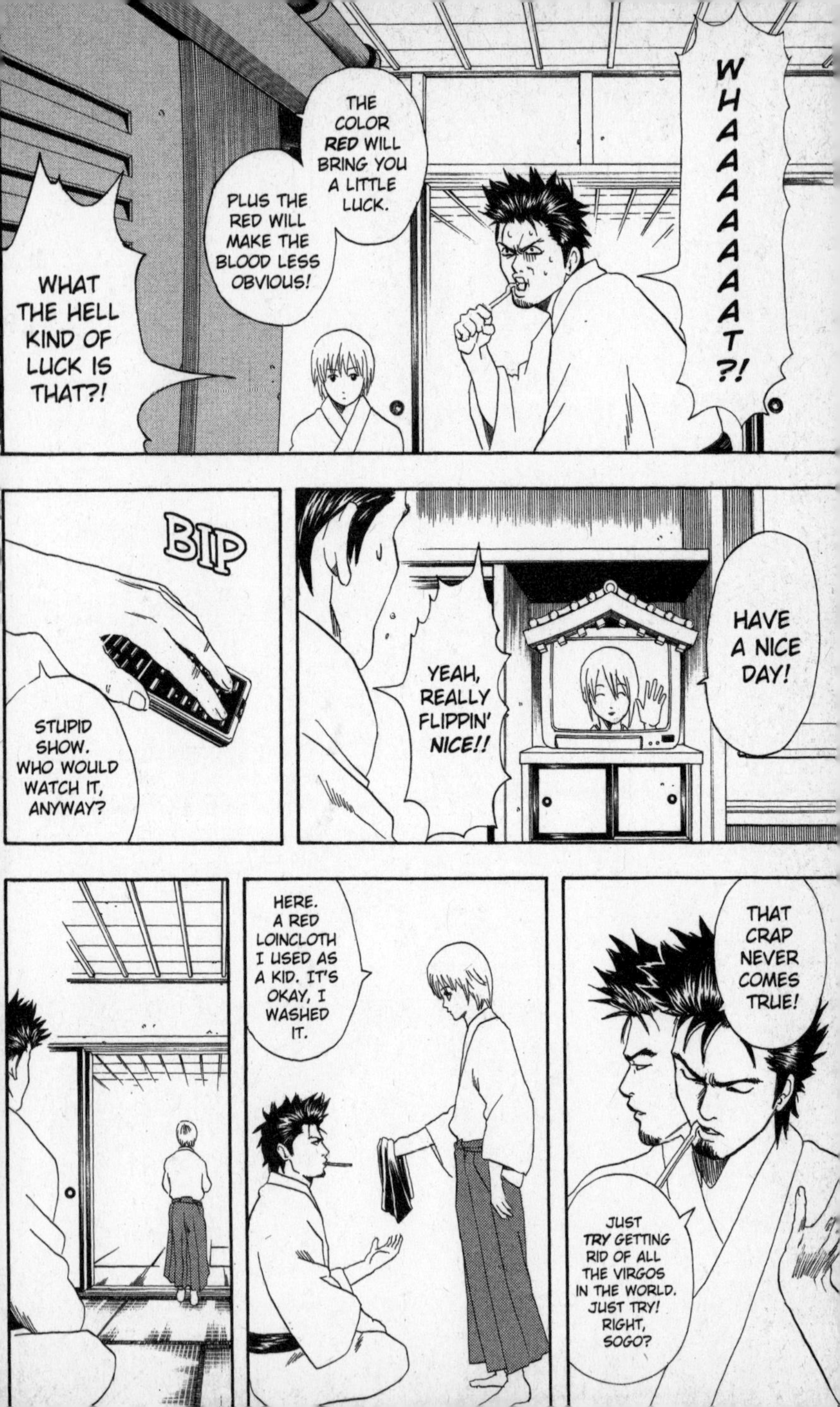
WHAAAAAAAT?!
THE COLOR RED WILL BRING YOU A LITTLE LUCK.
PLUS THE RED WILL MAKE THE BLOOD LESS OBVIOUS!
WHAT THE HELL KIND OF LUCK IS THAT?!
HAVE A NICE DAY!
YEAH, REALLY FLIPPIN' NICE!!
BIP
STUPID SHOW. WHO WOULD WATCH IT, ANYWAY?
THAT CRAP NEVER COMES TRUE!
JUST TRY GETTING RID OF ALL THE VIRGOS IN THE WORLD. JUST TRY! RIGHT, SOGO?
HERE. A RED LOINCLOTH I USED AS A KID. IT'S OKAY, I WASHED IT.

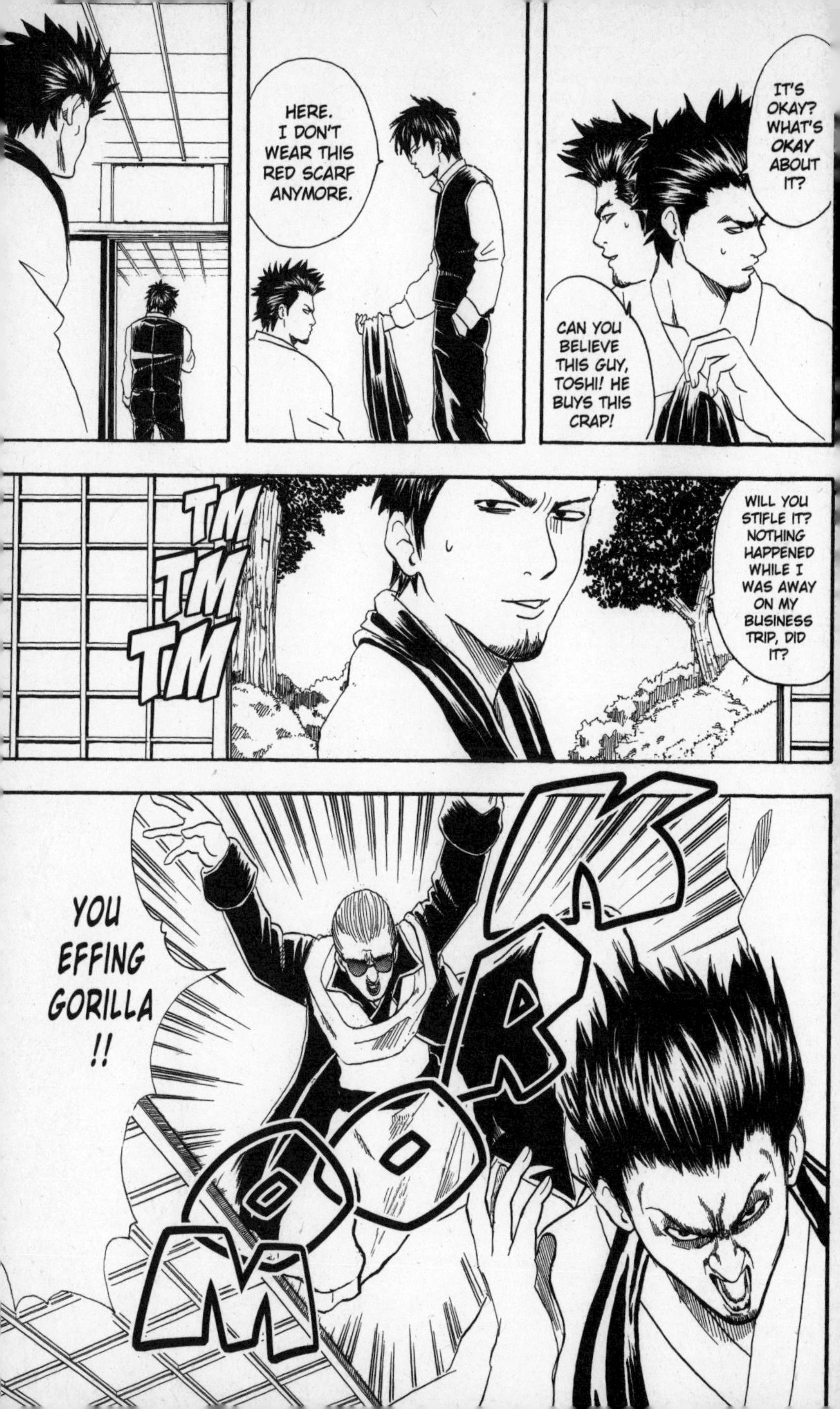
IT'S OKAY? WHAT'S OKAY ABOUT IT?
CAN YOU BELIEVE THIS GUY, TOSHI! HE BUYS THIS CRAP!
HERE. I DON'T WEAR THIS RED SCARF ANYMORE.
WILL YOU STIFLE IT? NOTHING HAPPENED WHILE I WAS AWAY ON MY BUSINESS TRIP, DID IT?
TM TM TM
KROOM
YOU EFFING GORILLA !!

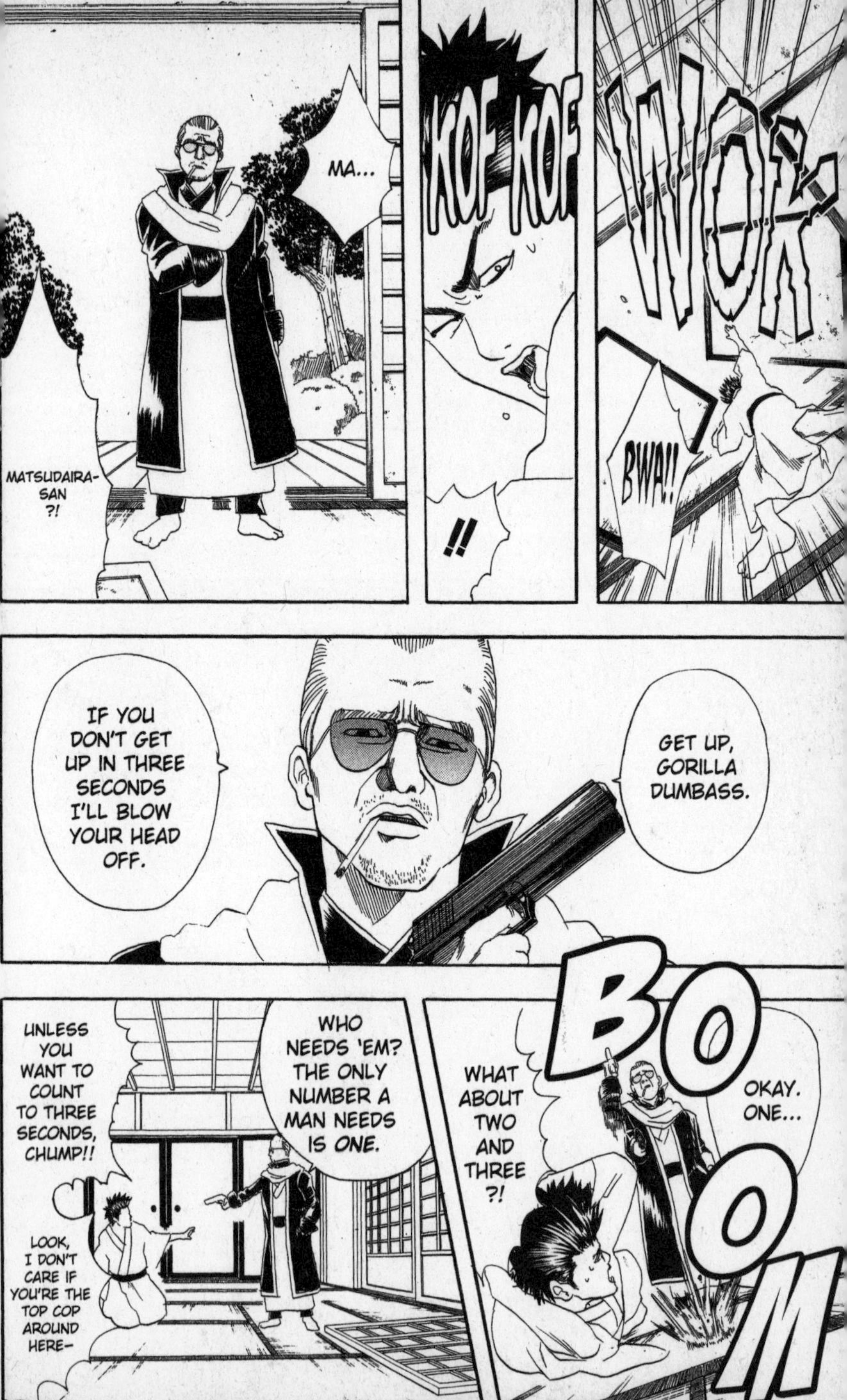
WOK
BWA!!
KOF KOF
!!
MA...
MATSUDAIRA-SAN ?!
GET UP, GORILLA DUMBASS.
IF YOU DON'T GET UP IN THREE SECONDS I'LL BLOW YOUR HEAD OFF.
OKAY. ONE...
BOOM
WHAT ABOUT TWO AND THREE ?!
WHO NEEDS 'EM? THE ONLY NUMBER A MAN NEEDS IS ONE.
LOOK, I DON'T CARE IF YOU'RE THE TOP COP AROUND HERE-
UNLESS YOU WANT TO COUNT TO THREE SECONDS, CHUMP!!

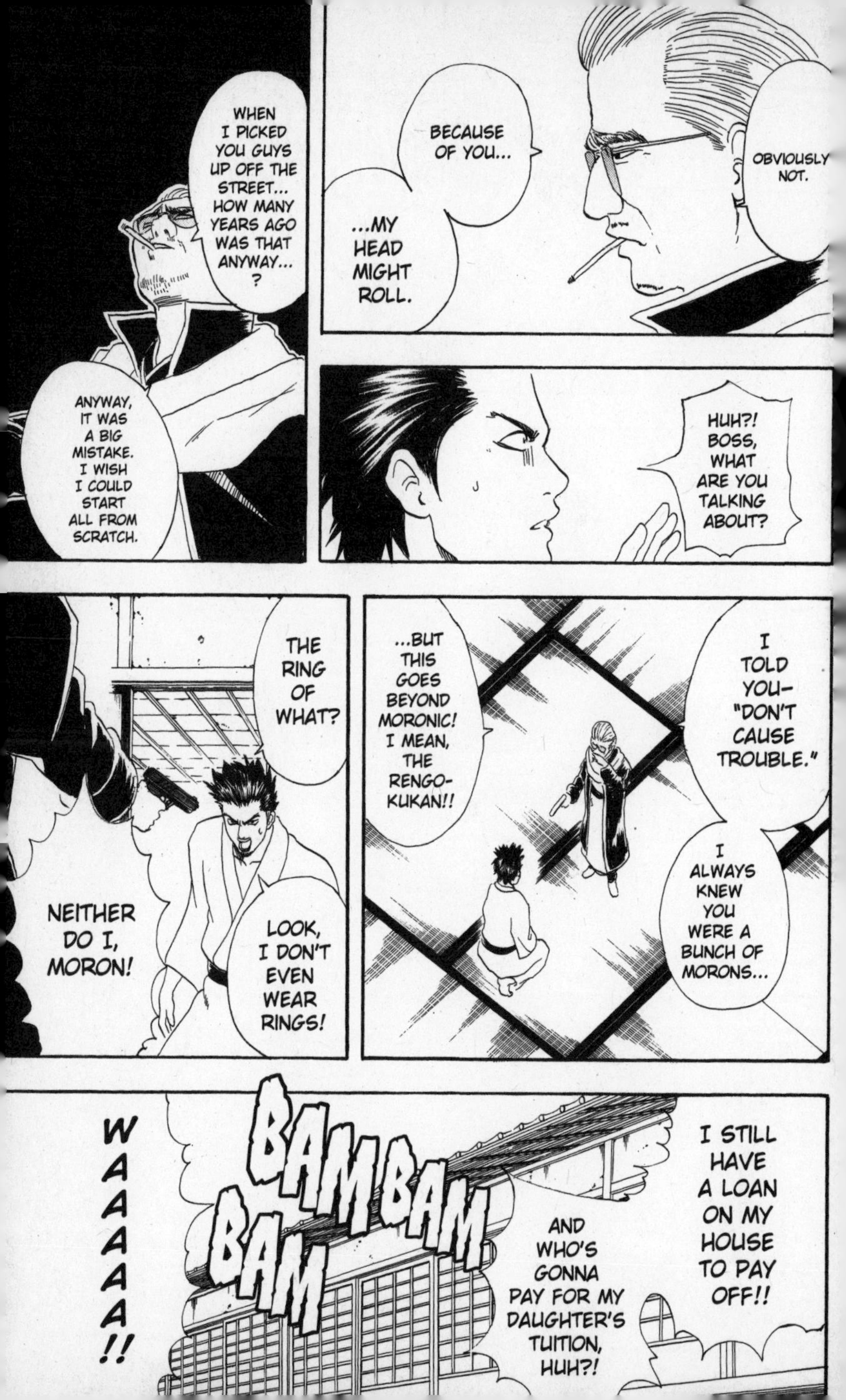
OBVIOUSLY NOT.
BECAUSE OF YOU...
...MY HEAD MIGHT ROLL.
HUH?! BOSS, WHAT ARE YOU TALKING ABOUT?
WHEN I PICKED YOU GUYS UP OFF THE STREET... HOW MANY YEARS AGO WAS THAT ANYWAY...?
ANYWAY, IT WAS A BIG MISTAKE. I WISH I COULD START ALL FROM SCRATCH.
I TOLD YOU—"DON'T CAUSE TROUBLE."
I ALWAYS KNEW YOU WERE A BUNCH OF MORONS...
...BUT THIS GOES BEYOND MORONIC! I MEAN, THE RENGOKUKAN!!
THE RING OF WHAT?
LOOK, I DON'T EVEN WEAR RINGS!
NEITHER DO I, MORON!
I STILL HAVE A LOAN ON MY HOUSE TO PAY OFF!!
AND WHO'S GONNA PAY FOR MY DAUGHTER'S TUITION, HUH?!
BAM BAM BAM
WAAAAAAA!!

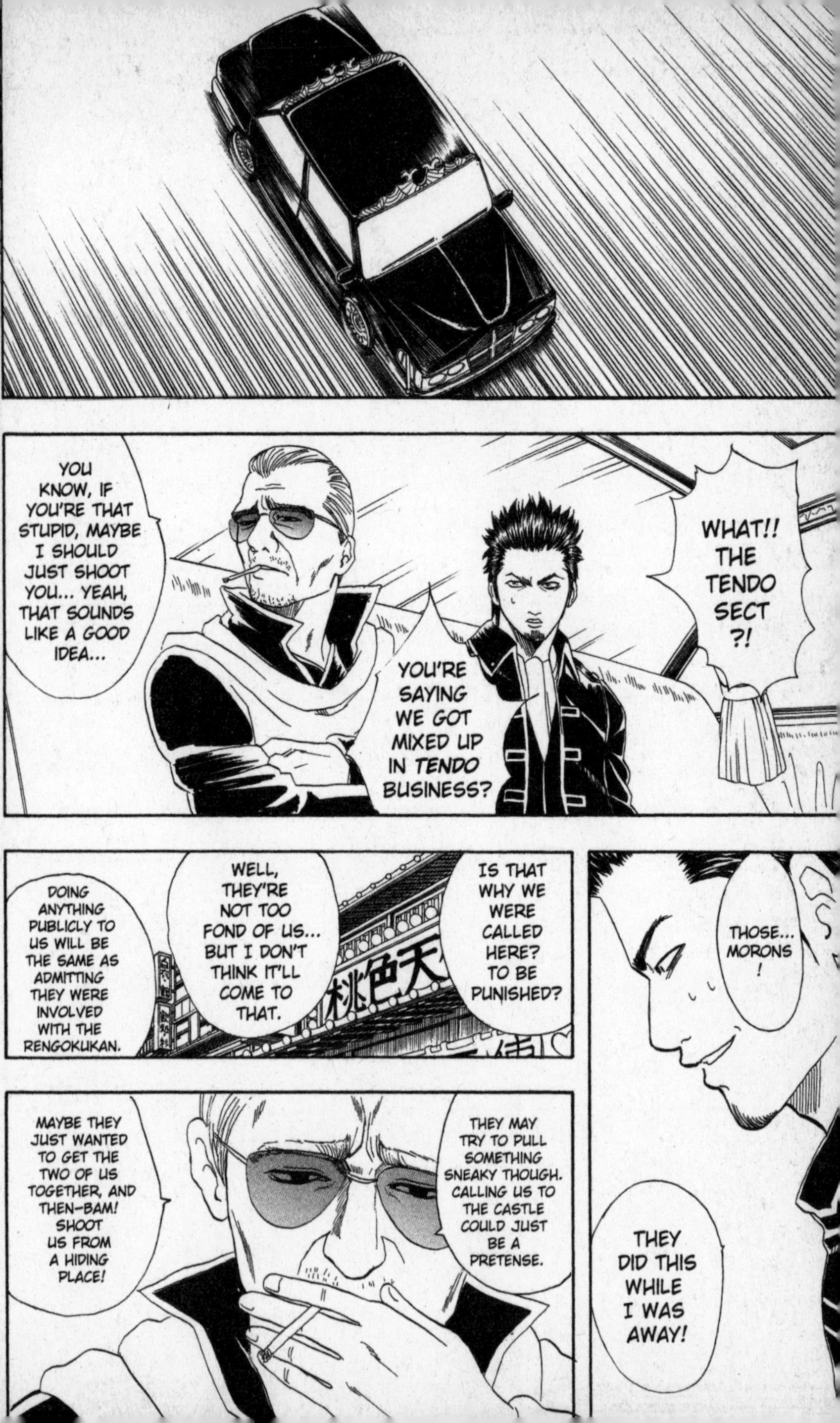
WHAT!! THE TENDO SECT ?!
YOU'RE SAYING WE GOT MIXED UP IN *TENDO* BUSINESS?
YOU KNOW, IF YOU'RE THAT STUPID, MAYBE I SHOULD JUST SHOOT YOU... YEAH, THAT SOUNDS LIKE A GOOD IDEA...
THOSE... MORONS!
THEY DID THIS WHILE I WAS AWAY!
IS THAT WHY WE WERE CALLED HERE? TO BE PUNISHED?
WELL, THEY'RE NOT TOO FOND OF US... BUT I DON'T THINK IT'LL COME TO THAT.
DOING ANYTHING PUBLICLY TO US WILL BE THE SAME AS ADMITTING THEY WERE INVOLVED WITH THE RENGOKUKAN.
THEY MAY TRY TO PULL SOMETHING SNEAKY THOUGH. CALLING US TO THE CASTLE COULD JUST BE A PRETENSE.
MAYBE THEY JUST WANTED TO GET THE TWO OF US TOGETHER, AND THEN-BAM! SHOOT US FROM A HIDING PLACE!

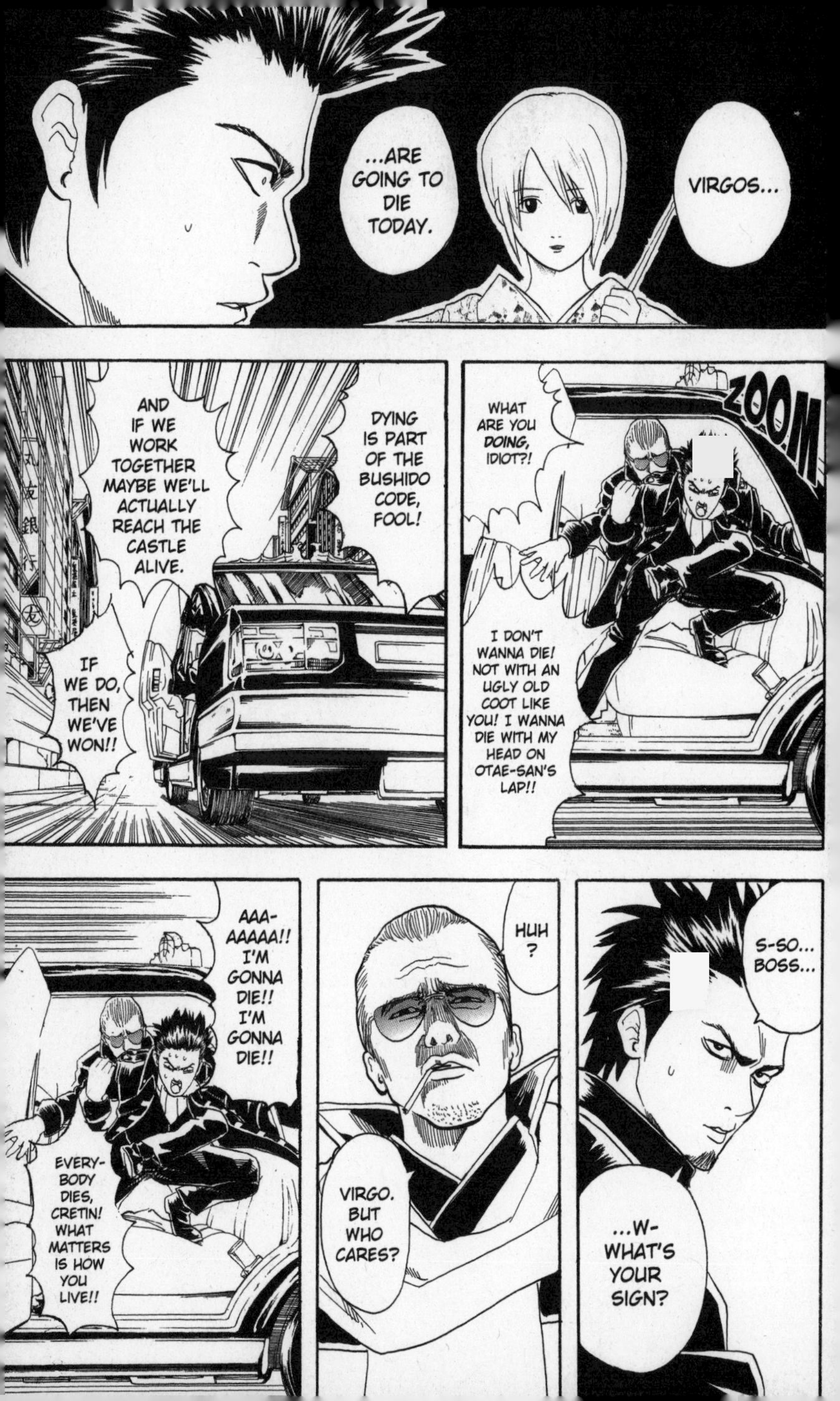
VIRGOS...
...ARE GOING TO DIE TODAY.
ZOOM
WHAT ARE YOU *DOING*, IDIOT?!
I DON'T WANNA DIE! NOT WITH AN UGLY OLD COOT LIKE YOU! I WANNA DIE WITH MY HEAD ON OTAE-SAN'S LAP!!
DYING IS PART OF THE BUSHIDO CODE, FOOL!
AND IF WE WORK TOGETHER MAYBE WE'LL ACTUALLY REACH THE CASTLE ALIVE.
IF WE DO, THEN WE'VE WON!!
S-SO... BOSS...
...W-WHAT'S YOUR SIGN?
HUH?
VIRGO. BUT WHO CARES?
AAA-AAAAA!! I'M GONNA DIE!! I'M GONNA DIE!!
EVERYBODY DIES, CRETIN! WHAT MATTERS IS HOW YOU LIVE!!

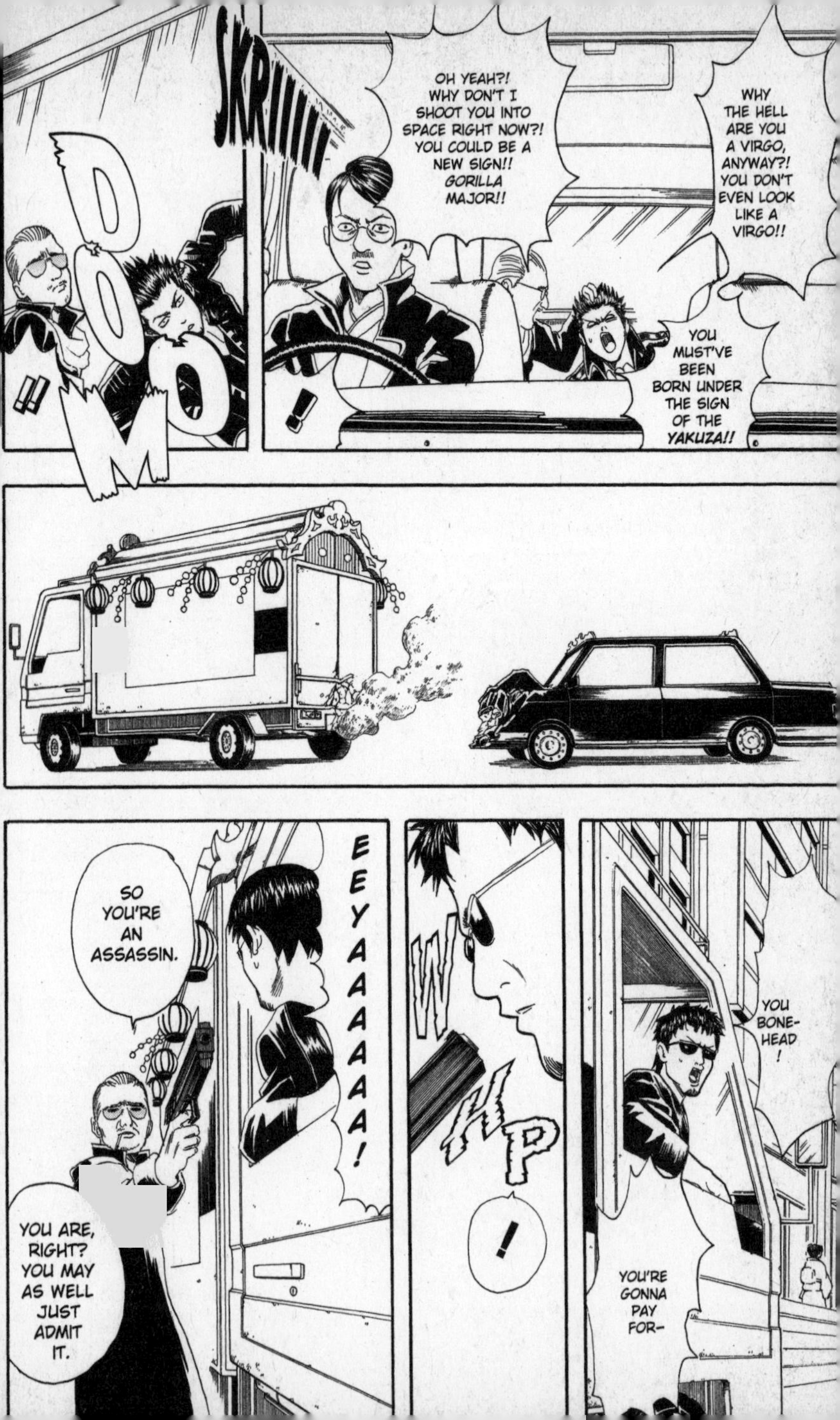

WHY THE HELL ARE YOU A VIRGO, ANYWAY?! YOU DON'T EVEN LOOK LIKE A VIRGO!!
YOU MUST'VE BEEN BORN UNDER THE SIGN OF THE *YAKUZA!!*
OH YEAH?! WHY DON'T I SHOOT YOU INTO SPACE RIGHT NOW?! YOU COULD BE A NEW SIGN!! GORILLA MAJOR!!
!
SKRIIIIII
DOOM
!!
YOU BONE-HEAD!
YOU'RE GONNA PAY FOR-
WHP
!
EEYAAAAAAA!
SO YOU'RE AN ASSASSIN.
YOU ARE, RIGHT? YOU MAY AS WELL JUST ADMIT IT.

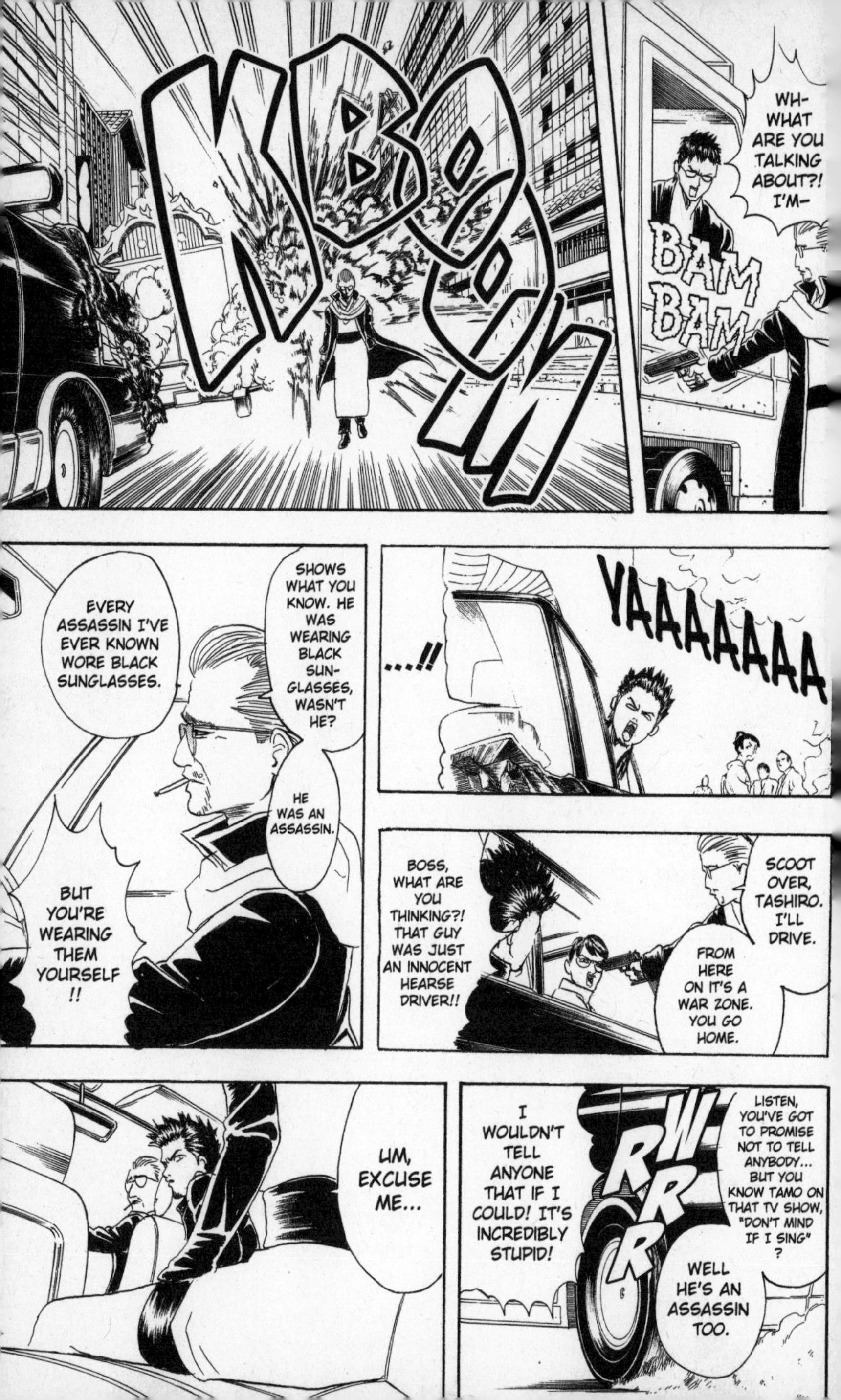
WH- WHAT ARE YOU TALKING ABOUT?! I'M—
BAM BAM
KBOOOM
YAAAAAAA
...!!
SCOOT OVER, TASHIRO. I'LL DRIVE.
FROM HERE ON IT'S A WAR ZONE. YOU GO HOME.
BOSS, WHAT ARE YOU THINKING?! THAT GUY WAS JUST AN INNOCENT HEARSE DRIVER!!
SHOWS WHAT YOU KNOW. HE WAS WEARING BLACK SUNGLASSES, WASN'T HE?
EVERY ASSASSIN I'VE EVER KNOWN WORE BLACK SUNGLASSES.
HE WAS AN ASSASSIN.
BUT YOU'RE WEARING THEM YOURSELF !!
LISTEN, YOU'VE GOT TO PROMISE NOT TO TELL ANYBODY... BUT YOU KNOW TAMO ON THAT TV SHOW, "DON'T MIND IF I SING" ?
WELL HE'S AN ASSASSIN TOO.
I WOULDN'T TELL ANYONE THAT IF I COULD! IT'S INCREDIBLY STUPID!
RWRR
UM, EXCUSE ME...

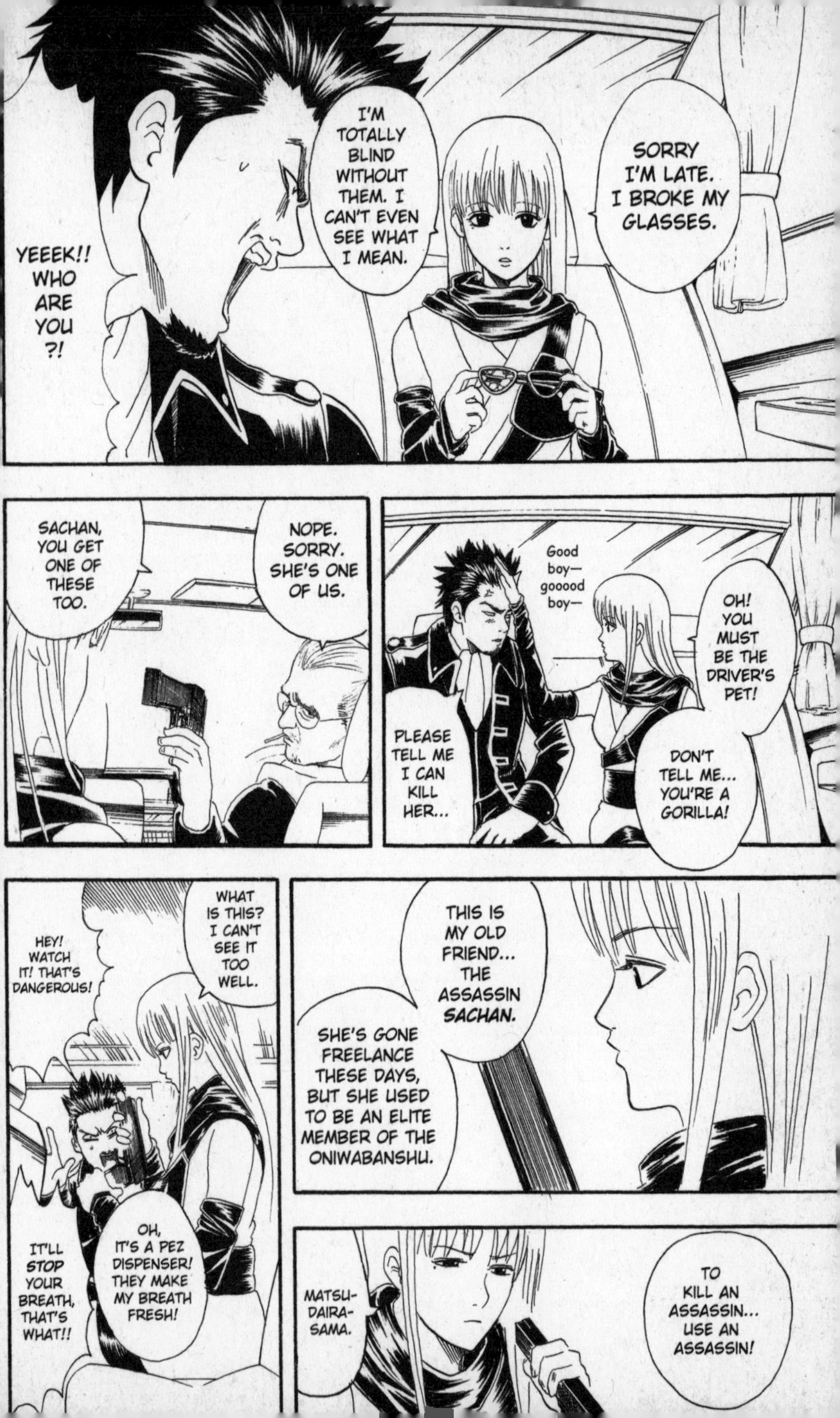
SORRY I'M LATE. I BROKE MY GLASSES.
I'M TOTALLY BLIND WITHOUT THEM. I CAN'T EVEN SEE WHAT I MEAN.
YEEEK!! WHO ARE YOU ?!
OH! YOU MUST BE THE DRIVER'S PET!
Good boy— gooood boy—
DON'T TELL ME... YOU'RE A GORILLA!
PLEASE TELL ME I CAN KILL HER...
NOPE. SORRY. SHE'S ONE OF US.
SACHAN, YOU GET ONE OF THESE TOO.
THIS IS MY OLD FRIEND... THE ASSASSIN SACHAN.
SHE'S GONE FREELANCE THESE DAYS, BUT SHE USED TO BE AN ELITE MEMBER OF THE ONIWABANSHU.
TO KILL AN ASSASSIN... USE AN ASSASSIN!
MATSU-DAIRA-SAMA.
WHAT IS THIS? I CAN'T SEE IT TOO WELL.
HEY! WATCH IT! THAT'S DANGEROUS!
OH, IT'S A PEZ DISPENSER! THEY MAKE MY BREATH FRESH!
IT'LL STOP YOUR BREATH, THAT'S WHAT!!

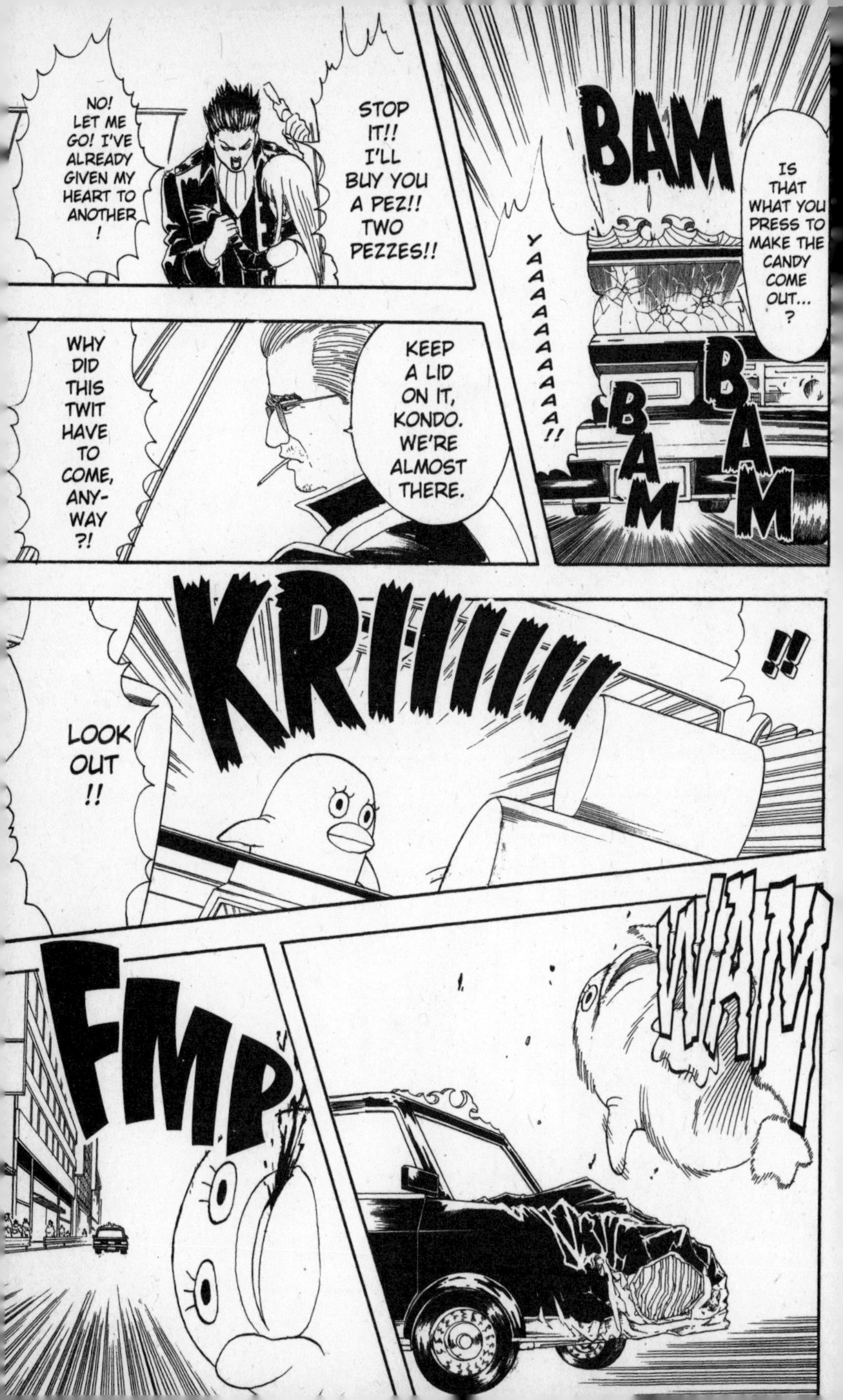

IS THAT WHAT YOU PRESS TO MAKE THE CANDY COME OUT...?
BAM
YAAAAAAAAAAAAA!!
BAM
BAM
STOP IT!! I'LL BUY YOU A PEZ!! TWO PEZZES!!
NO! LET ME GO! I'VE ALREADY GIVEN MY HEART TO ANOTHER!
KEEP A LID ON IT, KONDO. WE'RE ALMOST THERE.
WHY DID THIS TWIT HAVE TO COME, ANYWAY?!
KRIIIIIIII
!!
LOOK OUT!!
WAM
FMP

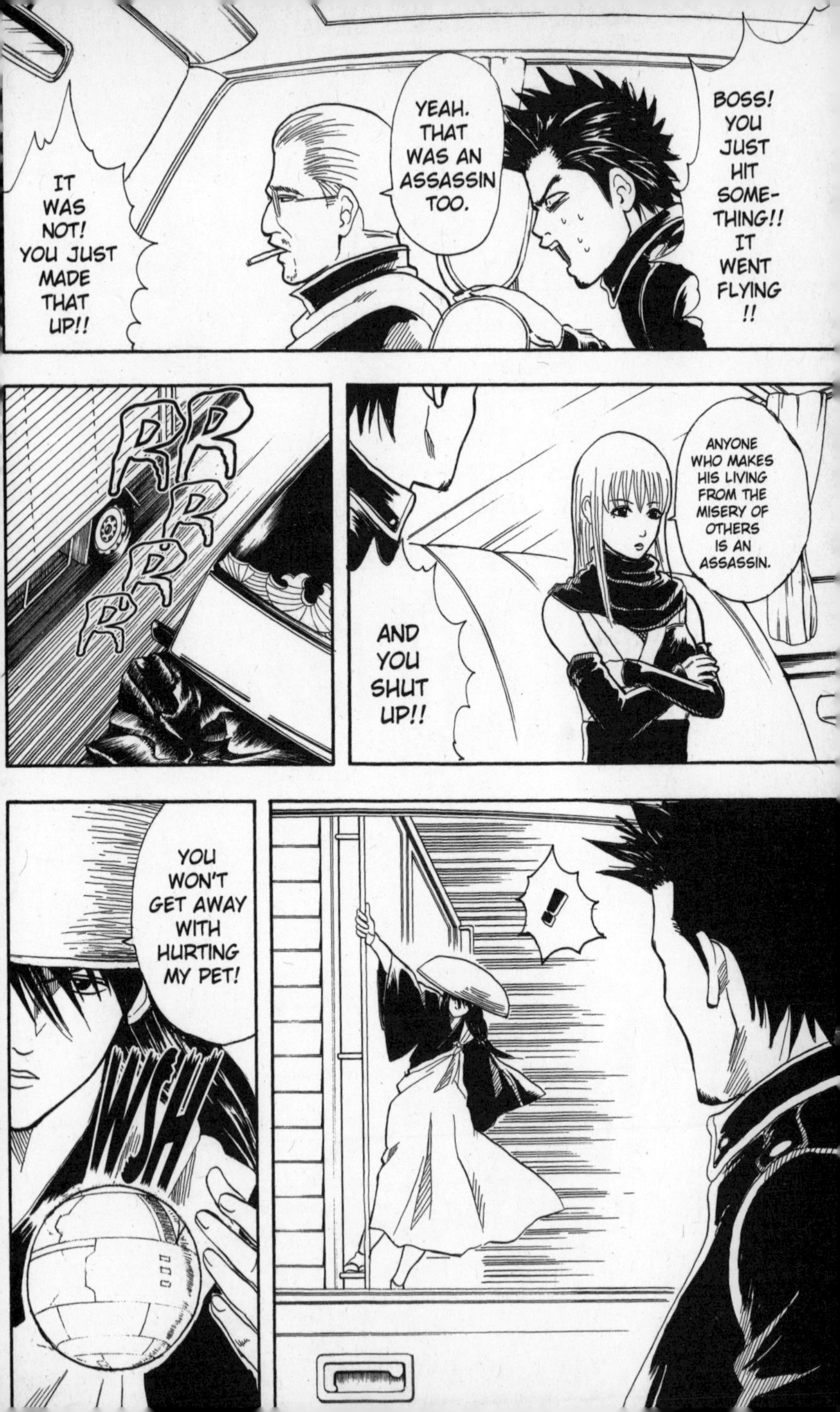
BOSS! YOU JUST HIT SOMETHING!! IT WENT FLYING!!
YEAH. THAT WAS AN ASSASSIN TOO.
IT WAS NOT! YOU JUST MADE THAT UP!!
ANYONE WHO MAKES HIS LIVING FROM THE MISERY OF OTHERS IS AN ASSASSIN.
AND YOU SHUT UP!!
RRRRR
!
YOU WON'T GET AWAY WITH HURTING MY PET!
WSH

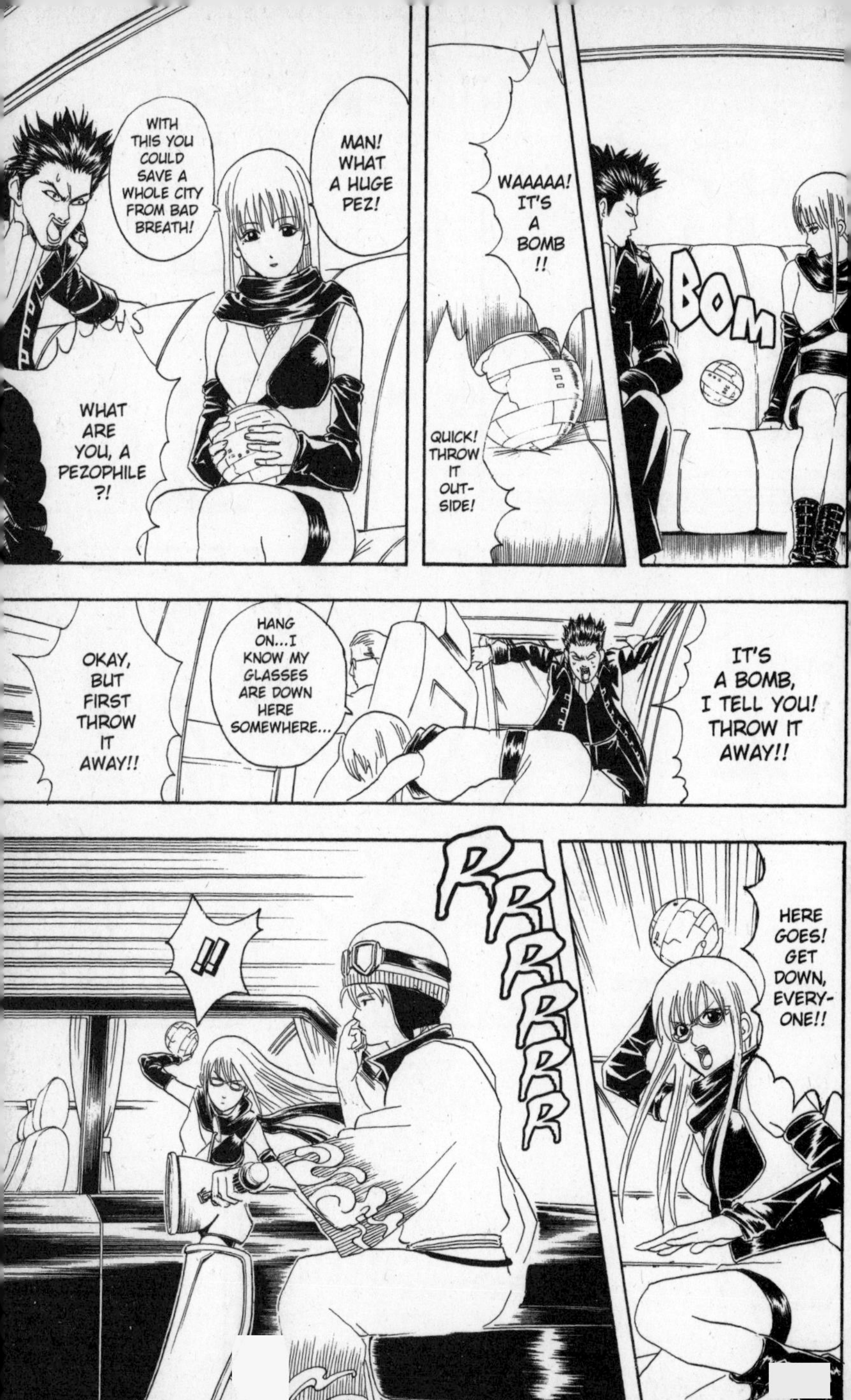
BOM
WAAAAA! IT'S A BOMB!!
QUICK! THROW IT OUTSIDE!
MAN! WHAT A HUGE PEZ!
WITH THIS YOU COULD SAVE A WHOLE CITY FROM BAD BREATH!
WHAT ARE YOU, A PEZOPHILE?!
IT'S A BOMB, I TELL YOU! THROW IT AWAY!!
HANG ON...I KNOW MY GLASSES ARE DOWN HERE SOMEWHERE...
OKAY, BUT FIRST THROW IT AWAY!!
HERE GOES! GET DOWN, EVERYONE!!
RRRRRRR
!!

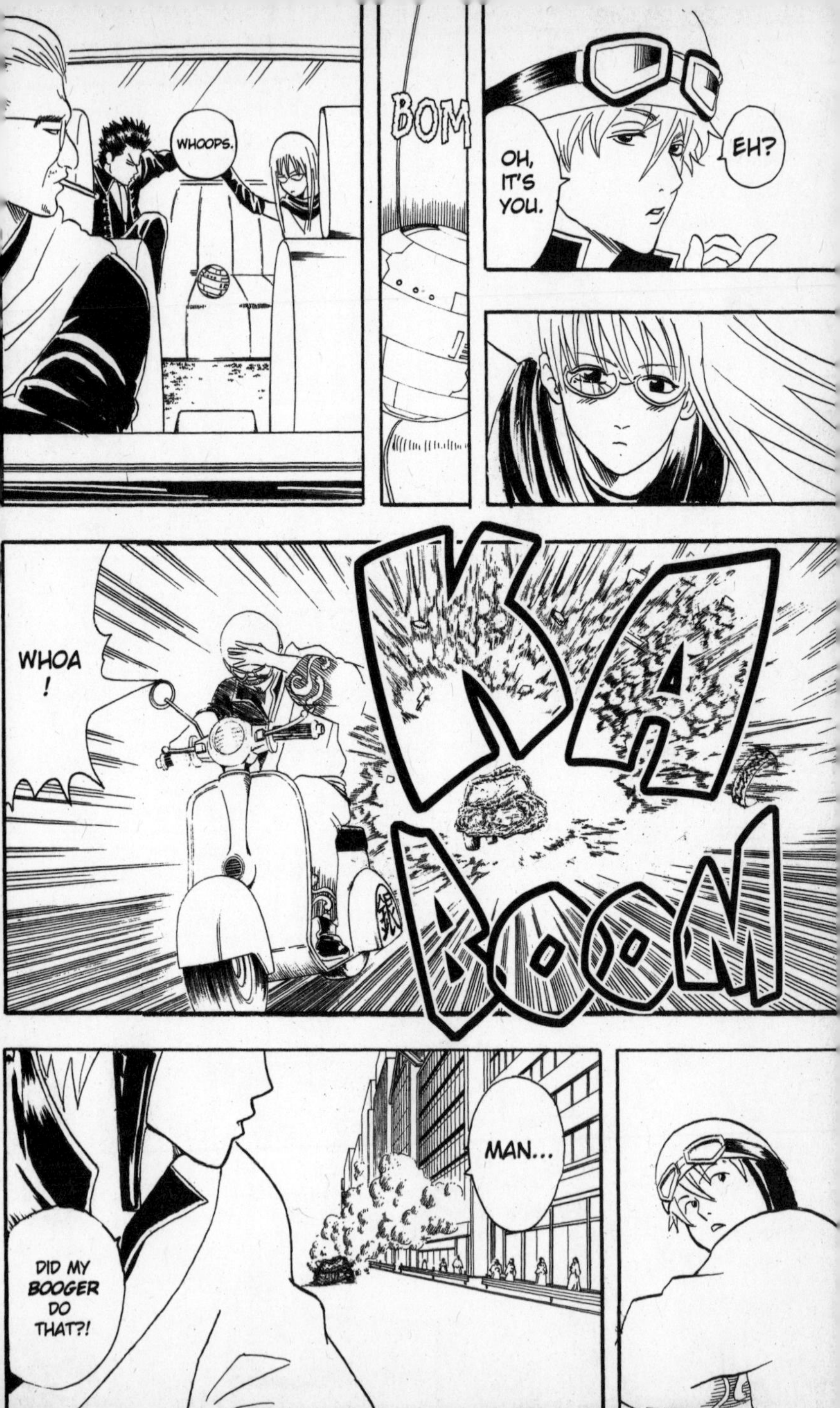
EH?
OH, IT'S YOU.
BOM
WHOOPS.
KA BOOM
WHOA!
MAN...
DID MY BOOGER DO THAT?!

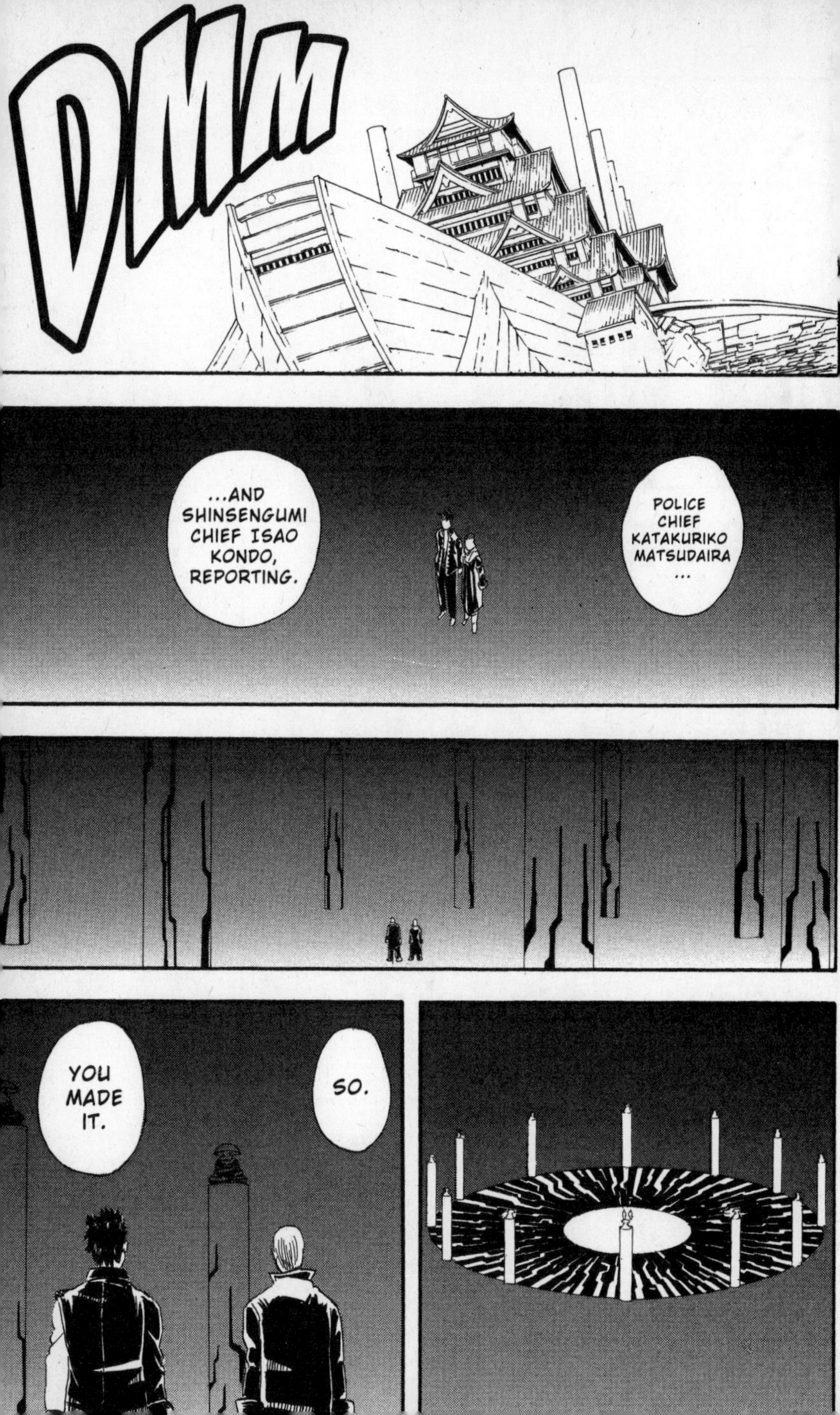
DMM
POLICE CHIEF KATAKURIKO MATSUDAIRA ...
...AND SHINSENGUMI CHIEF ISAO KONDO, REPORTING.
SO.
YOU MADE IT.

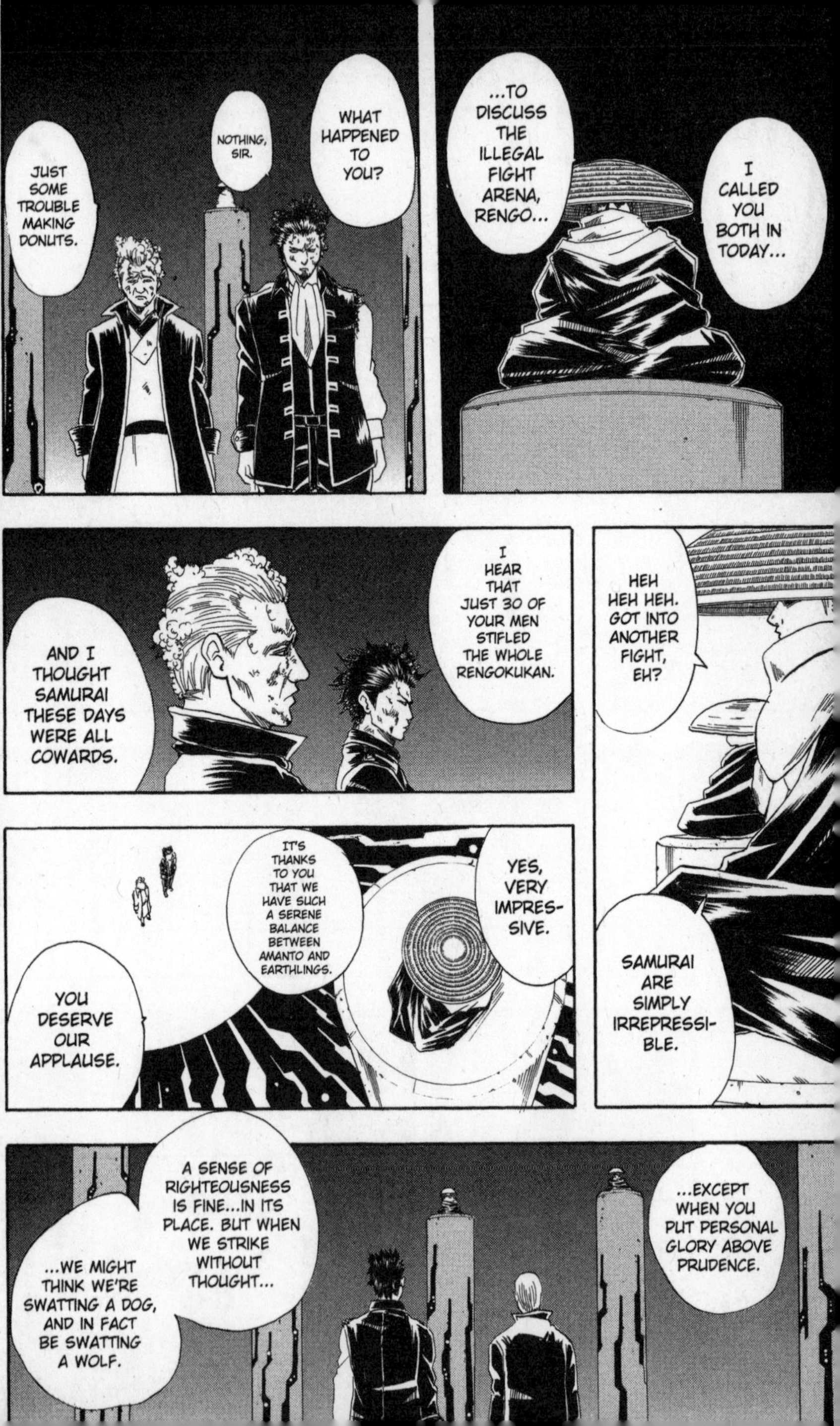
I CALLED YOU BOTH IN TODAY...
...TO DISCUSS THE ILLEGAL FIGHT ARENA, RENGO...
WHAT HAPPENED TO YOU?
NOTHING, SIR.
JUST SOME TROUBLE MAKING DONUTS.
HEH HEH HEH. GOT INTO ANOTHER FIGHT, EH?
SAMURAI ARE SIMPLY IRREPRESSI-BLE.
I HEAR THAT JUST 30 OF YOUR MEN STIFLED THE WHOLE RENGOKUKAN.
AND I THOUGHT SAMURAI THESE DAYS WERE ALL COWARDS.
YES, VERY IMPRES-SIVE.
IT'S THANKS TO YOU THAT WE HAVE SUCH A SERENE BALANCE BETWEEN AMANTO AND EARTHLINGS.
YOU DESERVE OUR APPLAUSE.
...EXCEPT WHEN YOU PUT PERSONAL GLORY ABOVE PRUDENCE.
A SENSE OF RIGHTEOUSNESS IS FINE...IN ITS PLACE. BUT WHEN WE STRIKE WITHOUT THOUGHT...
...WE MIGHT THINK WE'RE SWATTING A DOG, AND IN FACT BE SWATTING A WOLF.

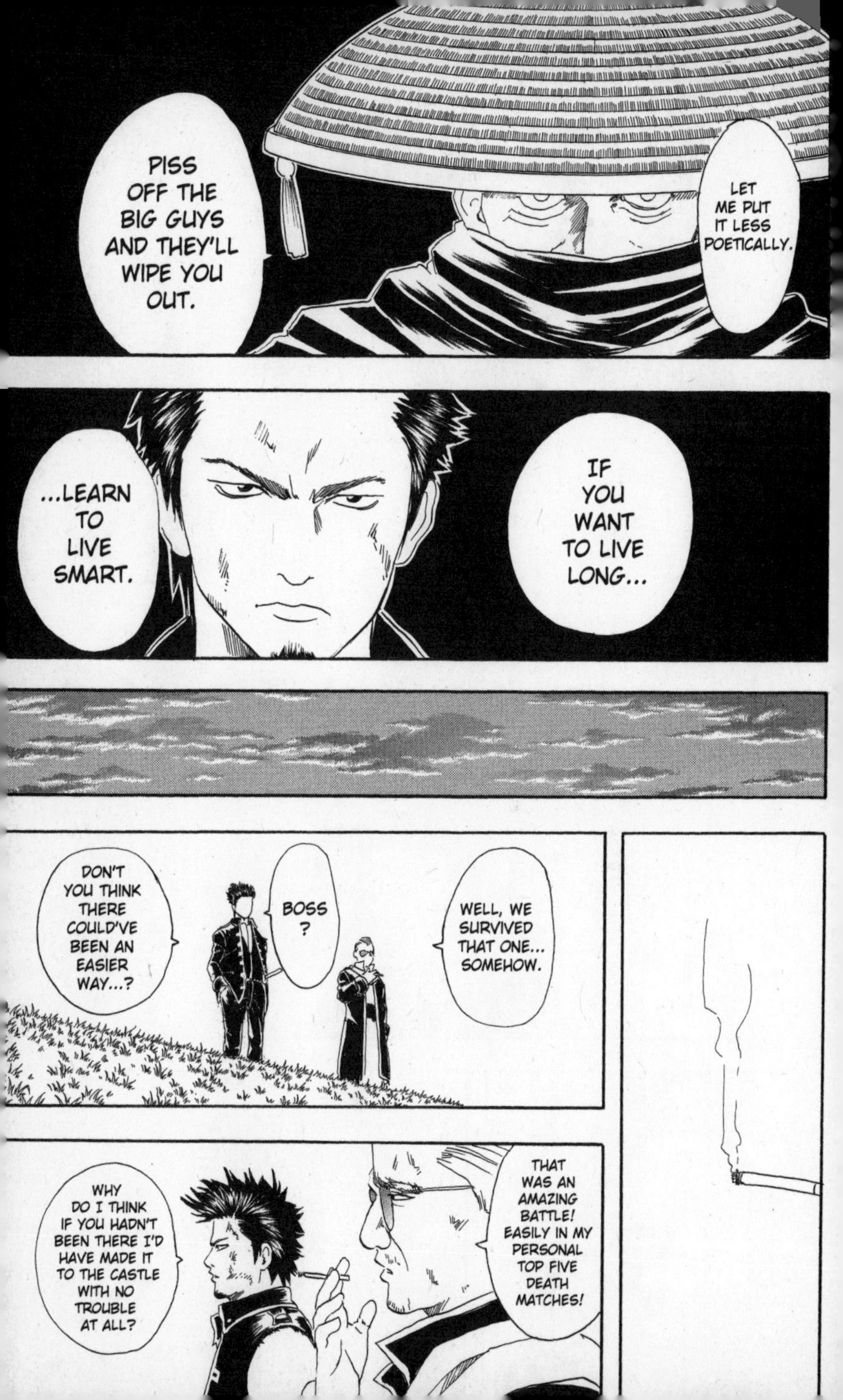
LET ME PUT IT LESS POETICALLY.
PISS OFF THE BIG GUYS AND THEY'LL WIPE YOU OUT.
IF YOU WANT TO LIVE LONG...
...LEARN TO LIVE SMART.
WELL, WE SURVIVED THAT ONE... SOMEHOW.
BOSS?
DON'T YOU THINK THERE COULD'VE BEEN AN EASIER WAY...?
THAT WAS AN AMAZING BATTLE! EASILY IN MY PERSONAL TOP FIVE DEATH MATCHES!
WHY DO I THINK IF YOU HADN'T BEEN THERE I'D HAVE MADE IT TO THE CASTLE WITH NO TROUBLE AT ALL?

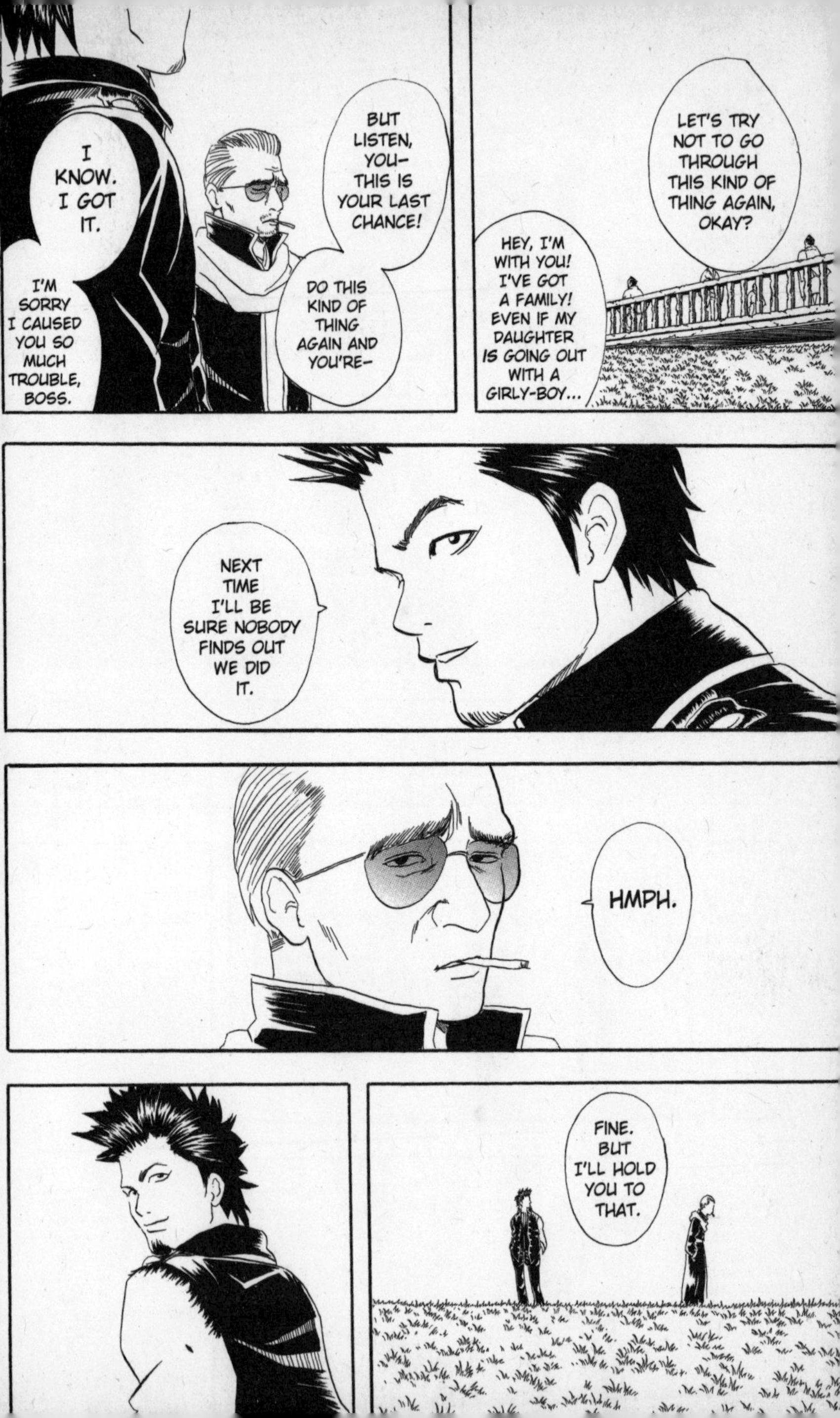
LET'S TRY NOT TO GO THROUGH THIS KIND OF THING AGAIN, OKAY?
HEY, I'M WITH YOU! I'VE GOT A FAMILY! EVEN IF MY DAUGHTER IS GOING OUT WITH A GIRLY-BOY...
BUT LISTEN, YOU— THIS IS YOUR LAST CHANCE!
DO THIS KIND OF THING AGAIN AND YOU'RE—
I KNOW. I GOT IT.
I'M SORRY I CAUSED YOU SO MUCH TROUBLE, BOSS.
NEXT TIME I'LL BE SURE NOBODY FINDS OUT WE DID IT.
HMPH.
FINE. BUT I'LL HOLD YOU TO THAT.

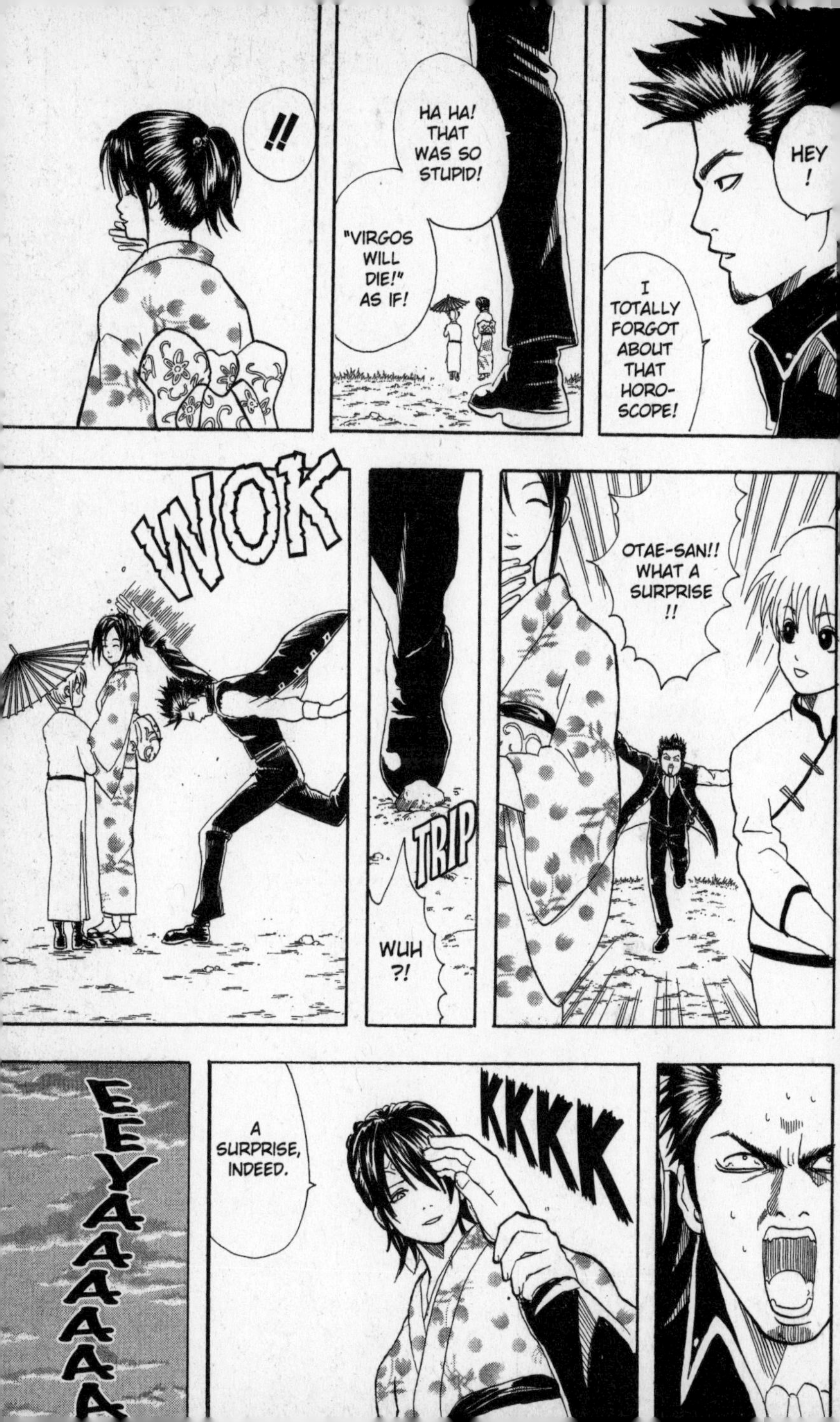
HEY!
I TOTALLY FORGOT ABOUT THAT HOROSCOPE!
HA HA! THAT WAS SO STUPID!
"VIRGOS WILL DIE!" AS IF!
!!
OTAE-SAN!! WHAT A SURPRISE !!
TRIP
WUH ?!
WOK
KKKK
A SURPRISE, INDEED.
EEYAAAAA

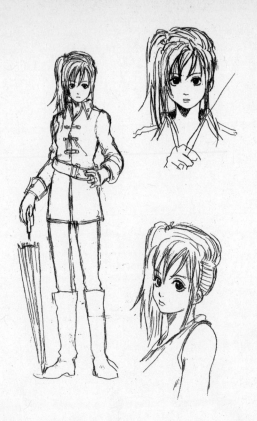

This is Okita. He used to be a woman.
Looks like Otsu-chan, doesn't it? The
fighting-with-an-umbrella gimmick got
handed down to Kagura. I realized the
Shinsengumi was all guys, so out of
despair this is what I got. Her
character's a bit thorny...prickly, you
know?

By the way, Kagura also used to be this
big in the beginning. But my editor said,
"She's not cute. Make her smaller!"
He's got such a Lolita complex.
Next up: Hijikata!

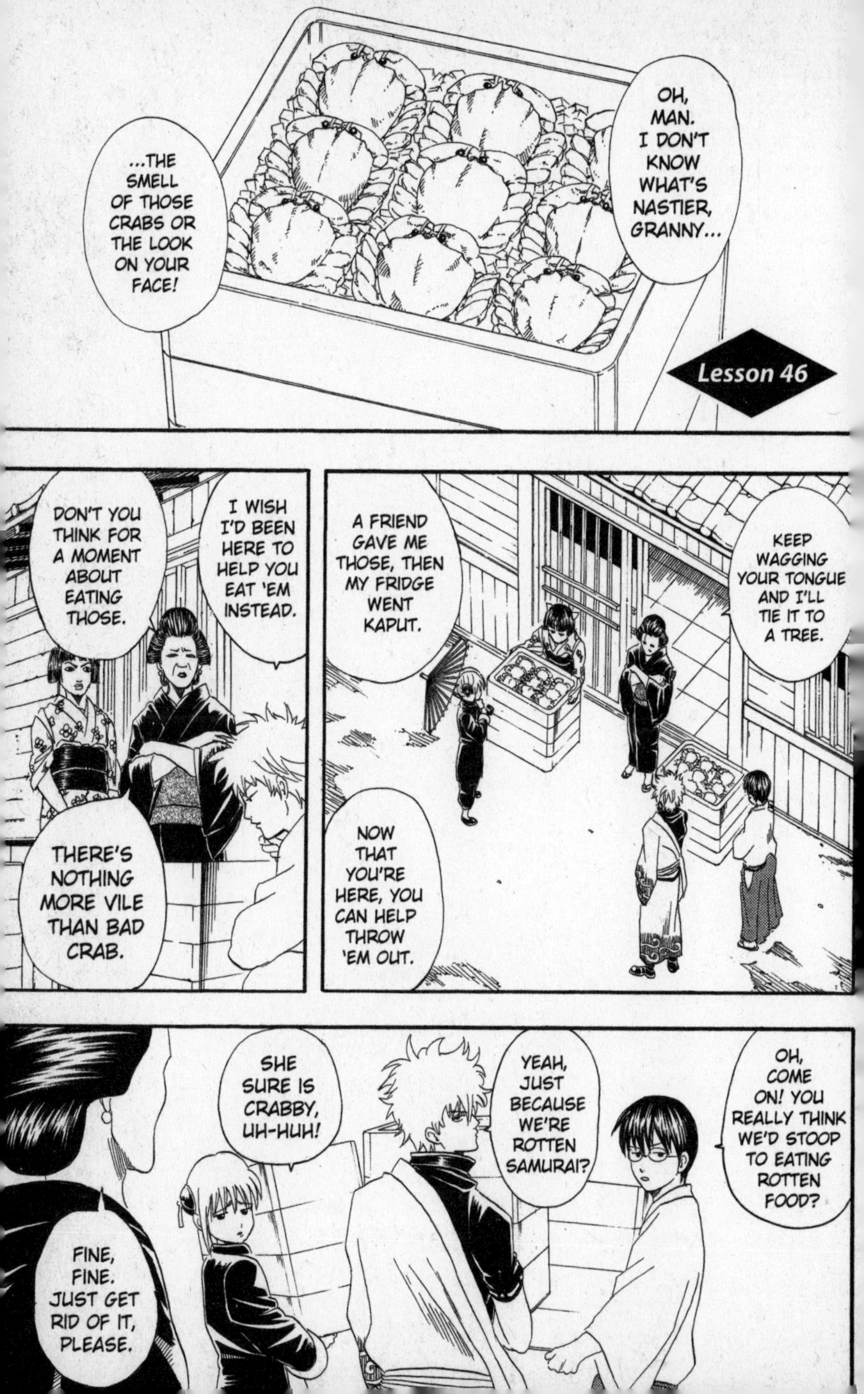
OH, MAN. I DON'T KNOW WHAT'S NASTIER, GRANNY...
...THE SMELL OF THOSE CRABS OR THE LOOK ON YOUR FACE!
Lesson 46
KEEP WAGGING YOUR TONGUE AND I'LL TIE IT TO A TREE.
A FRIEND GAVE ME THOSE, THEN MY FRIDGE WENT KAPUT.
NOW THAT YOU'RE HERE, YOU CAN HELP THROW 'EM OUT.
I WISH I'D BEEN HERE TO HELP YOU EAT 'EM INSTEAD.
DON'T YOU THINK FOR A MOMENT ABOUT EATING THOSE.
THERE'S NOTHING MORE VILE THAN BAD CRAB.
OH, COME ON! YOU REALLY THINK WE'D STOOP TO EATING ROTTEN FOOD?
YEAH, JUST BECAUSE WE'RE ROTTEN SAMURAI?
SHE SURE IS CRABBY, UH-HUH!
FINE, FINE. JUST GET RID OF IT, PLEASE.

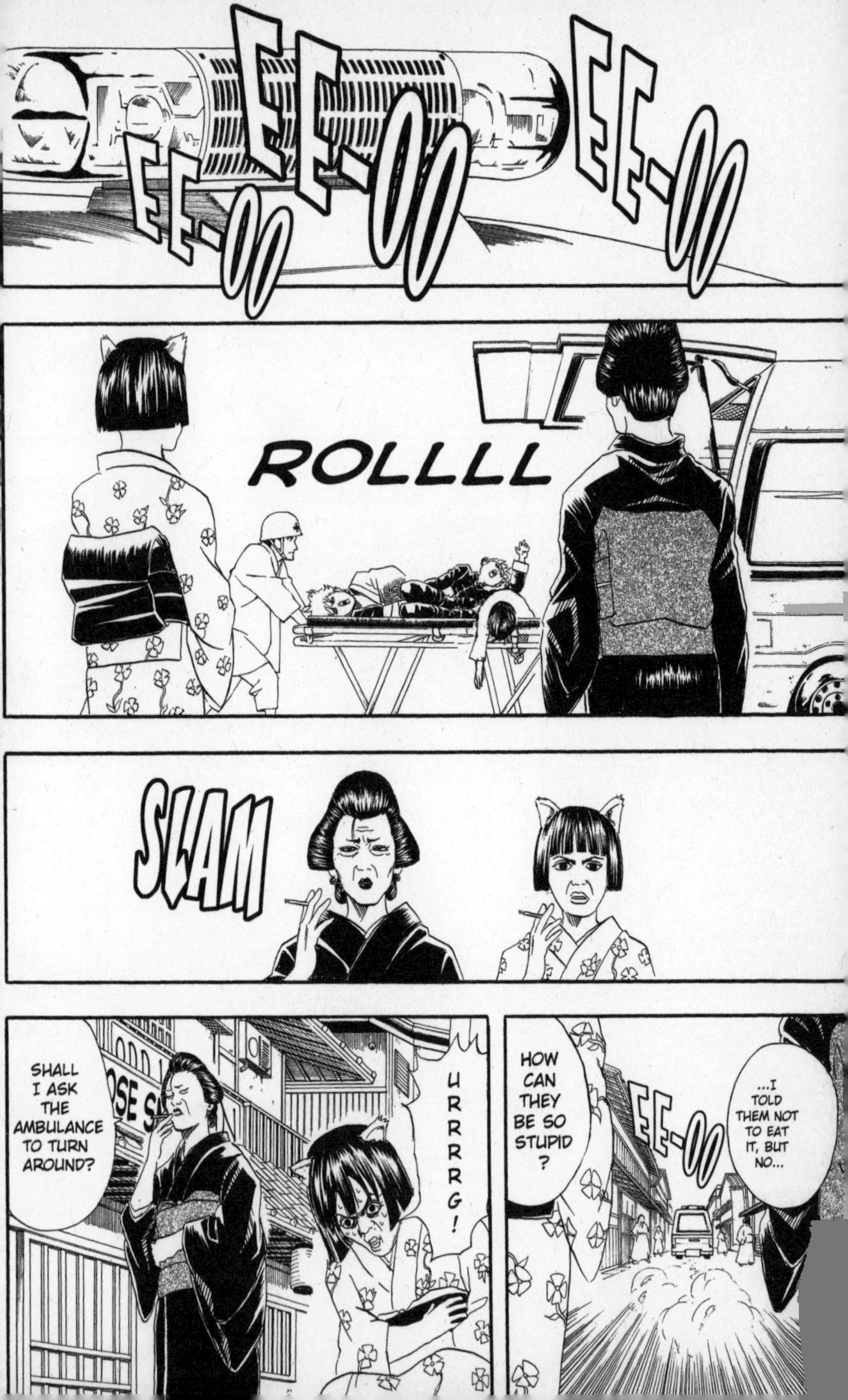
EE-OO
EE-OO
EE-OO
ROLLLL
SLAM
...I TOLD THEM NOT TO EAT IT, BUT NO...
EE-OO
HOW CAN THEY BE SO STUPID?
URRRRG!
SHALL I ASK THE AMBULANCE TO TURN AROUND?

Lesson 46: The More Delicious the Food, the Nastier It Is When It Goes Bad

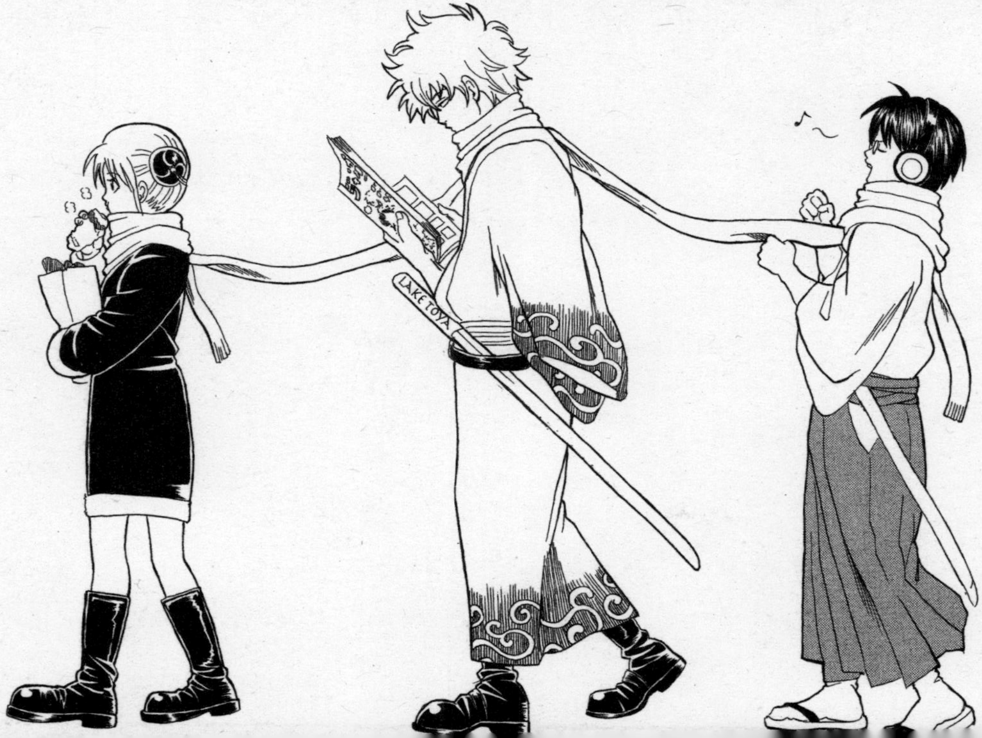
LAKE TOYA

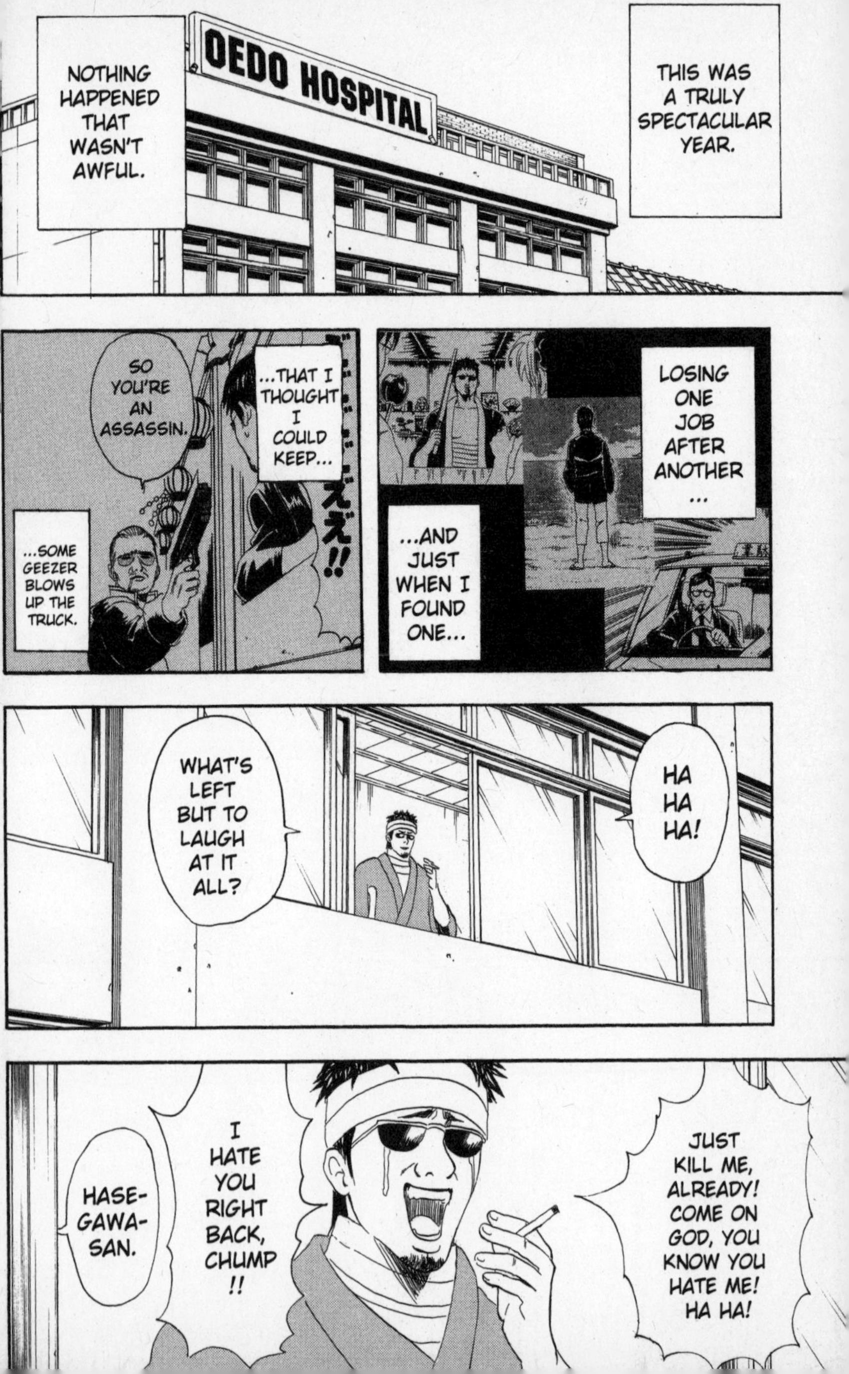
THIS WAS A TRULY SPECTACULAR YEAR.
OEDO HOSPITAL
NOTHING HAPPENED THAT WASN'T AWFUL.
LOSING ONE JOB AFTER ANOTHER ...
...AND JUST WHEN I FOUND ONE...
...THAT I THOUGHT I COULD KEEP...
SO YOU'RE AN ASSASSIN.
ええ!!
...SOME GEEZER BLOWS UP THE TRUCK.
HA HA HA!
WHAT'S LEFT BUT TO LAUGH AT IT ALL?
JUST KILL ME, ALREADY! COME ON GOD, YOU KNOW YOU HATE ME! HA HA!
I HATE YOU RIGHT BACK, CHUMP!!
HASE-GAWA-SAN.

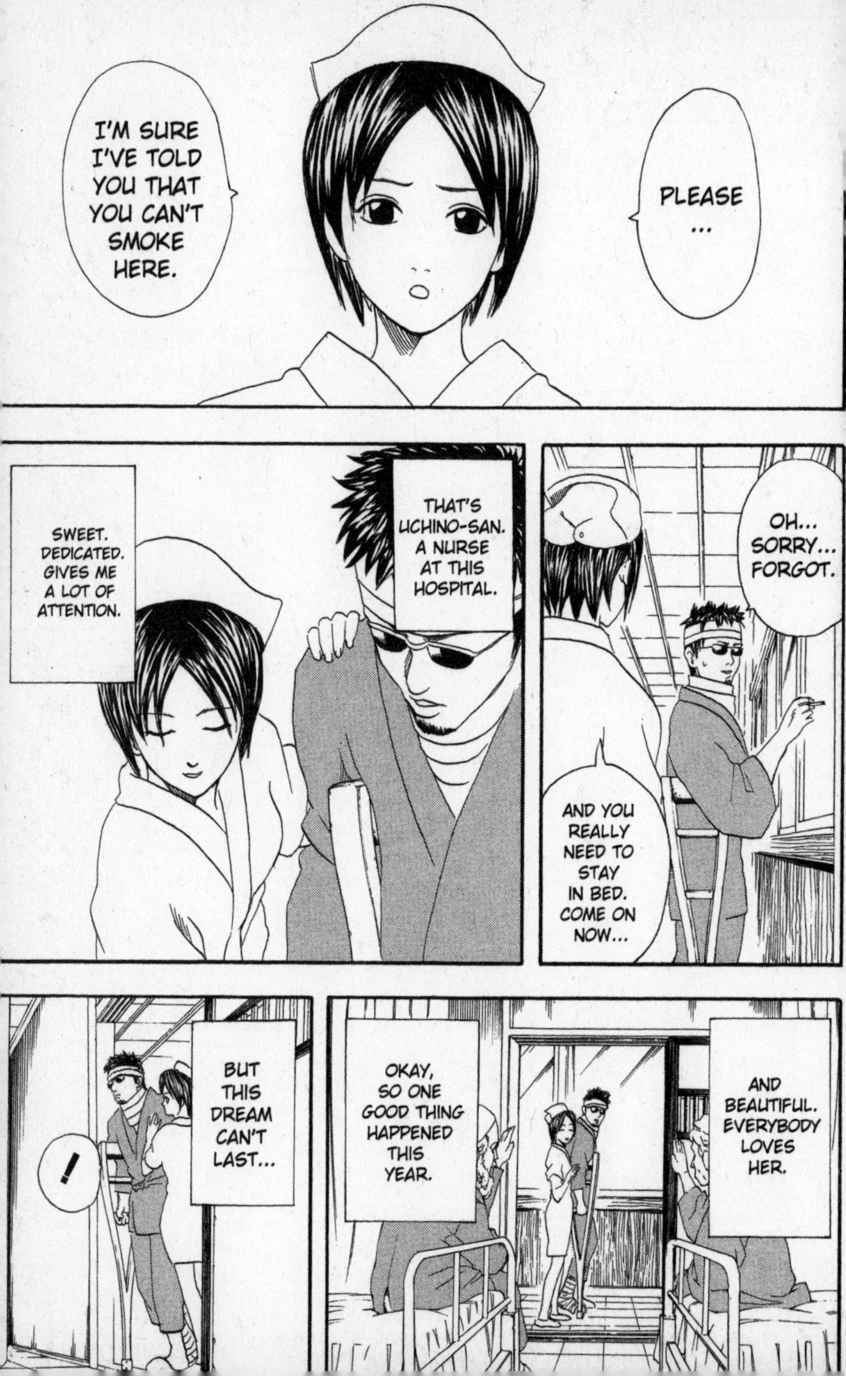
I'M SURE I'VE TOLD YOU THAT YOU CAN'T SMOKE HERE.
PLEASE ...
OH... SORRY... FORGOT.
AND YOU REALLY NEED TO STAY IN BED. COME ON NOW...
THAT'S UCHINO-SAN. A NURSE AT THIS HOSPITAL.
SWEET. DEDICATED. GIVES ME A LOT OF ATTENTION.
AND BEAUTIFUL. EVERYBODY LOVES HER.
OKAY, SO ONE GOOD THING HAPPENED THIS YEAR.
BUT THIS DREAM CAN'T LAST...
!

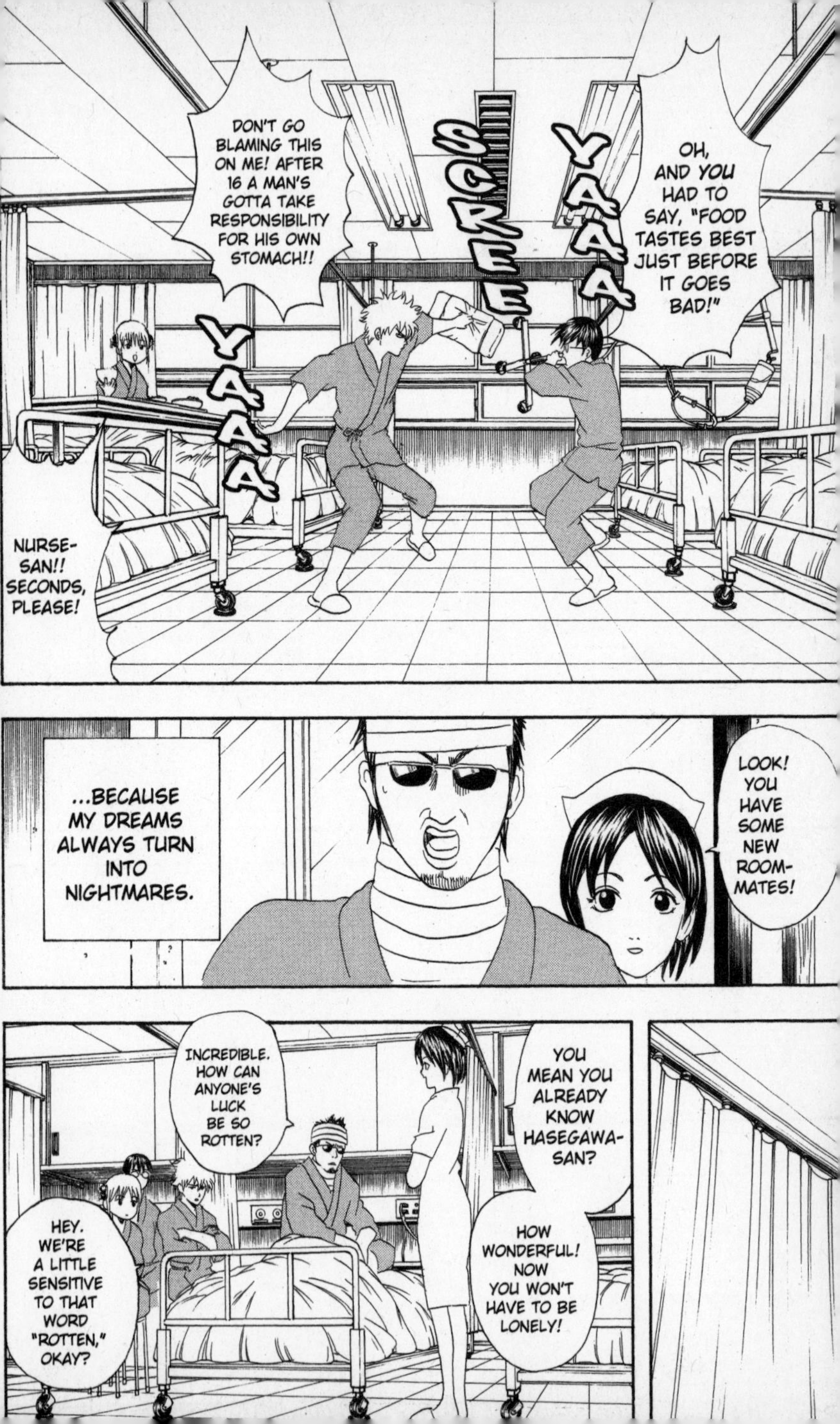
OH, AND YOU HAD TO SAY, "FOOD TASTES BEST JUST BEFORE IT GOES BAD!"
YAAAA
SCREE
DON'T GO BLAMING THIS ON ME! AFTER 16 A MAN'S GOTTA TAKE RESPONSIBILITY FOR HIS OWN STOMACH!!
YAAAA
NURSE-SAN!! SECONDS, PLEASE!
LOOK! YOU HAVE SOME NEW ROOMMATES!
...BECAUSE MY DREAMS ALWAYS TURN INTO NIGHTMARES.
YOU MEAN YOU ALREADY KNOW HASEGAWA-SAN?
INCREDIBLE. HOW CAN ANYONE'S LUCK BE SO ROTTEN?
HOW WONDERFUL! NOW YOU WON'T HAVE TO BE LONELY!
HEY. WE'RE A LITTLE SENSITIVE TO THAT WORD "ROTTEN," OKAY?

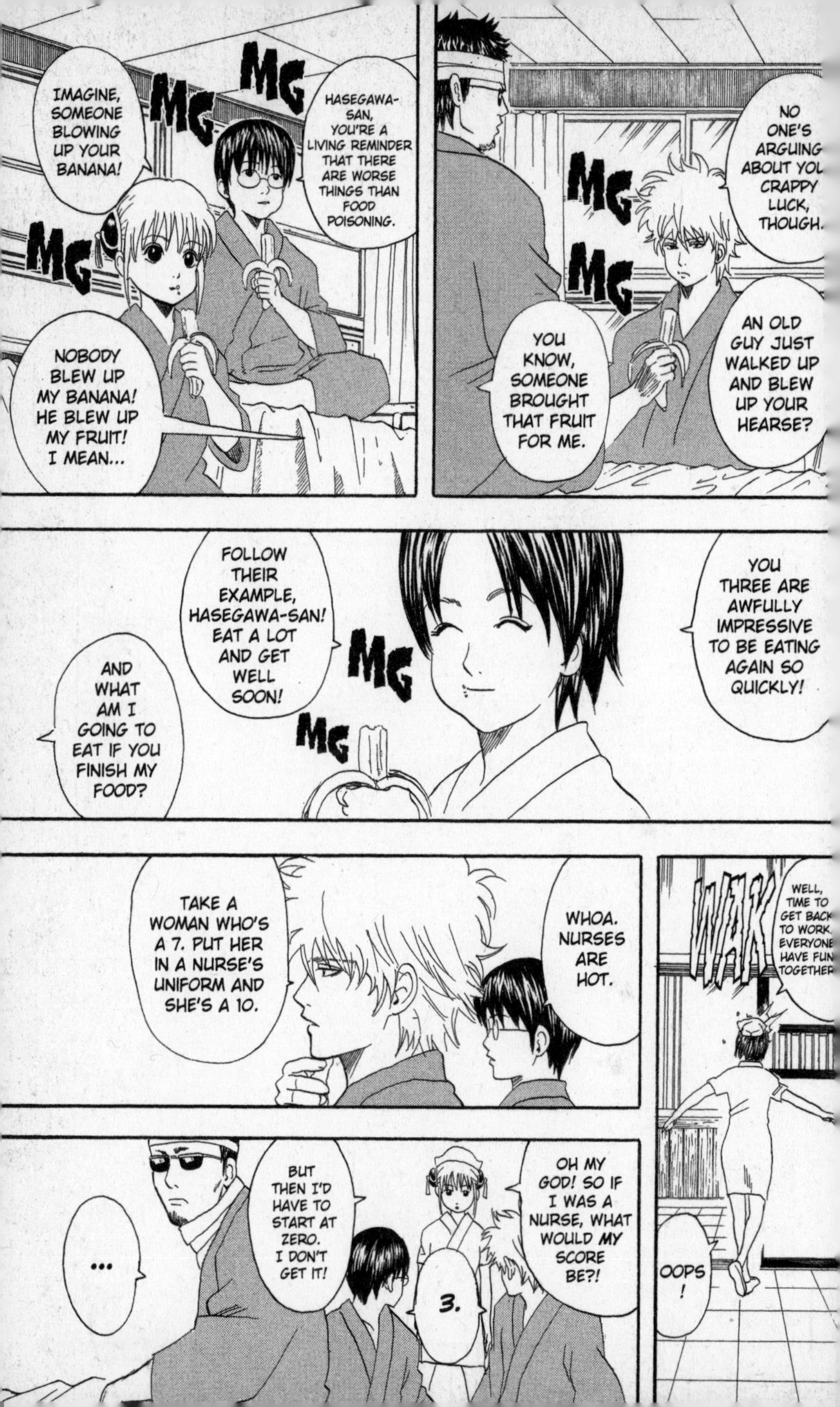
NO ONE'S ARGUING ABOUT YOU CRAPPY LUCK, THOUGH.
AN OLD GUY JUST WALKED UP AND BLEW UP YOUR HEARSE?
MG
MG
YOU KNOW, SOMEONE BROUGHT THAT FRUIT FOR ME.
HASEGAWA-SAN, YOU'RE A LIVING REMINDER THAT THERE ARE WORSE THINGS THAN FOOD POISONING.
MG
MG
IMAGINE, SOMEONE BLOWING UP YOUR BANANA!
MG
NOBODY BLEW UP MY BANANA! HE BLEW UP MY FRUIT! I MEAN...
YOU THREE ARE AWFULLY IMPRESSIVE TO BE EATING AGAIN SO QUICKLY!
MG
MG
FOLLOW THEIR EXAMPLE, HASEGAWA-SAN! EAT A LOT AND GET WELL SOON!
AND WHAT AM I GOING TO EAT IF YOU FINISH MY FOOD?
WAK
WELL, TIME TO GET BACK TO WORK. EVERYONE HAVE FUN TOGETHER
OOPS!
WHOA. NURSES ARE HOT.
TAKE A WOMAN WHO'S A 7. PUT HER IN A NURSE'S UNIFORM AND SHE'S A 10.
OH MY GOD! SO IF I WAS A NURSE, WHAT WOULD MY SCORE BE?!
3.
BUT THEN I'D HAVE TO START AT ZERO. I DON'T GET IT!
...

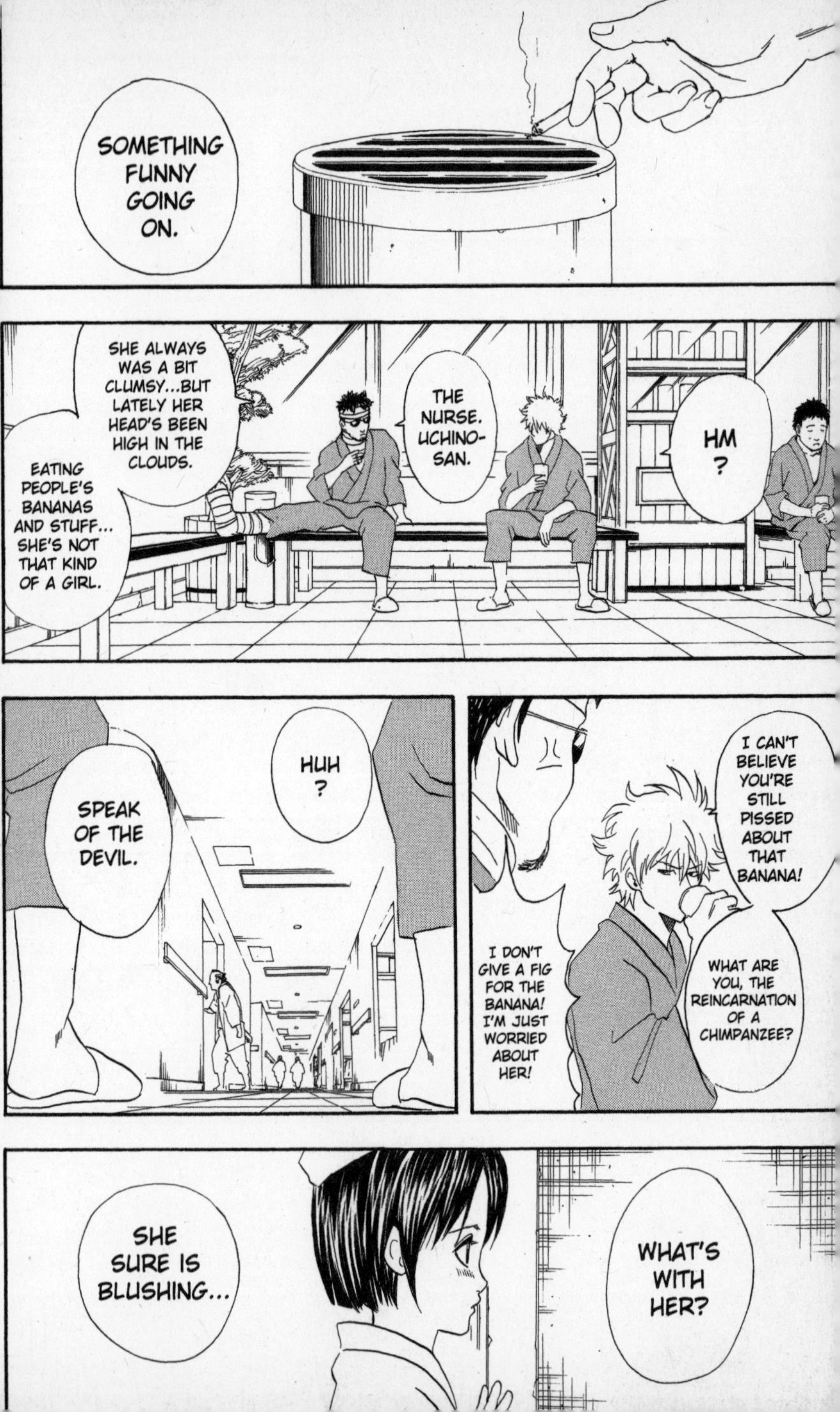
SOMETHING FUNNY GOING ON.
HM?
THE NURSE. UCHINO-SAN.
SHE ALWAYS WAS A BIT CLUMSY...BUT LATELY HER HEAD'S BEEN HIGH IN THE CLOUDS.
EATING PEOPLE'S BANANAS AND STUFF... SHE'S NOT THAT KIND OF A GIRL.
I CAN'T BELIEVE YOU'RE STILL PISSED ABOUT THAT BANANA!
WHAT ARE YOU, THE REINCARNATION OF A CHIMPANZEE?
I DON'T GIVE A FIG FOR THE BANANA! I'M JUST WORRIED ABOUT HER!
HUH?
SPEAK OF THE DEVIL.
WHAT'S WITH HER?
SHE SURE IS BLUSHING...

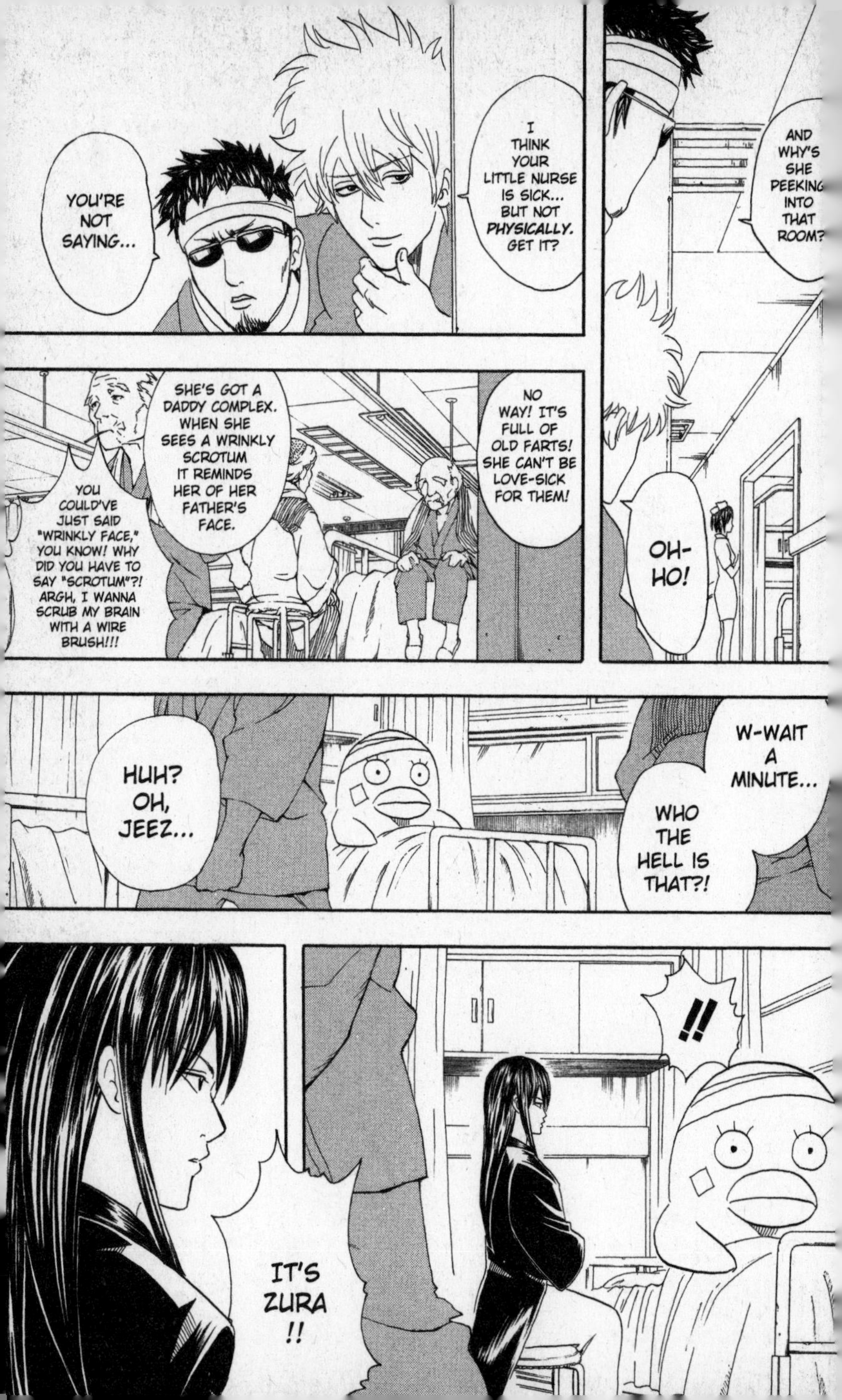
AND WHY'S SHE PEEKING INTO THAT ROOM?
OH-HO!
I THINK YOUR LITTLE NURSE IS SICK... BUT NOT *PHYSICALLY.* GET IT?
YOU'RE NOT SAYING...
NO WAY! IT'S FULL OF OLD FARTS! SHE CAN'T BE LOVE-SICK FOR THEM!
SHE'S GOT A DADDY COMPLEX. WHEN SHE SEES A WRINKLY SCROTUM IT REMINDS HER OF HER FATHER'S FACE.
YOU COULD'VE JUST SAID "WRINKLY FACE," YOU KNOW! WHY DID YOU HAVE TO SAY "SCROTUM"?! ARGH, I WANNA SCRUB MY BRAIN WITH A WIRE BRUSH!!!
W-WAIT A MINUTE...
WHO THE HELL IS THAT?!
HUH? OH, JEEZ...
!!
IT'S ZURA !!

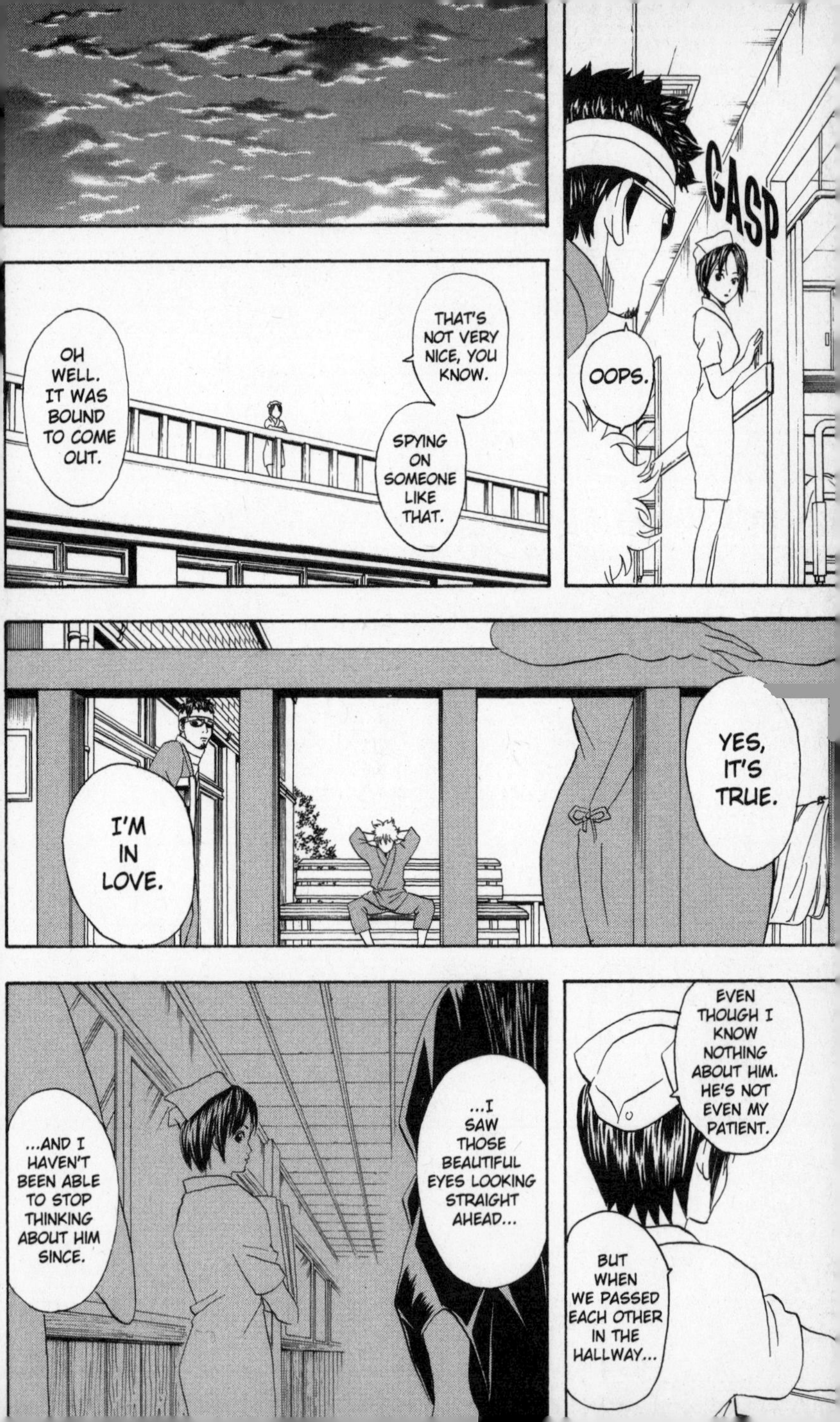
GASP
OOPS.
THAT'S NOT VERY NICE, YOU KNOW.
SPYING ON SOMEONE LIKE THAT.
OH WELL. IT WAS BOUND TO COME OUT.
YES, IT'S TRUE.
I'M IN LOVE.
EVEN THOUGH I KNOW NOTHING ABOUT HIM. HE'S NOT EVEN MY PATIENT.
BUT WHEN WE PASSED EACH OTHER IN THE HALLWAY...
...I SAW THOSE BEAUTIFUL EYES LOOKING STRAIGHT AHEAD...
...AND I HAVEN'T BEEN ABLE TO STOP THINKING ABOUT HIM SINCE.

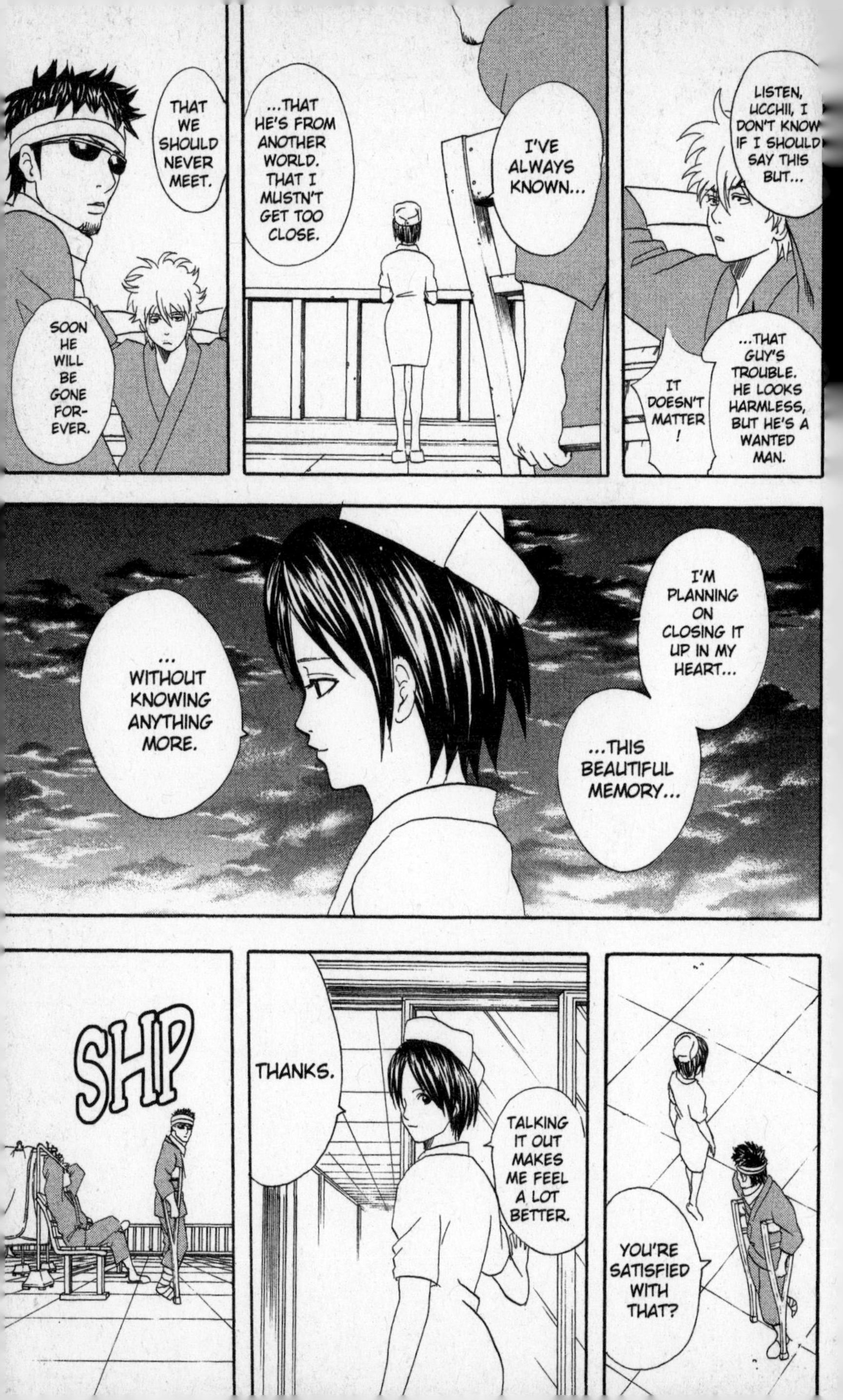
LISTEN, UCCHII, I DON'T KNOW IF I SHOULD SAY THIS BUT...
...THAT GUY'S TROUBLE. HE LOOKS HARMLESS, BUT HE'S A WANTED MAN.
IT DOESN'T MATTER!
I'VE ALWAYS KNOWN...
...THAT HE'S FROM ANOTHER WORLD. THAT I MUSTN'T GET TOO CLOSE.
THAT WE SHOULD NEVER MEET.
SOON HE WILL BE GONE FOR-EVER.
I'M PLANNING ON CLOSING IT UP IN MY HEART...
...THIS BEAUTIFUL MEMORY...
... WITHOUT KNOWING ANYTHING MORE.
YOU'RE SATISFIED WITH THAT?
TALKING IT OUT MAKES ME FEEL A LOT BETTER.
THANKS.
SHP

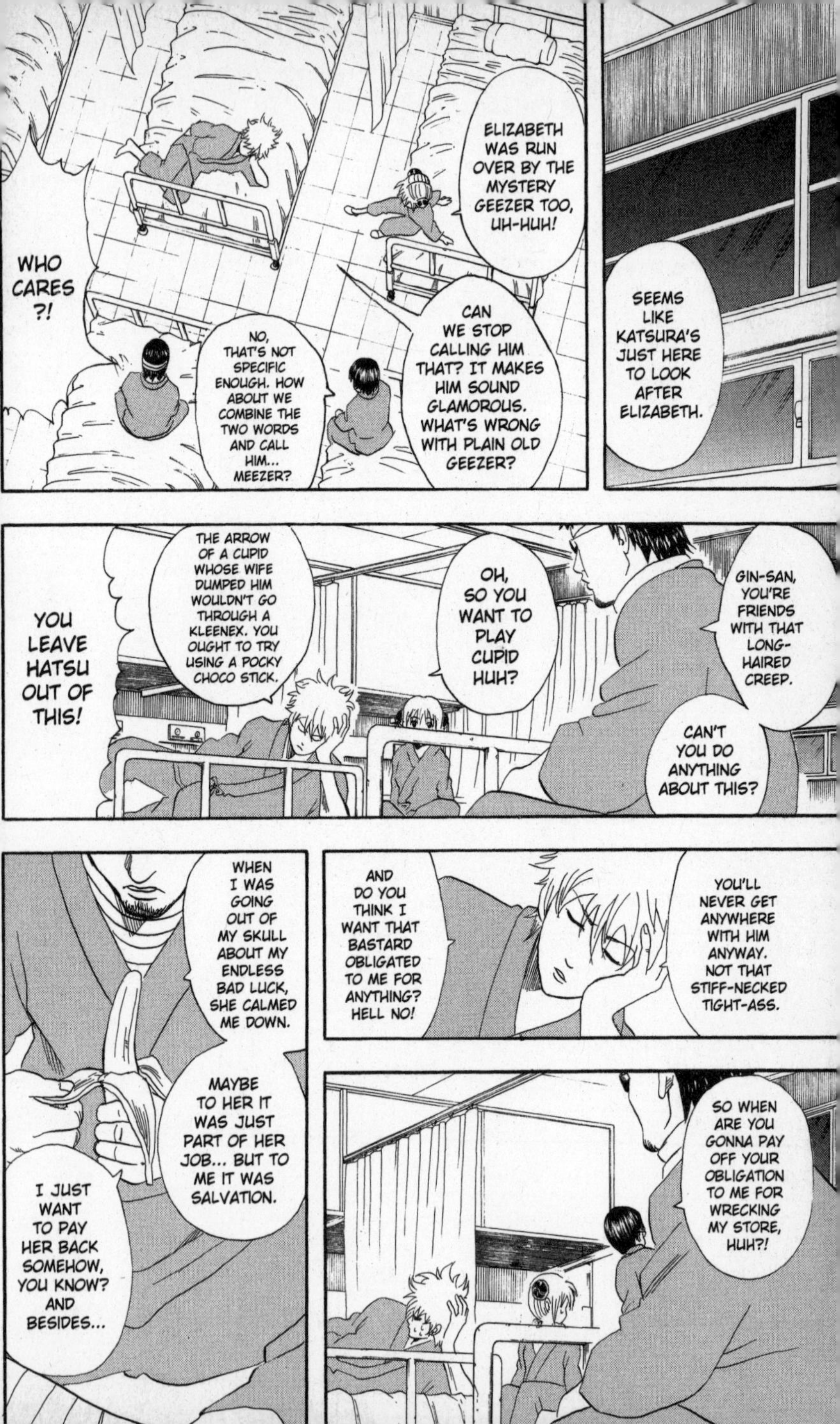
SEEMS LIKE KATSURA'S JUST HERE TO LOOK AFTER ELIZABETH.
ELIZABETH WAS RUN OVER BY THE MYSTERY GEEZER TOO, UH-HUH!
CAN WE STOP CALLING HIM THAT? IT MAKES HIM SOUND GLAMOROUS. WHAT'S WRONG WITH PLAIN OLD GEEZER?
NO, THAT'S NOT SPECIFIC ENOUGH. HOW ABOUT WE COMBINE THE TWO WORDS AND CALL HIM... MEEZER?
WHO CARES?!
GIN-SAN, YOU'RE FRIENDS WITH THAT LONG-HAIRED CREEP.
CAN'T YOU DO ANYTHING ABOUT THIS?
OH, SO YOU WANT TO PLAY CUPID HUH?
THE ARROW OF A CUPID WHOSE WIFE DUMPED HIM WOULDN'T GO THROUGH A KLEENEX. YOU OUGHT TO TRY USING A POCKY CHOCO STICK.
YOU LEAVE HATSU OUT OF THIS!
YOU'LL NEVER GET ANYWHERE WITH HIM ANYWAY. NOT THAT STIFF-NECKED TIGHT-ASS.
AND DO YOU THINK I WANT THAT BASTARD OBLIGATED TO ME FOR ANYTHING? HELL NO!
SO WHEN ARE YOU GONNA PAY OFF YOUR OBLIGATION TO ME FOR WRECKING MY STORE, HUH?!
WHEN I WAS GOING OUT OF MY SKULL ABOUT MY ENDLESS BAD LUCK, SHE CALMED ME DOWN.
MAYBE TO HER IT WAS JUST PART OF HER JOB... BUT TO ME IT WAS SALVATION.
I JUST WANT TO PAY HER BACK SOMEHOW, YOU KNOW? AND BESIDES...

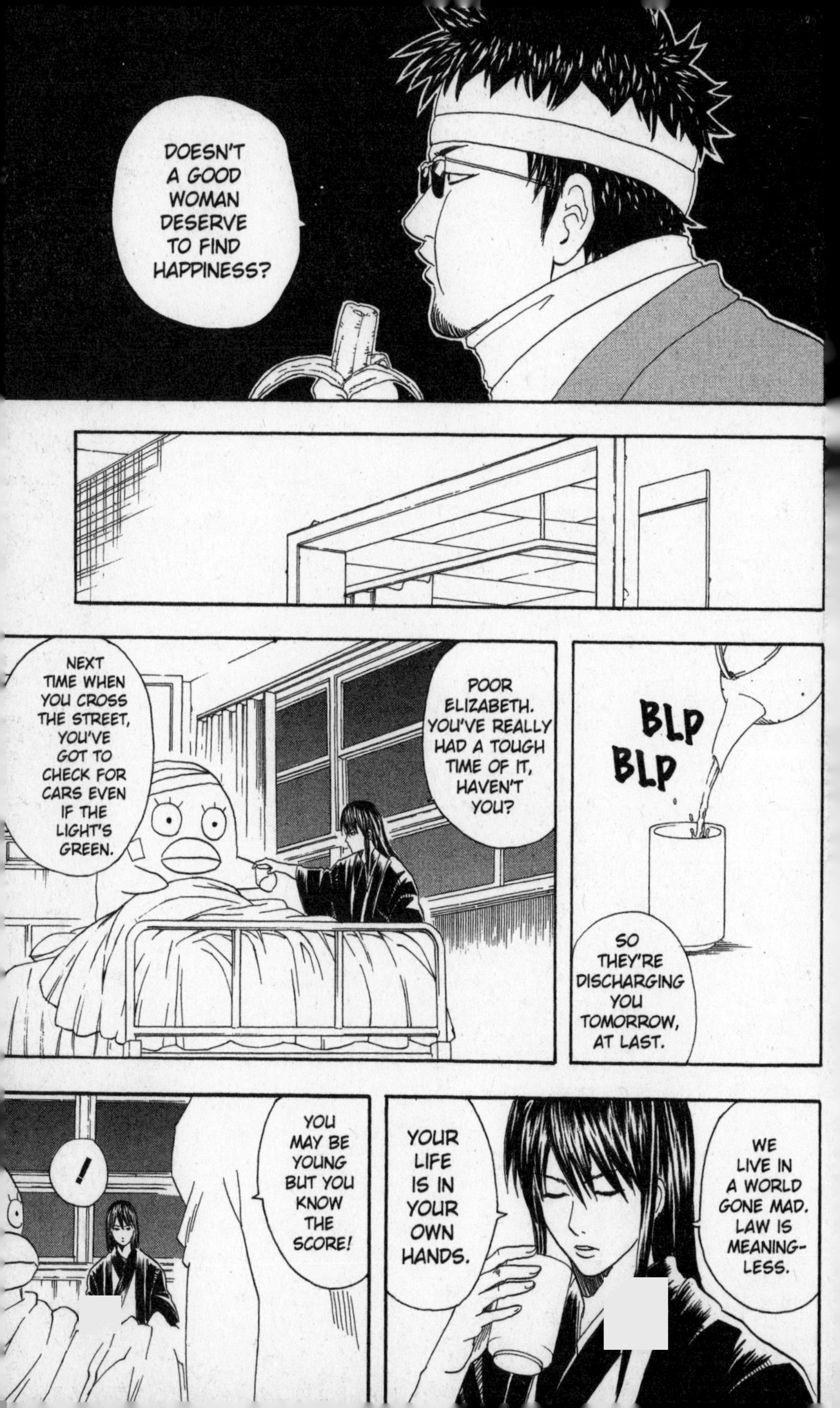
DOESN'T A GOOD WOMAN DESERVE TO FIND HAPPINESS?
BLP BLP
SO THEY'RE DISCHARGING YOU TOMORROW, AT LAST.
POOR ELIZABETH. YOU'VE REALLY HAD A TOUGH TIME OF IT, HAVEN'T YOU?
NEXT TIME WHEN YOU CROSS THE STREET, YOU'VE GOT TO CHECK FOR CARS EVEN IF THE LIGHT'S GREEN.
WE LIVE IN A WORLD GONE MAD. LAW IS MEANING-LESS.
YOUR LIFE IS IN YOUR OWN HANDS.
YOU MAY BE YOUNG BUT YOU KNOW THE SCORE!
!

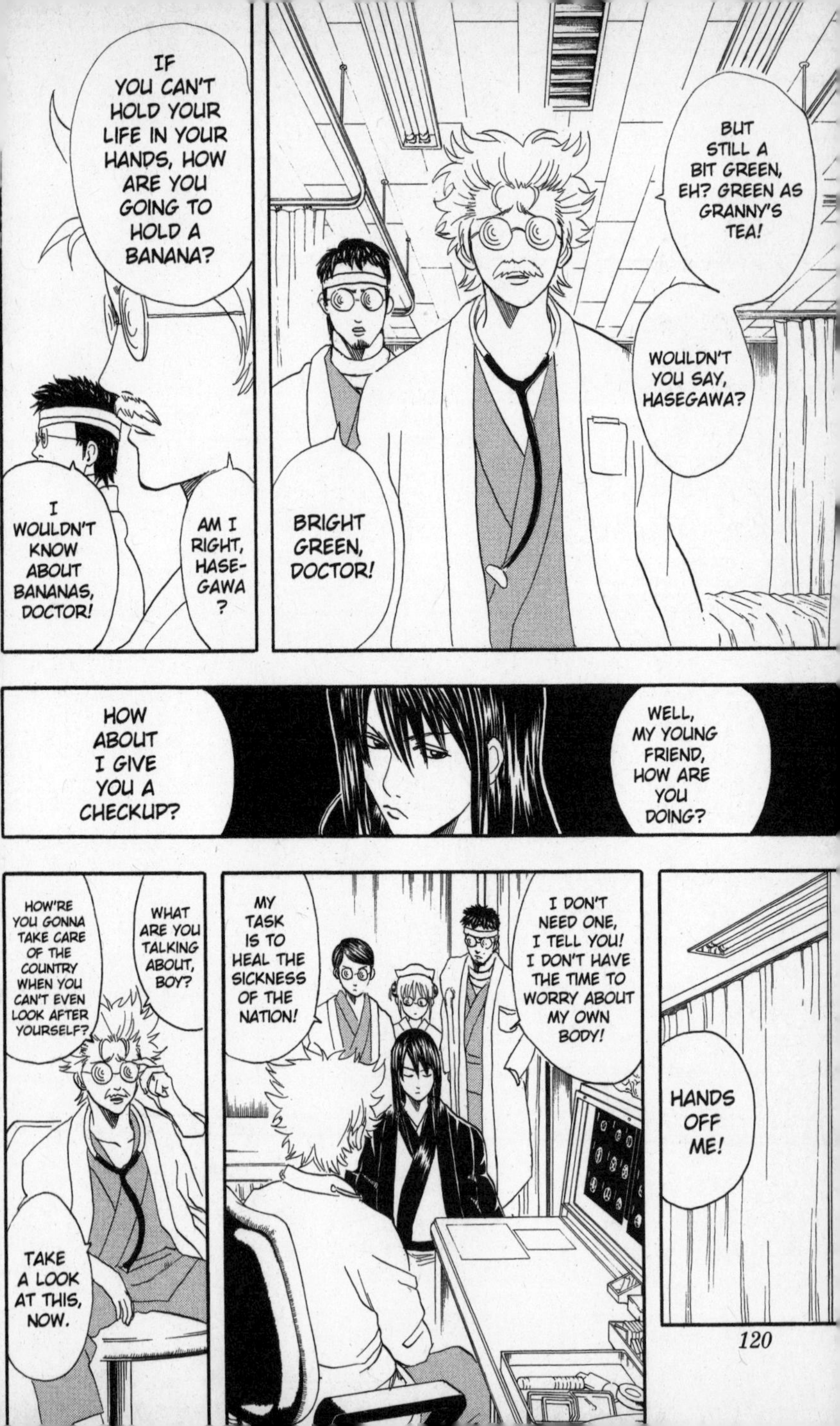
BUT STILL A BIT GREEN, EH? GREEN AS GRANNY'S TEA!
WOULDN'T YOU SAY, HASEGAWA?
BRIGHT GREEN, DOCTOR!
IF YOU CAN'T HOLD YOUR LIFE IN YOUR HANDS, HOW ARE YOU GOING TO HOLD A BANANA?
AM I RIGHT, HASEGAWA?
I WOULDN'T KNOW ABOUT BANANAS, DOCTOR!
WELL, MY YOUNG FRIEND, HOW ARE YOU DOING?
HOW ABOUT I GIVE YOU A CHECKUP?
HANDS OFF ME!
I DON'T NEED ONE, I TELL YOU! I DON'T HAVE THE TIME TO WORRY ABOUT MY OWN BODY!
MY TASK IS TO HEAL THE SICKNESS OF THE NATION!
WHAT ARE YOU TALKING ABOUT, BOY?
HOW'RE YOU GONNA TAKE CARE OF THE COUNTRY WHEN YOU CAN'T EVEN LOOK AFTER YOURSELF?
TAKE A LOOK AT THIS, NOW.

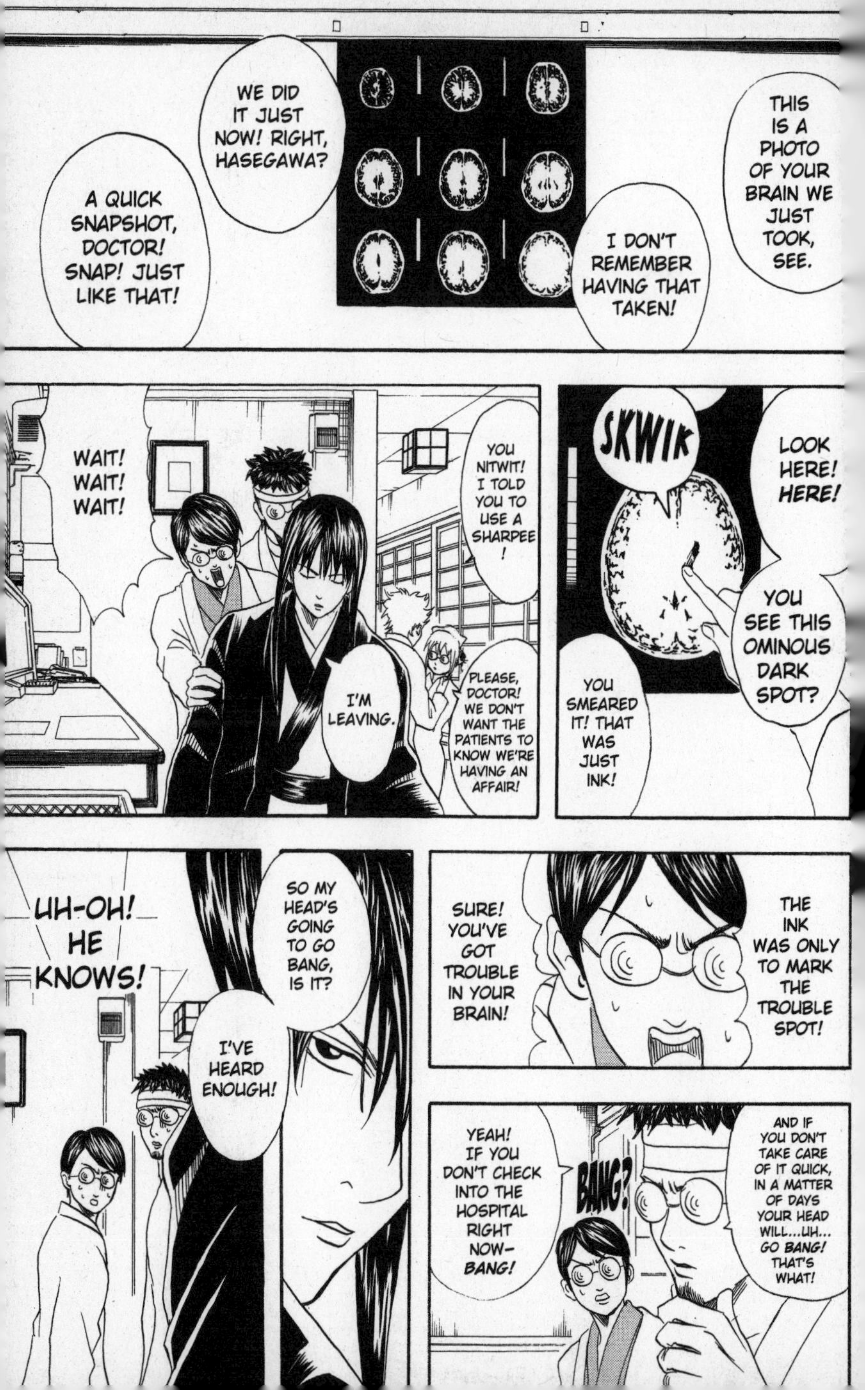
THIS IS A PHOTO OF YOUR BRAIN WE JUST TOOK, SEE.
I DON'T REMEMBER HAVING THAT TAKEN!
WE DID IT JUST NOW! RIGHT, HASEGAWA?
A QUICK SNAPSHOT, DOCTOR! SNAP! JUST LIKE THAT!
SKWIK
LOOK HERE! HERE!
YOU SEE THIS OMINOUS DARK SPOT?
YOU SMEARED IT! THAT WAS JUST INK!
YOU NITWIT! I TOLD YOU TO USE A SHARPEE!
WAIT! WAIT! WAIT!
PLEASE, DOCTOR! WE DON'T WANT THE PATIENTS TO KNOW WE'RE HAVING AN AFFAIR!
I'M LEAVING.
THE INK WAS ONLY TO MARK THE TROUBLE SPOT!
SURE! YOU'VE GOT TROUBLE IN YOUR BRAIN!
AND IF YOU DON'T TAKE CARE OF IT QUICK, IN A MATTER OF DAYS YOUR HEAD WILL...UH... GO BANG! THAT'S WHAT!
BANG?
YEAH! IF YOU DON'T CHECK INTO THE HOSPITAL RIGHT NOW– BANG!
SO MY HEAD'S GOING TO GO BANG, IS IT?
UH-OH! HE KNOWS!
I'VE HEARD ENOUGH!

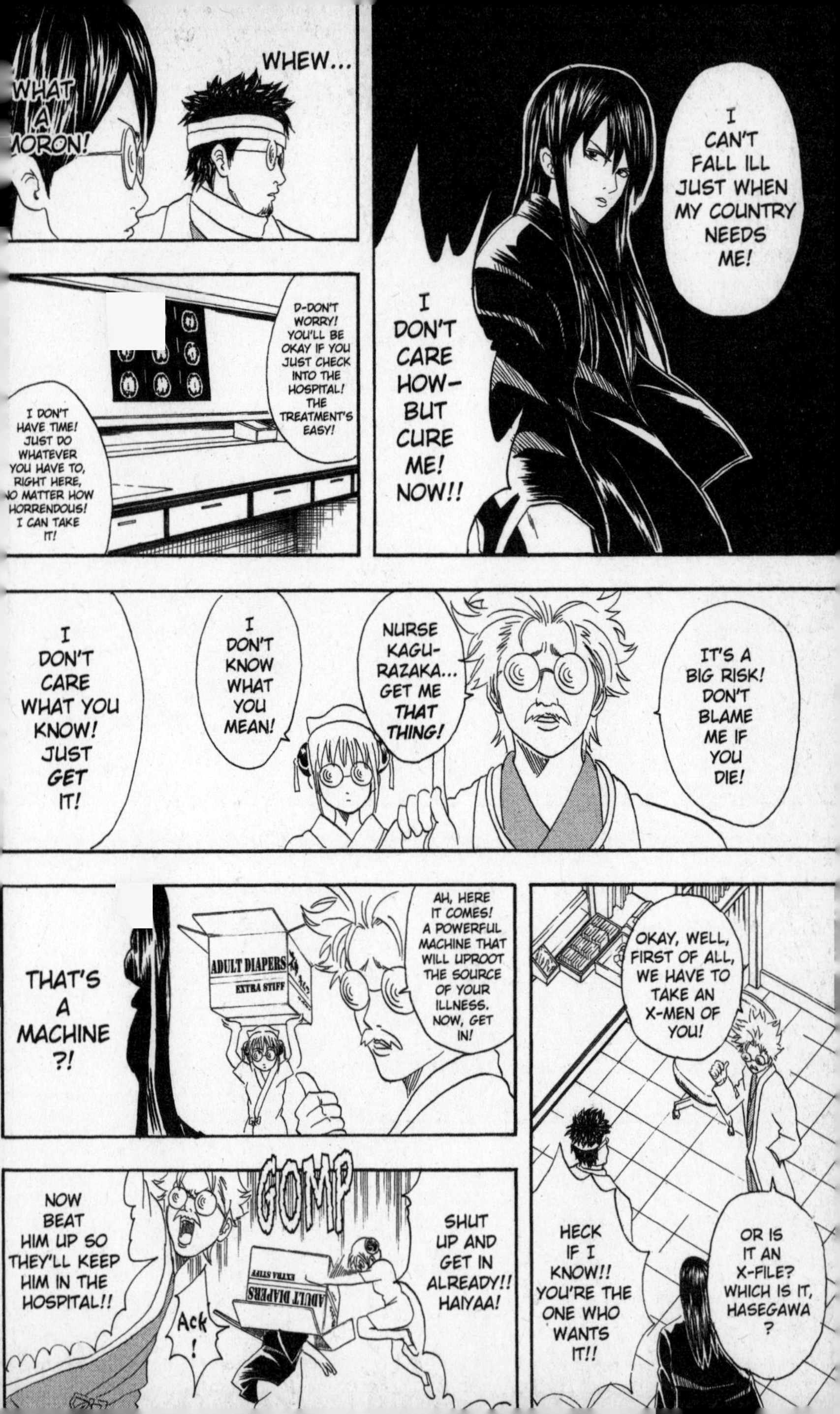
I CAN'T FALL ILL JUST WHEN MY COUNTRY NEEDS ME!
I DON'T CARE HOW— BUT CURE ME! NOW!!
WHEW...
WHAT A MORON!
D-DON'T WORRY! YOU'LL BE OKAY IF YOU JUST CHECK INTO THE HOSPITAL! THE TREATMENT'S EASY!
I DON'T HAVE TIME! JUST DO WHATEVER YOU HAVE TO, RIGHT HERE, NO MATTER HOW HORRENDOUS! I CAN TAKE IT!
IT'S A BIG RISK! DON'T BLAME ME IF YOU DIE!
NURSE KAGURAZAKA... GET ME THAT THING!
I DON'T KNOW WHAT YOU MEAN!
I DON'T CARE WHAT YOU KNOW! JUST GET IT!
OKAY, WELL, FIRST OF ALL, WE HAVE TO TAKE AN X-MEN OF YOU!
OR IS IT AN X-FILE? WHICH IS IT, HASEGAWA?
HECK IF I KNOW!! YOU'RE THE ONE WHO WANTS IT!!
AH, HERE IT COMES! A POWERFUL MACHINE THAT WILL UPROOT THE SOURCE OF YOUR ILLNESS. NOW, GET IN!
ADULT DIAPERS
EXTRA STIFF
THAT'S A MACHINE?!
SHUT UP AND GET IN ALREADY!! HAIYAA!
GOMP
NOW BEAT HIM UP SO THEY'LL KEEP HIM IN THE HOSPITAL!!
Ack!

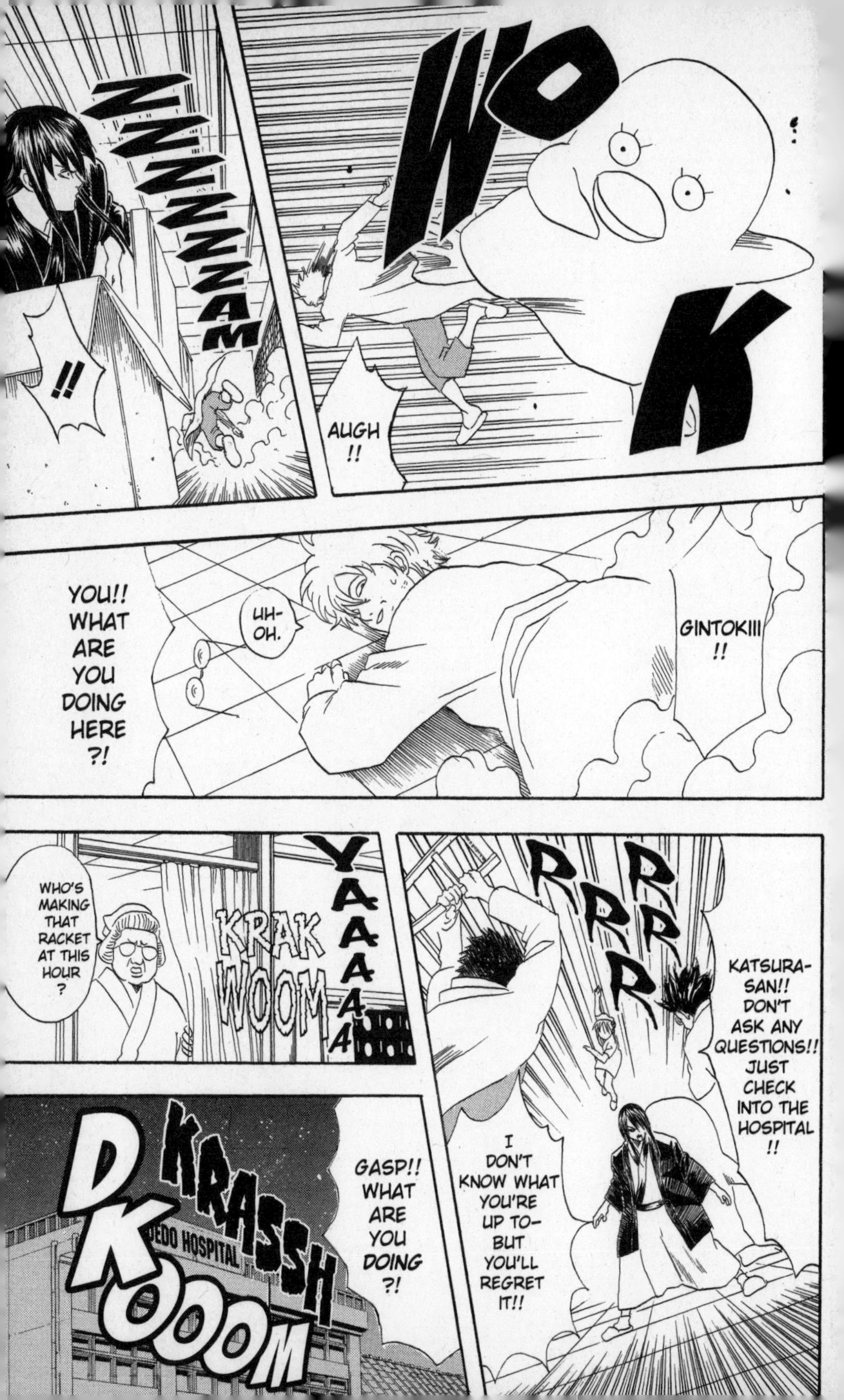
WOK
AUGH!!
ZZZZZAM
!!
GINTOKIII!!
UH-OH.
YOU!! WHAT ARE YOU DOING HERE?!
RRRRRR
KATSURA-SAN!! DON'T ASK ANY QUESTIONS!! JUST CHECK INTO THE HOSPITAL!!
I DON'T KNOW WHAT YOU'RE UP TO-BUT YOU'LL REGRET IT!!
YAAAAA
KRAK WOOM
WHO'S MAKING THAT RACKET AT THIS HOUR?
DKRASSH KOOOM
GASP!! WHAT ARE YOU DOING?!
OEDO HOSPITAL

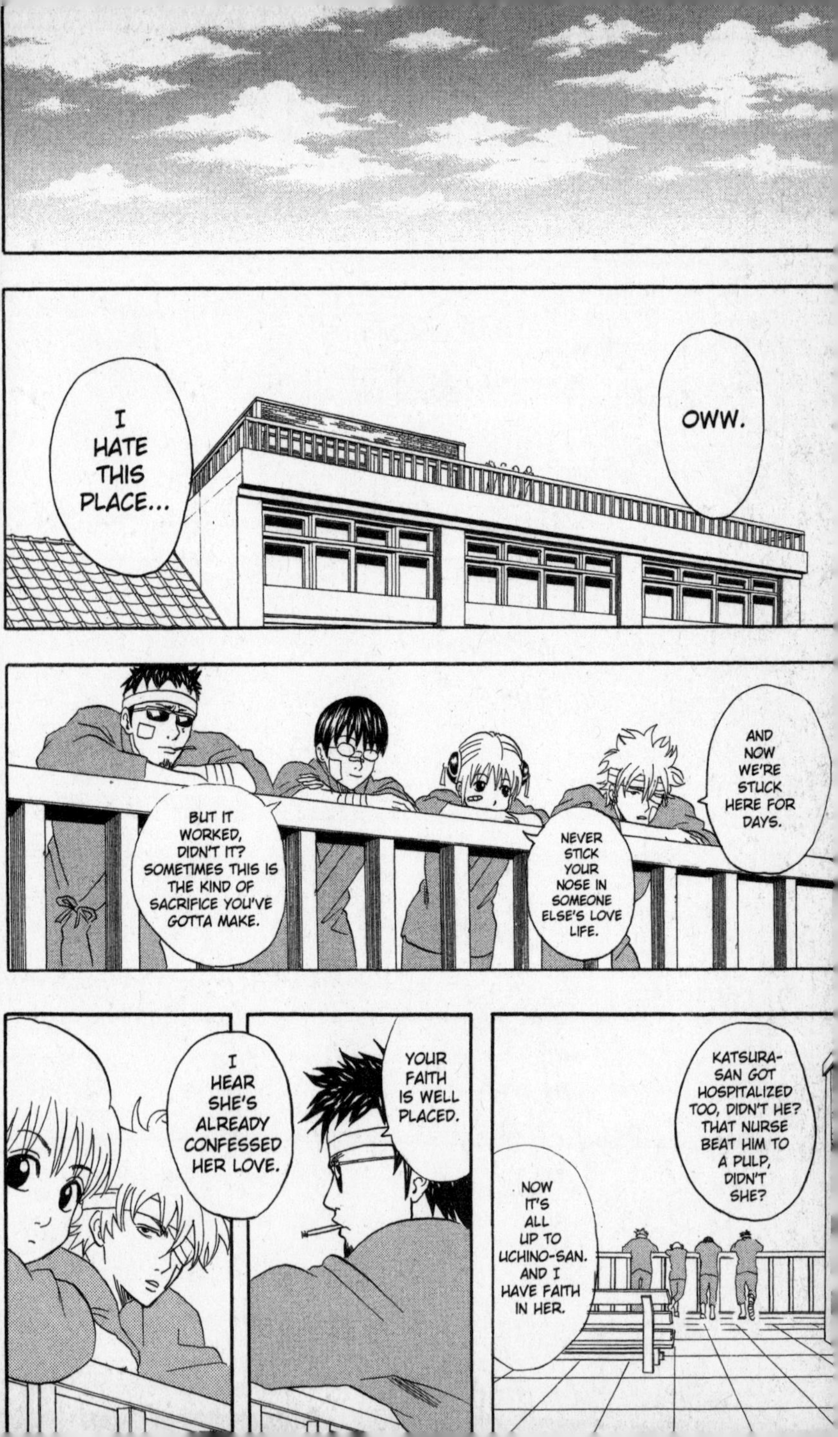
OWW.
I HATE THIS PLACE...
AND NOW WE'RE STUCK HERE FOR DAYS.
NEVER STICK YOUR NOSE IN SOMEONE ELSE'S LOVE LIFE.
BUT IT WORKED, DIDN'T IT? SOMETIMES THIS IS THE KIND OF SACRIFICE YOU'VE GOTTA MAKE.
KATSURA-SAN GOT HOSPITALIZED TOO, DIDN'T HE? THAT NURSE BEAT HIM TO A PULP, DIDN'T SHE?
NOW IT'S ALL UP TO UCHINO-SAN. AND I HAVE FAITH IN HER.
YOUR FAITH IS WELL PLACED.
I HEAR SHE'S ALREADY CONFESSED HER LOVE.

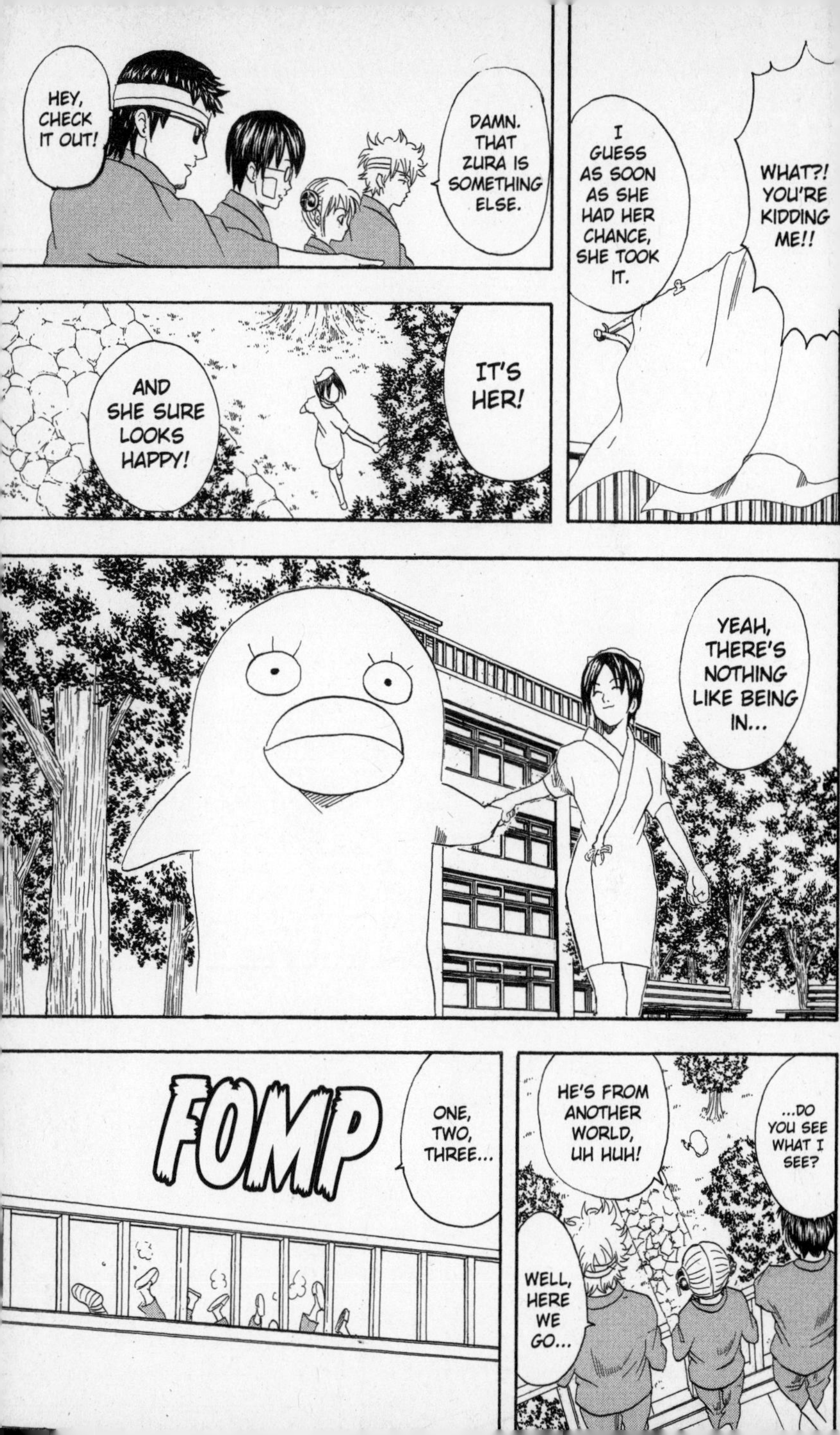
WHAT?! YOU'RE KIDDING ME!!
I GUESS AS SOON AS SHE HAD HER CHANCE, SHE TOOK IT.
DAMN. THAT ZURA IS SOMETHING ELSE.
HEY, CHECK IT OUT!
IT'S HER!
AND SHE SURE LOOKS HAPPY!
YEAH, THERE'S NOTHING LIKE BEING IN...
...DO YOU SEE WHAT I SEE?
HE'S FROM ANOTHER WORLD, UH HUH!
WELL, HERE WE GO...
ONE, TWO, THREE...
FOMP

Yeah, this is Hijikata. He was originally my lead character, but I couldn't find the character sheet I did for him, so I just drew him from memory here. And, yeah, it's Gin-san. A Gin-san with his hair parted on one side and eyes that aren't dead-looking. I love everything about the real Shinsengumi, especially Hijikata, ever since I read "Burn, My Sword." I just can't get the original image out of my head.

I failed to draw out the hero's character and told myself if I couldn't get away from that image I'd have to drop it, and my editor was giving me crap about it—but then he told me it would be okay if the Shinsengumi had a role like Zenigata's in Lupin, so I could separate this hero-image from Hijikata and name him Gin-san, which led me to totally shatter that character. Amazing the power names have! I think I finally understand what people mean by breathing life into something through words. Still, destroying Hijikata was beyond me...unless you count destroying him with mayonnaise.

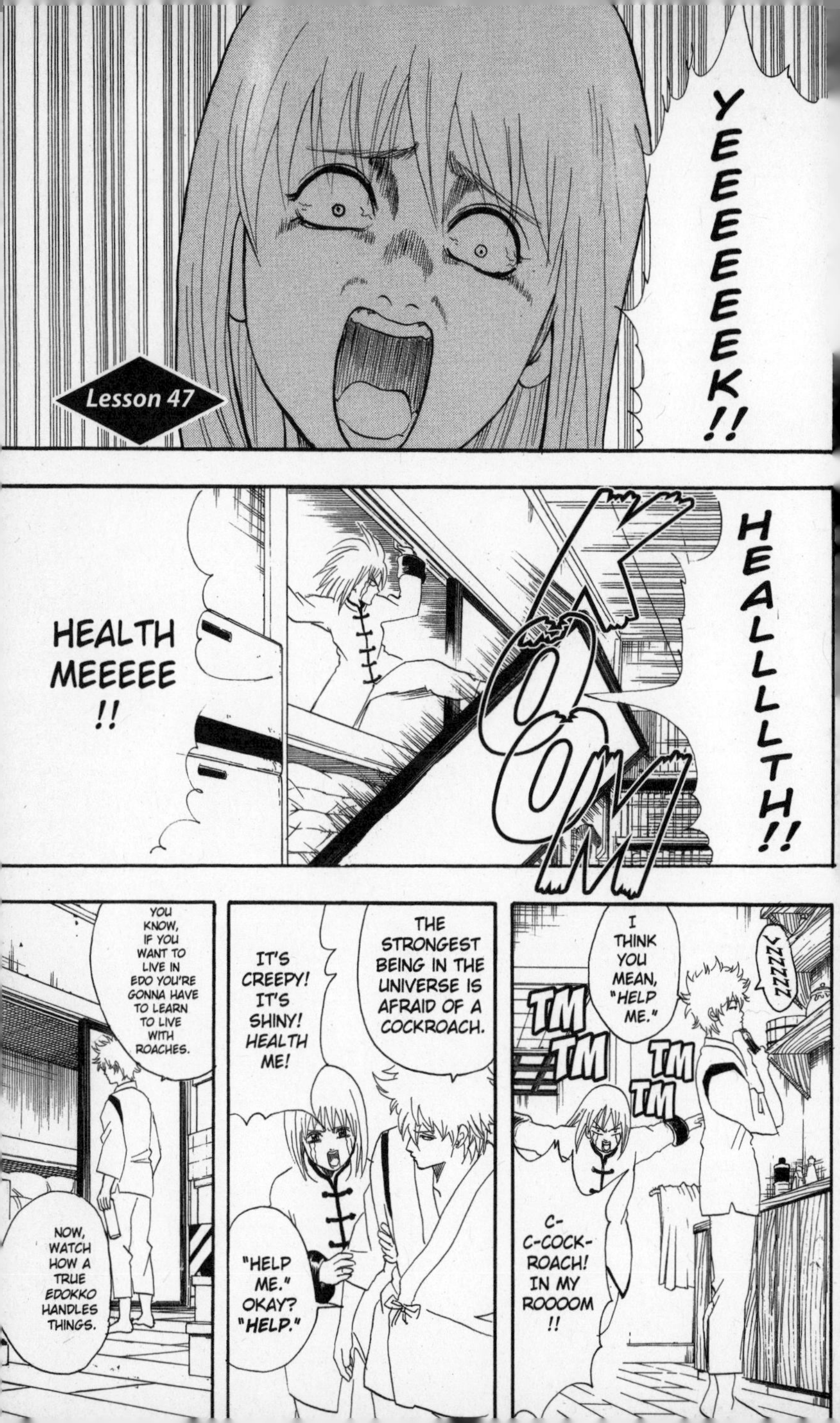
YEEEEEEEK!!
Lesson 47
HEALLLLTH!!
KOOM
HEALTH MEEEEE!!
VZZZZZ
I THINK YOU MEAN, "HELP ME."
TM TM
TM TM
C-C-COCK-ROACH! IN MY ROOOOM!!
THE STRONGEST BEING IN THE UNIVERSE IS AFRAID OF A COCKROACH.
IT'S CREEPY! IT'S SHINY! HEALTH ME!
"HELP ME." OKAY? "HELP."
YOU KNOW, IF YOU WANT TO LIVE IN EDO YOU'RE GONNA HAVE TO LEARN TO LIVE WITH ROACHES.
NOW, WATCH HOW A TRUE EDOKKO HANDLES THINGS.

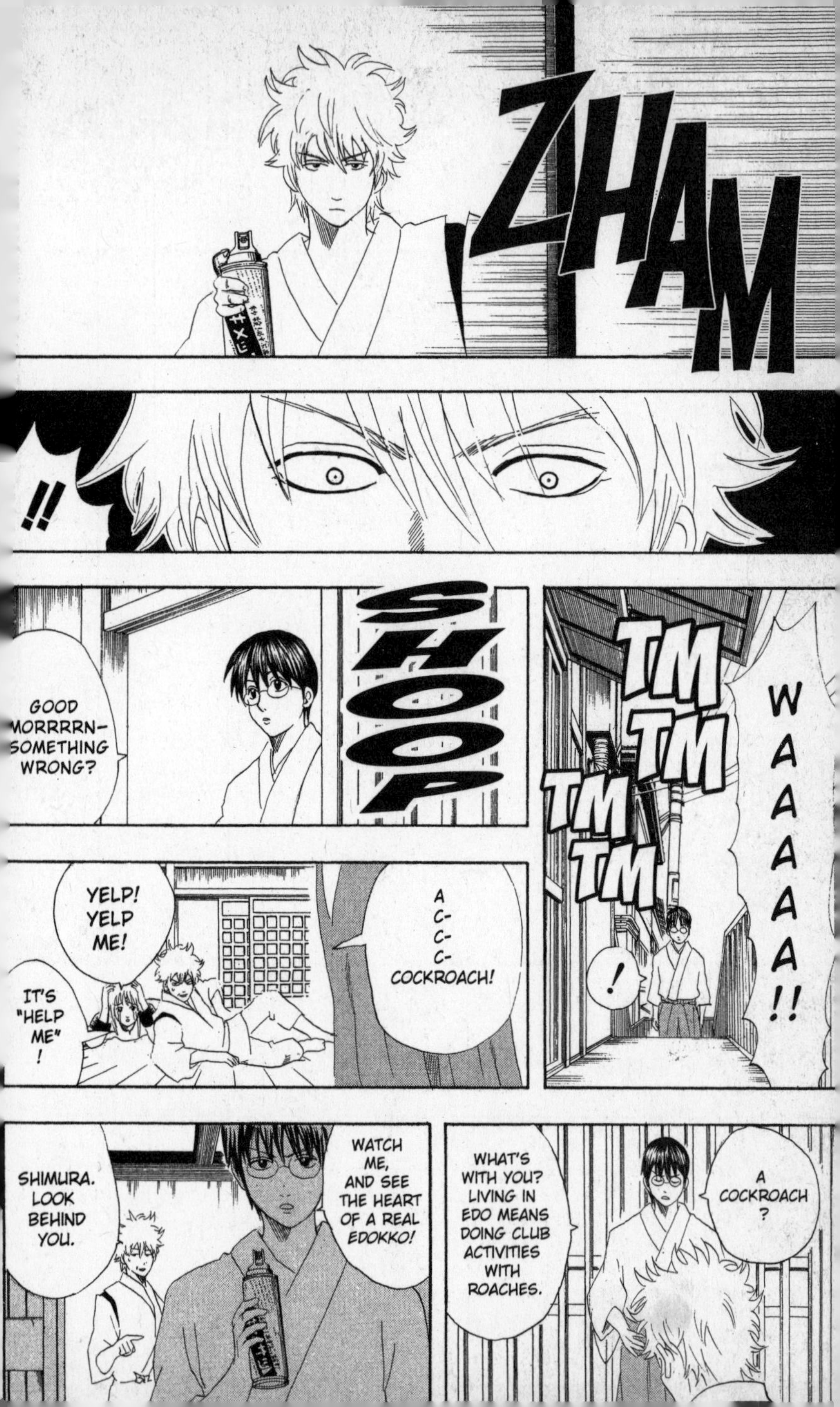
ZHAM
!!
WAAAAAA!!
TM TM TM TM
!
SHOOP
GOOD MORRRRN-SOMETHING WRONG?
A C- C- C- COCKROACH!
YELP! YELP ME!
IT'S "HELP ME"!
A COCKROACH?
WHAT'S WITH YOU? LIVING IN EDO MEANS DOING CLUB ACTIVITIES WITH ROACHES.
WATCH ME, AND SEE THE HEART OF A REAL EDOKKO!
SHIMURA. LOOK BEHIND YOU.

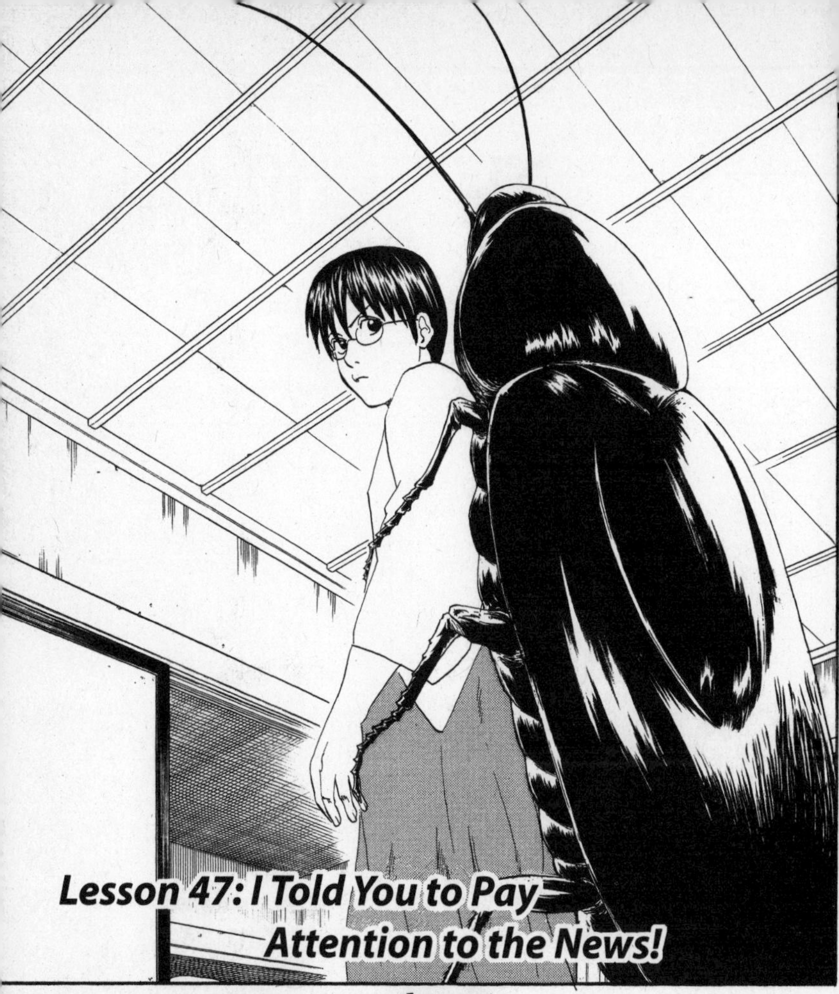
Lesson 47: I Told You to Pay Attention to the News!

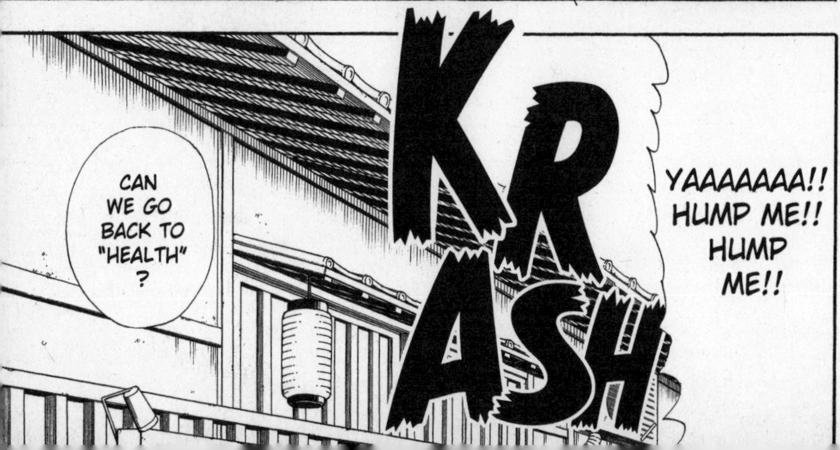
YAAAAAAA!! HUMP ME!! HUMP ME!!
KRASH
CAN WE GO BACK TO "HEALTH" ?

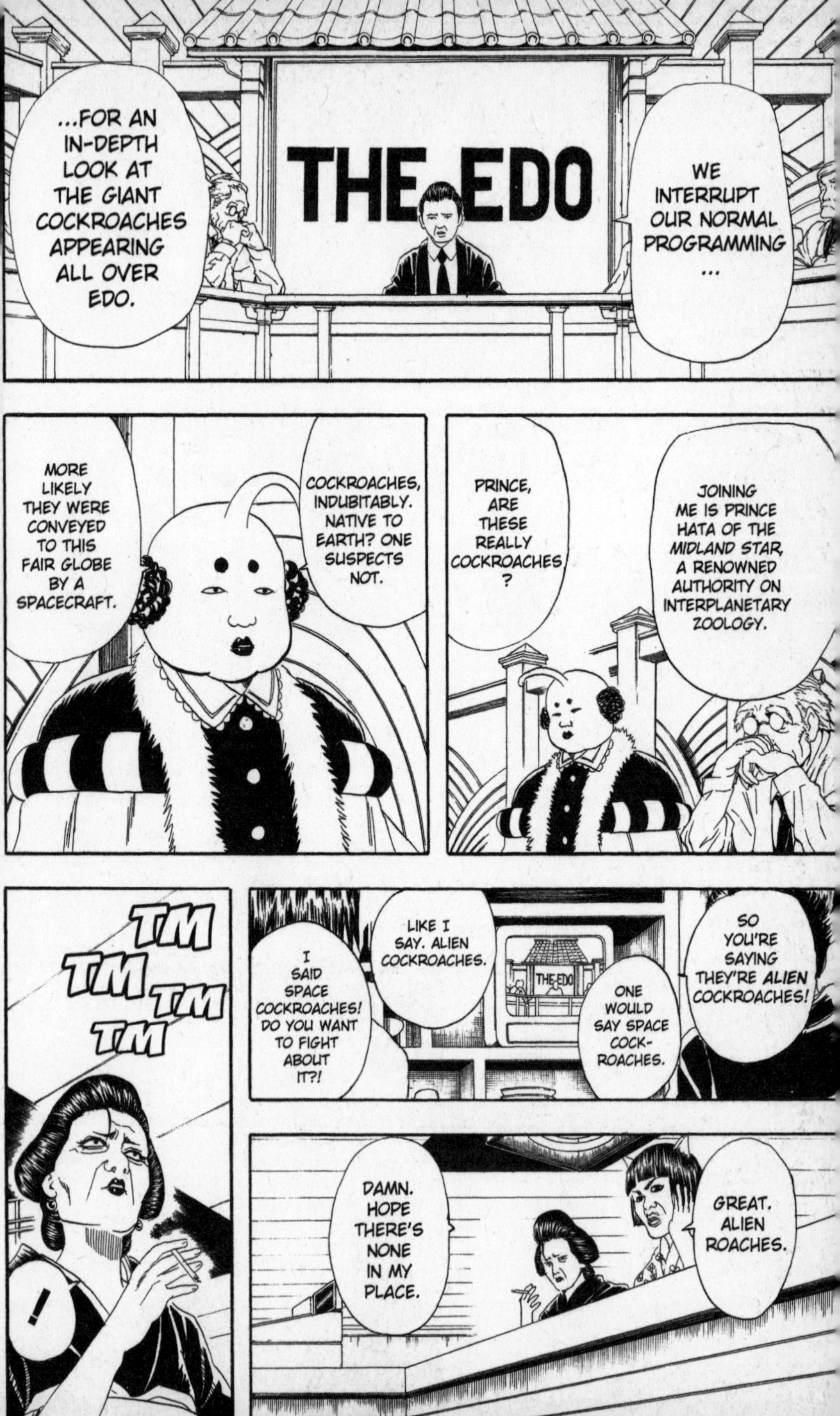
WE INTERRUPT OUR NORMAL PROGRAMMING...
THE EDO
...FOR AN IN-DEPTH LOOK AT THE GIANT COCKROACHES APPEARING ALL OVER EDO.
JOINING ME IS PRINCE HATA OF THE *MIDLAND STAR*, A RENOWNED AUTHORITY ON INTERPLANETARY ZOOLOGY.
PRINCE, ARE THESE REALLY COCKROACHES?
COCKROACHES, INDUBITABLY. NATIVE TO EARTH? ONE SUSPECTS NOT.
MORE LIKELY THEY WERE CONVEYED TO THIS FAIR GLOBE BY A SPACECRAFT.
SO YOU'RE SAYING THEY'RE *ALIEN* COCKROACHES!
ONE WOULD SAY SPACE COCK-ROACHES.
THE EDO
LIKE I SAY. ALIEN COCKROACHES.
I SAID SPACE COCKROACHES! DO YOU WANT TO FIGHT ABOUT IT?!
GREAT. ALIEN ROACHES.
DAMN. HOPE THERE'S NONE IN MY PLACE.
TM
TM
TM
TM
!

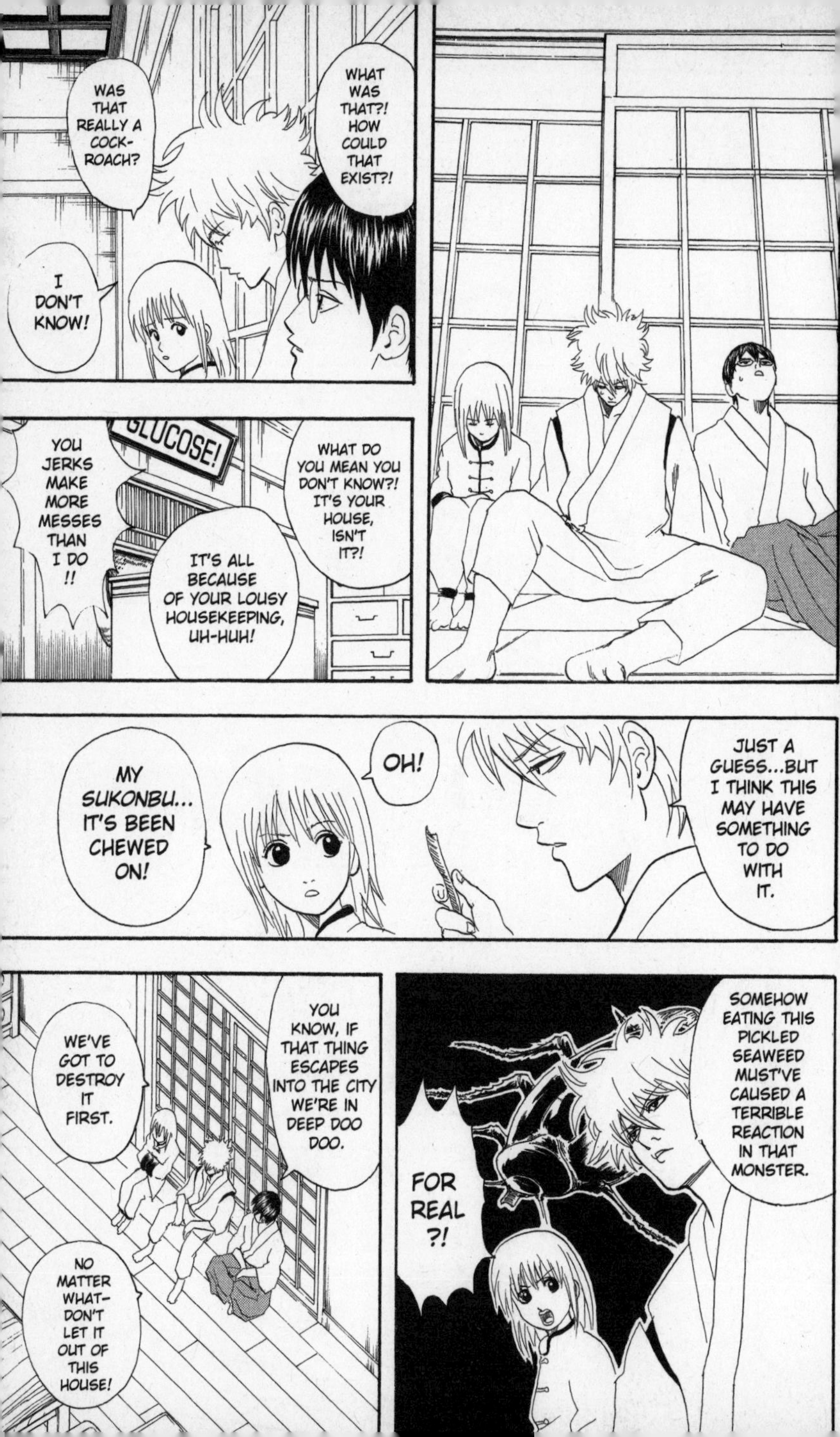
WHAT WAS THAT?! HOW COULD THAT EXIST?!
WAS THAT REALLY A COCK-ROACH?
I DON'T KNOW!
WHAT DO YOU MEAN YOU DON'T KNOW?! IT'S YOUR HOUSE, ISN'T IT?!
GLUCOSE!
IT'S ALL BECAUSE OF YOUR LOUSY HOUSEKEEPING, UH-HUH!
YOU JERKS MAKE MORE MESSES THAN I DO!!
JUST A GUESS...BUT I THINK THIS MAY HAVE SOMETHING TO DO WITH IT.
OH!
MY SUKONBU... IT'S BEEN CHEWED ON!
SOMEHOW EATING THIS PICKLED SEAWEED MUST'VE CAUSED A TERRIBLE REACTION IN THAT MONSTER.
FOR REAL?!
YOU KNOW, IF THAT THING ESCAPES INTO THE CITY WE'RE IN DEEP DOO DOO.
WE'VE GOT TO DESTROY IT FIRST.
NO MATTER WHAT-DON'T LET IT OUT OF THIS HOUSE!

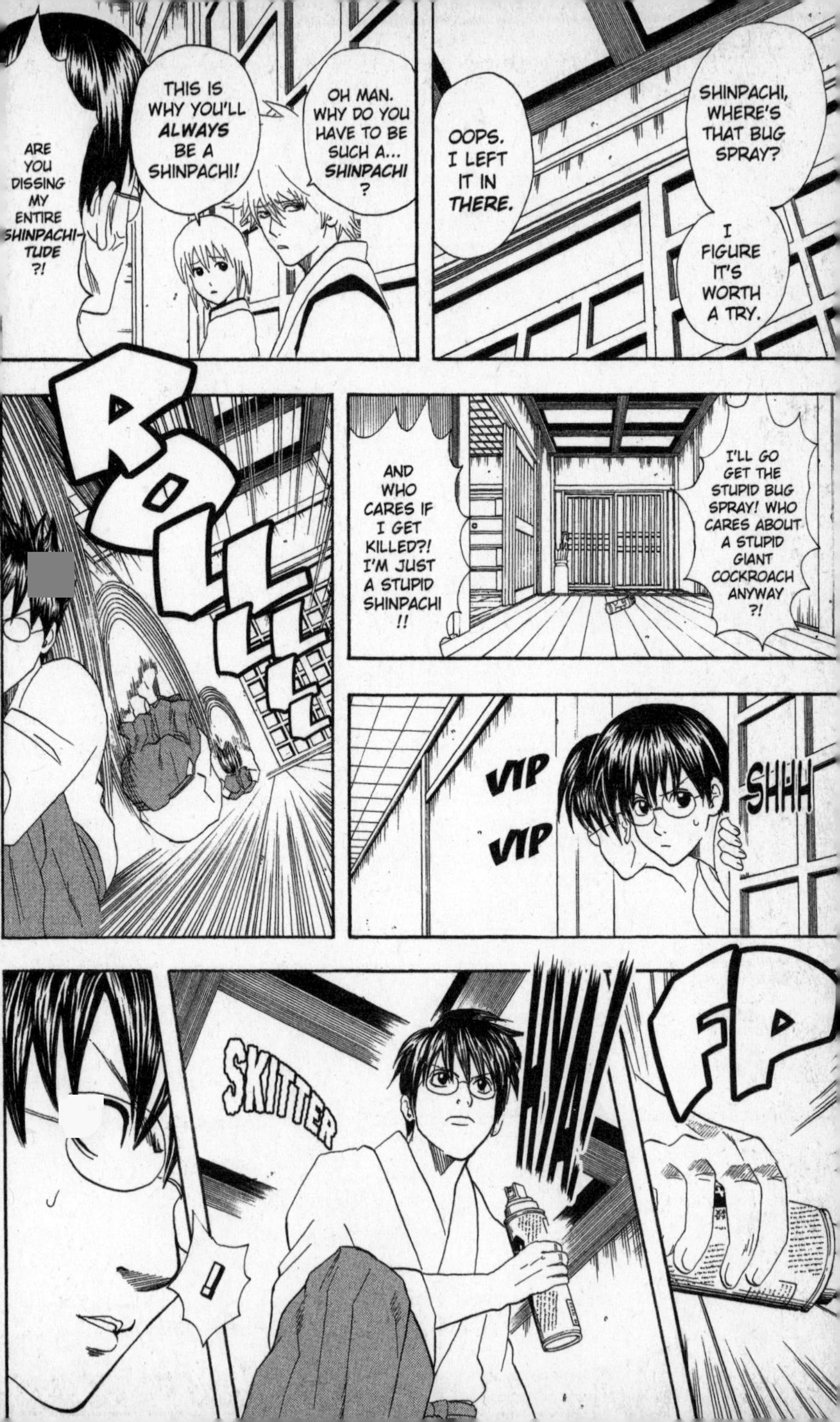

SHINPACHI, WHERE'S THAT BUG SPRAY?
I FIGURE IT'S WORTH A TRY.
OOPS. I LEFT IT IN THERE.
OH MAN. WHY DO YOU HAVE TO BE SUCH A... SHINPACHI?
THIS IS WHY YOU'LL ALWAYS BE A SHINPACHI!
ARE YOU DISSING MY ENTIRE SHINPACHI-TUDE?!
I'LL GO GET THE STUPID BUG SPRAY! WHO CARES ABOUT A STUPID GIANT COCKROACH ANYWAY?!
AND WHO CARES IF I GET KILLED?! I'M JUST A STUPID SHINPACHI!!
SHHH
VIP VIP
ROLLLL
FP
SKITTER
!

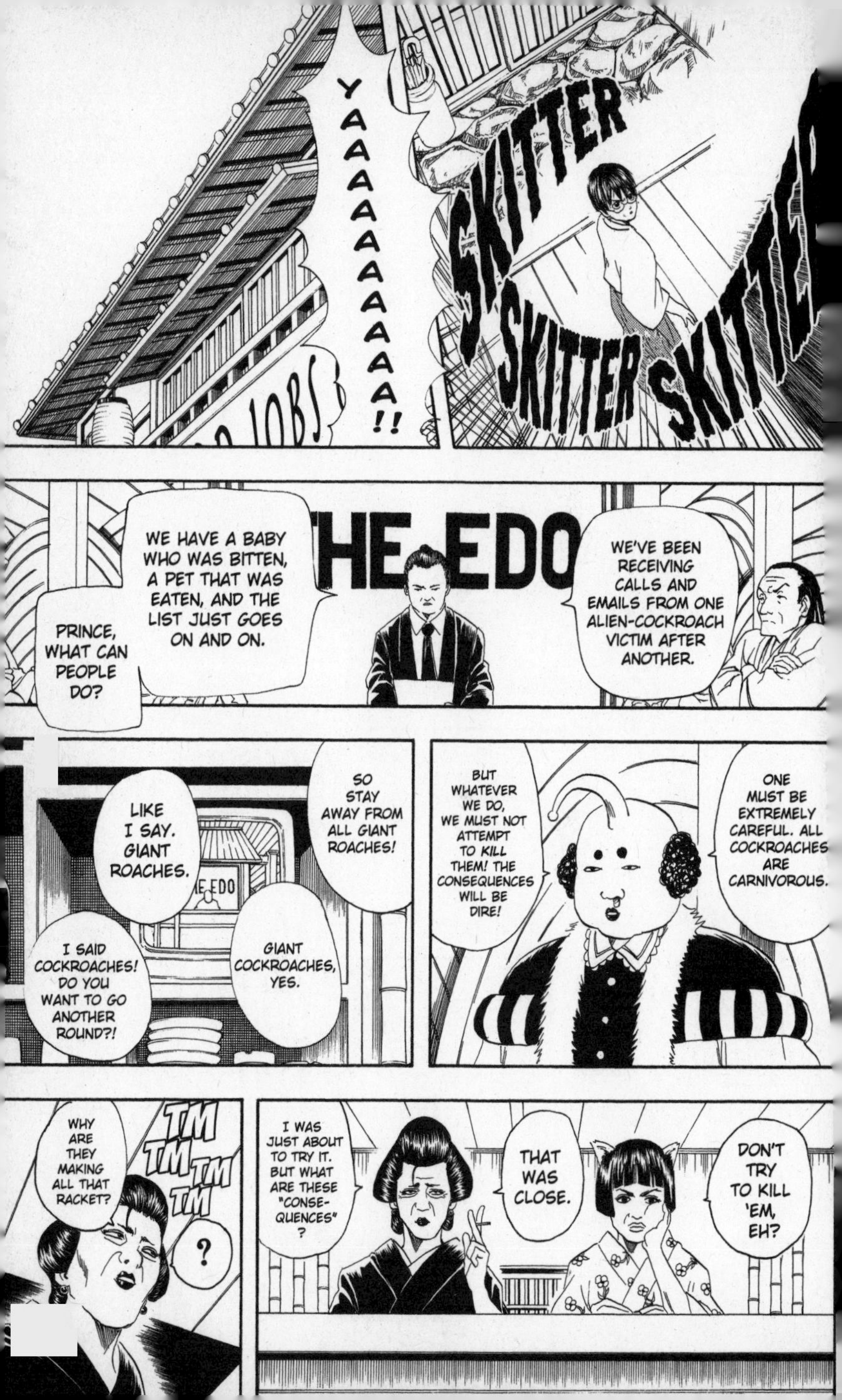
SKITTER SKITTER SKITTER
YAAAAAAAAAA!!
JOBS
WE'VE BEEN RECEIVING CALLS AND EMAILS FROM ONE ALIEN-COCKROACH VICTIM AFTER ANOTHER.
THE EDO
WE HAVE A BABY WHO WAS BITTEN, A PET THAT WAS EATEN, AND THE LIST JUST GOES ON AND ON.
PRINCE, WHAT CAN PEOPLE DO?
ONE MUST BE EXTREMELY CAREFUL. ALL COCKROACHES ARE CARNIVOROUS.
BUT WHATEVER WE DO, WE MUST NOT ATTEMPT TO KILL THEM! THE CONSEQUENCES WILL BE DIRE!
SO STAY AWAY FROM ALL GIANT ROACHES!
LIKE I SAY. GIANT ROACHES.
GIANT COCKROACHES, YES.
I SAID COCKROACHES! DO YOU WANT TO GO ANOTHER ROUND?!
DON'T TRY TO KILL 'EM, EH?
THAT WAS CLOSE.
I WAS JUST ABOUT TO TRY IT. BUT WHAT ARE THESE "CONSE-QUENCES"?
TM TM TM TM
WHY ARE THEY MAKING ALL THAT RACKET?
?

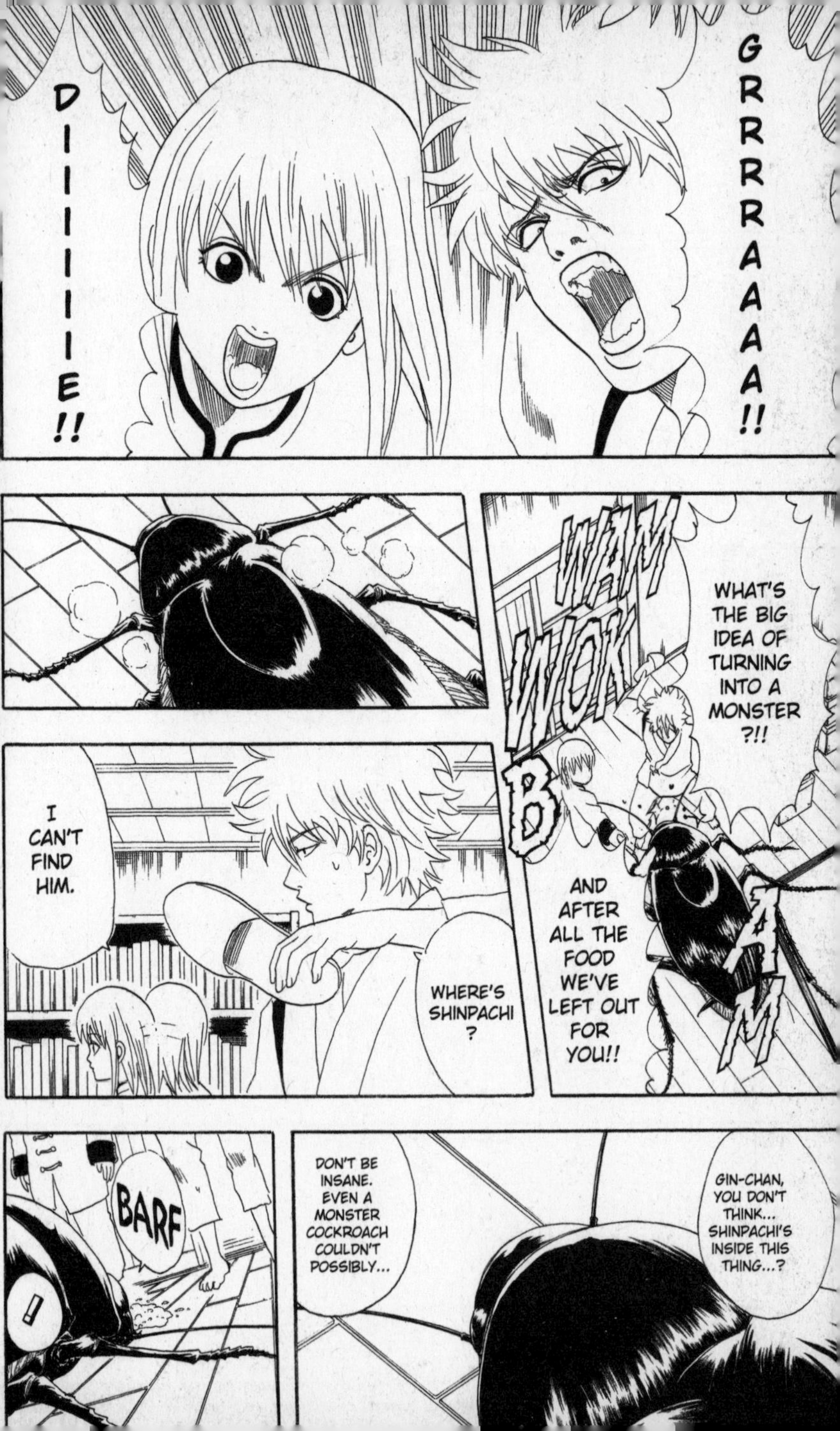
GRRRRAAAA!!
DIIIIIIE!!
WAM
WOK
WHAT'S THE BIG IDEA OF TURNING INTO A MONSTER?!!
BAM
AND AFTER ALL THE FOOD WE'VE LEFT OUT FOR YOU!!
WHERE'S SHINPACHI?
I CAN'T FIND HIM.
GIN-CHAN, YOU DON'T THINK... SHINPACHI'S INSIDE THIS THING...?
DON'T BE INSANE. EVEN A MONSTER COCKROACH COULDN'T POSSIBLY...
BARF
!

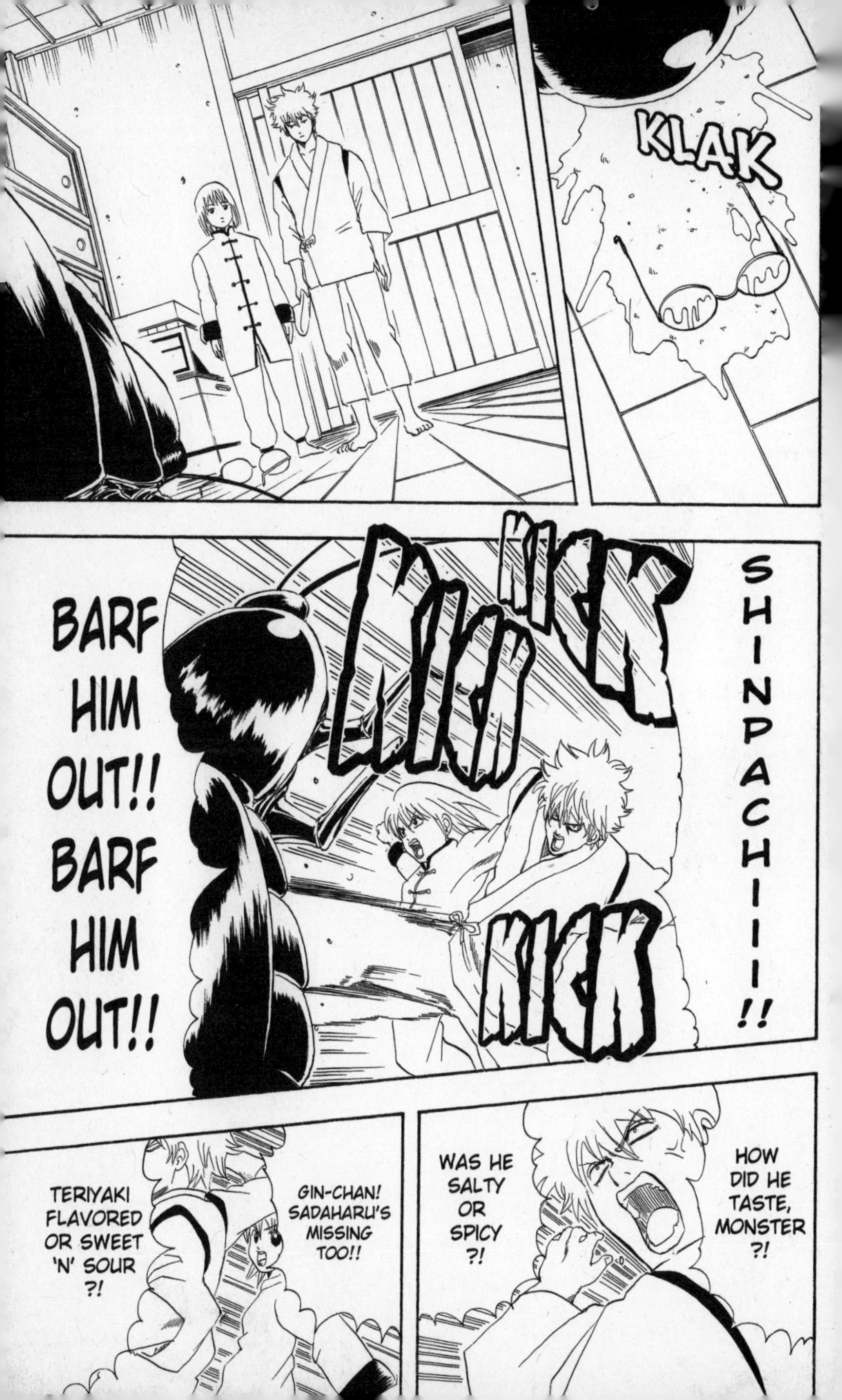

KLAK
SHINPACHIII!!
KICK KICK
KICK
BARF HIM OUT!! BARF HIM OUT!!
HOW DID HE TASTE, MONSTER?!
WAS HE SALTY OR SPICY?!
GIN-CHAN! SADAHARU'S MISSING TOO!!
TERIYAKI FLAVORED OR SWEET 'N' SOUR?!

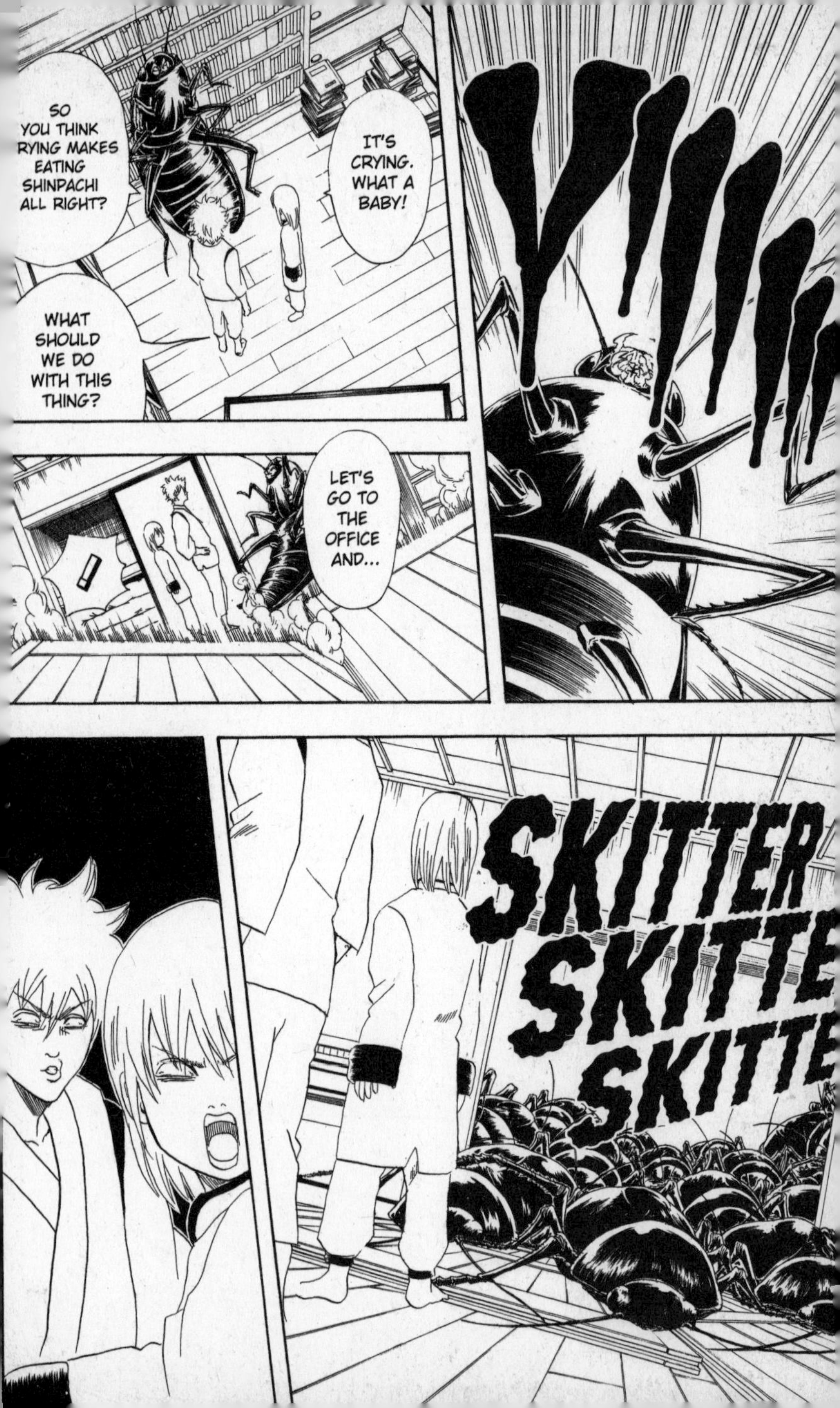

YIIIIII
IT'S CRYING. WHAT A BABY!
SO YOU THINK RYING MAKES EATING SHINPACHI ALL RIGHT?
WHAT SHOULD WE DO WITH THIS THING?
LET'S GO TO THE OFFICE AND...
!
SKITTER
SKITTE
SKITTE

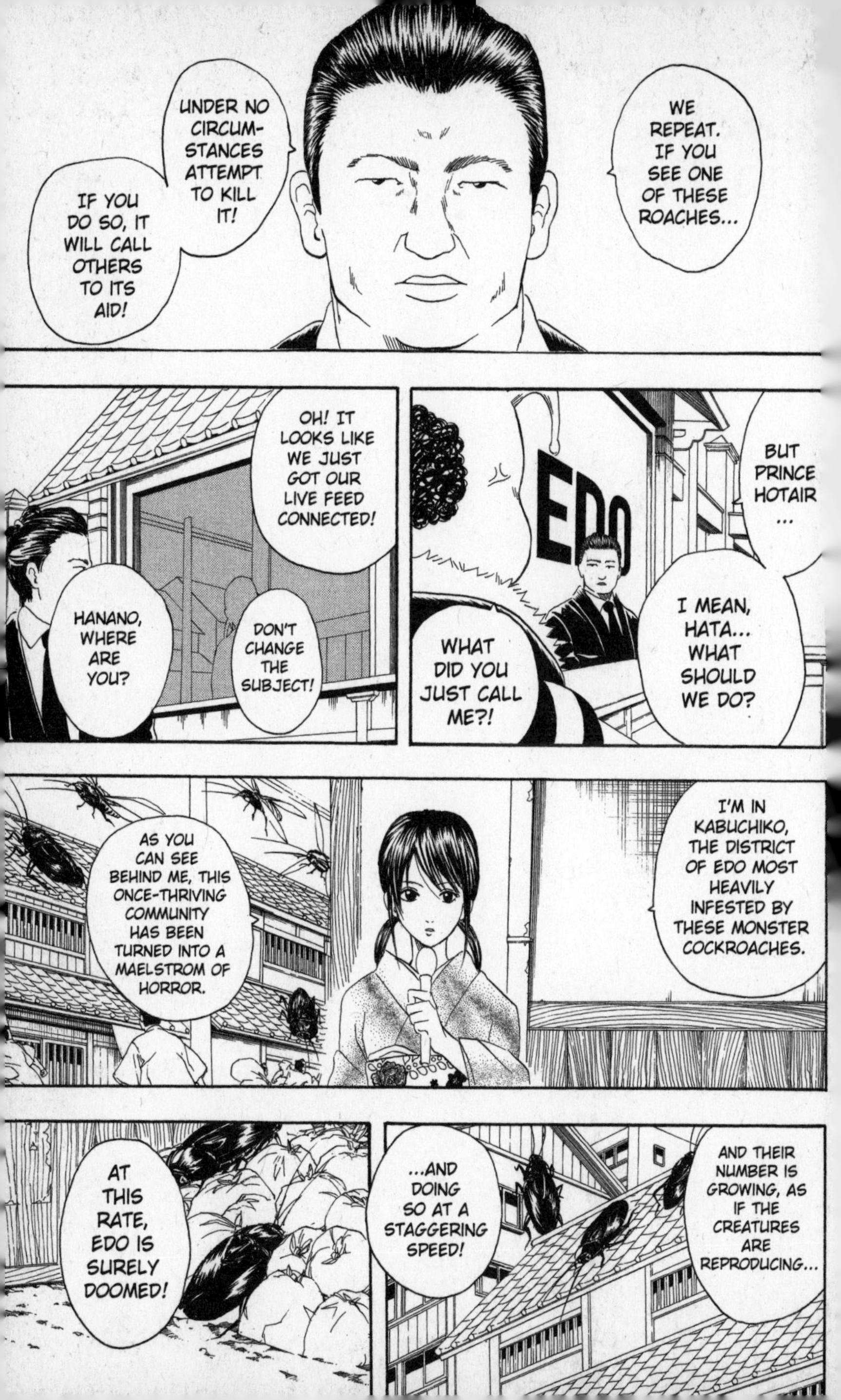
WE REPEAT. IF YOU SEE ONE OF THESE ROACHES...
UNDER NO CIRCUM-STANCES ATTEMPT TO KILL IT!
IF YOU DO SO, IT WILL CALL OTHERS TO ITS AID!
BUT PRINCE HOTAIR ...
EDO
I MEAN, HATA... WHAT SHOULD WE DO?
WHAT DID YOU JUST CALL ME?!
OH! IT LOOKS LIKE WE JUST GOT OUR LIVE FEED CONNECTED!
DON'T CHANGE THE SUBJECT!
HANANO, WHERE ARE YOU?
I'M IN KABUCHIKO, THE DISTRICT OF EDO MOST HEAVILY INFESTED BY THESE MONSTER COCKROACHES.
AS YOU CAN SEE BEHIND ME, THIS ONCE-THRIVING COMMUNITY HAS BEEN TURNED INTO A MAELSTROM OF HORROR.
AND THEIR NUMBER IS GROWING, AS IF THE CREATURES ARE REPRODUCING...
...AND DOING SO AT A STAGGERING SPEED!
AT THIS RATE, EDO IS SURELY DOOMED!

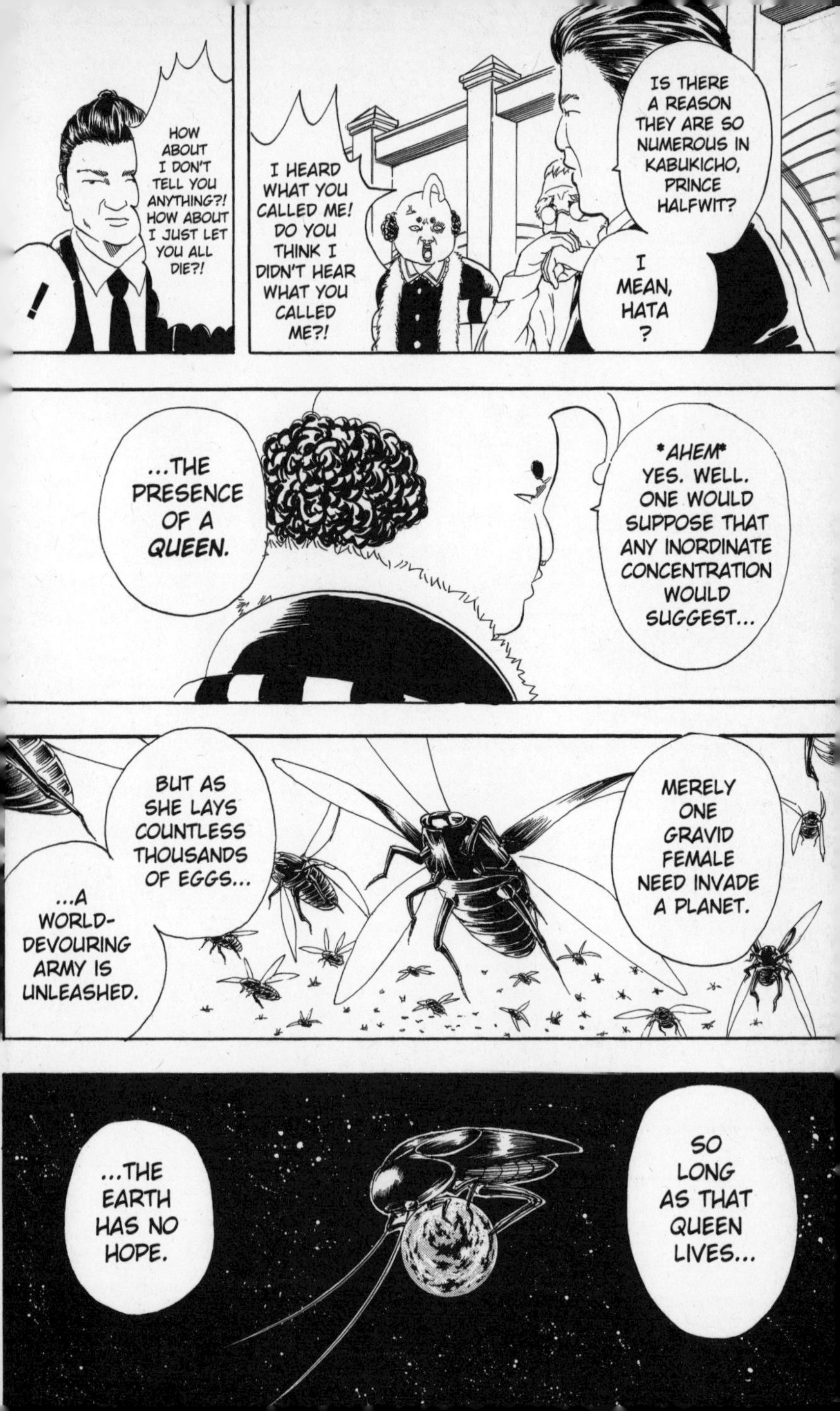
IS THERE A REASON THEY ARE SO NUMEROUS IN KABUKICHO, PRINCE HALFWIT?
I MEAN, HATA ?
I HEARD WHAT YOU CALLED ME! DO YOU THINK I DIDN'T HEAR WHAT YOU CALLED ME?!
HOW ABOUT I DON'T TELL YOU ANYTHING?! HOW ABOUT I JUST LET YOU ALL DIE?!
!
AHEM YES. WELL. ONE WOULD SUPPOSE THAT ANY INORDINATE CONCENTRATION WOULD SUGGEST...
...THE PRESENCE OF A QUEEN.
MERELY ONE GRAVID FEMALE NEED INVADE A PLANET.
BUT AS SHE LAYS COUNTLESS THOUSANDS OF EGGS...
...A WORLD-DEVOURING ARMY IS UNLEASHED.
SO LONG AS THAT QUEEN LIVES...
...THE EARTH HAS NO HOPE.

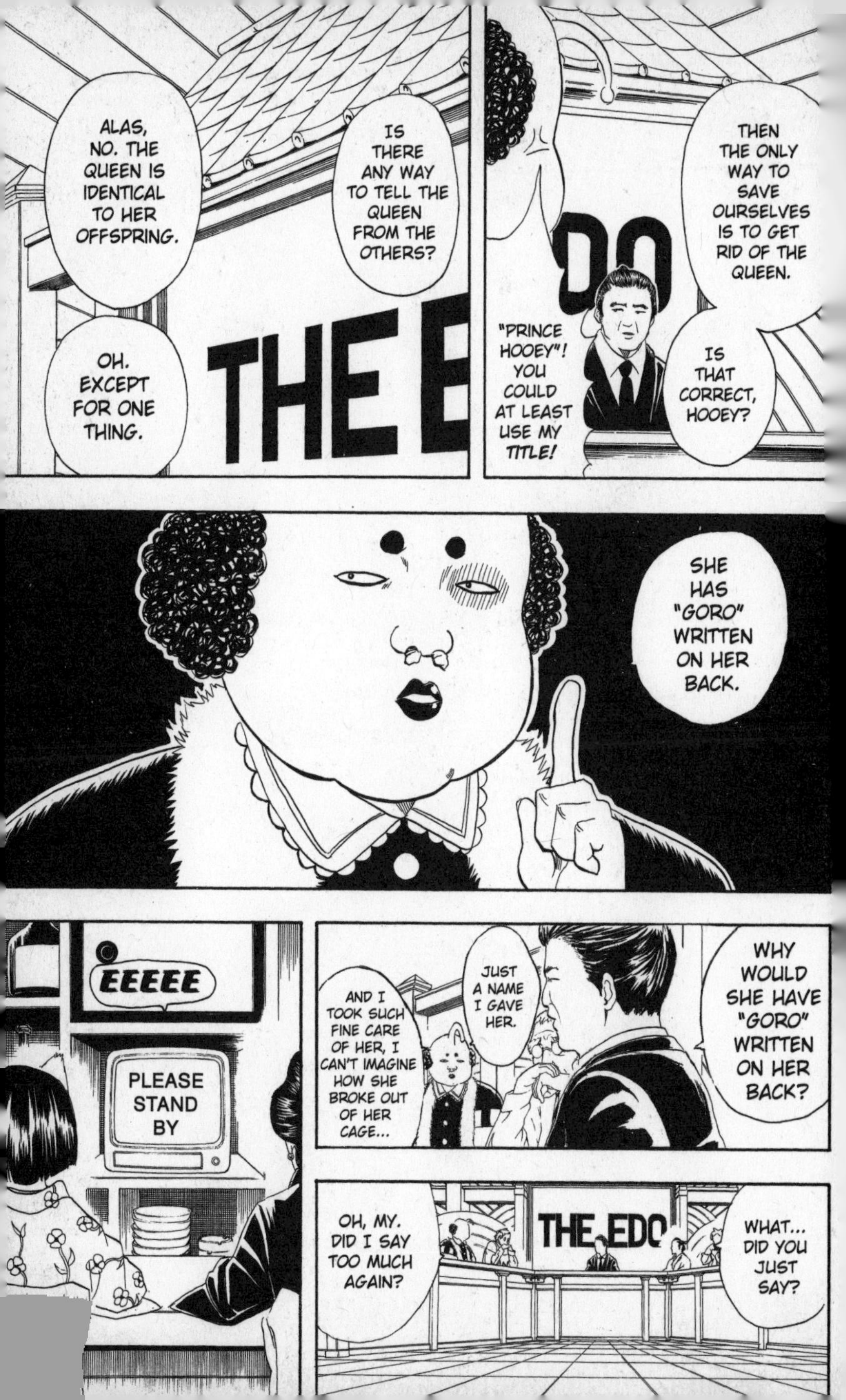
IS THERE ANY WAY TO TELL THE QUEEN FROM THE OTHERS?
ALAS, NO. THE QUEEN IS IDENTICAL TO HER OFFSPRING.
OH. EXCEPT FOR ONE THING.
THE E
DO
THEN THE ONLY WAY TO SAVE OURSELVES IS TO GET RID OF THE QUEEN.
IS THAT CORRECT, HOOEY?
"PRINCE HOOEY"! YOU COULD AT LEAST USE MY TITLE!
SHE HAS "GORO" WRITTEN ON HER BACK.
EEEEE
PLEASE STAND BY
WHY WOULD SHE HAVE "GORO" WRITTEN ON HER BACK?
JUST A NAME I GAVE HER.
AND I TOOK SUCH FINE CARE OF HER, I CAN'T IMAGINE HOW SHE BROKE OUT OF HER CAGE...
THE EDO
WHAT... DID YOU JUST SAY?
OH, MY. DID I SAY TOO MUCH AGAIN?

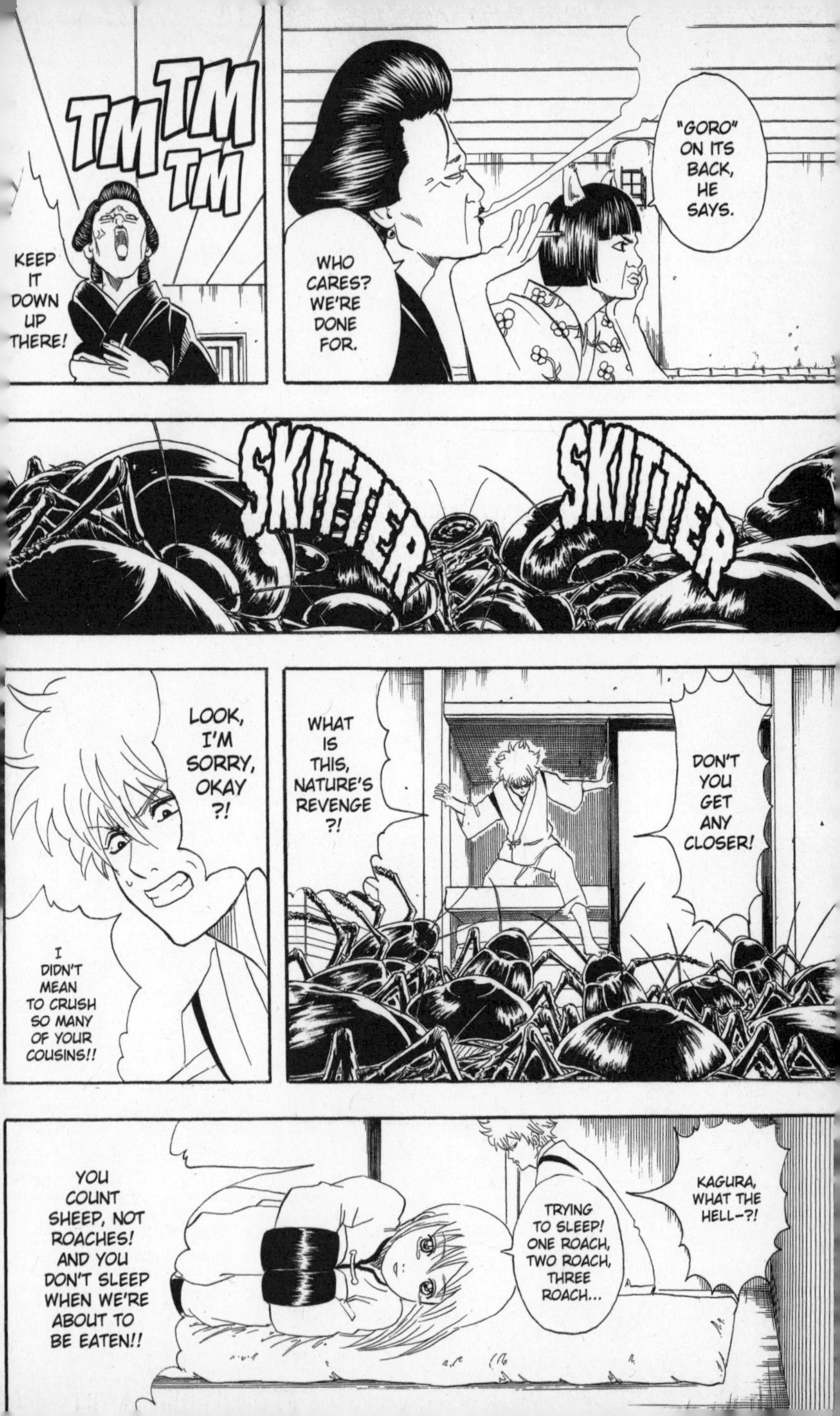
"GORO" ON ITS BACK, HE SAYS.
WHO CARES? WE'RE DONE FOR.
TM TM TM TM
KEEP IT DOWN UP THERE!
SKITTER SKITTER
DON'T YOU GET ANY CLOSER!
WHAT IS THIS, NATURE'S REVENGE?!
LOOK, I'M SORRY, OKAY?!
I DIDN'T MEAN TO CRUSH SO MANY OF YOUR COUSINS!!
KAGURA, WHAT THE HELL-?!
TRYING TO SLEEP! ONE ROACH, TWO ROACH, THREE ROACH...
YOU COUNT SHEEP, NOT ROACHES! AND YOU DON'T SLEEP WHEN WE'RE ABOUT TO BE EATEN!!

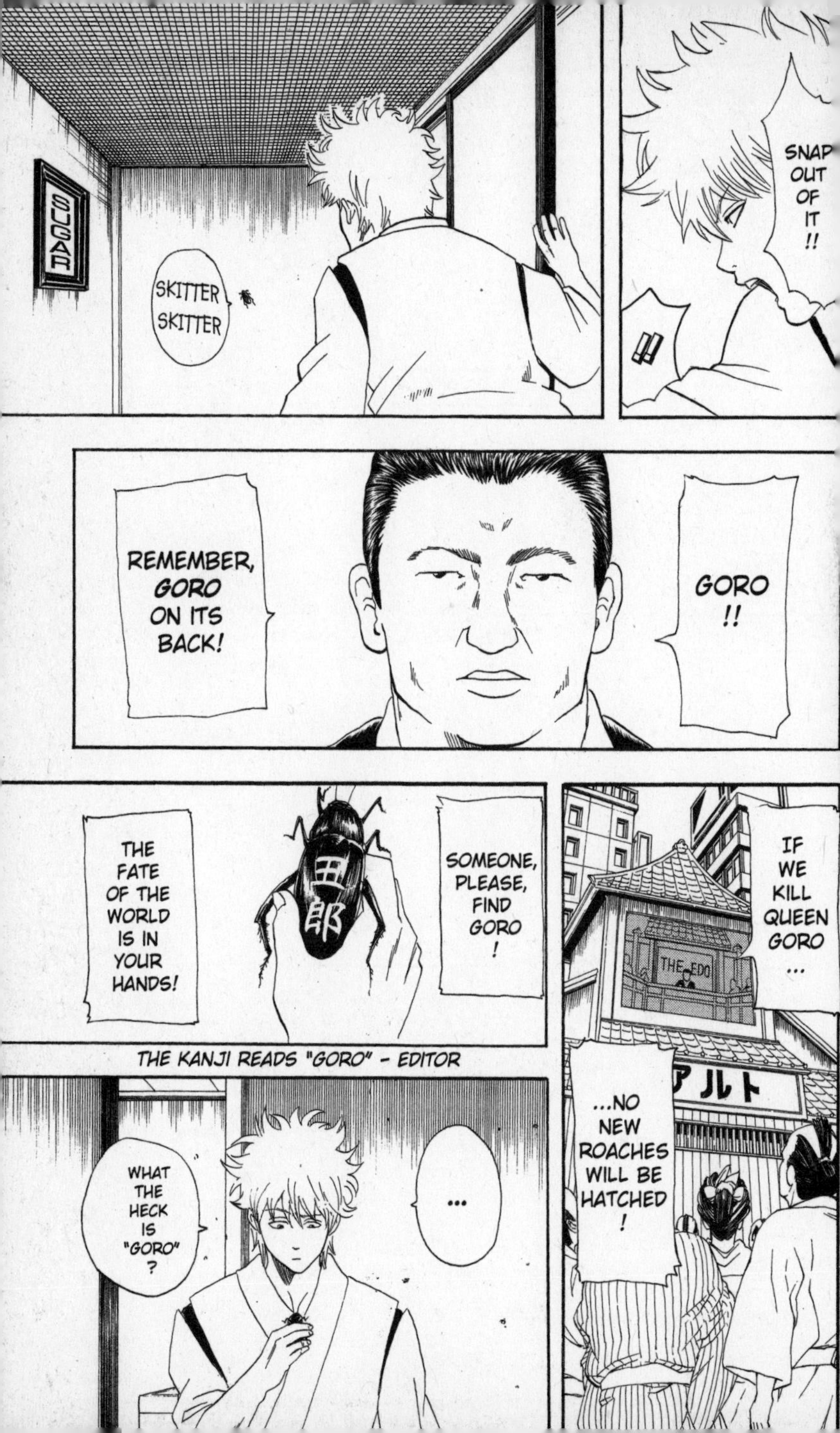
SNAP OUT OF IT!!
!!
SUGAR
SKITTER SKITTER
GORO!!
REMEMBER, GORO ON ITS BACK!
IF WE KILL QUEEN GORO...
THE EDO
アルト
...NO NEW ROACHES WILL BE HATCHED!
SOMEONE, PLEASE, FIND GORO!
五郎
THE FATE OF THE WORLD IS IN YOUR HANDS!
THE KANJI READS "GORO" - EDITOR
...
WHAT THE HECK IS "GORO"?

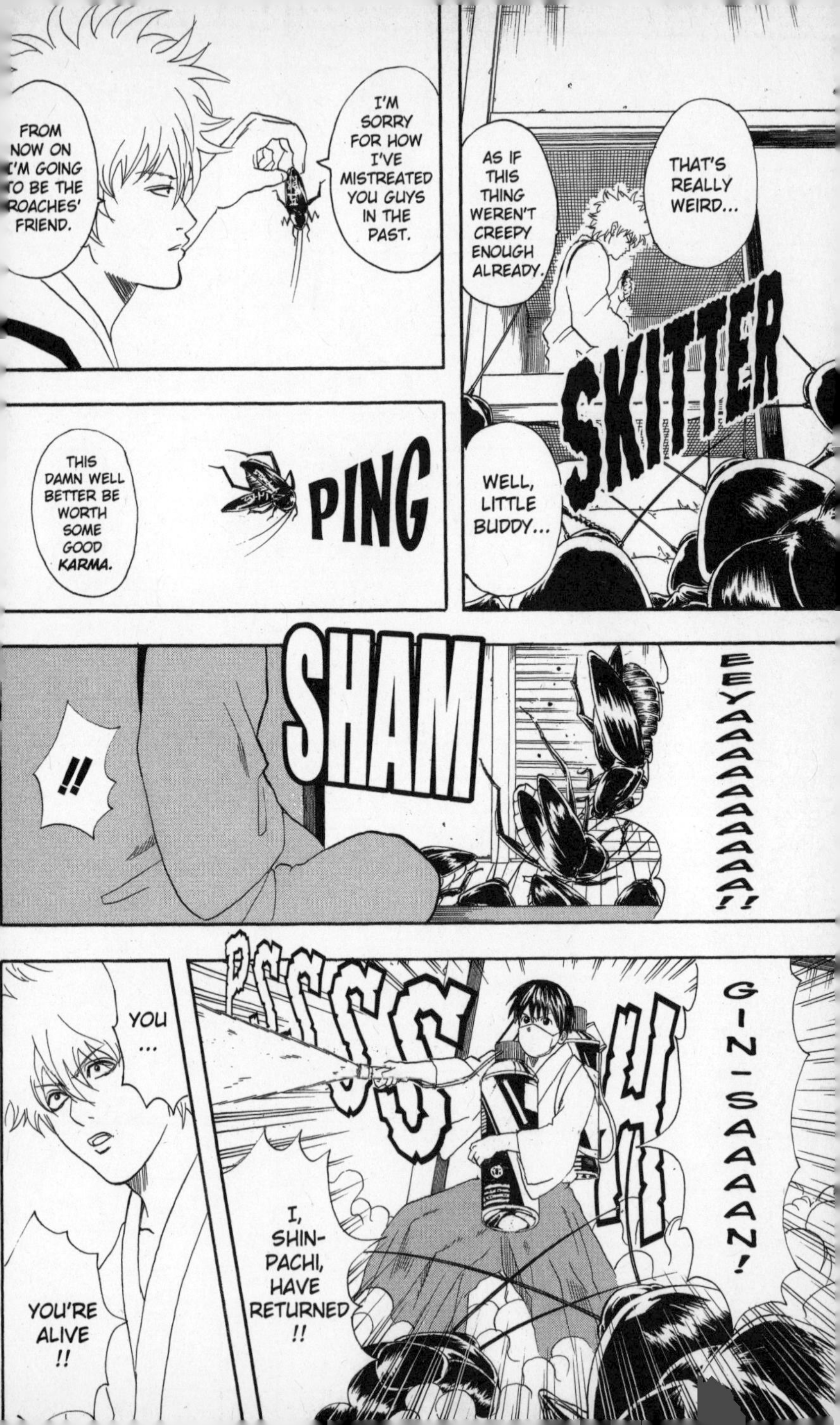
THAT'S REALLY WEIRD...
AS IF THIS THING WEREN'T CREEPY ENOUGH ALREADY.
SKITTER
WELL, LITTLE BUDDY...
I'M SORRY FOR HOW I'VE MISTREATED YOU GUYS IN THE PAST.
FROM NOW ON I'M GOING TO BE THE ROACHES' FRIEND.
PING
THIS DAMN WELL BETTER BE WORTH SOME GOOD KARMA.
EEYAAAAAAAAAAAA!!
SHAM
!!
GIN-SAAAAN!
PSSSSH
I, SHIN-PACHI, HAVE RETURNED!!
YOU...
YOU'RE ALIVE!!

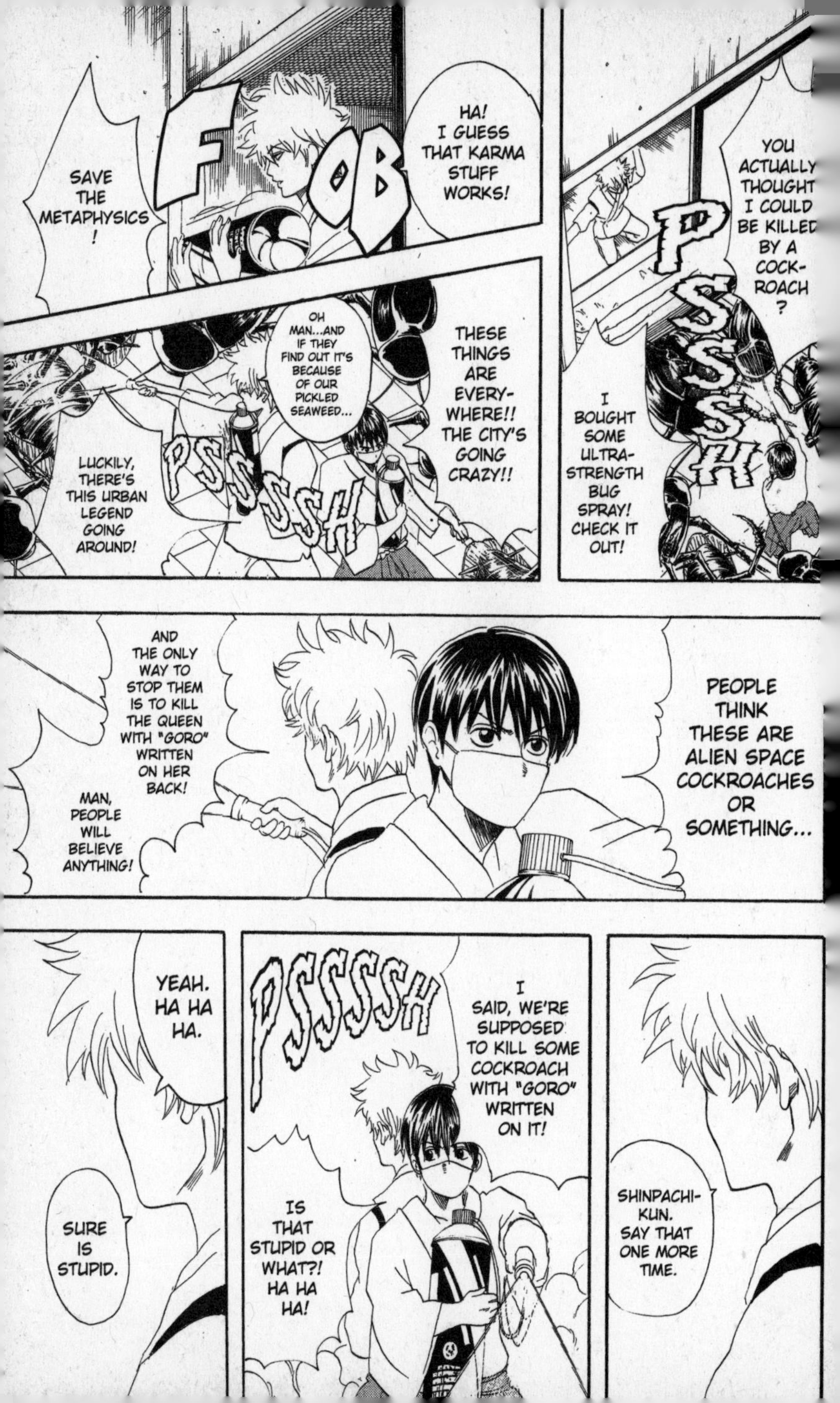
YOU ACTUALLY THOUGHT I COULD BE KILLED BY A COCK-ROACH?
PSSSH
I BOUGHT SOME ULTRA-STRENGTH BUG SPRAY! CHECK IT OUT!
HA! I GUESS THAT KARMA STUFF WORKS!
FOB
SAVE THE METAPHYSICS!
THESE THINGS ARE EVERY-WHERE!! THE CITY'S GOING CRAZY!!
OH MAN...AND IF THEY FIND OUT IT'S BECAUSE OF OUR PICKLED SEAWEED...
PSSSH
LUCKILY, THERE'S THIS URBAN LEGEND GOING AROUND!
PEOPLE THINK THESE ARE ALIEN SPACE COCKROACHES OR SOMETHING...
AND THE ONLY WAY TO STOP THEM IS TO KILL THE QUEEN WITH "GORO" WRITTEN ON HER BACK!
MAN, PEOPLE WILL BELIEVE ANYTHING!
SHINPACHI-KUN. SAY THAT ONE MORE TIME.
I SAID, WE'RE SUPPOSED TO KILL SOME COCKROACH WITH "GORO" WRITTEN ON IT!
PSSSSH
IS THAT STUPID OR WHAT?! HA HA HA!
YEAH. HA HA HA.
SURE IS STUPID.

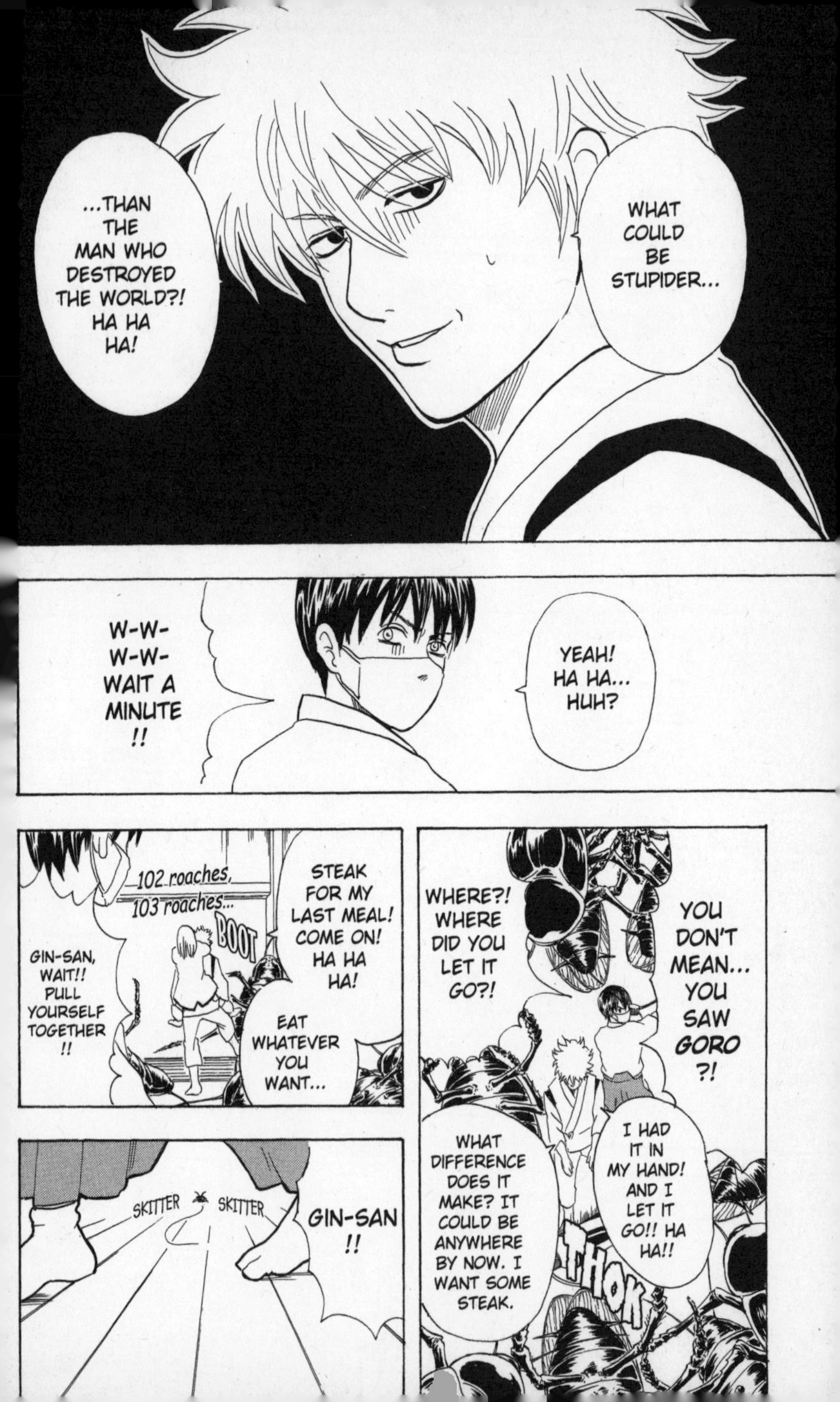
WHAT COULD BE STUPIDER...
...THAN THE MAN WHO DESTROYED THE WORLD?! HA HA HA!
YEAH! HA HA... HUH?
W-W-W-W-WAIT A MINUTE!!
YOU DON'T MEAN... YOU SAW GORO?!
WHERE?! WHERE DID YOU LET IT GO?!
I HAD IT IN MY HAND! AND I LET IT GO!! HA HA!!
THOK
WHAT DIFFERENCE DOES IT MAKE? IT COULD BE ANYWHERE BY NOW. I WANT SOME STEAK.
STEAK FOR MY LAST MEAL! COME ON! HA HA HA!
BOOT
102 roaches, 103 roaches...
EAT WHATEVER YOU WANT...
GIN-SAN, WAIT!! PULL YOURSELF TOGETHER!!
GIN-SAN!!
SKITTER SKITTER

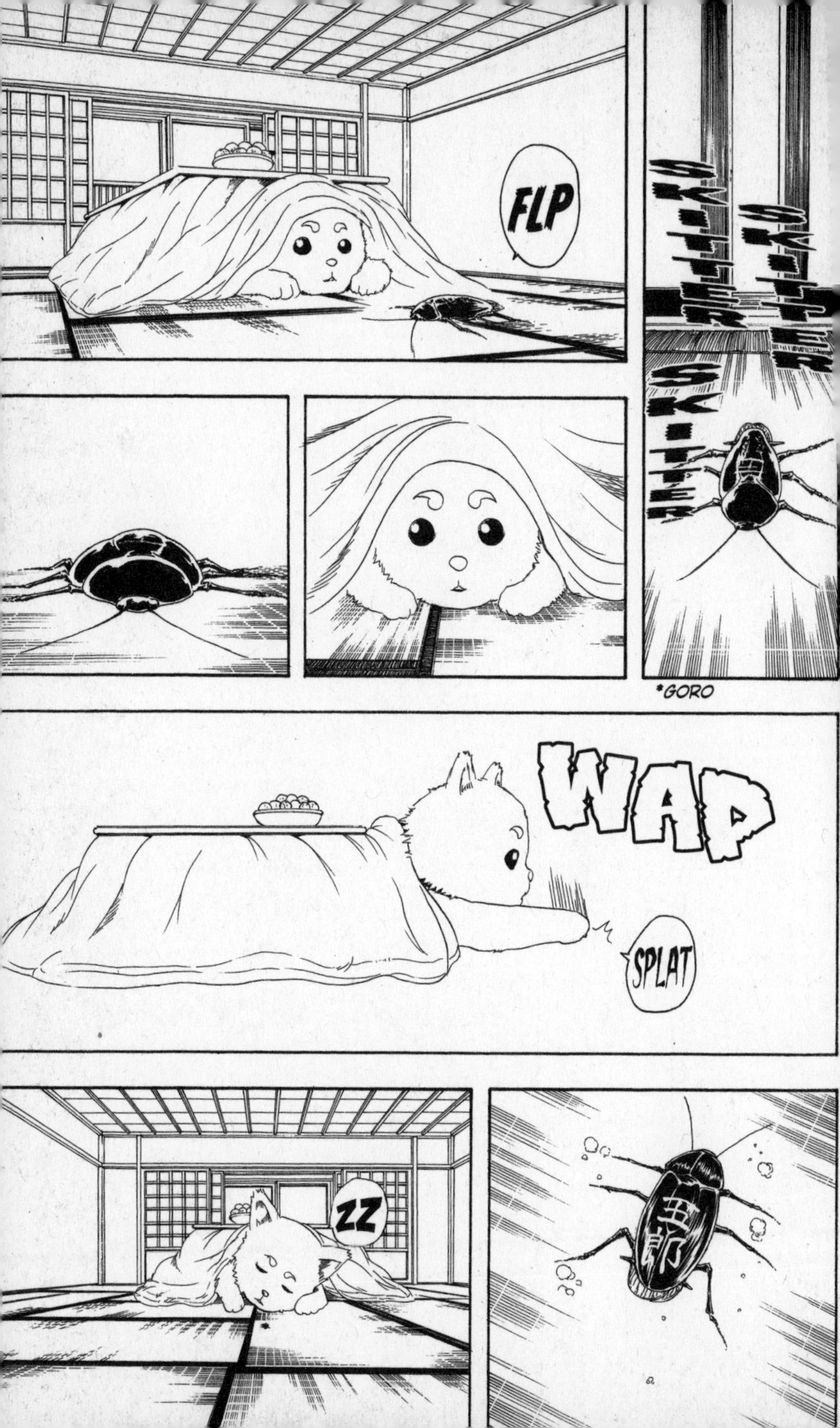
SKITTER
SKITTER
SKITTER
FLP
WAP
SPLAT
ZZ
*GORO

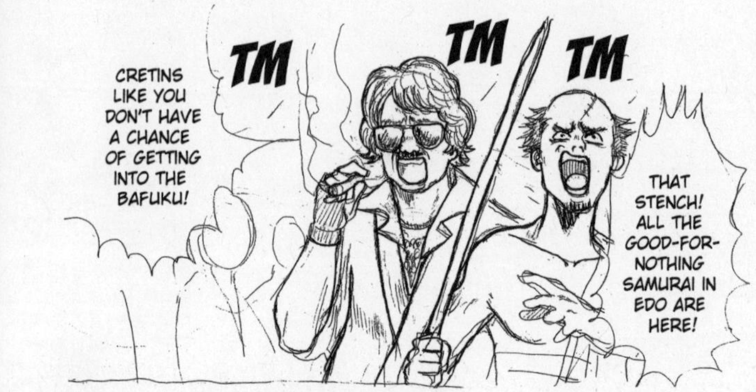
TM
TM
TM
CRETINS LIKE YOU DON'T HAVE A CHANCE OF GETTING INTO THE BAFUKU!
THAT STENCH! ALL THE GOOD-FOR-NOTHING SAMURAI IN EDO ARE HERE!

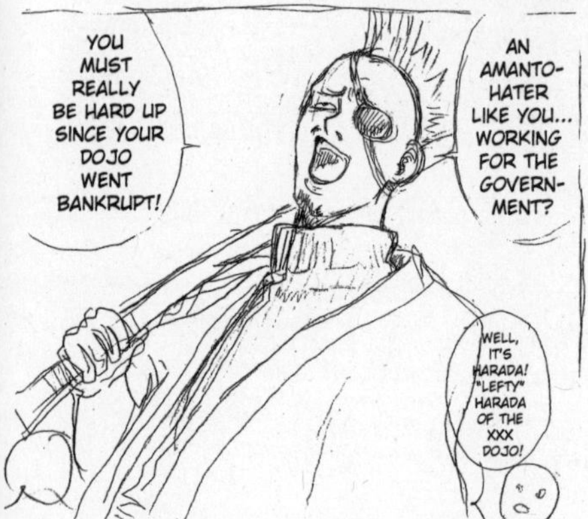
AN AMANTO-HATER LIKE YOU... WORKING FOR THE GOVERN-MENT?
YOU MUST REALLY BE HARD UP SINCE YOUR DOJO WENT BANKRUPT!
WELL, IT'S HARADA! "LEFTY" HARADA OF THE XXX DOJO!

On top is "Mad Bull" Kamo Serizawa and on the bottom, Hidarinosuke Harada. You can see I thought up all different variations...

Gin Tama was basically born out of messing around with guys like this. In my original Gin Tama episode, Shinpachi was already a member of the Yorozuya, and together with Gin-san he saved a samurai who resembled Kato Cha, the comedian. My publisher accepted it, but I started thinking a cast of just old guys would be boring, so I changed it again. I have to watch out, because my manga all seem to end up being about a bunch of old guys together...

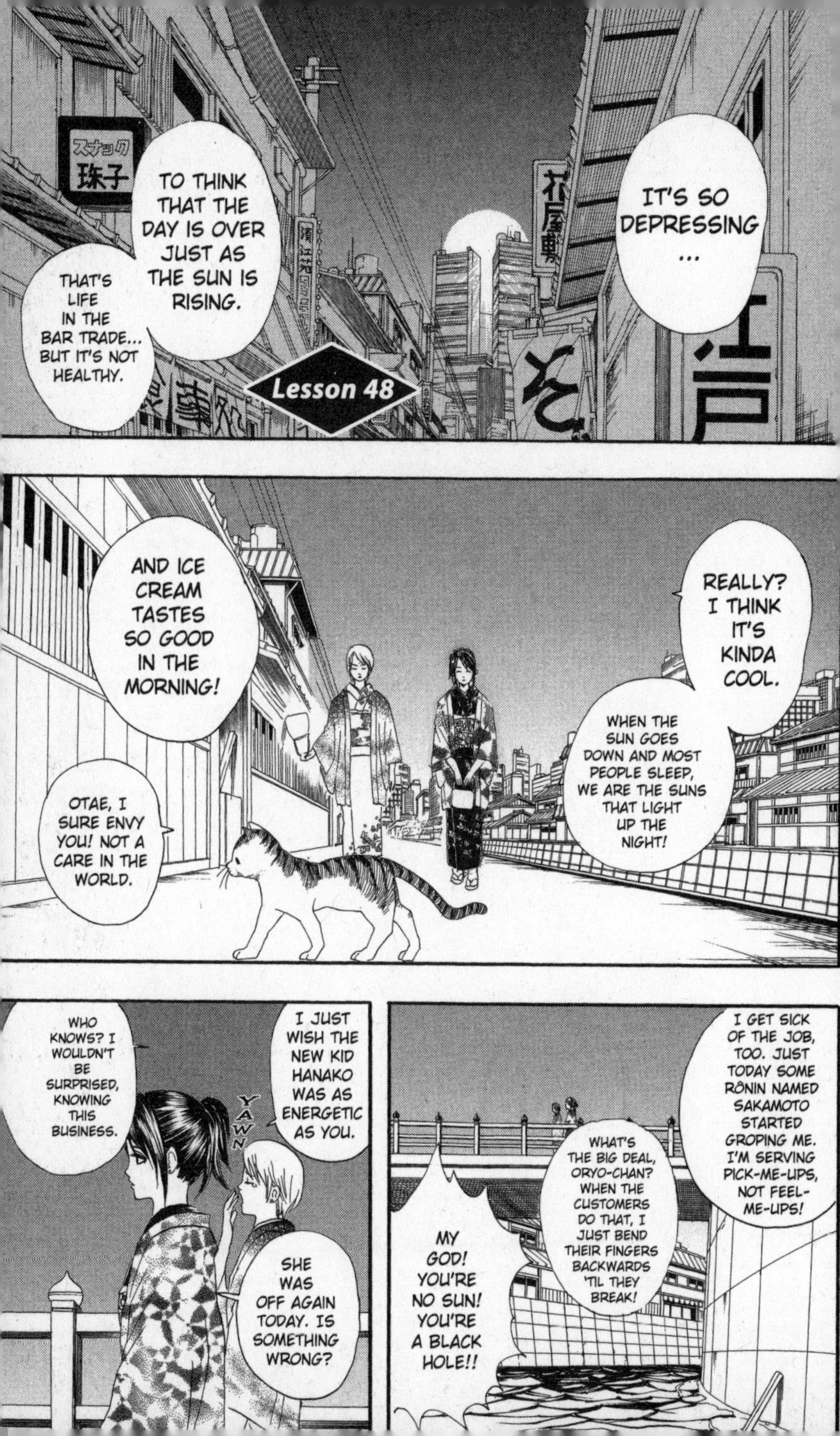
IT'S SO DEPRESSING ...
TO THINK THAT THE DAY IS OVER JUST AS THE SUN IS RISING.
THAT'S LIFE IN THE BAR TRADE... BUT IT'S NOT HEALTHY.
スナック 珠子
江戸
Lesson 48
REALLY? I THINK IT'S KINDA COOL.
WHEN THE SUN GOES DOWN AND MOST PEOPLE SLEEP, WE ARE THE SUNS THAT LIGHT UP THE NIGHT!
AND ICE CREAM TASTES SO GOOD IN THE MORNING!
OTAE, I SURE ENVY YOU! NOT A CARE IN THE WORLD.
I GET SICK OF THE JOB, TOO. JUST TODAY SOME RÔNIN NAMED SAKAMOTO STARTED GROPING ME. I'M SERVING PICK-ME-UPS, NOT FEEL-ME-UPS!
WHAT'S THE BIG DEAL, ORYO-CHAN? WHEN THE CUSTOMERS DO THAT, I JUST BEND THEIR FINGERS BACKWARDS 'TIL THEY BREAK!
MY GOD! YOU'RE NO SUN! YOU'RE A BLACK HOLE!!
I JUST WISH THE NEW KID HANAKO WAS AS ENERGETIC AS YOU.
YAWN
SHE WAS OFF AGAIN TODAY. IS SOMETHING WRONG?
WHO KNOWS? I WOULDN'T BE SURPRISED, KNOWING THIS BUSINESS.

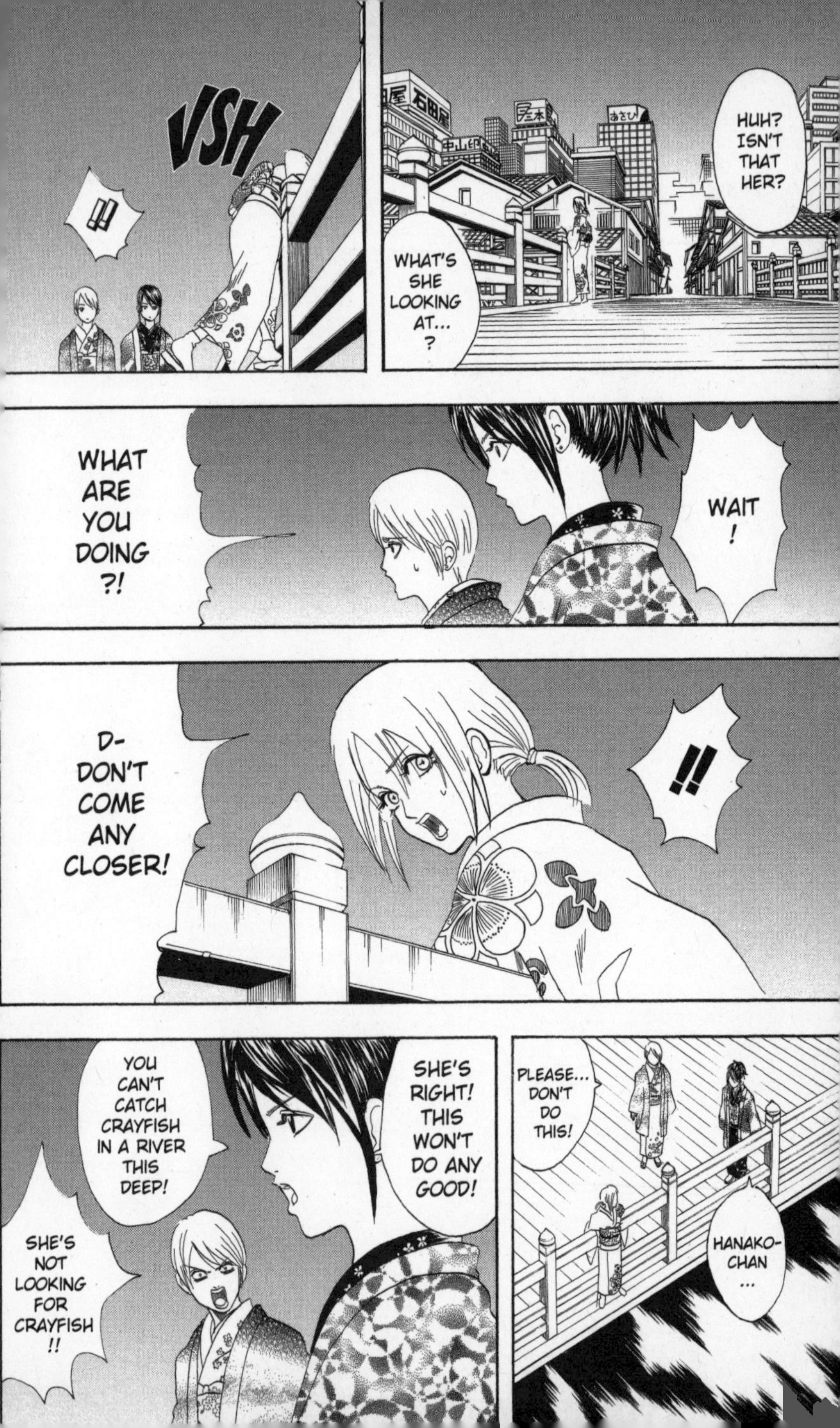

HUH? ISN'T THAT HER?
WHAT'S SHE LOOKING AT...?
VSH
!!
WAIT!
WHAT ARE YOU DOING?!
!!
D-DON'T COME ANY CLOSER!
PLEASE... DON'T DO THIS!
HANAKO-CHAN...
SHE'S RIGHT! THIS WON'T DO ANY GOOD!
YOU CAN'T CATCH CRAYFISH IN A RIVER THIS DEEP!
SHE'S NOT LOOKING FOR CRAYFISH!!

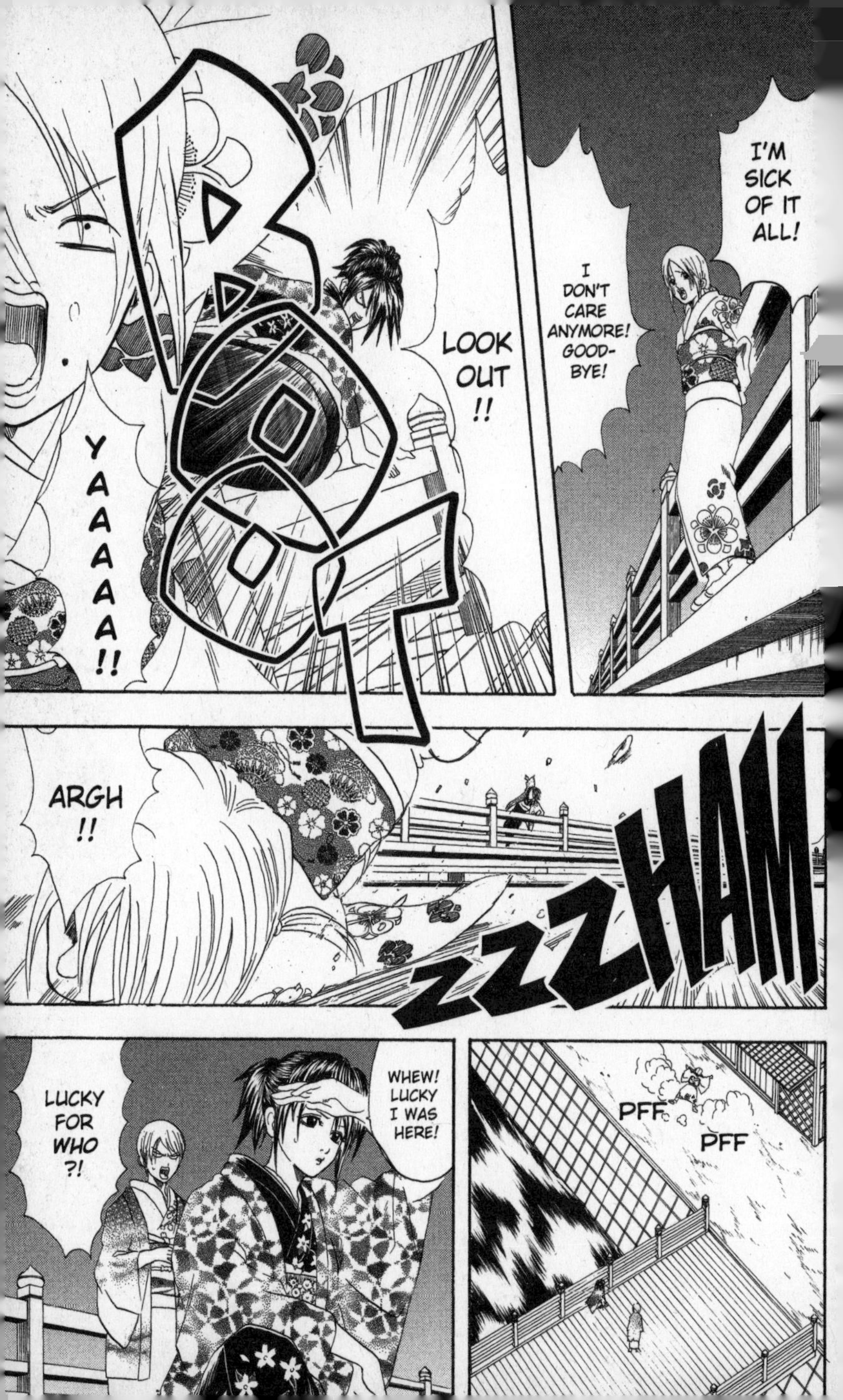
I'M SICK OF IT ALL!
I DON'T CARE ANYMORE! GOOD-BYE!
LOOK OUT!!
YAAAAAA!!
BOOT
ZZZHAM
ARGH!!
PFF
PFF
WHEW! LUCKY I WAS HERE!
LUCKY FOR WHO?!

Lesson 48: People with Dark Pasts Can't Shut Up

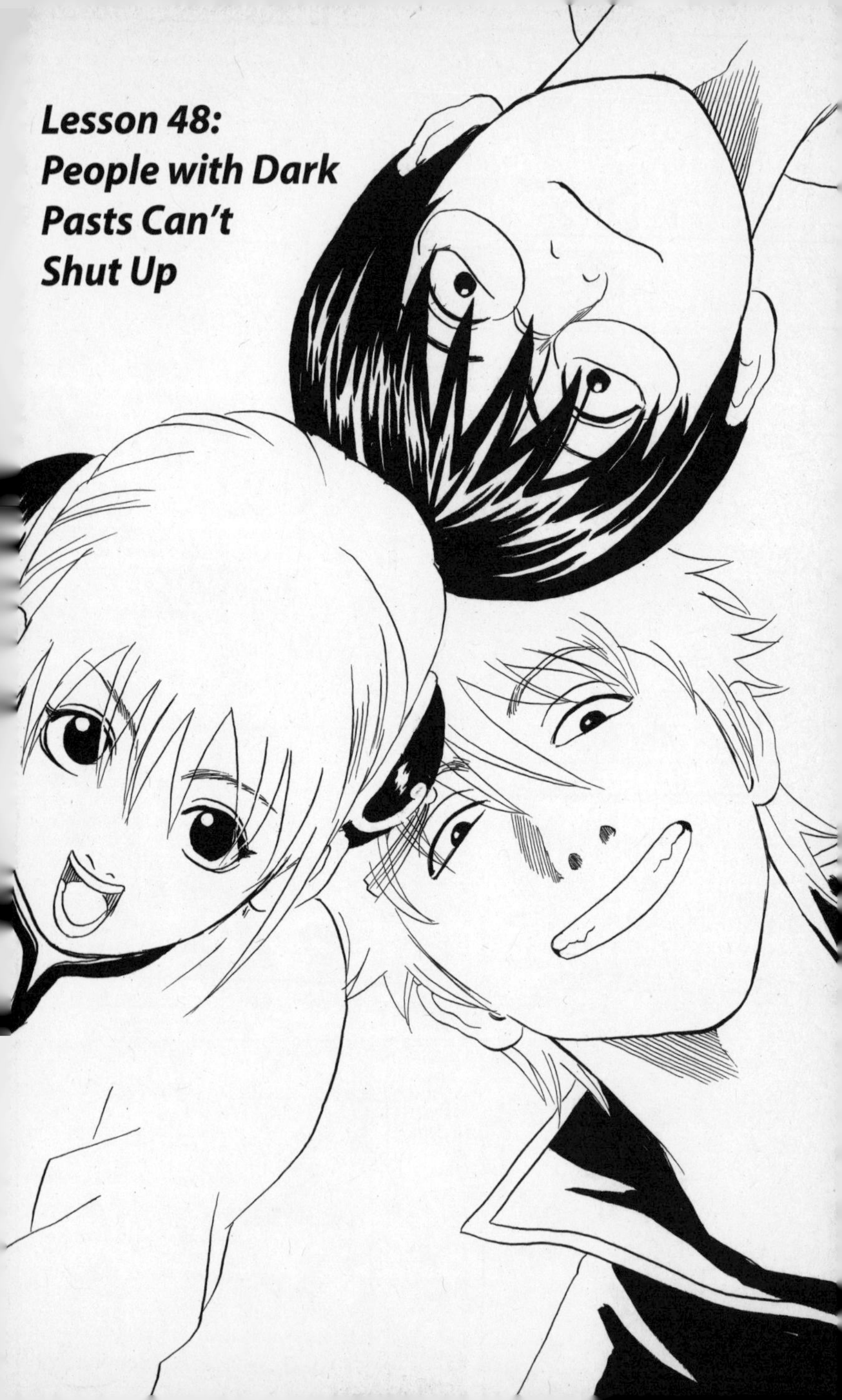

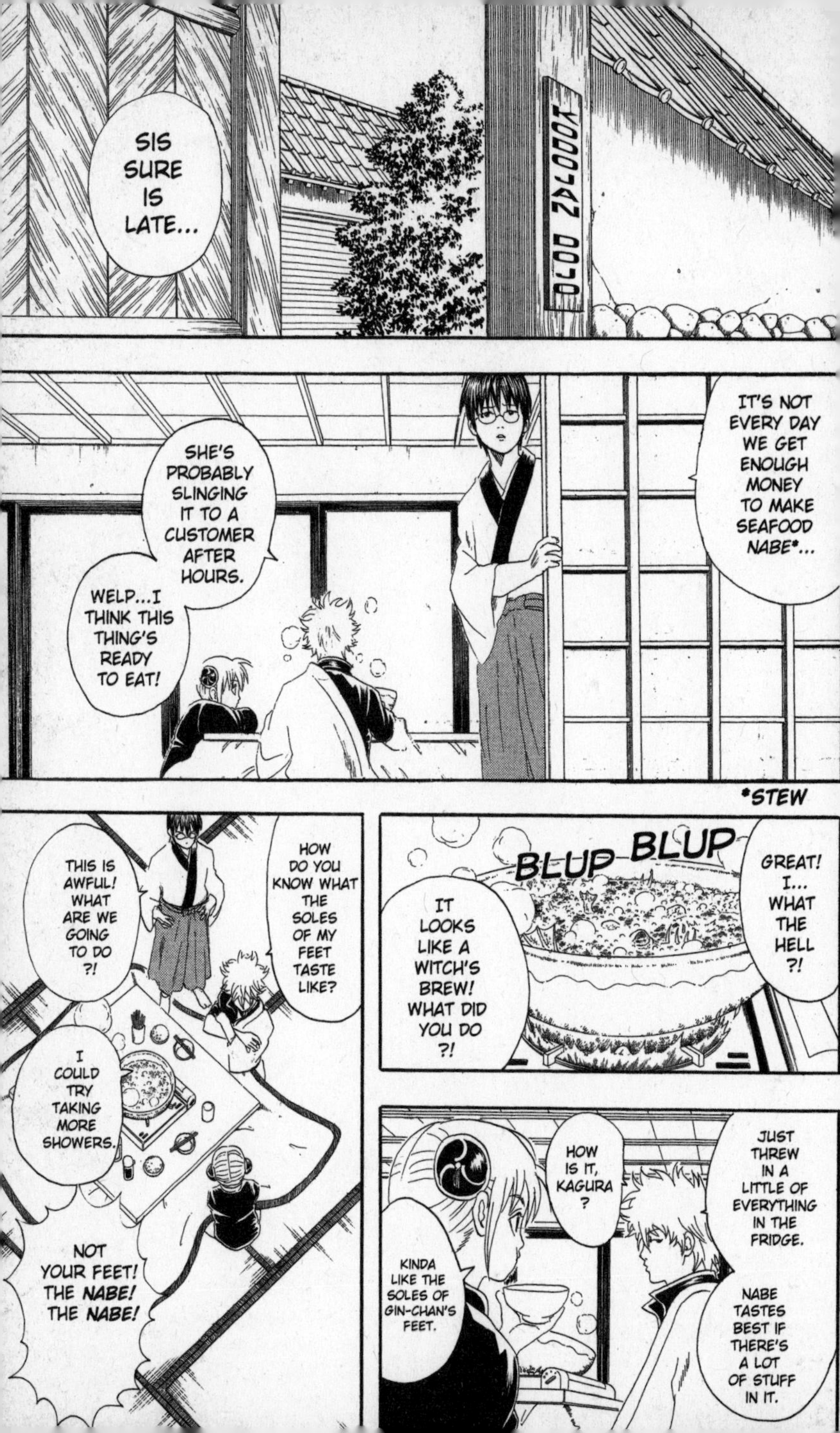
KODOJAN DOJO
SIS SURE IS LATE...
IT'S NOT EVERY DAY WE GET ENOUGH MONEY TO MAKE SEAFOOD NABE*...
SHE'S PROBABLY SLINGING IT TO A CUSTOMER AFTER HOURS.
WELP...I THINK THIS THING'S READY TO EAT!
*STEW
GREAT! I... WHAT THE HELL?!
BLUP BLUP
IT LOOKS LIKE A WITCH'S BREW! WHAT DID YOU DO?!
JUST THREW IN A LITTLE OF EVERYTHING IN THE FRIDGE.
NABE TASTES BEST IF THERE'S A LOT OF STUFF IN IT.
HOW IS IT, KAGURA?
KINDA LIKE THE SOLES OF GIN-CHAN'S FEET.
HOW DO YOU KNOW WHAT THE SOLES OF MY FEET TASTE LIKE?
THIS IS AWFUL! WHAT ARE WE GOING TO DO?!
I COULD TRY TAKING MORE SHOWERS.
NOT YOUR FEET! THE NABE! THE NABE!

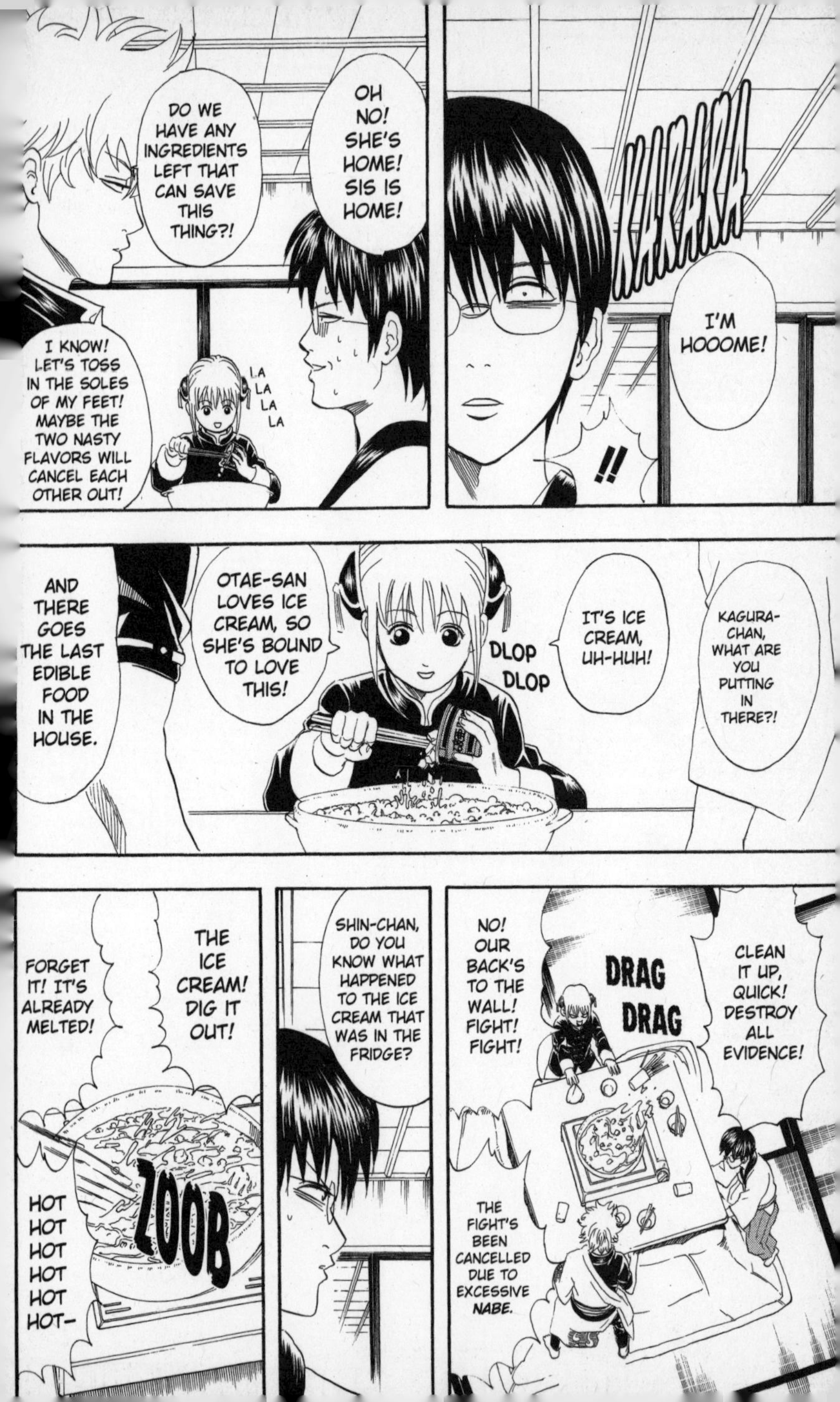
I'M HOOOME!
!!
OH NO! SHE'S HOME! SIS IS HOME!
DO WE HAVE ANY INGREDIENTS LEFT THAT CAN SAVE THIS THING?!
LA LA LA LA
I KNOW! LET'S TOSS IN THE SOLES OF MY FEET! MAYBE THE TWO NASTY FLAVORS WILL CANCEL EACH OTHER OUT!
KAGURA-CHAN, WHAT ARE YOU PUTTING IN THERE?!
IT'S ICE CREAM, UH-HUH!
DLOP DLOP
OTAE-SAN LOVES ICE CREAM, SO SHE'S BOUND TO LOVE THIS!
AND THERE GOES THE LAST EDIBLE FOOD IN THE HOUSE.
CLEAN IT UP, QUICK! DESTROY ALL EVIDENCE!
DRAG DRAG
NO! OUR BACK'S TO THE WALL! FIGHT! FIGHT!
THE FIGHT'S BEEN CANCELLED DUE TO EXCESSIVE NABE.
SHIN-CHAN, DO YOU KNOW WHAT HAPPENED TO THE ICE CREAM THAT WAS IN THE FRIDGE?
THE ICE CREAM! DIG IT OUT!
FORGET IT! IT'S ALREADY MELTED!
ZOOB
HOT HOT HOT HOT HOT HOT-

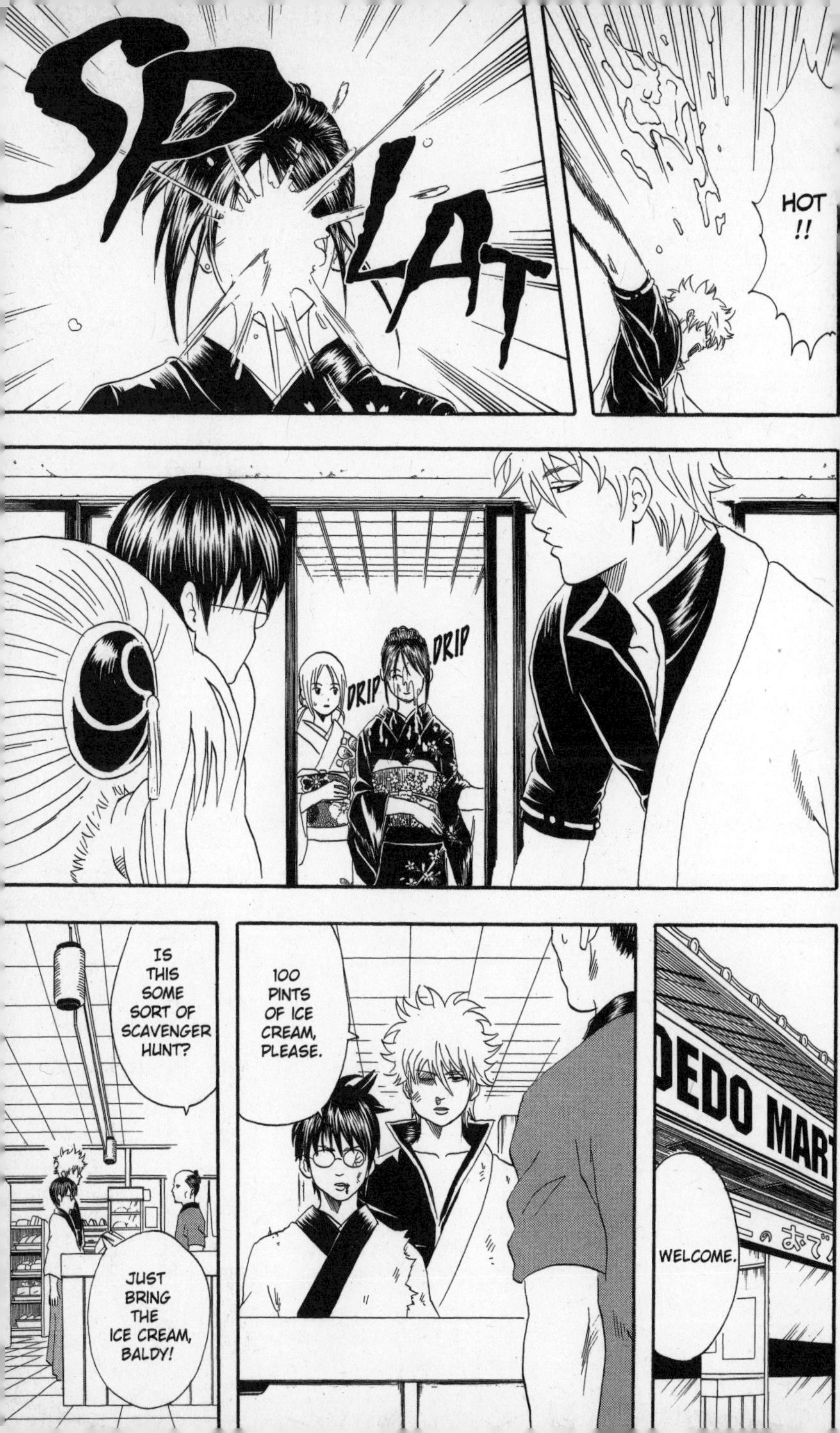
HOT !!
SPLAT
DRIP
DRIP
OEDO MART
WELCOME.
100 PINTS OF ICE CREAM, PLEASE.
IS THIS SOME SORT OF SCAVENGER HUNT?
JUST BRING THE ICE CREAM, BALDY!

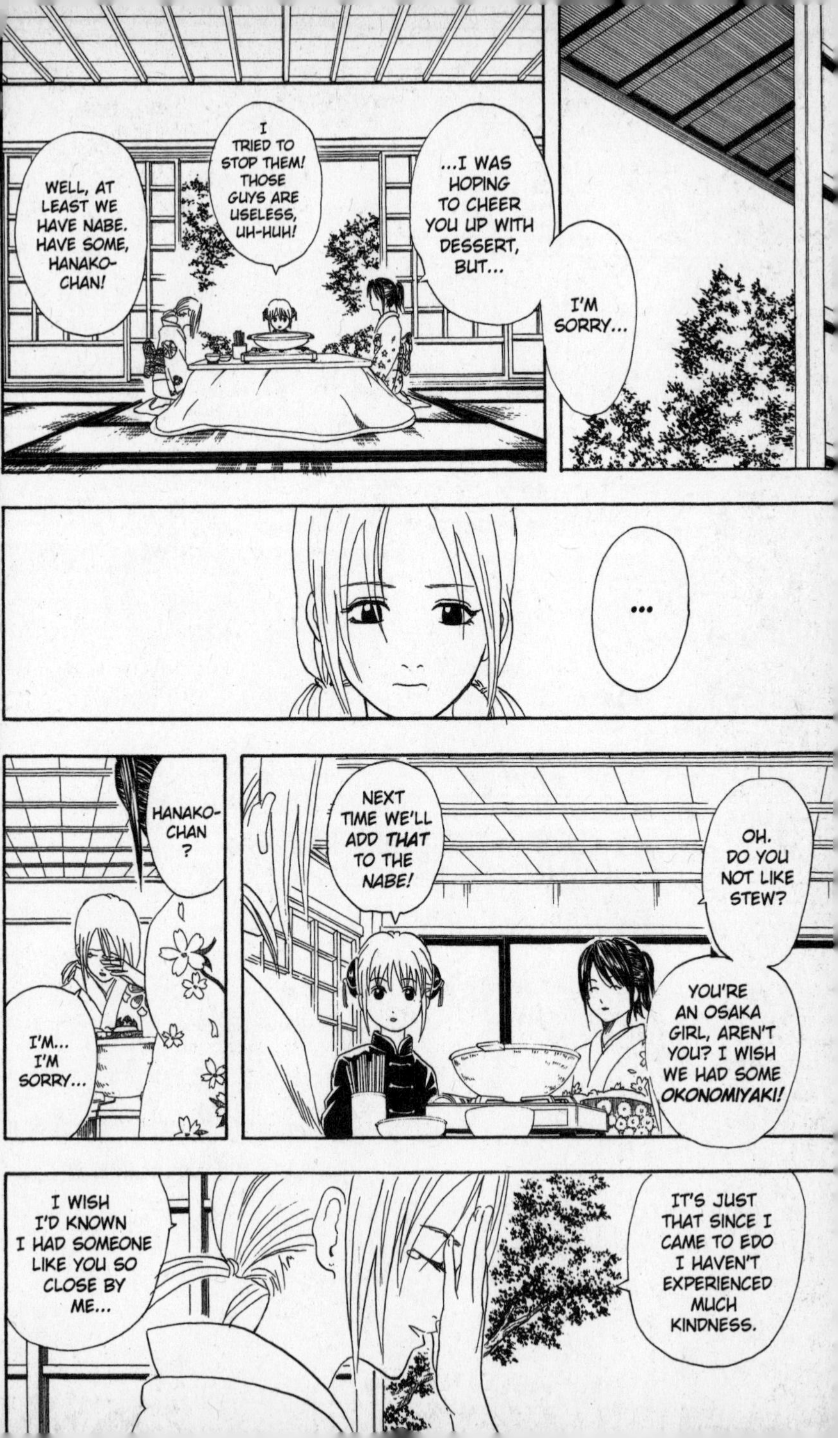
I'M SORRY...
...I WAS HOPING TO CHEER YOU UP WITH DESSERT, BUT...
I TRIED TO STOP THEM! THOSE GUYS ARE USELESS, UH-HUH!
WELL, AT LEAST WE HAVE NABE. HAVE SOME, HANAKO-CHAN!
...
OH. DO YOU NOT LIKE STEW?
YOU'RE AN OSAKA GIRL, AREN'T YOU? I WISH WE HAD SOME *OKONOMIYAKI*!
NEXT TIME WE'LL ADD *THAT* TO THE NABE!
HANAKO-CHAN?
I'M... I'M SORRY...
IT'S JUST THAT SINCE I CAME TO EDO I HAVEN'T EXPERIENCED MUCH KINDNESS.
I WISH I'D KNOWN I HAD SOMEONE LIKE YOU SO CLOSE BY ME...

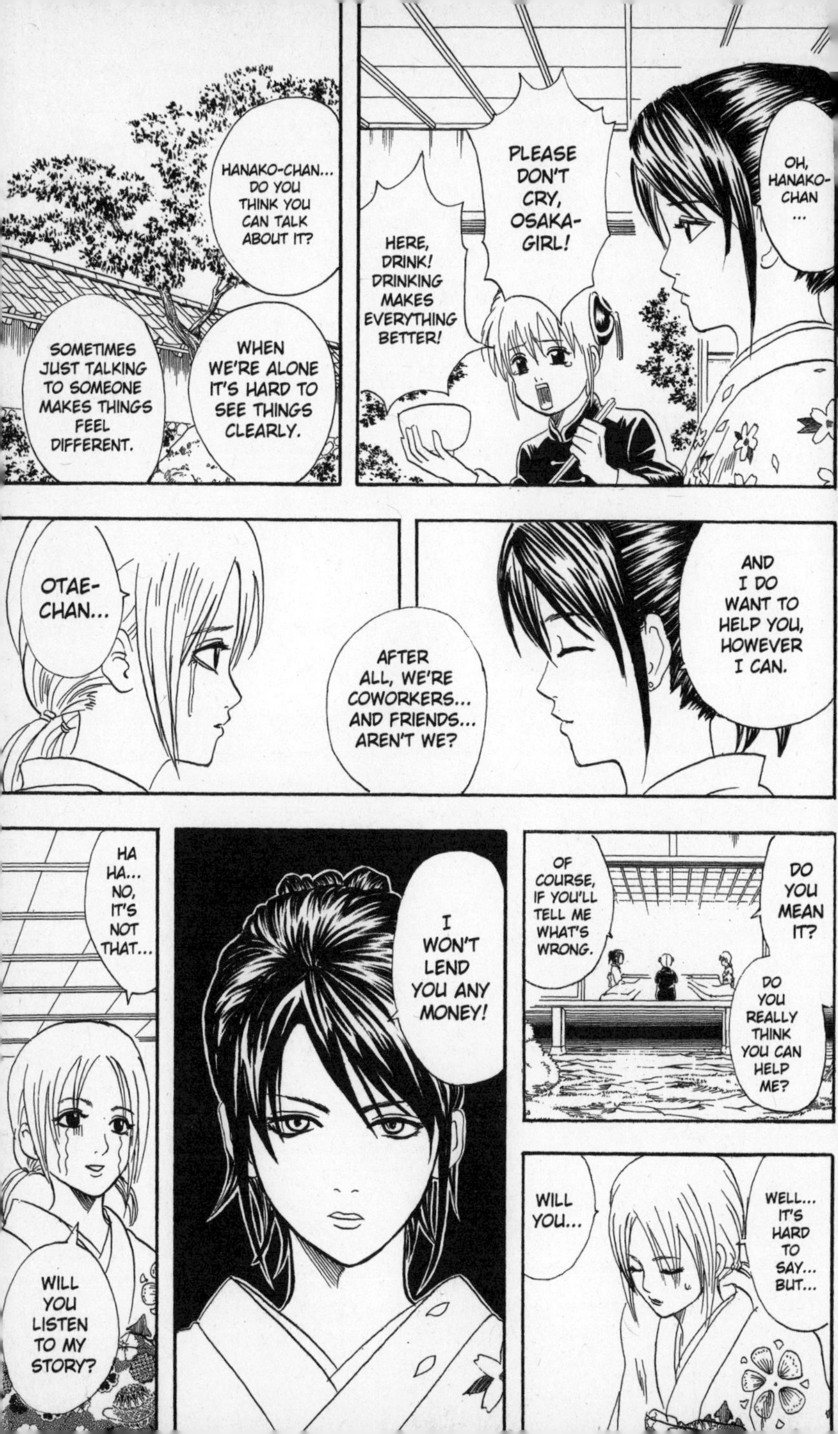
OH, HANAKO-CHAN...
PLEASE DON'T CRY, OSAKA-GIRL!
HERE, DRINK! DRINKING MAKES EVERYTHING BETTER!
HANAKO-CHAN... DO YOU THINK YOU CAN TALK ABOUT IT?
WHEN WE'RE ALONE IT'S HARD TO SEE THINGS CLEARLY.
SOMETIMES JUST TALKING TO SOMEONE MAKES THINGS FEEL DIFFERENT.
AND I DO WANT TO HELP YOU, HOWEVER I CAN.
AFTER ALL, WE'RE COWORKERS... AND FRIENDS... AREN'T WE?
OTAE-CHAN...
DO YOU MEAN IT?
DO YOU REALLY THINK YOU CAN HELP ME?
OF COURSE, IF YOU'LL TELL ME WHAT'S WRONG.
WELL... IT'S HARD TO SAY... BUT...
WILL YOU...
I WON'T LEND YOU ANY MONEY!
HA HA... NO, IT'S NOT THAT...
WILL YOU LISTEN TO MY STORY?

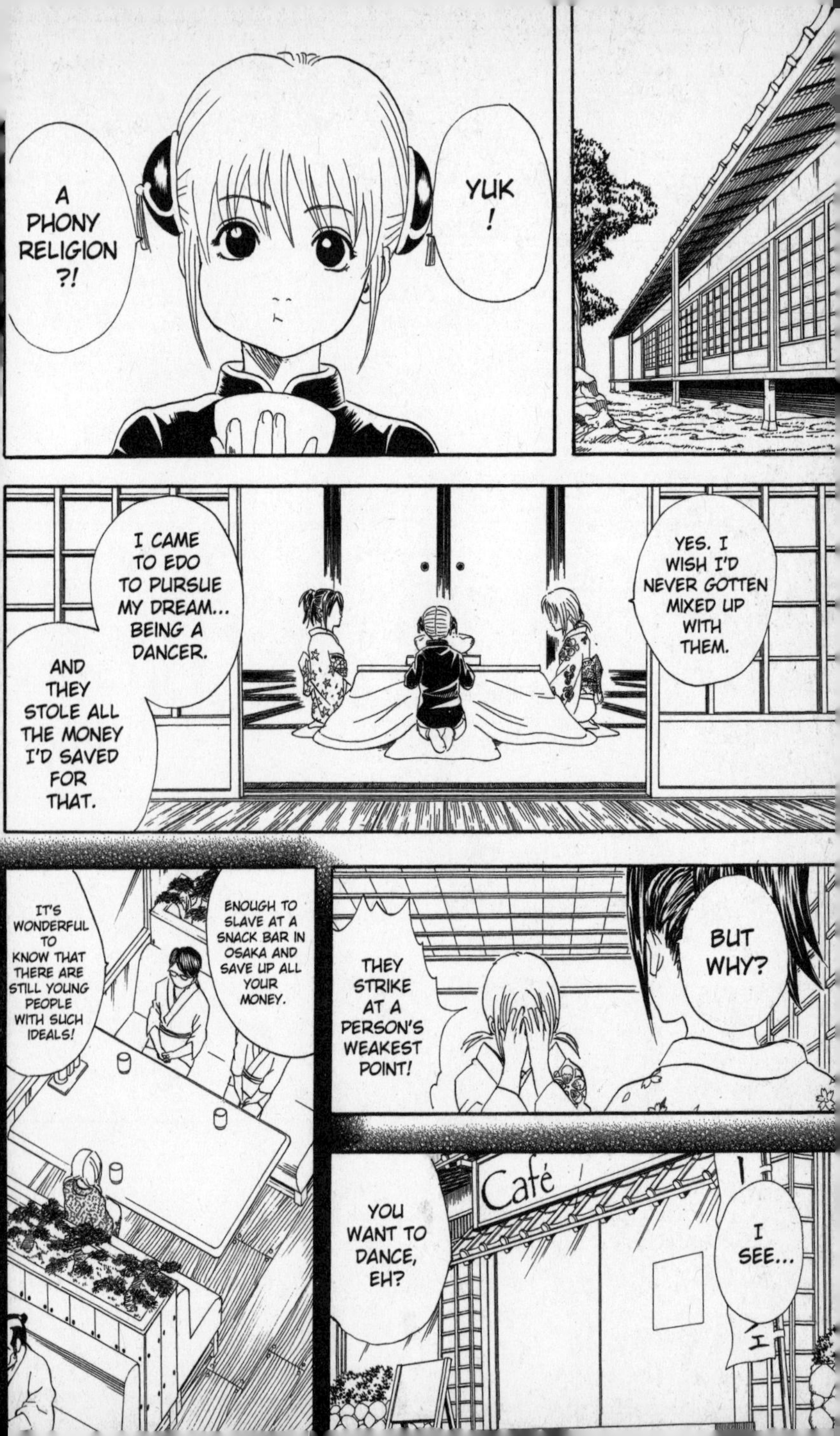
YUK!
A PHONY RELIGION?!
YES. I WISH I'D NEVER GOTTEN MIXED UP WITH THEM.
I CAME TO EDO TO PURSUE MY DREAM... BEING A DANCER.
AND THEY STOLE ALL THE MONEY I'D SAVED FOR THAT.
BUT WHY?
THEY STRIKE AT A PERSON'S WEAKEST POINT!
Café
I SEE...
YOU WANT TO DANCE, EH?
ENOUGH TO SLAVE AT A SNACK BAR IN OSAKA AND SAVE UP ALL YOUR MONEY.
IT'S WONDERFUL TO KNOW THAT THERE ARE STILL YOUNG PEOPLE WITH SUCH IDEALS!

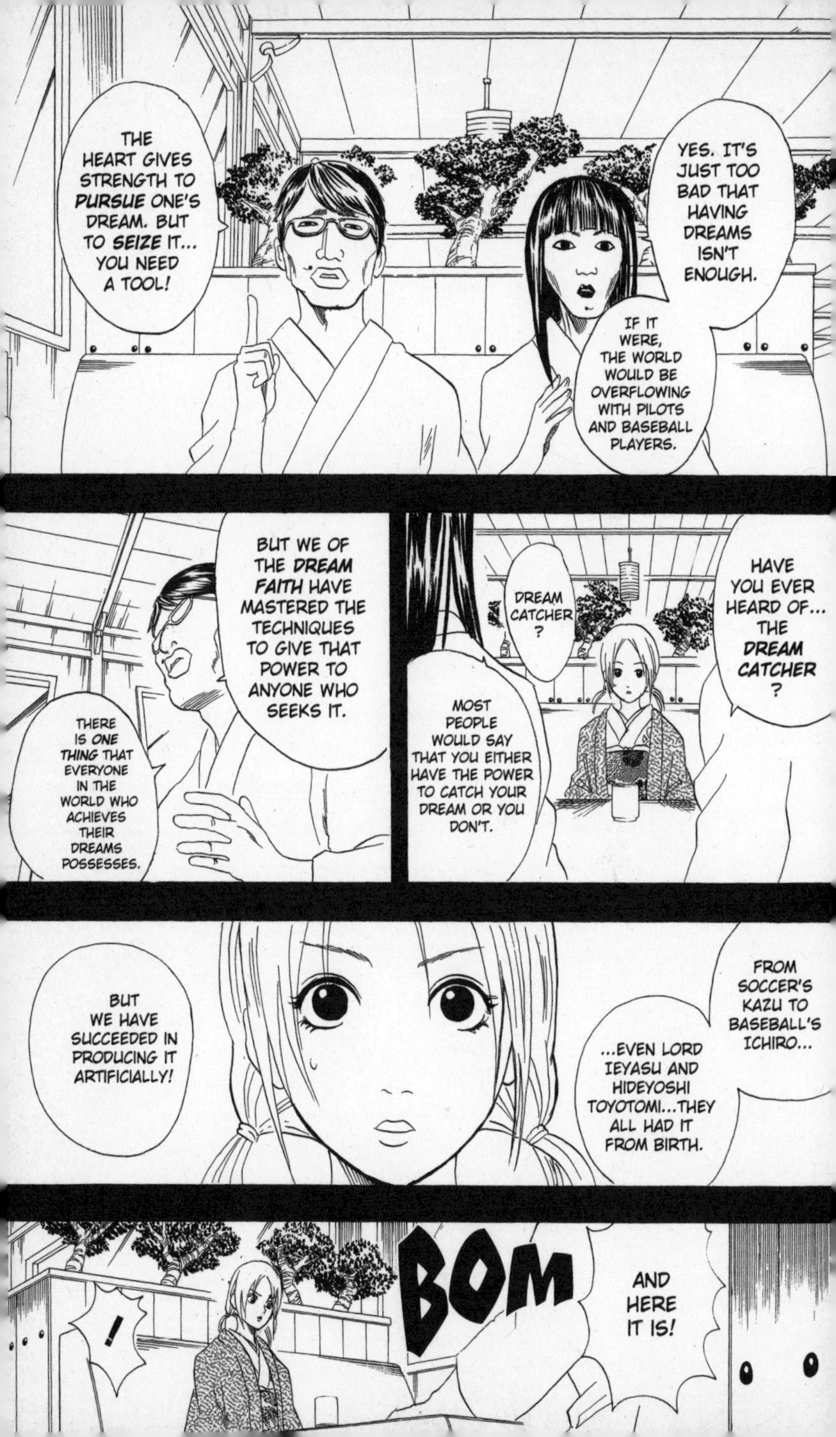
THE HEART GIVES STRENGTH TO *PURSUE* ONE'S DREAM. BUT TO *SEIZE* IT... YOU NEED A TOOL!
YES. IT'S JUST TOO BAD THAT HAVING DREAMS ISN'T ENOUGH.
IF IT WERE, THE WORLD WOULD BE OVERFLOWING WITH PILOTS AND BASEBALL PLAYERS.
HAVE YOU EVER HEARD OF... THE *DREAM CATCHER*?
DREAM CATCHER?
MOST PEOPLE WOULD SAY THAT YOU EITHER HAVE THE POWER TO CATCH YOUR DREAM OR YOU DON'T.
BUT WE OF THE *DREAM FAITH* HAVE MASTERED THE TECHNIQUES TO GIVE THAT POWER TO ANYONE WHO SEEKS IT.
THERE IS *ONE THING* THAT EVERYONE IN THE WORLD WHO ACHIEVES THEIR DREAMS POSSESSES.
FROM SOCCER'S KAZU TO BASEBALL'S ICHIRO...
...EVEN LORD IEYASU AND HIDEYOSHI TOYOTOMI...THEY ALL HAD IT FROM BIRTH.
BUT WE HAVE SUCCEEDED IN PRODUCING IT ARTIFICIALLY!
AND HERE IT IS!
BOM
!

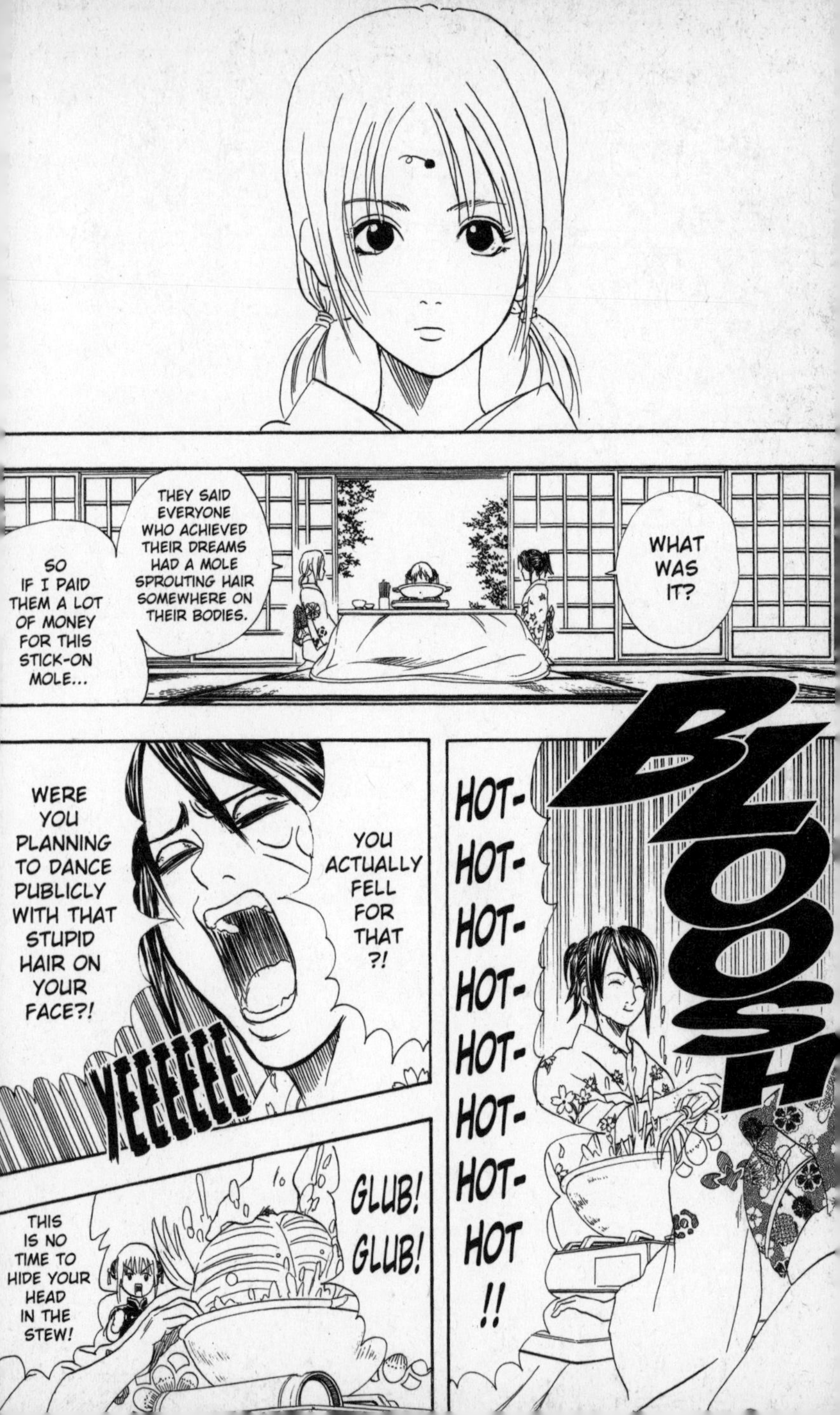
WHAT WAS IT?
THEY SAID EVERYONE WHO ACHIEVED THEIR DREAMS HAD A MOLE SPROUTING HAIR SOMEWHERE ON THEIR BODIES.
SO IF I PAID THEM A LOT OF MONEY FOR THIS STICK-ON MOLE...
BLOOSH
HOT-HOT-HOT-HOT-HOT-HOT-HOT-HOT-HOT-HOT!!
YOU ACTUALLY FELL FOR THAT?!
WERE YOU PLANNING TO DANCE PUBLICLY WITH THAT STUPID HAIR ON YOUR FACE?!
YEEEEEE
GLUB! GLUB!
THIS IS NO TIME TO HIDE YOUR HEAD IN THE STEW!

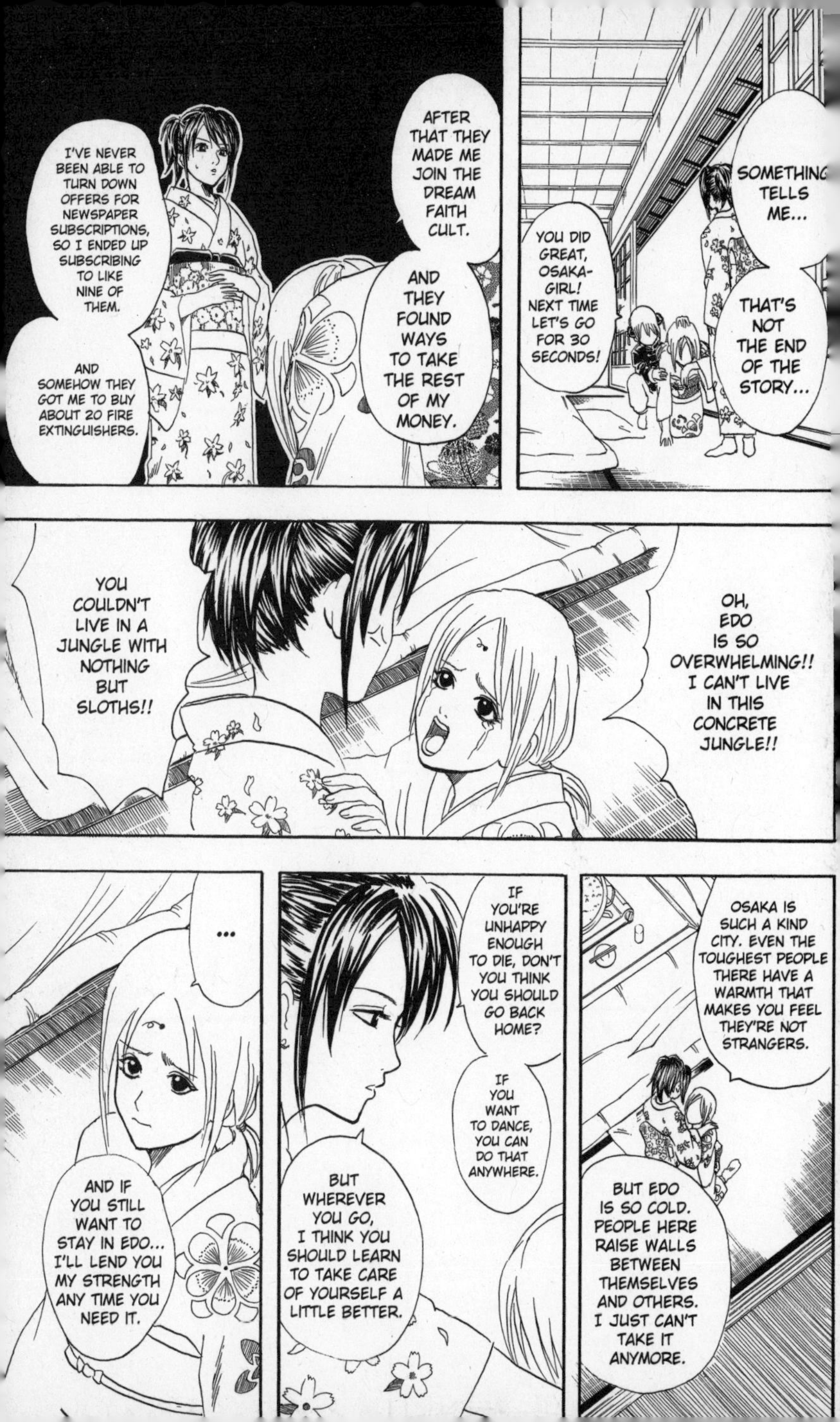
SOMETHING TELLS ME...
THAT'S NOT THE END OF THE STORY...
YOU DID GREAT, OSAKA-GIRL! NEXT TIME LET'S GO FOR 30 SECONDS!
AFTER THAT THEY MADE ME JOIN THE DREAM FAITH CULT.
AND THEY FOUND WAYS TO TAKE THE REST OF MY MONEY.
I'VE NEVER BEEN ABLE TO TURN DOWN OFFERS FOR NEWSPAPER SUBSCRIPTIONS, SO I ENDED UP SUBSCRIBING TO LIKE NINE OF THEM.
AND SOMEHOW THEY GOT ME TO BUY ABOUT 20 FIRE EXTINGUISHERS.
OH, EDO IS SO OVERWHELMING!! I CAN'T LIVE IN THIS CONCRETE JUNGLE!!
YOU COULDN'T LIVE IN A JUNGLE WITH NOTHING BUT SLOTHS!!
OSAKA IS SUCH A KIND CITY. EVEN THE TOUGHEST PEOPLE THERE HAVE A WARMTH THAT MAKES YOU FEEL THEY'RE NOT STRANGERS.
BUT EDO IS SO COLD. PEOPLE HERE RAISE WALLS BETWEEN THEMSELVES AND OTHERS. I JUST CAN'T TAKE IT ANYMORE.
IF YOU'RE UNHAPPY ENOUGH TO DIE, DON'T YOU THINK YOU SHOULD GO BACK HOME?
IF YOU WANT TO DANCE, YOU CAN DO THAT ANYWHERE.
BUT WHEREVER YOU GO, I THINK YOU SHOULD LEARN TO TAKE CARE OF YOURSELF A LITTLE BETTER.
...
AND IF YOU STILL WANT TO STAY IN EDO... I'LL LEND YOU MY STRENGTH ANY TIME YOU NEED IT.

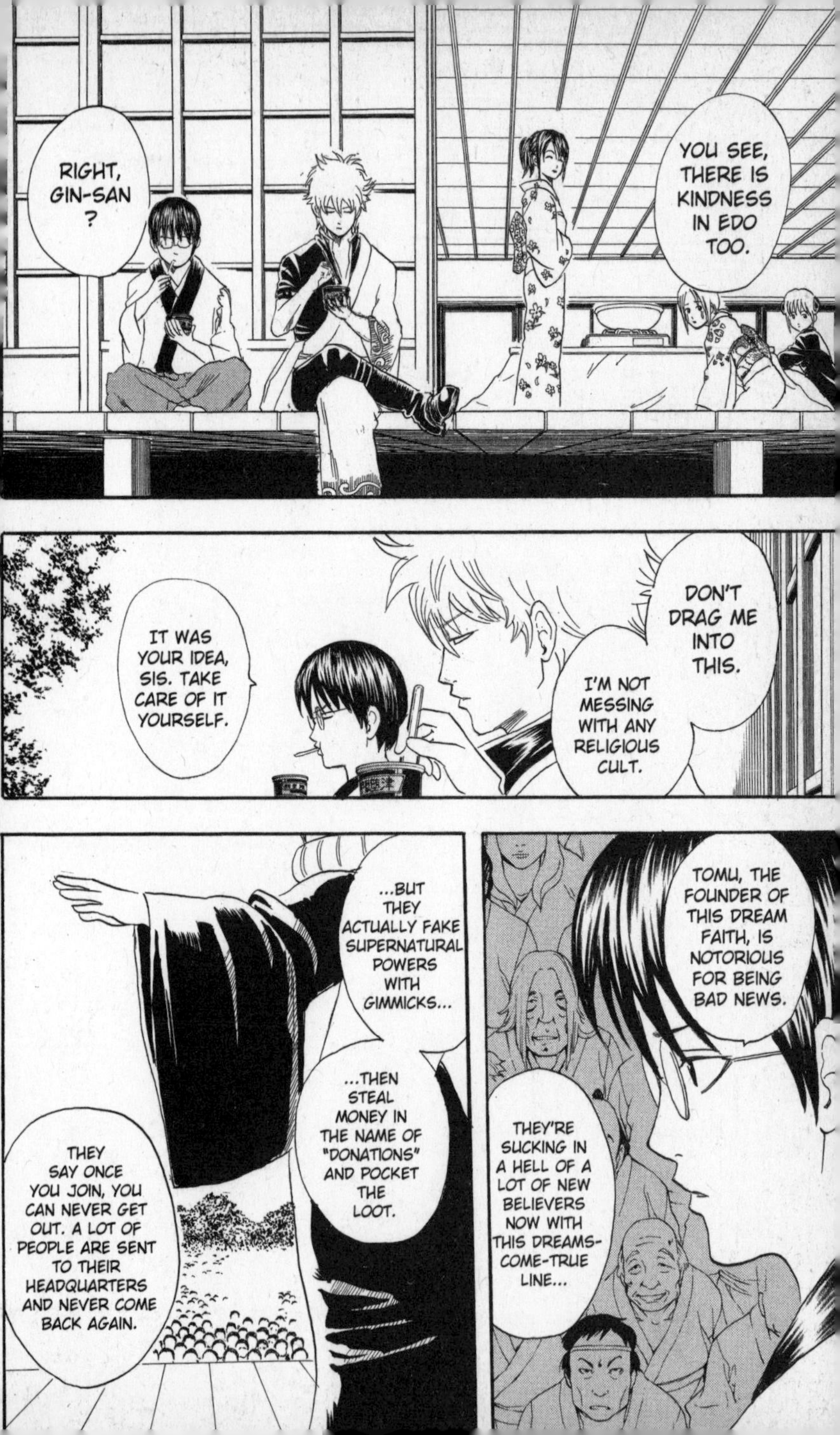
YOU SEE, THERE IS KINDNESS IN EDO TOO.
RIGHT, GIN-SAN ?
DON'T DRAG ME INTO THIS.
I'M NOT MESSING WITH ANY RELIGIOUS CULT.
IT WAS YOUR IDEA, SIS. TAKE CARE OF IT YOURSELF.
TOMU, THE FOUNDER OF THIS DREAM FAITH, IS NOTORIOUS FOR BEING BAD NEWS.
THEY'RE SUCKING IN A HELL OF A LOT OF NEW BELIEVERS NOW WITH THIS DREAMS-COME-TRUE LINE...
...BUT THEY ACTUALLY FAKE SUPERNATURAL POWERS WITH GIMMICKS...
...THEN STEAL MONEY IN THE NAME OF "DONATIONS" AND POCKET THE LOOT.
THEY SAY ONCE YOU JOIN, YOU CAN NEVER GET OUT. A LOT OF PEOPLE ARE SENT TO THEIR HEADQUARTERS AND NEVER COME BACK AGAIN.

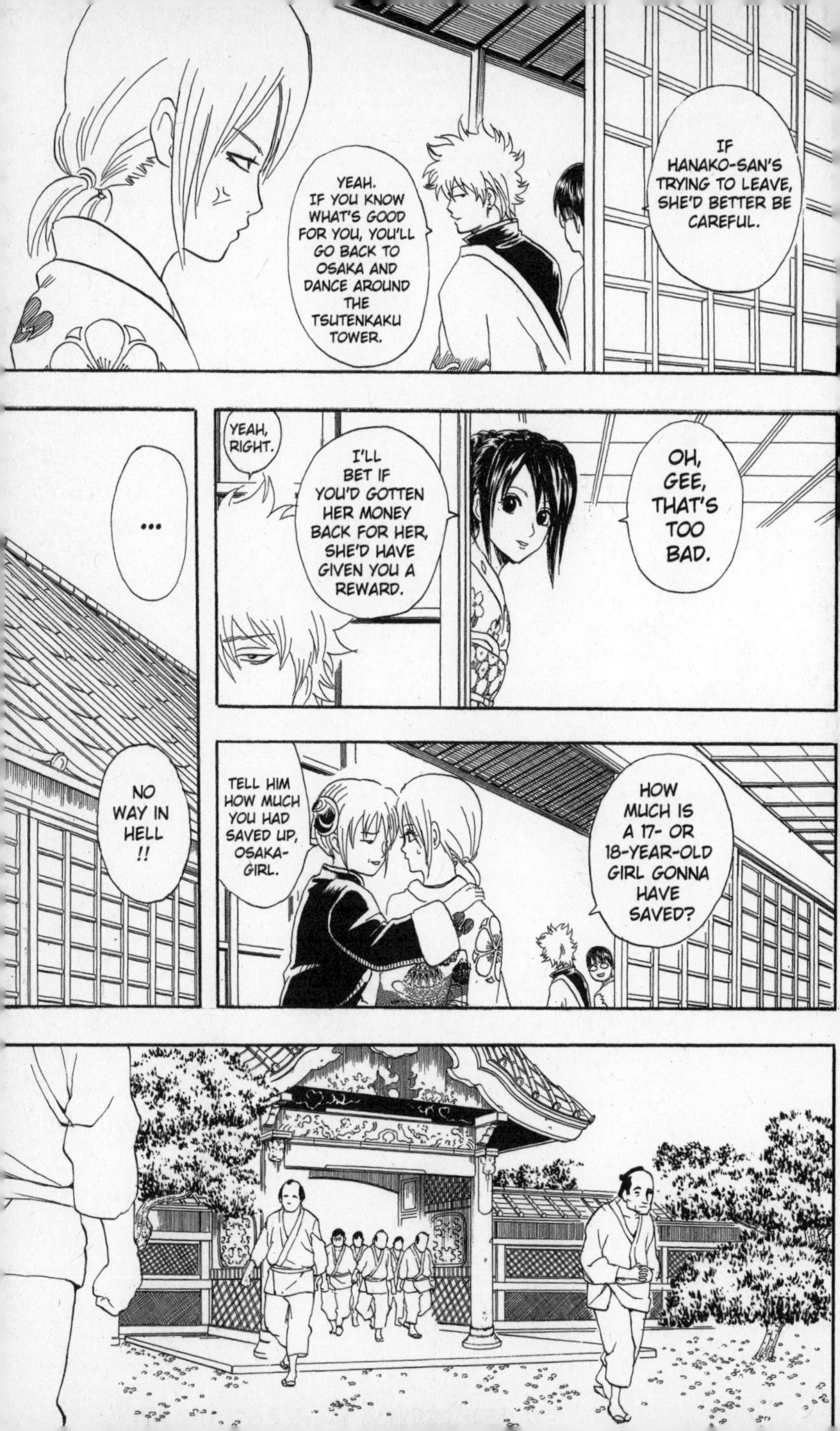
IF HANAKO-SAN'S TRYING TO LEAVE, SHE'D BETTER BE CAREFUL.
YEAH. IF YOU KNOW WHAT'S GOOD FOR YOU, YOU'LL GO BACK TO OSAKA AND DANCE AROUND THE TSUTENKAKU TOWER.
OH, GEE, THAT'S TOO BAD.
I'LL BET IF YOU'D GOTTEN HER MONEY BACK FOR HER, SHE'D HAVE GIVEN YOU A REWARD.
YEAH, RIGHT.
HOW MUCH IS A 17- OR 18-YEAR-OLD GIRL GONNA HAVE SAVED?
TELL HIM HOW MUCH YOU HAD SAVED UP, OSAKA-GIRL.
...
NO WAY IN HELL !!

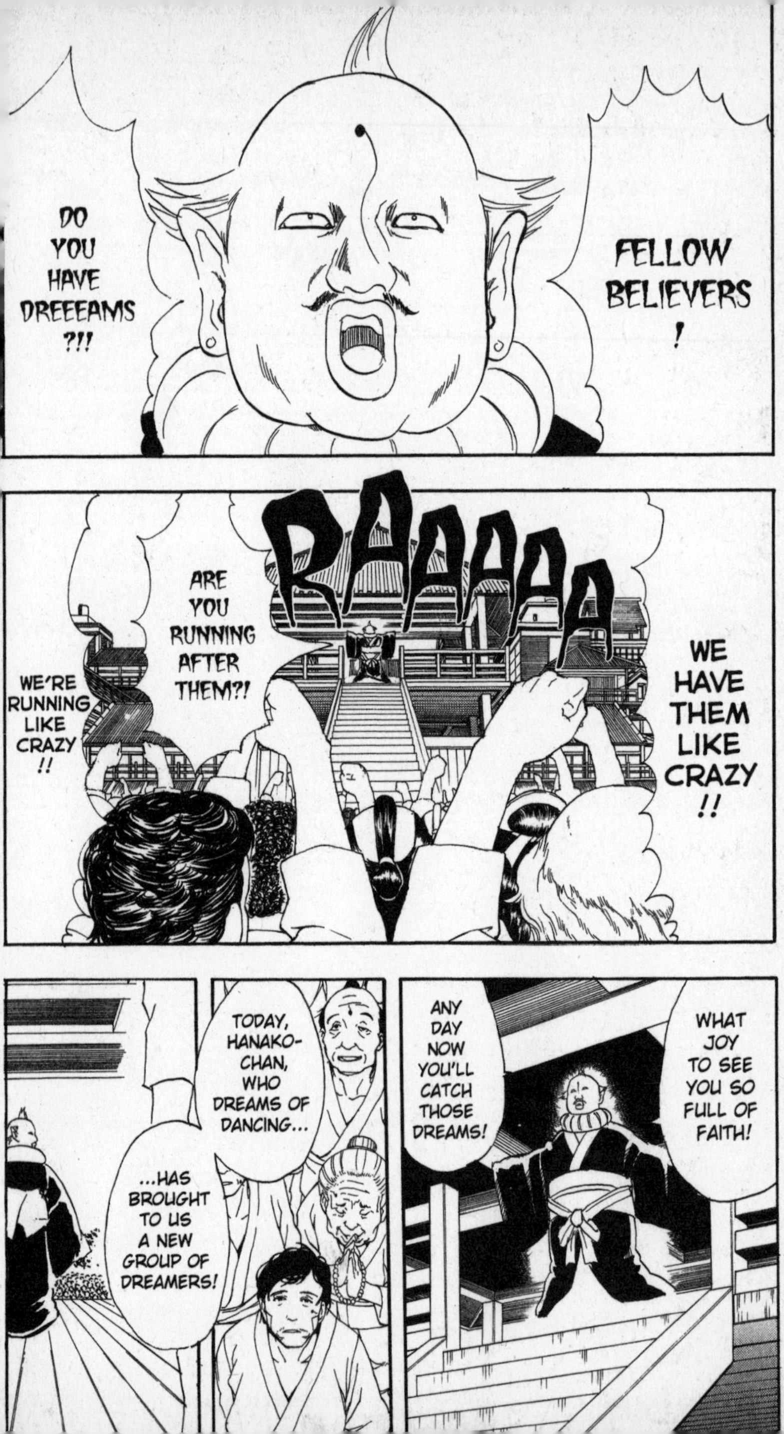

FELLOW BELIEVERS!
DO YOU HAVE DREEEAMS?!!
WE HAVE THEM LIKE CRAZY!!
RAAAAA
ARE YOU RUNNING AFTER THEM?!
WE'RE RUNNING LIKE CRAZY!!
WHAT JOY TO SEE YOU SO FULL OF FAITH!
ANY DAY NOW YOU'LL CATCH THOSE DREAMS!
TODAY, HANAKO-CHAN, WHO DREAMS OF DANCING...
...HAS BROUGHT TO US A NEW GROUP OF DREAMERS!

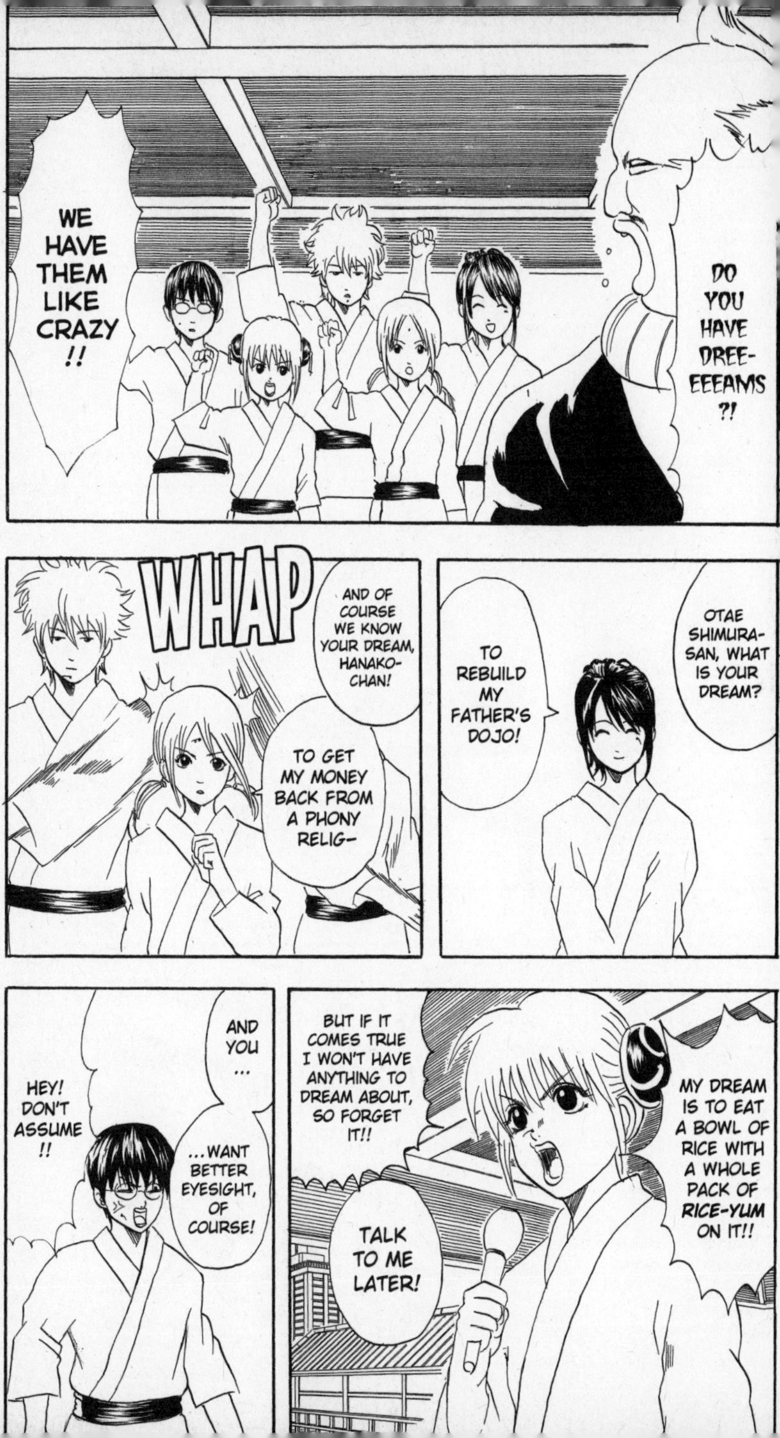
DO YOU HAVE DREE-EEEAMS ?!
WE HAVE THEM LIKE CRAZY !!
OTAE SHIMURA-SAN, WHAT IS YOUR DREAM?
TO REBUILD MY FATHER'S DOJO!
AND OF COURSE WE KNOW YOUR DREAM, HANAKO-CHAN!
WHAP
TO GET MY MONEY BACK FROM A PHONY RELIG-
MY DREAM IS TO EAT A BOWL OF RICE WITH A WHOLE PACK OF RICE-YUM ON IT!!
BUT IF IT COMES TRUE I WON'T HAVE ANYTHING TO DREAM ABOUT, SO FORGET IT!!
TALK TO ME LATER!
AND YOU ...
...WANT BETTER EYESIGHT, OF COURSE!
HEY! DON'T ASSUME !!

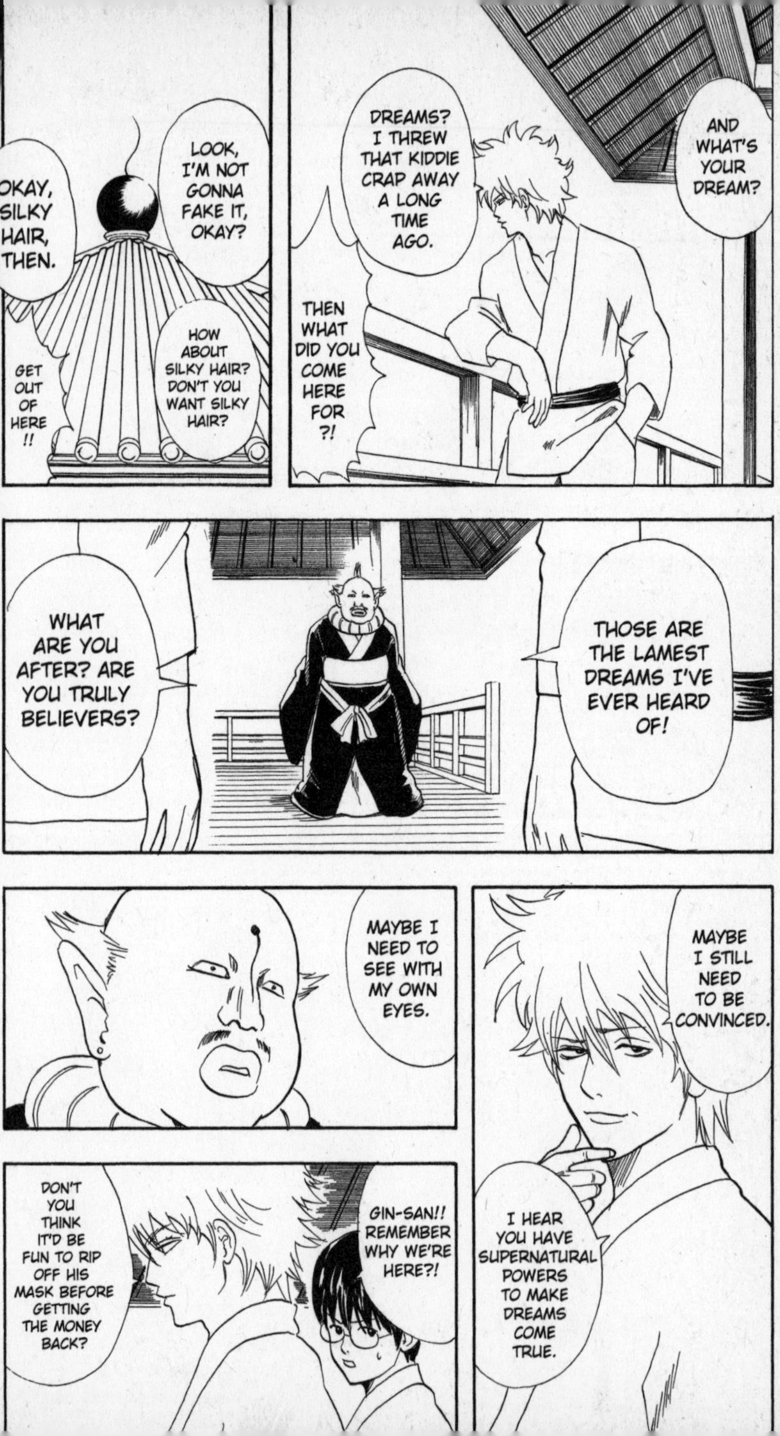
AND WHAT'S YOUR DREAM?
DREAMS? I THREW THAT KIDDIE CRAP AWAY A LONG TIME AGO.
THEN WHAT DID YOU COME HERE FOR ?!
LOOK, I'M NOT GONNA FAKE IT, OKAY?
OKAY, SILKY HAIR, THEN.
HOW ABOUT SILKY HAIR? DON'T YOU WANT SILKY HAIR?
GET OUT OF HERE !!
THOSE ARE THE LAMEST DREAMS I'VE EVER HEARD OF!
WHAT ARE YOU AFTER? ARE YOU TRULY BELIEVERS?
MAYBE I STILL NEED TO BE CONVINCED.
I HEAR YOU HAVE SUPERNATURAL POWERS TO MAKE DREAMS COME TRUE.
MAYBE I NEED TO SEE WITH MY OWN EYES.
GIN-SAN!! REMEMBER WHY WE'RE HERE?!
DON'T YOU THINK IT'D BE FUN TO RIP OFF HIS MASK BEFORE GETTING THE MONEY BACK?

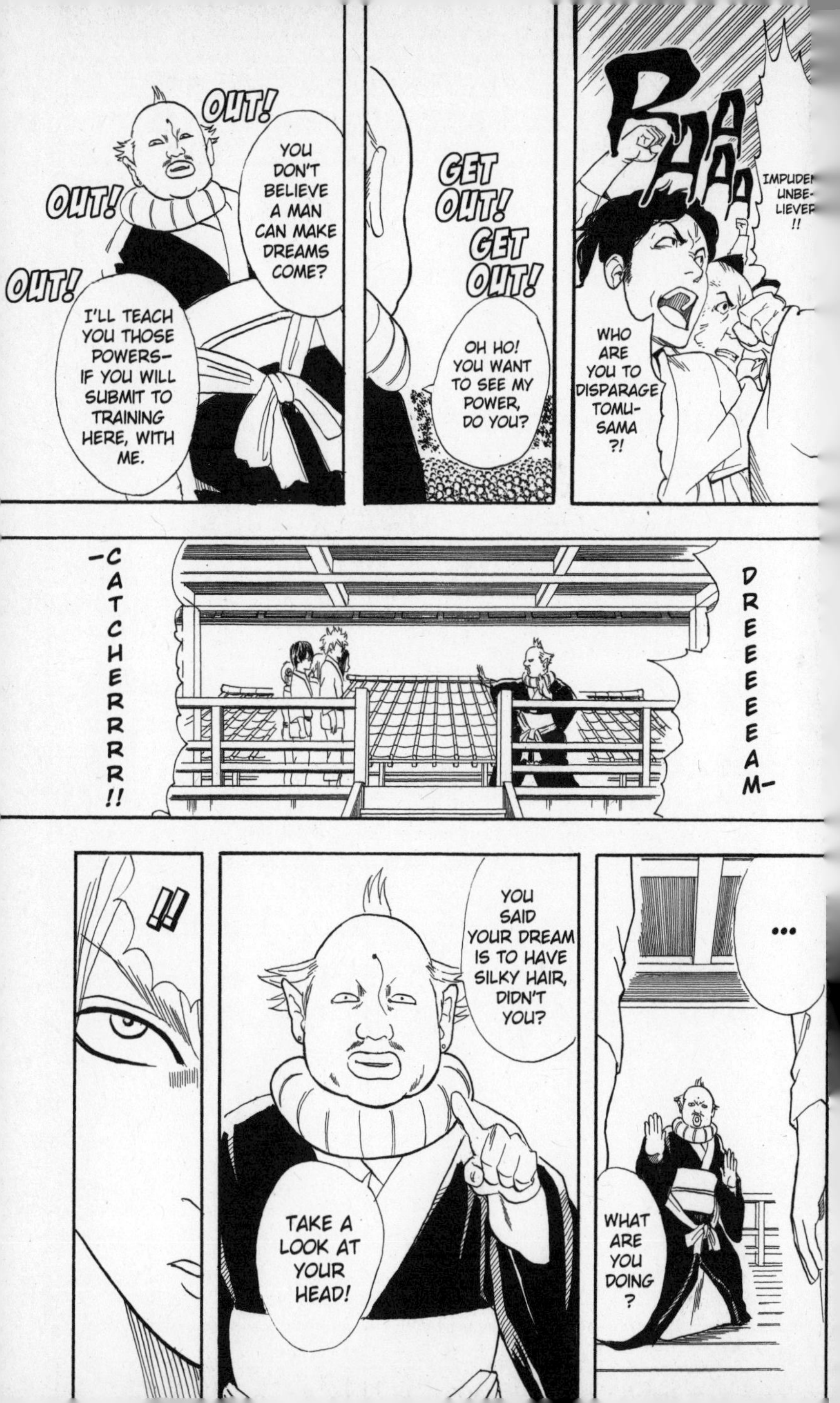
IMPUDEN UNBE-LIEVER !!
WHO ARE YOU TO DISPARAGE TOMU-SAMA ?!
GET OUT! GET OUT!
OH HO! YOU WANT TO SEE MY POWER, DO YOU?
OUT!
OUT!
YOU DON'T BELIEVE A MAN CAN MAKE DREAMS COME?
OUT!
I'LL TEACH YOU THOSE POWERS— IF YOU WILL SUBMIT TO TRAINING HERE, WITH ME.
DREEEEEEAM—
—CATCHERRRR!!
...
WHAT ARE YOU DOING?
YOU SAID YOUR DREAM IS TO HAVE SILKY HAIR, DIDN'T YOU?
TAKE A LOOK AT YOUR HEAD!
!!

Sorachi's Q&A Corner

<From T2 — Gunma Prefecture>

Your answers are too long! They're hard to read! Write whatever you want, Sensei, but keep it short, okay? (And give more space to Yamazaki!)

Of course I wrote this guy a really long reply...
So how was Volume 6? I feel like I laid my ass on the line with this one—so I'd be real happy if you took it like, "Wow, I can see a manga artist's butt for $7.99! What a great deal!"
You don't get to see those things every day, you know!

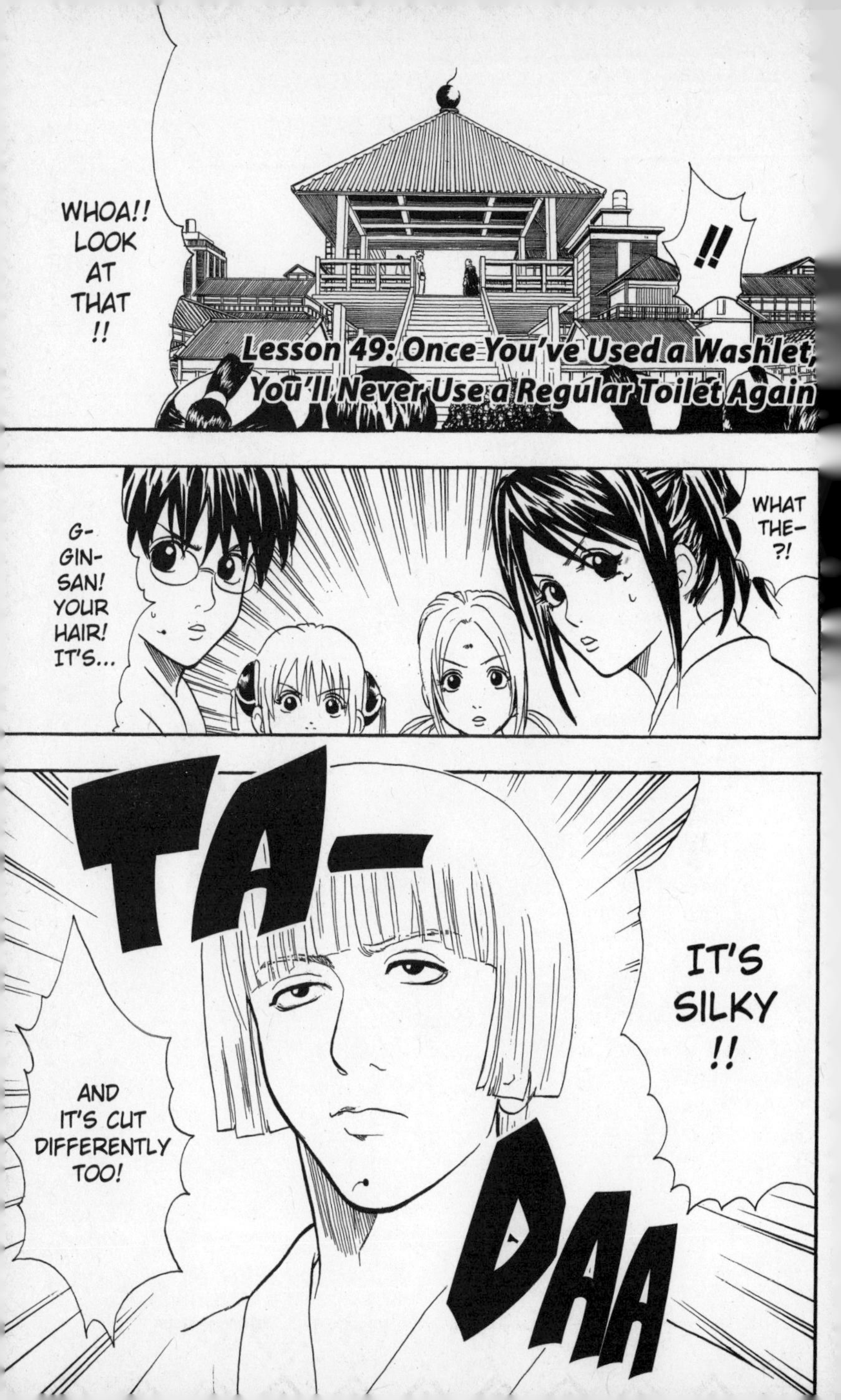
!!
WHOA!! LOOK AT THAT!!
Lesson 49: Once You've Used a Washlet, You'll Never Use a Regular Toilet Again
WHAT THE-?!
G-GIN-SAN! YOUR HAIR! IT'S...
IT'S SILKY!!
TA-DAA
AND IT'S CUT DIFFERENTLY TOO!

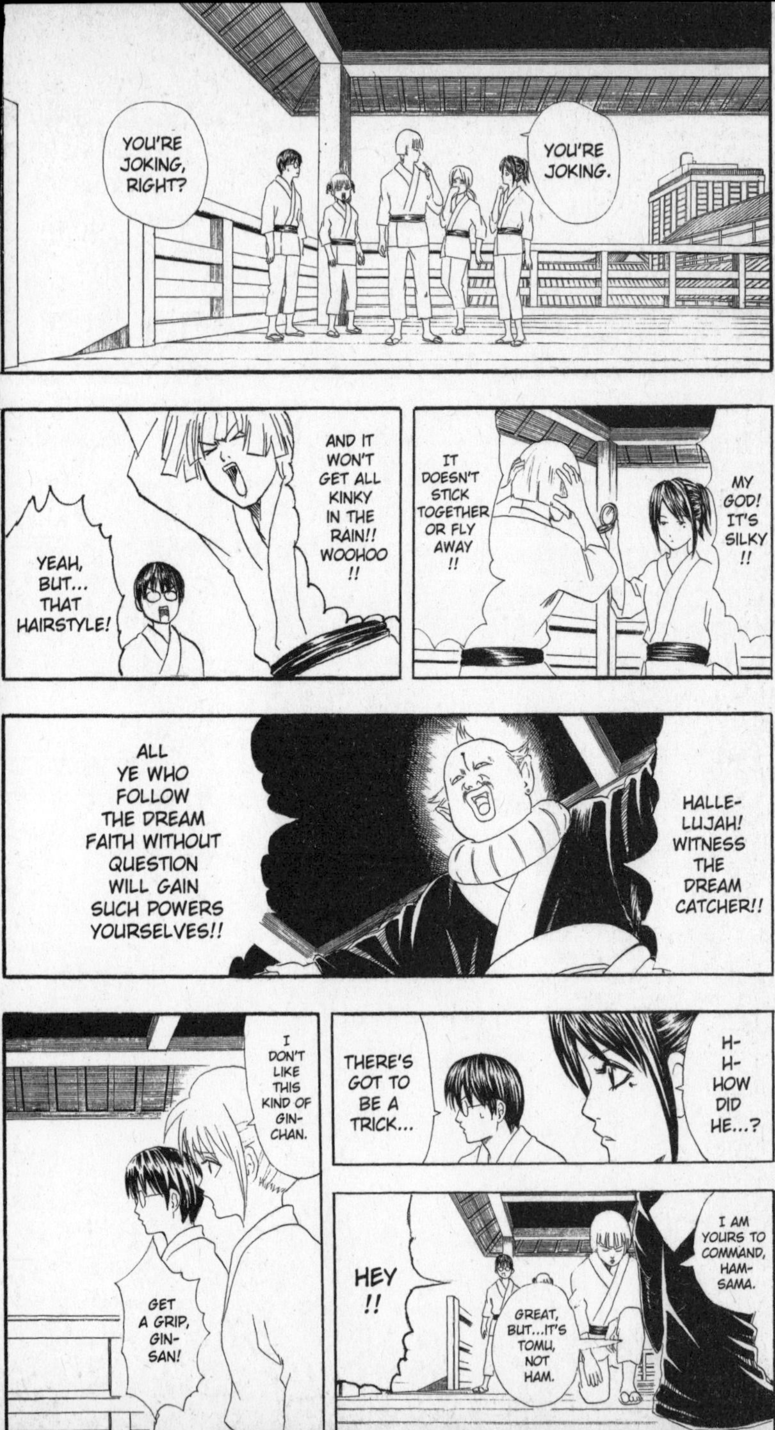

YOU'RE JOKING.
YOU'RE JOKING, RIGHT?
MY GOD! IT'S SILKY!!
IT DOESN'T STICK TOGETHER OR FLY AWAY!!
AND IT WON'T GET ALL KINKY IN THE RAIN!! WOOHOO!!
YEAH, BUT... THAT HAIRSTYLE!
HALLE-LUJAH! WITNESS THE DREAM CATCHER!!
ALL YE WHO FOLLOW THE DREAM FAITH WITHOUT QUESTION WILL GAIN SUCH POWERS YOURSELVES!!
H-H-HOW DID HE...?
THERE'S GOT TO BE A TRICK...
I AM YOURS TO COMMAND, HAM-SAMA.
GREAT, BUT...IT'S TOMU, NOT HAM.
HEY!!
I DON'T LIKE THIS KIND OF GIN-CHAN.
GET A GRIP, GIN-SAN!

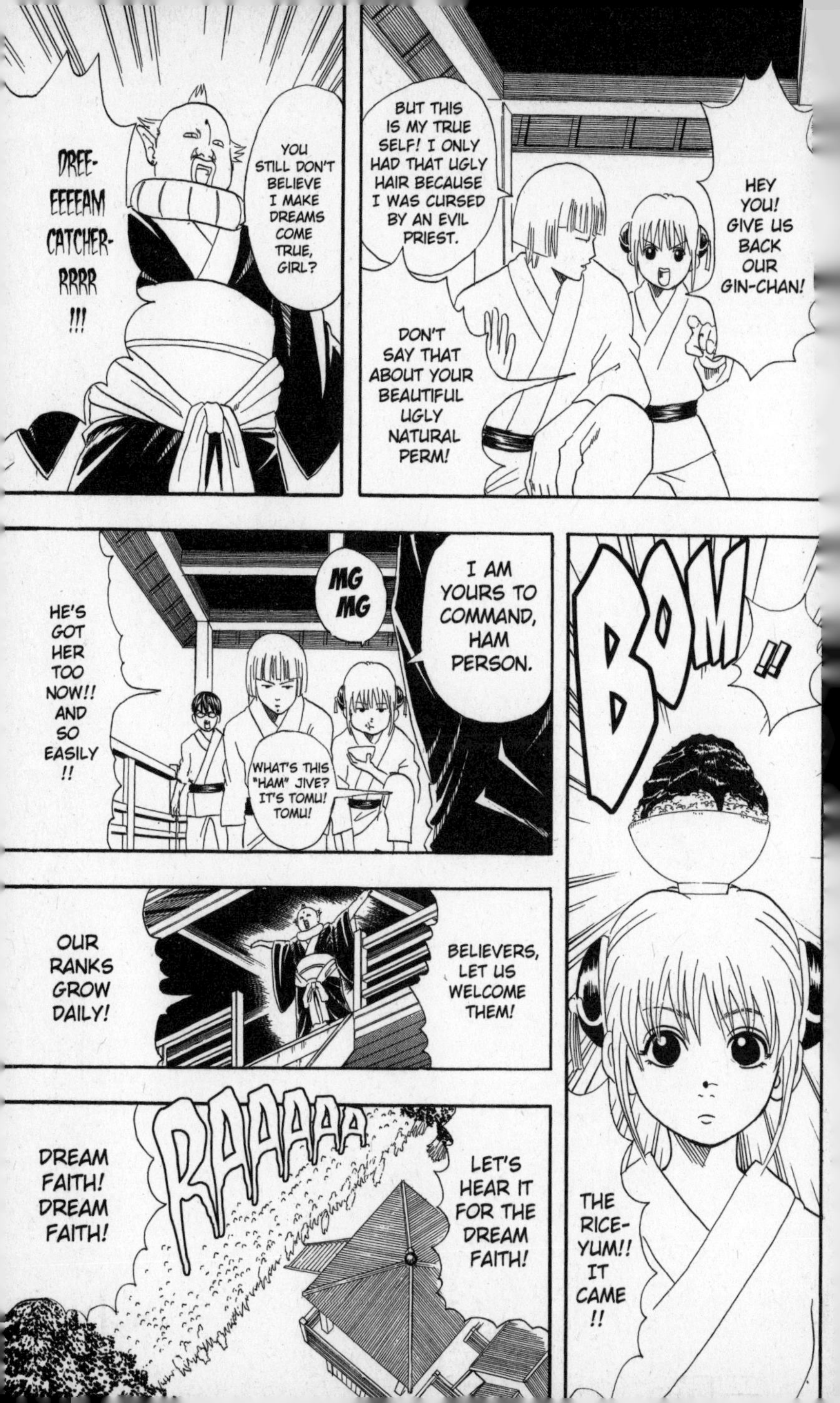
HEY YOU! GIVE US BACK OUR GIN-CHAN!
BUT THIS IS MY TRUE SELF! I ONLY HAD THAT UGLY HAIR BECAUSE I WAS CURSED BY AN EVIL PRIEST.
DON'T SAY THAT ABOUT YOUR BEAUTIFUL UGLY NATURAL PERM!
YOU STILL DON'T BELIEVE I MAKE DREAMS COME TRUE, GIRL?
DREE-EEEEAM CATCHER-RRRR!!!
BOM!!
THE RICE-YUM!! IT CAME!!
I AM YOURS TO COMMAND, HAM PERSON.
MG MG
WHAT'S THIS "HAM" JIVE? IT'S TOMU! TOMU!
HE'S GOT HER TOO NOW!! AND SO EASILY!!
BELIEVERS, LET US WELCOME THEM!
OUR RANKS GROW DAILY!
LET'S HEAR IT FOR THE DREAM FAITH!
RAAAAA
DREAM FAITH! DREAM FAITH!

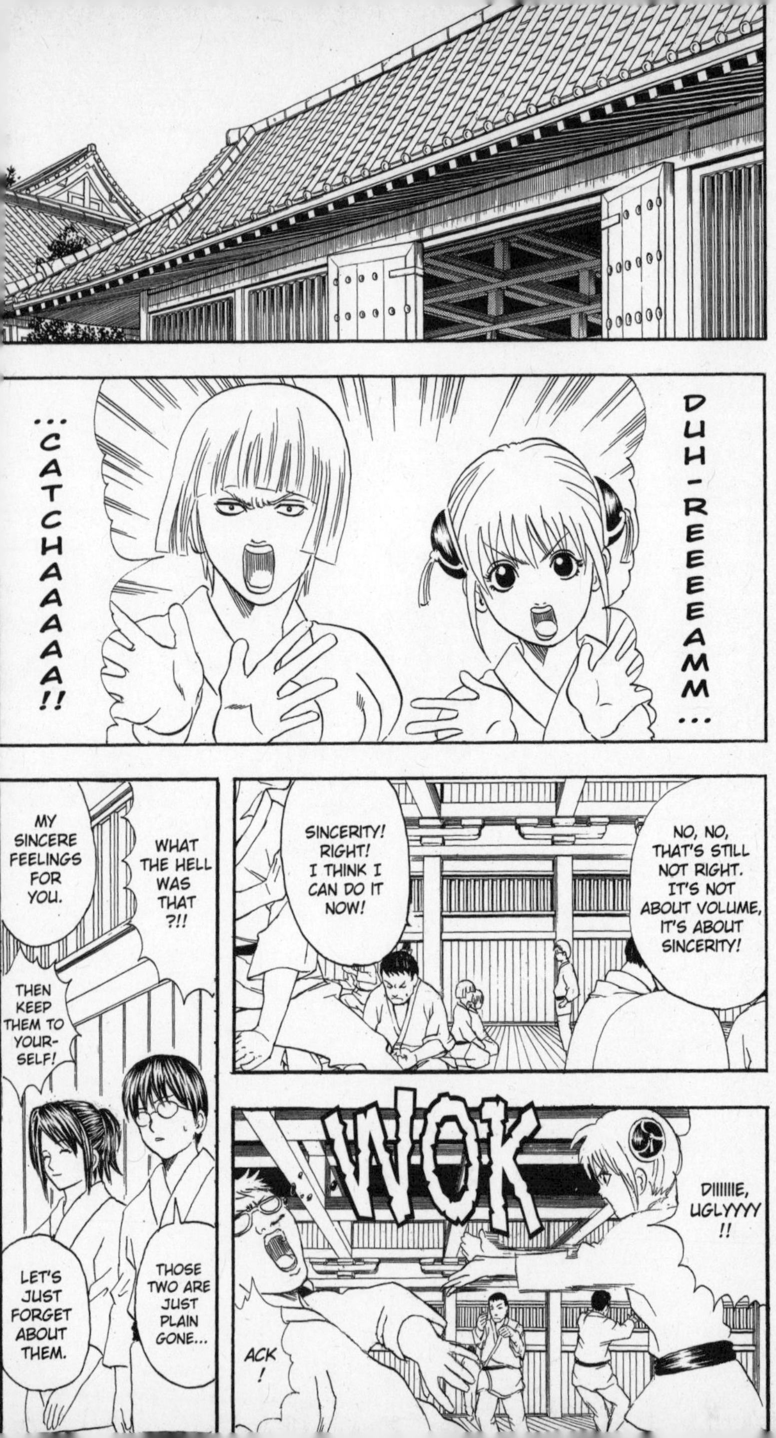
DUH-REEEEAMM...
...CATCHAAAAAAA!!
NO, NO, THAT'S STILL NOT RIGHT. IT'S NOT ABOUT VOLUME, IT'S ABOUT SINCERITY!
SINCERITY! RIGHT! I THINK I CAN DO IT NOW!
WOK
DIIIIIE, UGLYYYY!!
ACK!
WHAT THE HELL WAS THAT?!!
MY SINCERE FEELINGS FOR YOU.
THEN KEEP THEM TO YOUR-SELF!
THOSE TWO ARE JUST PLAIN GONE...
LET'S JUST FORGET ABOUT THEM.

READ THIS WAY

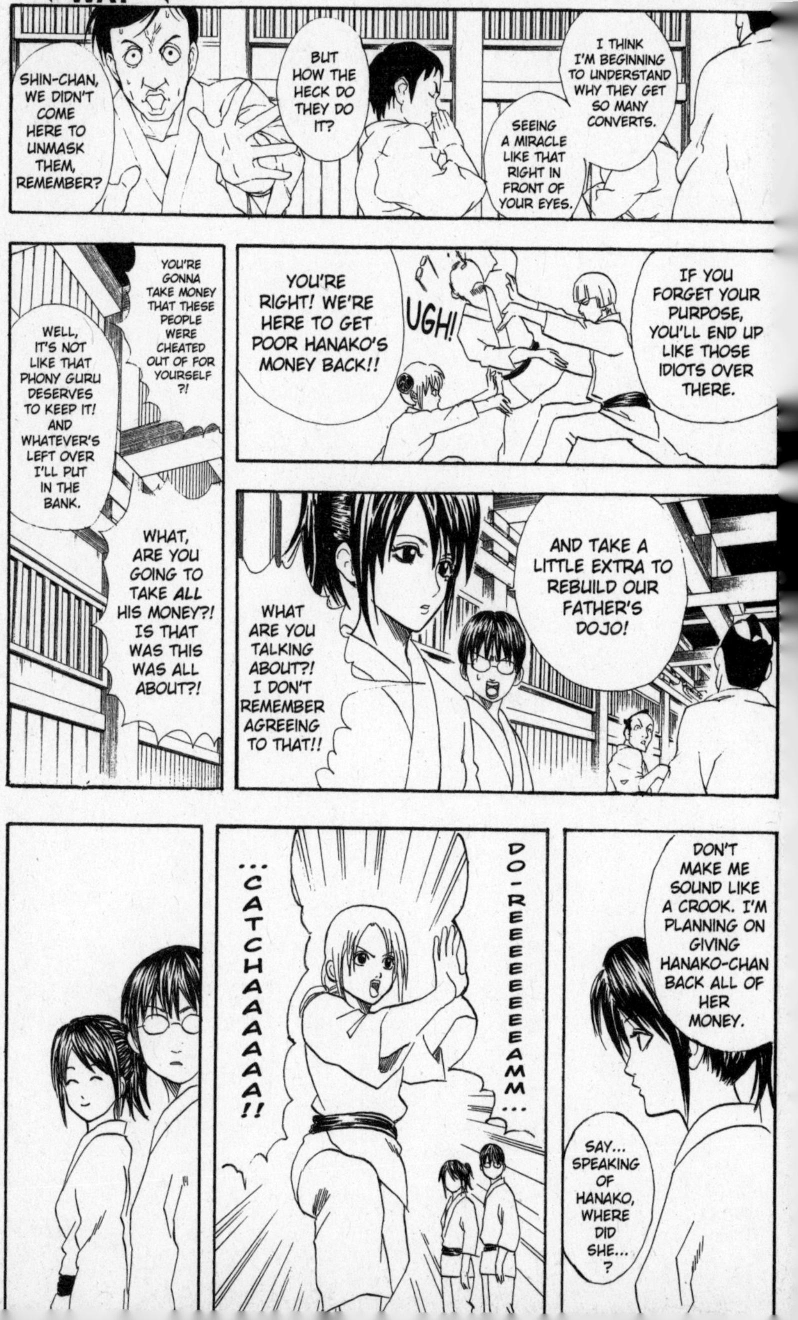
I THINK I'M BEGINNING TO UNDERSTAND WHY THEY GET SO MANY CONVERTS.
SEEING A MIRACLE LIKE THAT RIGHT IN FRONT OF YOUR EYES.
BUT HOW THE HECK DO THEY DO IT?
SHIN-CHAN, WE DIDN'T COME HERE TO UNMASK THEM, REMEMBER?
IF YOU FORGET YOUR PURPOSE, YOU'LL END UP LIKE THOSE IDIOTS OVER THERE.
UGH!
YOU'RE RIGHT! WE'RE HERE TO GET POOR HANAKO'S MONEY BACK!!
AND TAKE A LITTLE EXTRA TO REBUILD OUR FATHER'S DOJO!
WHAT ARE YOU TALKING ABOUT?! I DON'T REMEMBER AGREEING TO THAT!!
YOU'RE GONNA TAKE MONEY THAT THESE PEOPLE WERE CHEATED OUT OF FOR YOURSELF ?!
WELL, IT'S NOT LIKE THAT PHONY GURU DESERVES TO KEEP IT! AND WHATEVER'S LEFT OVER I'LL PUT IN THE BANK.
WHAT, ARE YOU GOING TO TAKE ALL HIS MONEY?! IS THAT WAS THIS WAS ALL ABOUT?!
DON'T MAKE ME SOUND LIKE A CROOK. I'M PLANNING ON GIVING HANAKO-CHAN BACK ALL OF HER MONEY.
SAY... SPEAKING OF HANAKO, WHERE DID SHE... ?
DO-REEEEEEEEEAMM...
...CATCHAAAAAAAA!!

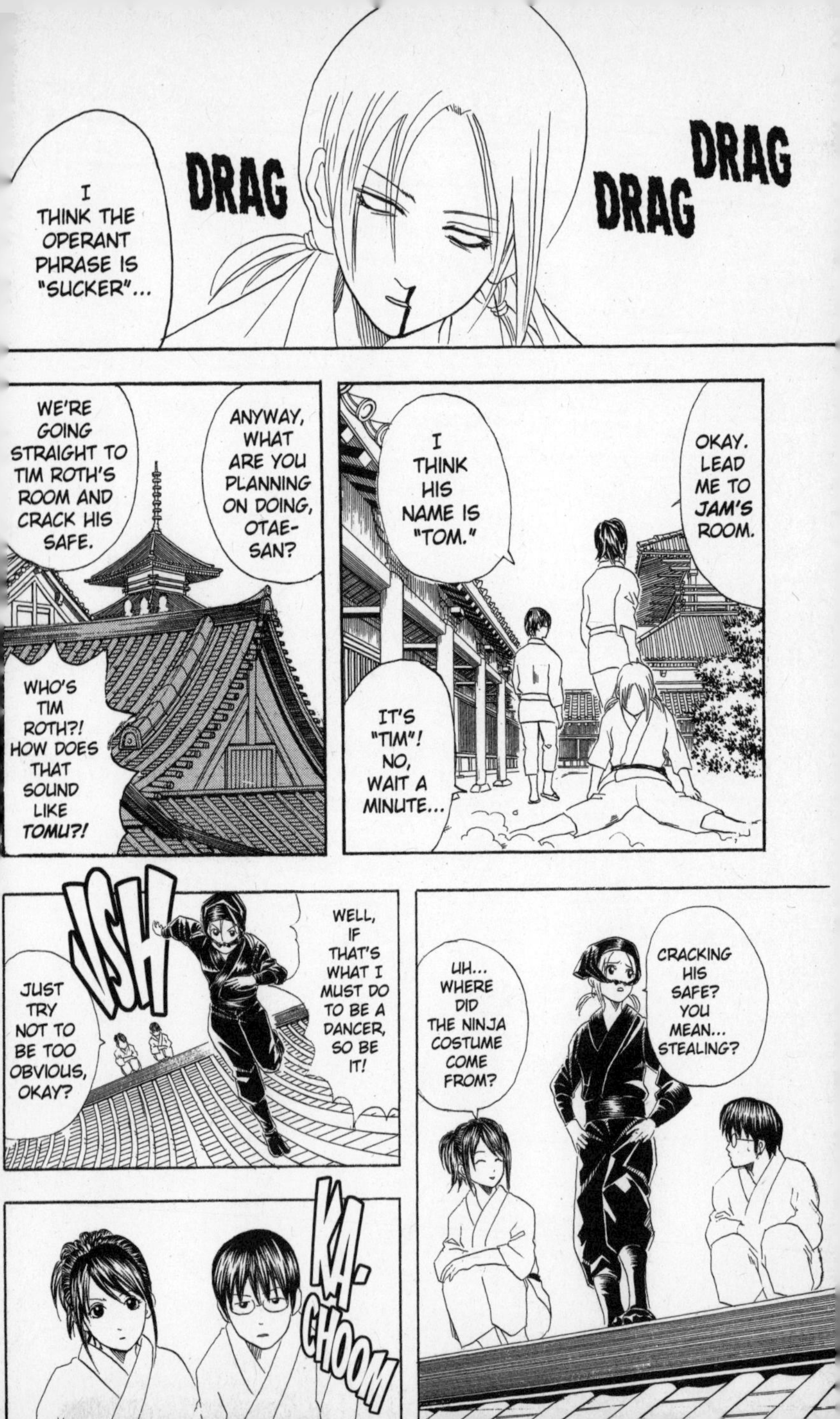
DRAG
DRAG
DRAG
I THINK THE OPERANT PHRASE IS "SUCKER"...
OKAY. LEAD ME TO JAM'S ROOM.
I THINK HIS NAME IS "TOM."
IT'S "TIM"! NO, WAIT A MINUTE...
ANYWAY, WHAT ARE YOU PLANNING ON DOING, OTAE-SAN?
WE'RE GOING STRAIGHT TO TIM ROTH'S ROOM AND CRACK HIS SAFE.
WHO'S TIM ROTH?! HOW DOES THAT SOUND LIKE TOMU?!
CRACKING HIS SAFE? YOU MEAN... STEALING?
UH... WHERE DID THE NINJA COSTUME COME FROM?
WELL, IF THAT'S WHAT I MUST DO TO BE A DANCER, SO BE IT!
VSH
JUST TRY NOT TO BE TOO OBVIOUS, OKAY?
KA-CHOOM

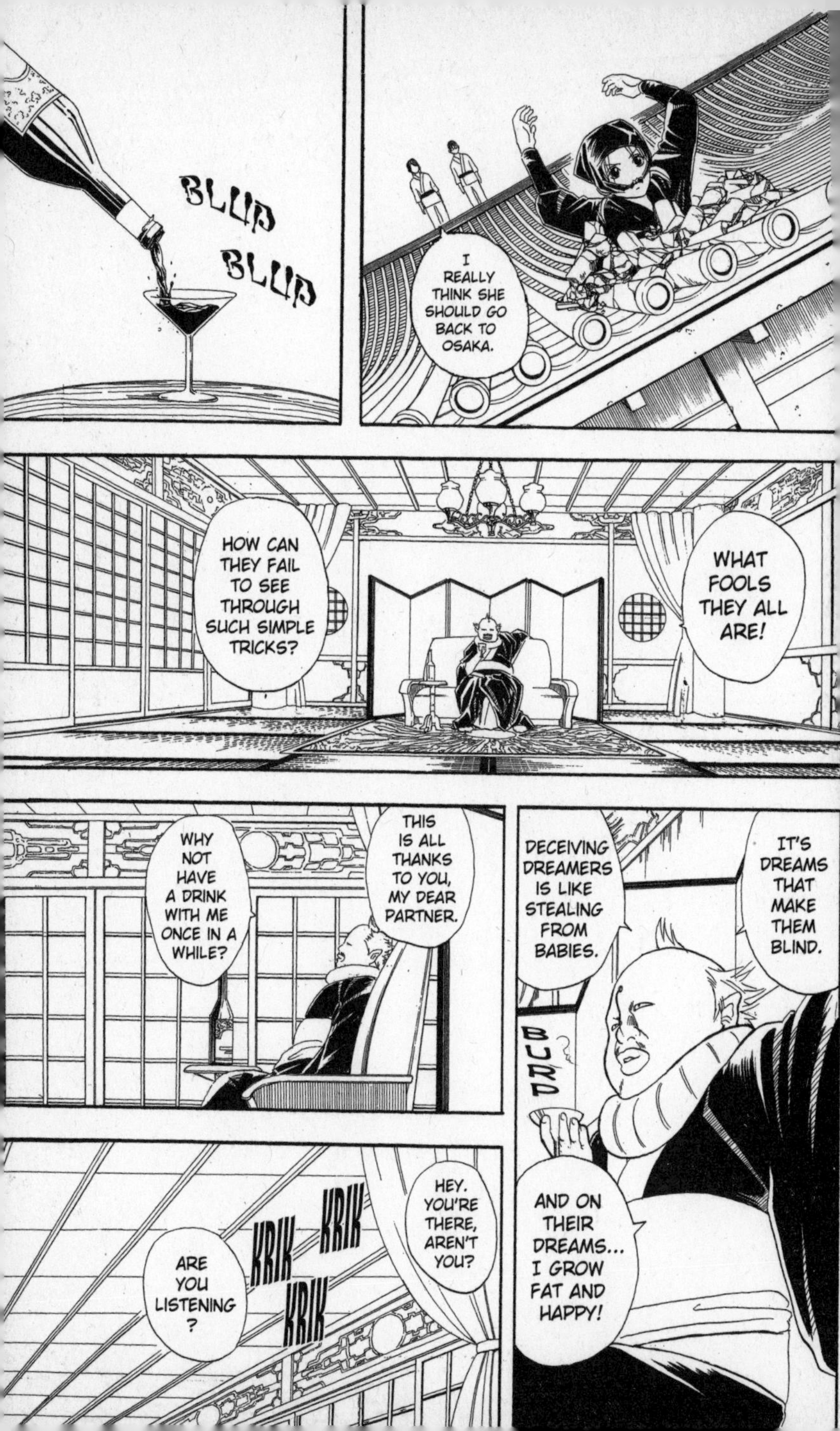

I REALLY THINK SHE SHOULD GO BACK TO OSAKA.
BLUP
BLUP
WHAT FOOLS THEY ALL ARE!
HOW CAN THEY FAIL TO SEE THROUGH SUCH SIMPLE TRICKS?
IT'S DREAMS THAT MAKE THEM BLIND.
DECEIVING DREAMERS IS LIKE STEALING FROM BABIES.
BURP
AND ON THEIR DREAMS... I GROW FAT AND HAPPY!
THIS IS ALL THANKS TO YOU, MY DEAR PARTNER.
WHY NOT HAVE A DRINK WITH ME ONCE IN A WHILE?
HEY. YOU'RE THERE, AREN'T YOU?
KRIK
KRIK
KRIK
ARE YOU LISTENING?

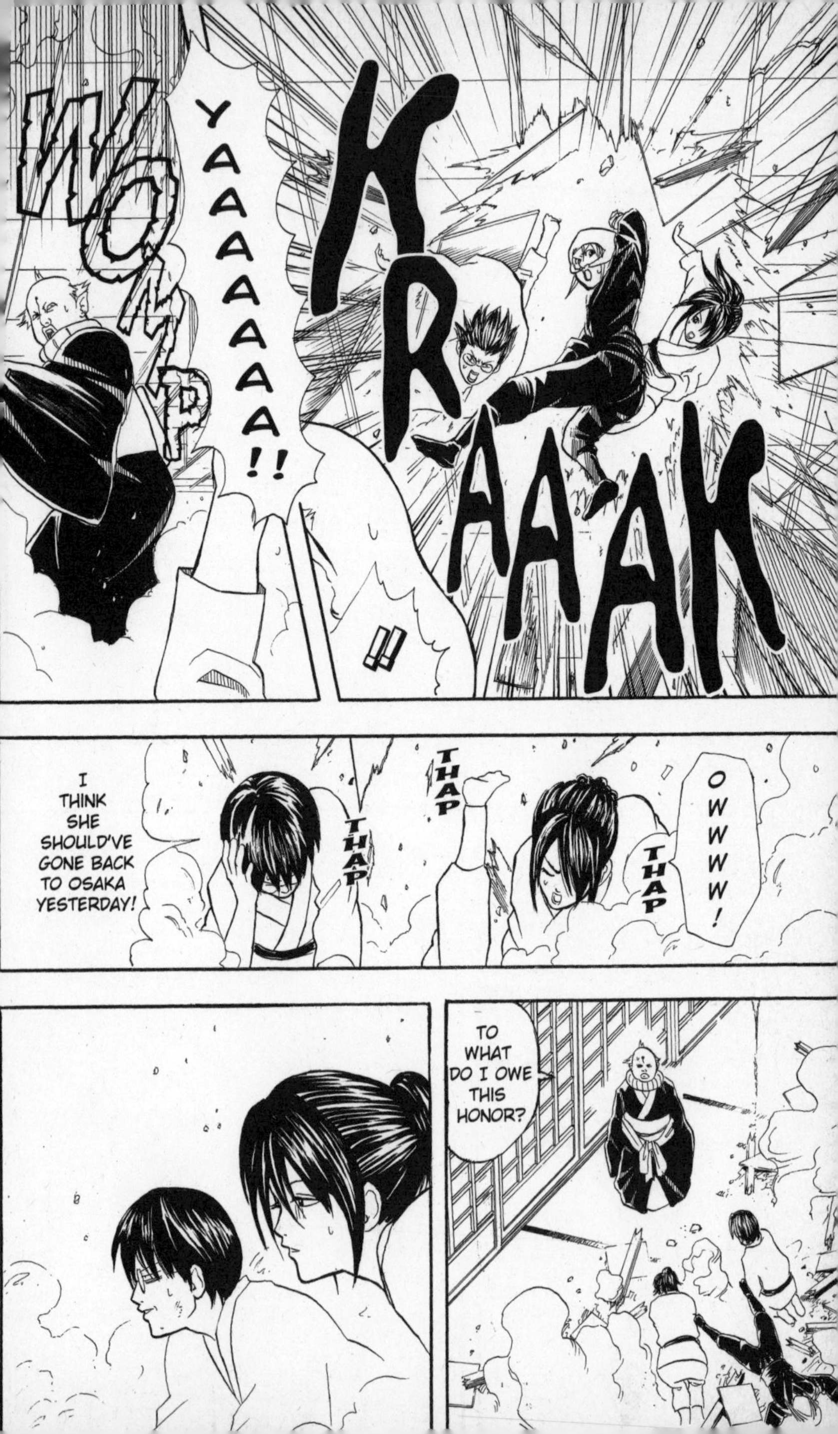
KRAAAK
!!
YAAAAAAA!!
WOMP
OWWWW!
THAP
THAP
THAP
I THINK SHE SHOULD'VE GONE BACK TO OSAKA YESTERDAY!
TO WHAT DO I OWE THIS HONOR?

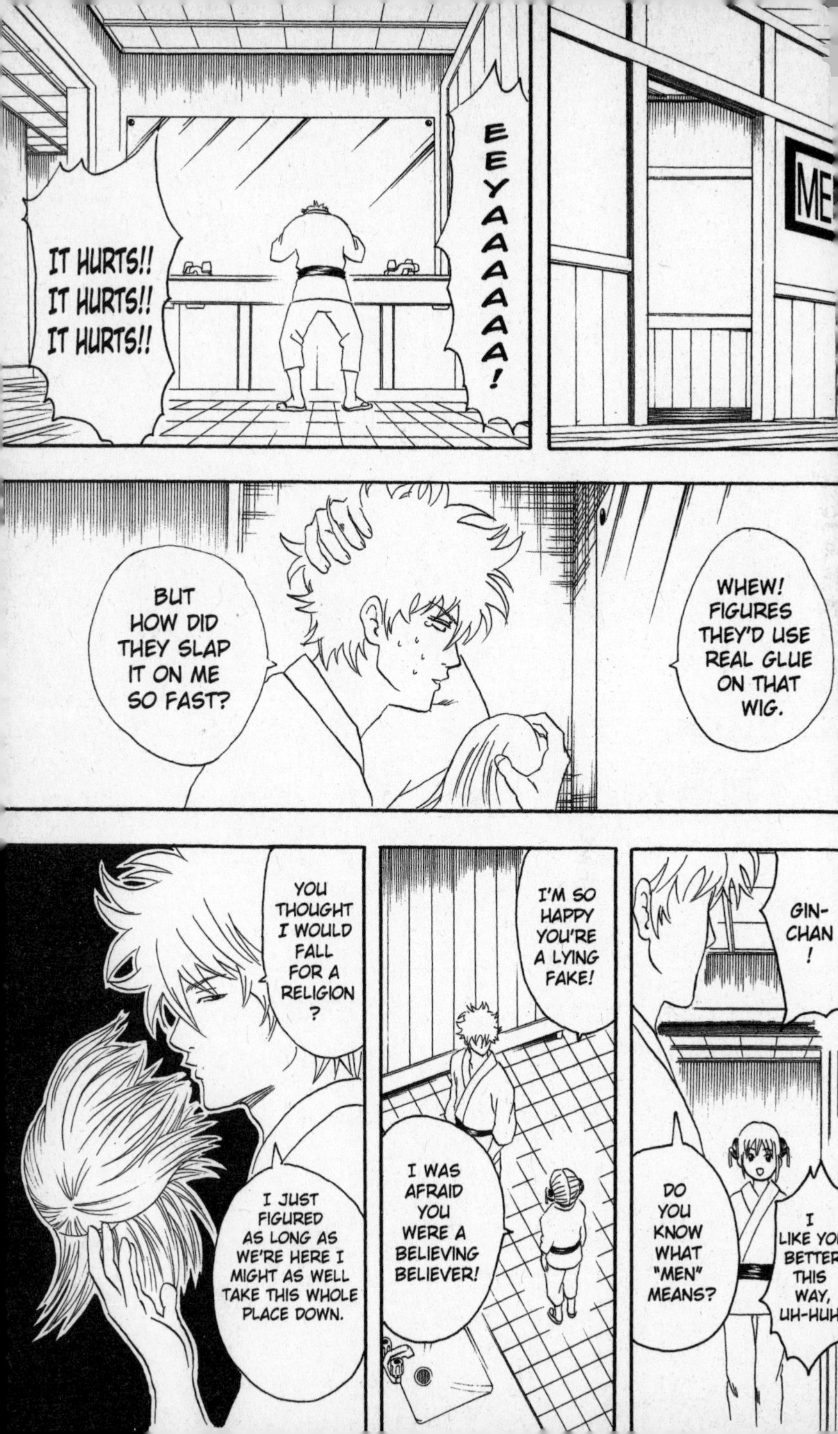
ME
EEYAAAAAAAA!
IT HURTS!! IT HURTS!! IT HURTS!!
WHEW! FIGURES THEY'D USE REAL GLUE ON THAT WIG.
BUT HOW DID THEY SLAP IT ON ME SO FAST?
GIN-CHAN!
I LIKE YOU BETTER THIS WAY, UH-HUH!
DO YOU KNOW WHAT "MEN" MEANS?
I'M SO HAPPY YOU'RE A LYING FAKE!
I WAS AFRAID YOU WERE A BELIEVING BELIEVER!
YOU THOUGHT I WOULD FALL FOR A RELIGION?
I JUST FIGURED AS LONG AS WE'RE HERE I MIGHT AS WELL TAKE THIS WHOLE PLACE DOWN.

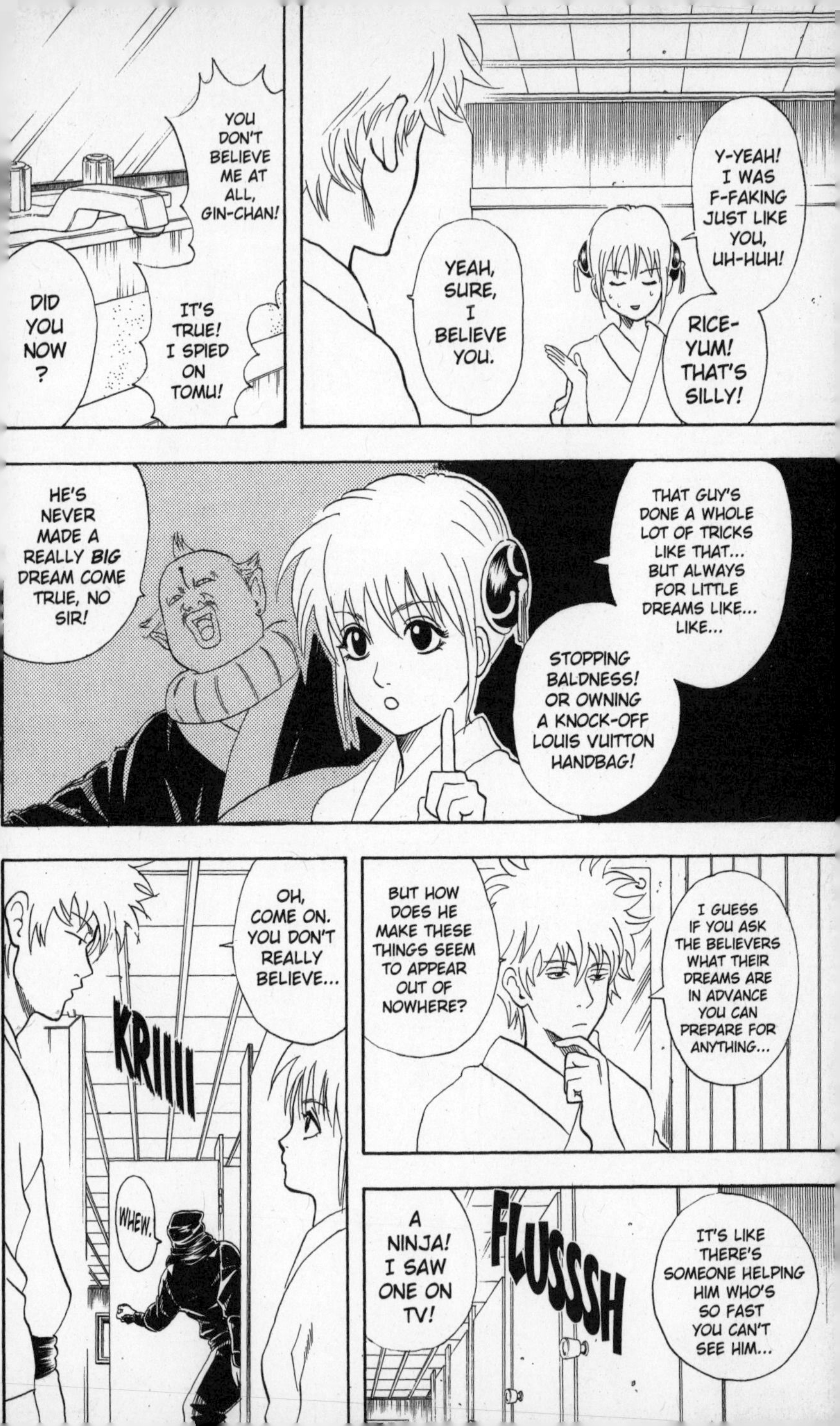
Y-YEAH! I WAS F-FAKING JUST LIKE YOU, UH-HUH!
YEAH, SURE, I BELIEVE YOU.
RICE-YUM! THAT'S SILLY!
YOU DON'T BELIEVE ME AT ALL, GIN-CHAN!
IT'S TRUE! I SPIED ON TOMU!
DID YOU NOW?
THAT GUY'S DONE A WHOLE LOT OF TRICKS LIKE THAT... BUT ALWAYS FOR LITTLE DREAMS LIKE... LIKE...
STOPPING BALDNESS! OR OWNING A KNOCK-OFF LOUIS VUITTON HANDBAG!
HE'S NEVER MADE A REALLY BIG DREAM COME TRUE, NO SIR!
I GUESS IF YOU ASK THE BELIEVERS WHAT THEIR DREAMS ARE IN ADVANCE YOU CAN PREPARE FOR ANYTHING...
BUT HOW DOES HE MAKE THESE THINGS SEEM TO APPEAR OUT OF NOWHERE?
IT'S LIKE THERE'S SOMEONE HELPING HIM WHO'S SO FAST YOU CAN'T SEE HIM...
FLUSSSH
A NINJA! I SAW ONE ON TV!
OH, COME ON. YOU DON'T REALLY BELIEVE...
KRIIII
WHEW.

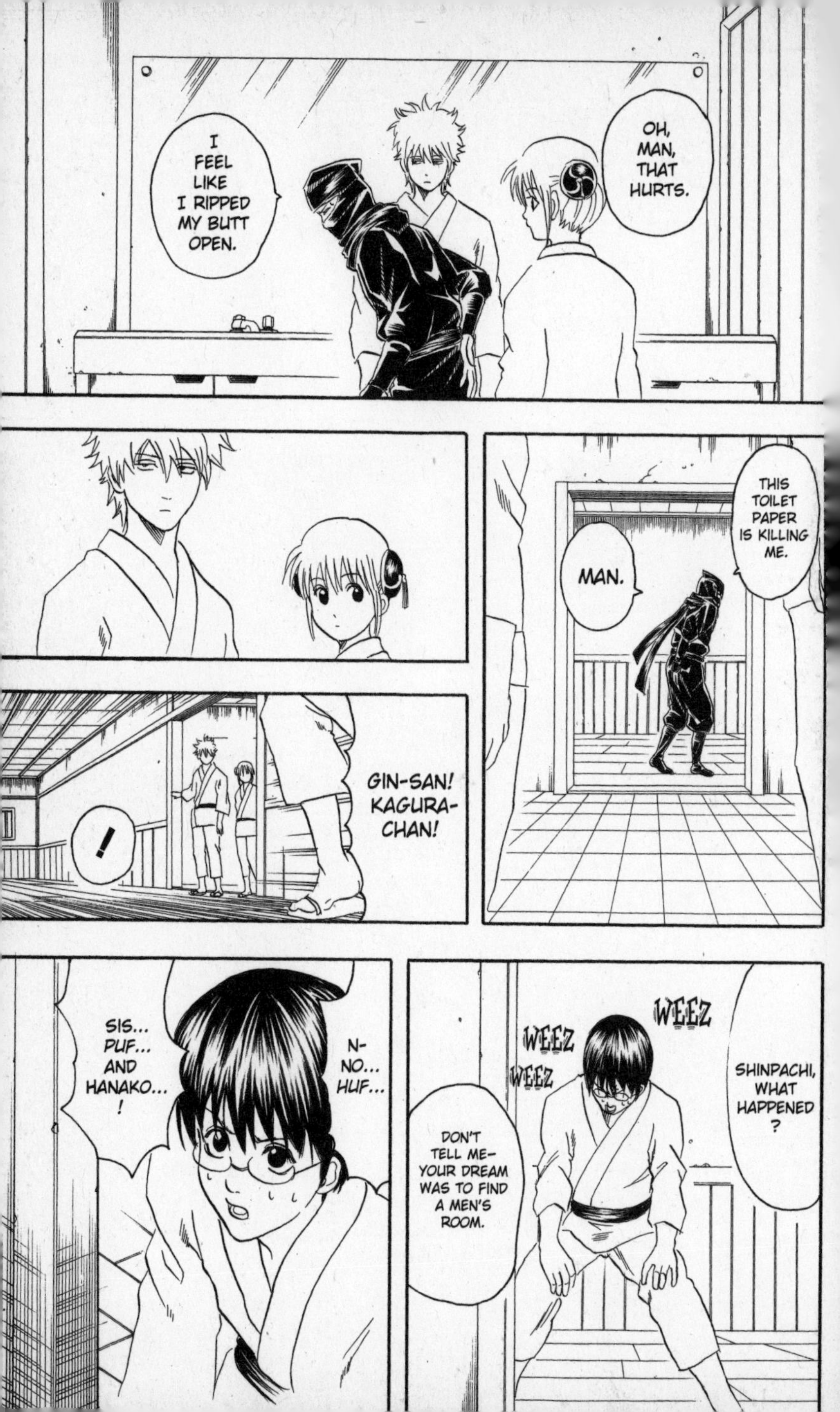
OH, MAN, THAT HURTS.
I FEEL LIKE I RIPPED MY BUTT OPEN.
THIS TOILET PAPER IS KILLING ME.
MAN.
GIN-SAN! KAGURA-CHAN!
!
SHINPACHI, WHAT HAPPENED?
WEEZ
WEEZ
WEEZ
DON'T TELL ME- YOUR DREAM WAS TO FIND A MEN'S ROOM.
N- NO... HUF...
SIS... PUF... AND HANAKO... !

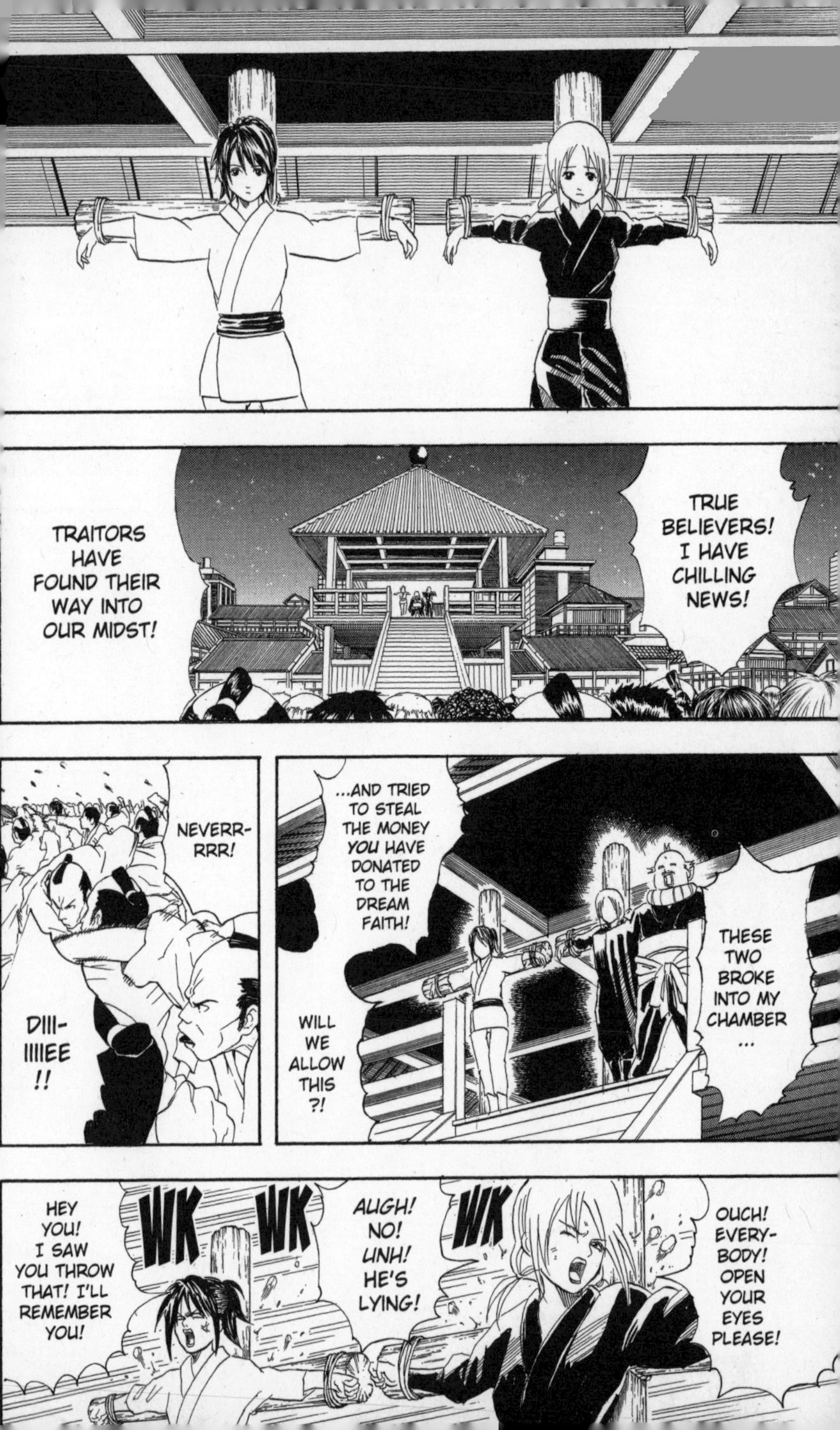
TRUE BELIEVERS! I HAVE CHILLING NEWS!
TRAITORS HAVE FOUND THEIR WAY INTO OUR MIDST!
THESE TWO BROKE INTO MY CHAMBER ...
...AND TRIED TO STEAL THE MONEY YOU HAVE DONATED TO THE DREAM FAITH!
WILL WE ALLOW THIS ?!
NEVERR-RRR!
DIII-IIIIEE !!
OUCH! EVERY-BODY! OPEN YOUR EYES PLEASE!
WK
AUGH! NO! UNH! HE'S LYING!
WK
WK
HEY YOU! I SAW YOU THROW THAT! I'LL REMEMBER YOU!

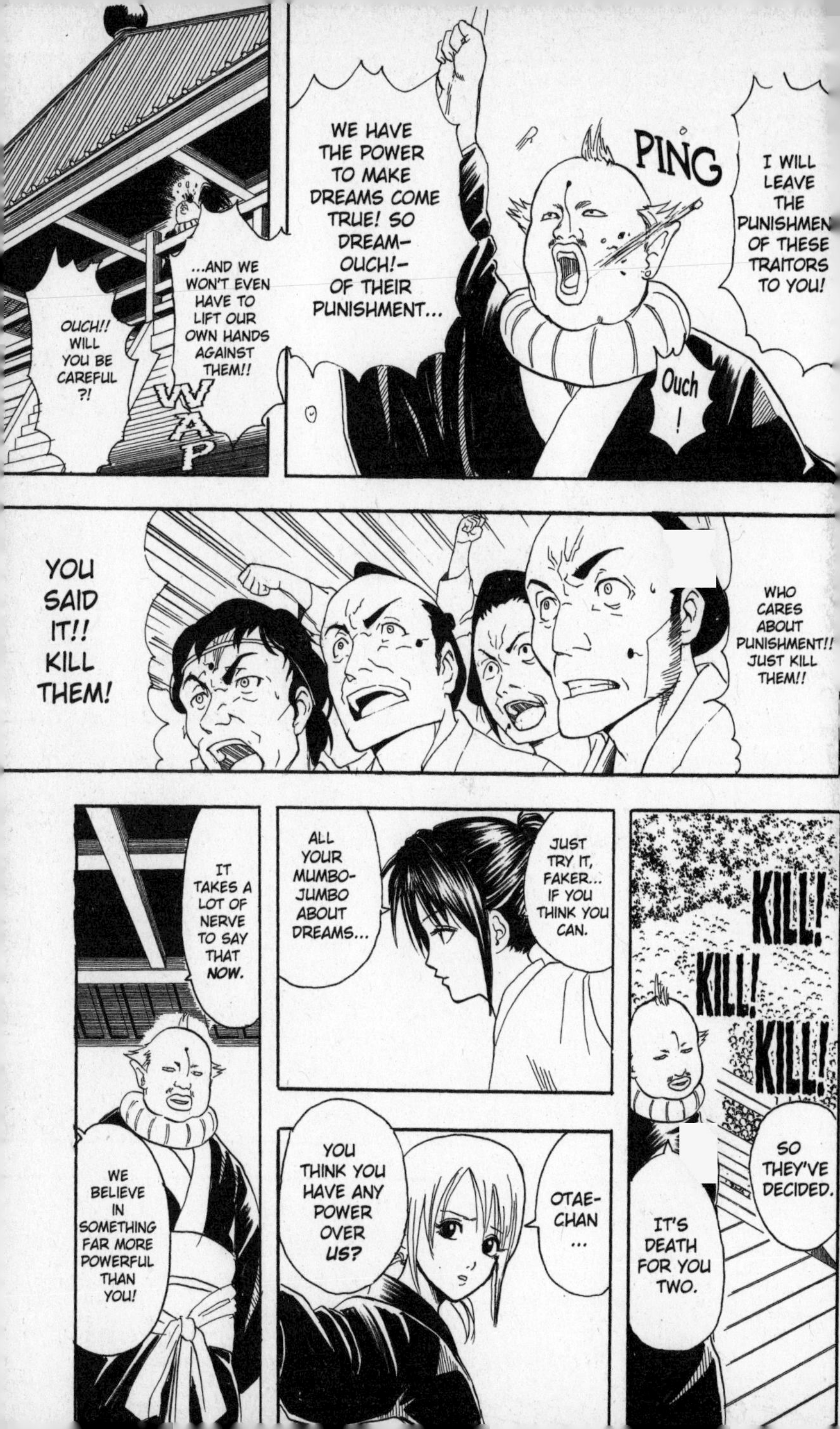
I WILL LEAVE THE PUNISHMEN OF THESE TRAITORS TO YOU!
PING
WE HAVE THE POWER TO MAKE DREAMS COME TRUE! SO DREAM–OUCH!–OF THEIR PUNISHMENT...
Ouch!
...AND WE WON'T EVEN HAVE TO LIFT OUR OWN HANDS AGAINST THEM!!
WAP
OUCH!! WILL YOU BE CAREFUL?!
WHO CARES ABOUT PUNISHMENT!! JUST KILL THEM!!
YOU SAID IT!! KILL THEM!
KILL! KILL! KILL!
SO THEY'VE DECIDED.
IT'S DEATH FOR YOU TWO.
JUST TRY IT, FAKER... IF YOU THINK YOU CAN.
ALL YOUR MUMBO-JUMBO ABOUT DREAMS...
OTAE-CHAN...
YOU THINK YOU HAVE ANY POWER OVER US?
IT TAKES A LOT OF NERVE TO SAY THAT NOW.
WE BELIEVE IN SOMETHING FAR MORE POWERFUL THAN YOU!

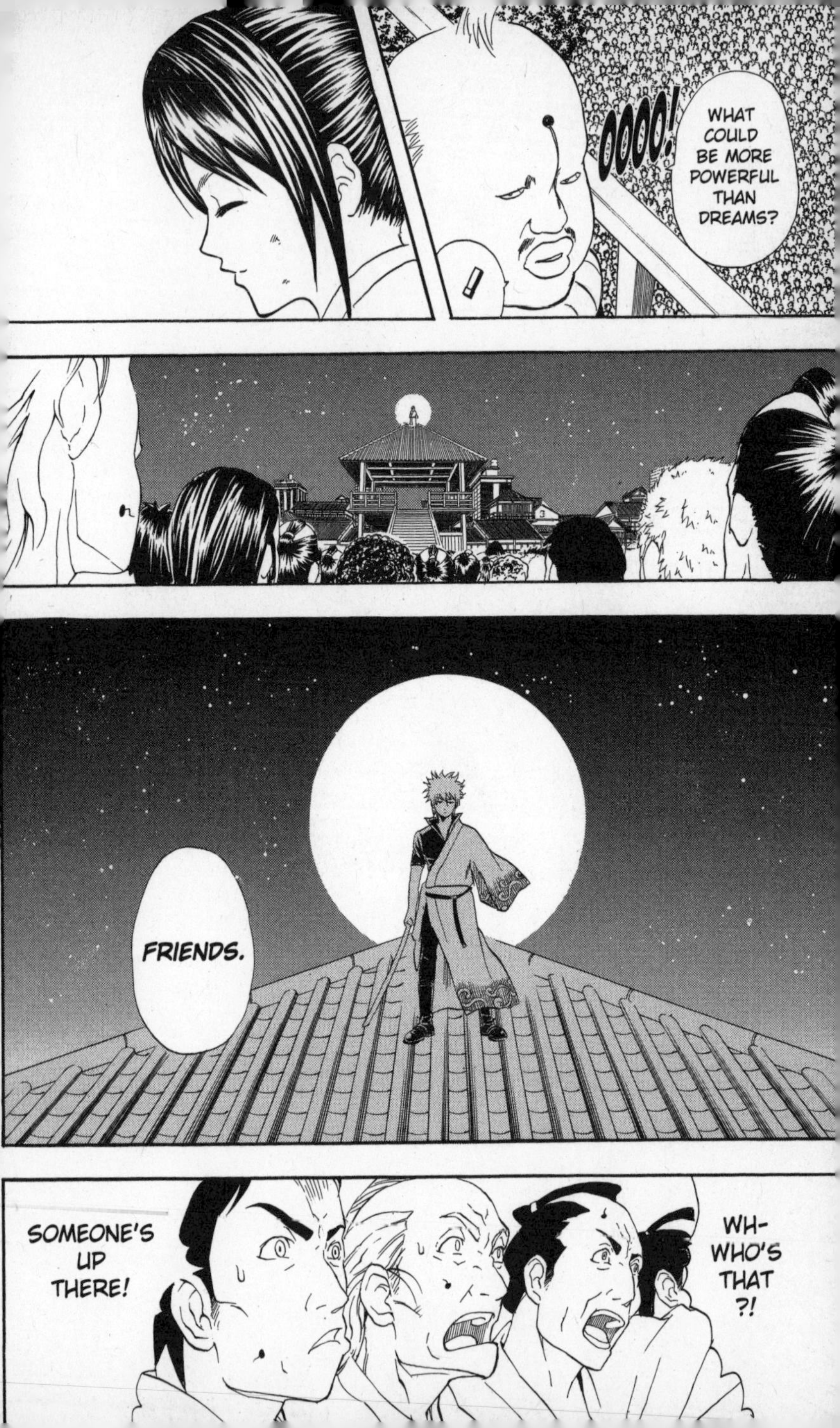
WHAT COULD BE MORE POWERFUL THAN DREAMS?
OOOO!
FRIENDS.
WH-WHO'S THAT ?!
SOMEONE'S UP THERE!

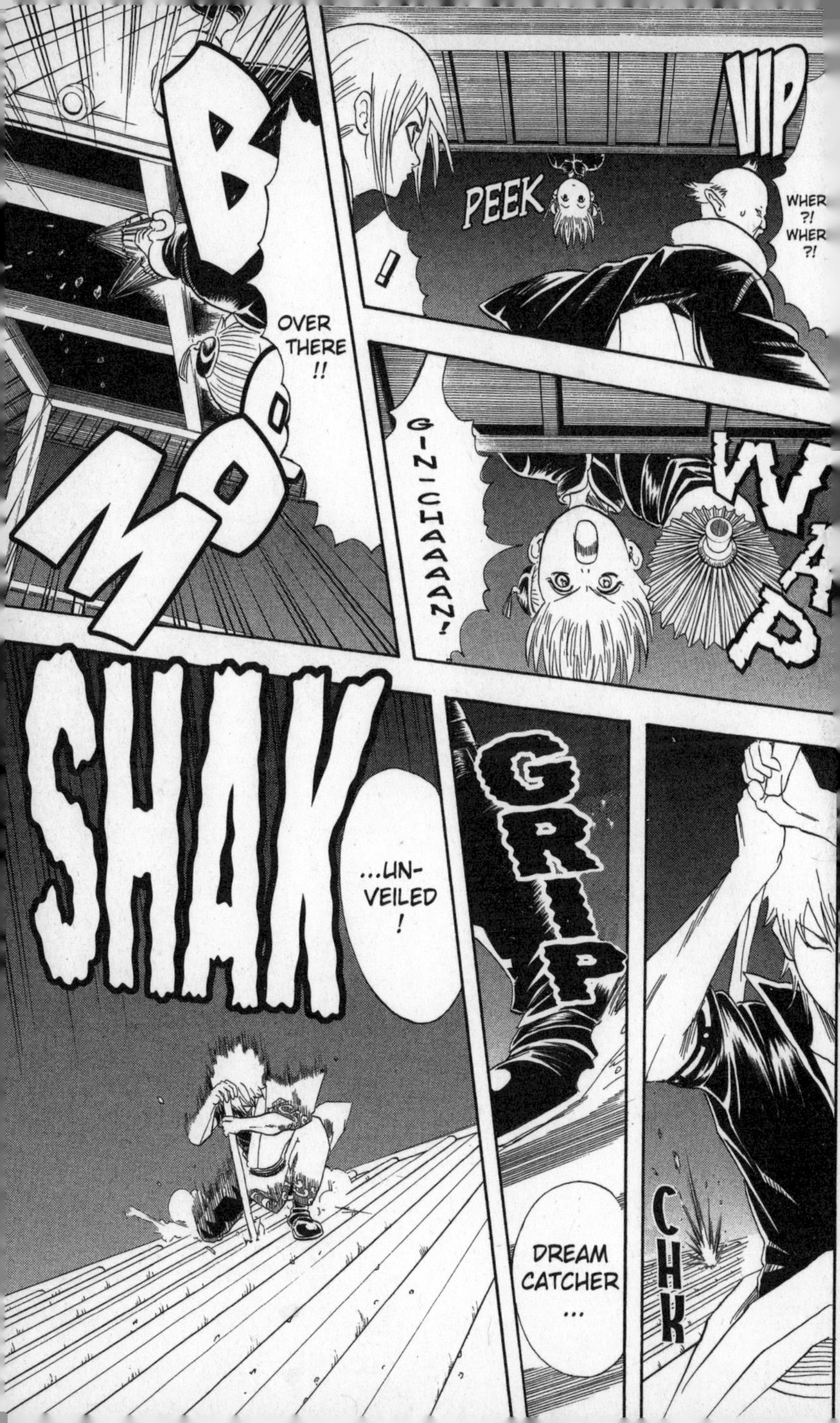

VIP
WHER?! WHER?!
PEEK
!
WAP
GIN-CHAAAAN!
OVER THERE!!
BOOM
CHK
DREAM CATCHER...
GRIP
...UN-VEILED!
SHAK

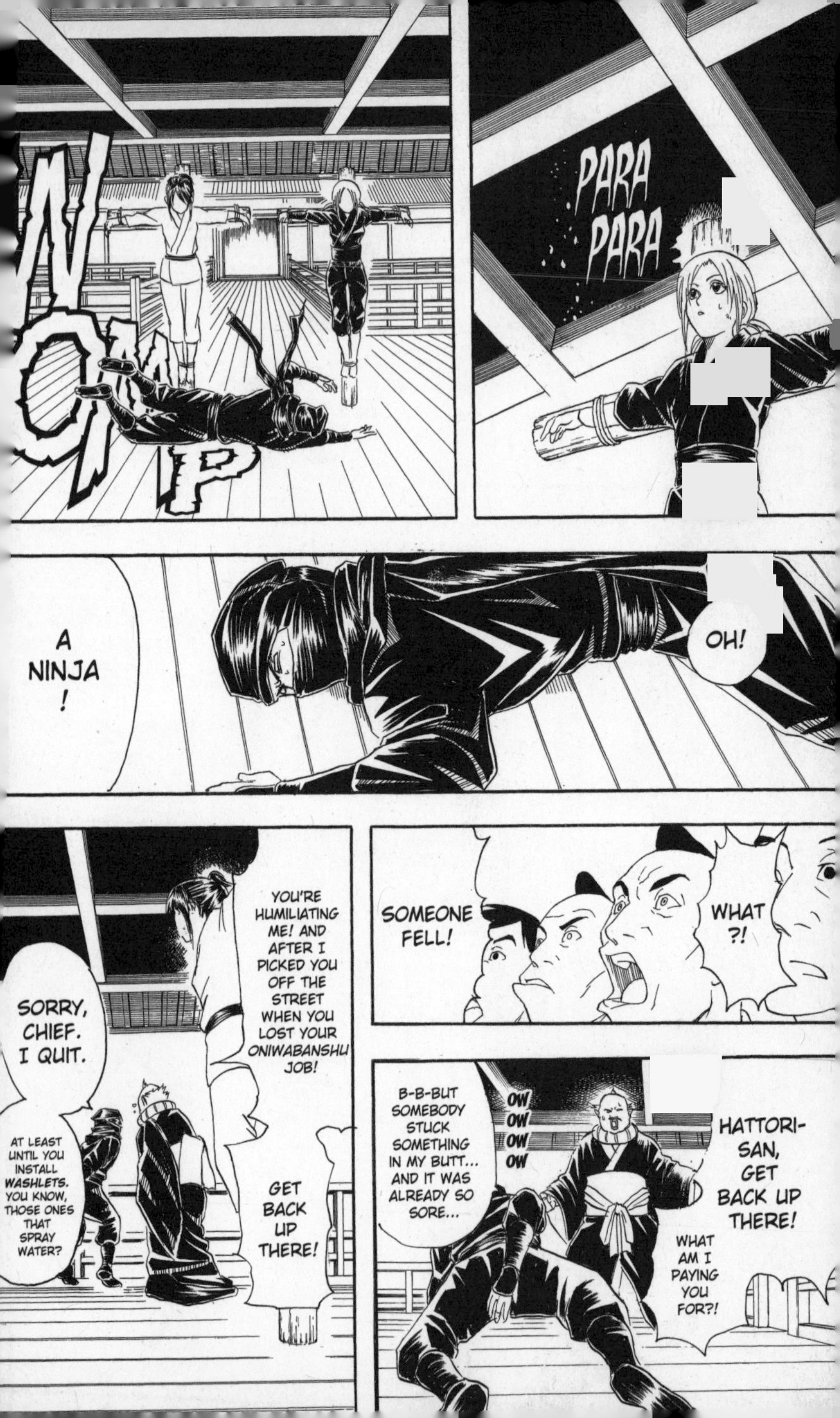

PARA PARA
OH!
A NINJA!
WHAT?!
SOMEONE FELL!
HATTORI-SAN, GET BACK UP THERE!
WHAT AM I PAYING YOU FOR?!
OW OW OW OW
B-B-BUT SOMEBODY STUCK SOMETHING IN MY BUTT... AND IT WAS ALREADY SO SORE...
YOU'RE HUMILIATING ME! AND AFTER I PICKED YOU OFF THE STREET WHEN YOU LOST YOUR ONIWABANSHU JOB!
SORRY, CHIEF. I QUIT.
GET BACK UP THERE!
AT LEAST UNTIL YOU INSTALL WASHLETS. YOU KNOW, THOSE ONES THAT SPRAY WATER?

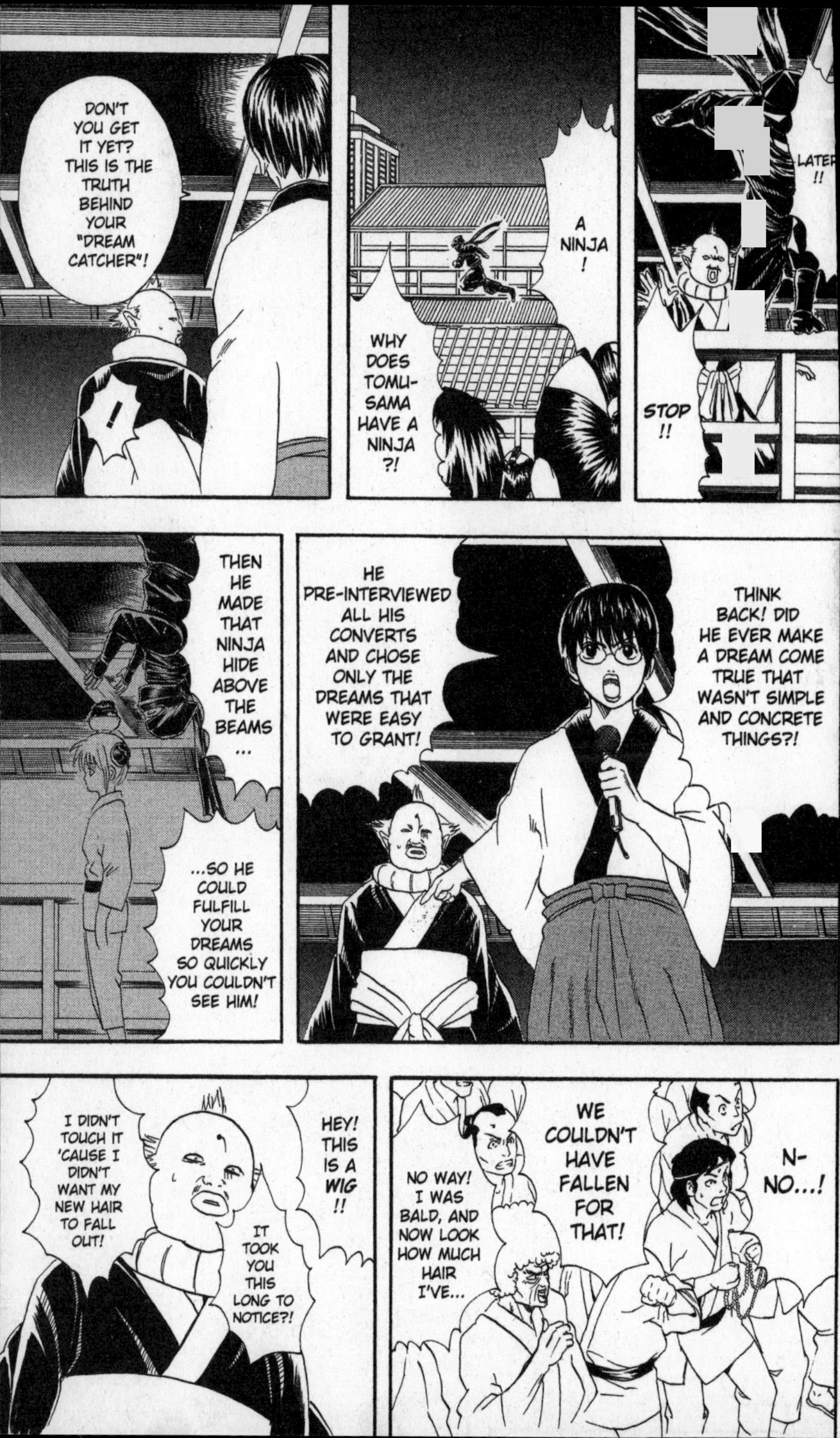
LATER !!
STOP !!
A NINJA !
WHY DOES TOMU-SAMA HAVE A NINJA ?!
DON'T YOU GET IT YET? THIS IS THE TRUTH BEHIND YOUR "DREAM CATCHER"!
!
THINK BACK! DID HE EVER MAKE A DREAM COME TRUE THAT WASN'T SIMPLE AND CONCRETE THINGS?!
HE PRE-INTERVIEWED ALL HIS CONVERTS AND CHOSE ONLY THE DREAMS THAT WERE EASY TO GRANT!
THEN HE MADE THAT NINJA HIDE ABOVE THE BEAMS ...
...SO HE COULD FULFILL YOUR DREAMS SO QUICKLY YOU COULDN'T SEE HIM!
N-NO...!
WE COULDN'T HAVE FALLEN FOR THAT!
NO WAY! I WAS BALD, AND NOW LOOK HOW MUCH HAIR I'VE...
HEY! THIS IS A *WIG* !!
IT TOOK YOU THIS LONG TO NOTICE?!
I DIDN'T TOUCH IT 'CAUSE I DIDN'T WANT MY NEW HAIR TO FALL OUT!

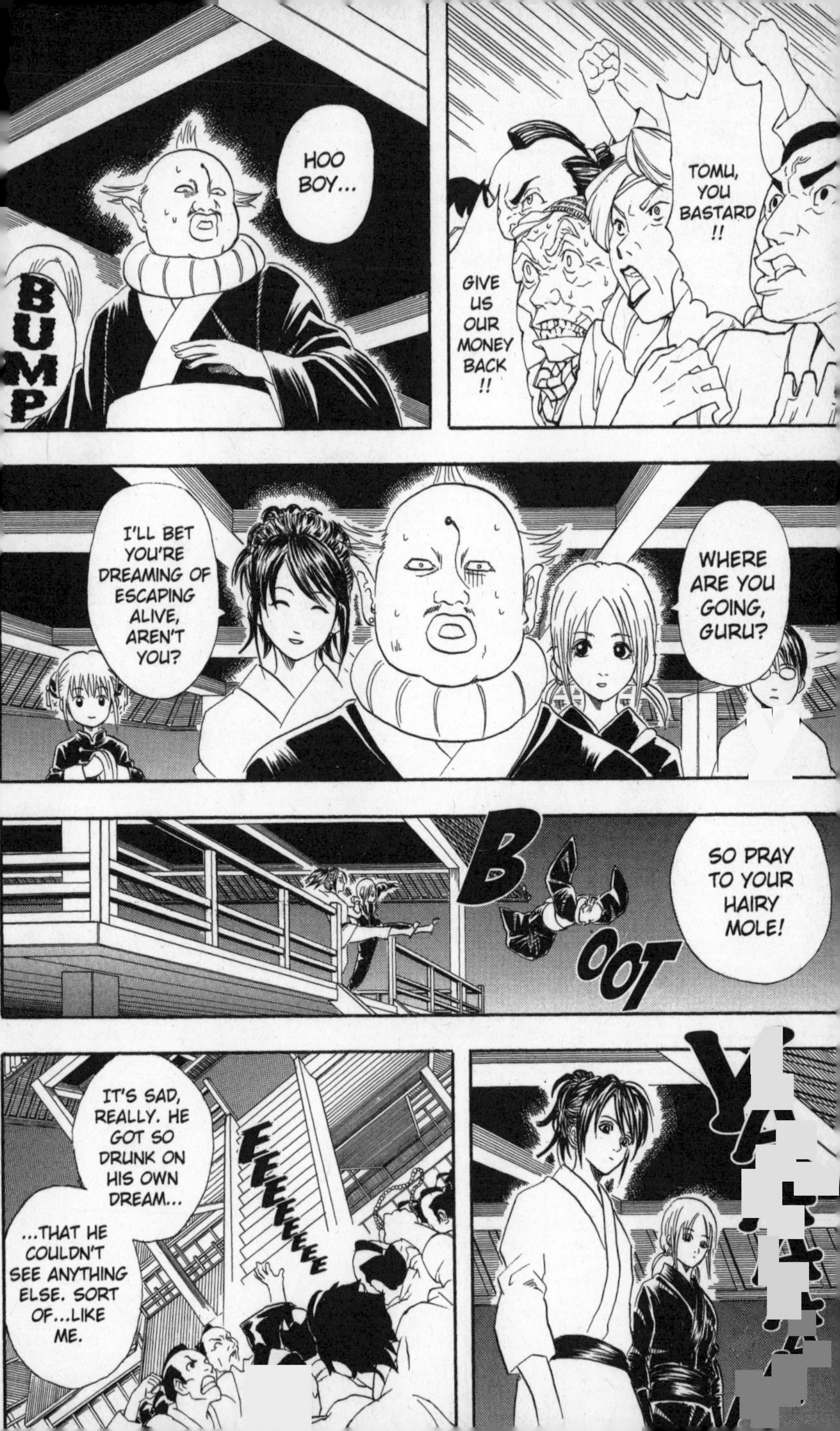
TOMU, YOU BASTARD!!
GIVE US OUR MONEY BACK!!
HOO BOY...
BUMP
WHERE ARE YOU GOING, GURU?
I'LL BET YOU'RE DREAMING OF ESCAPING ALIVE, AREN'T YOU?
SO PRAY TO YOUR HAIRY MOLE!
BOOT
IT'S SAD, REALLY. HE GOT SO DRUNK ON HIS OWN DREAM...
...THAT HE COULDN'T SEE ANYTHING ELSE. SORT OF...LIKE ME.
EEEEEEEE

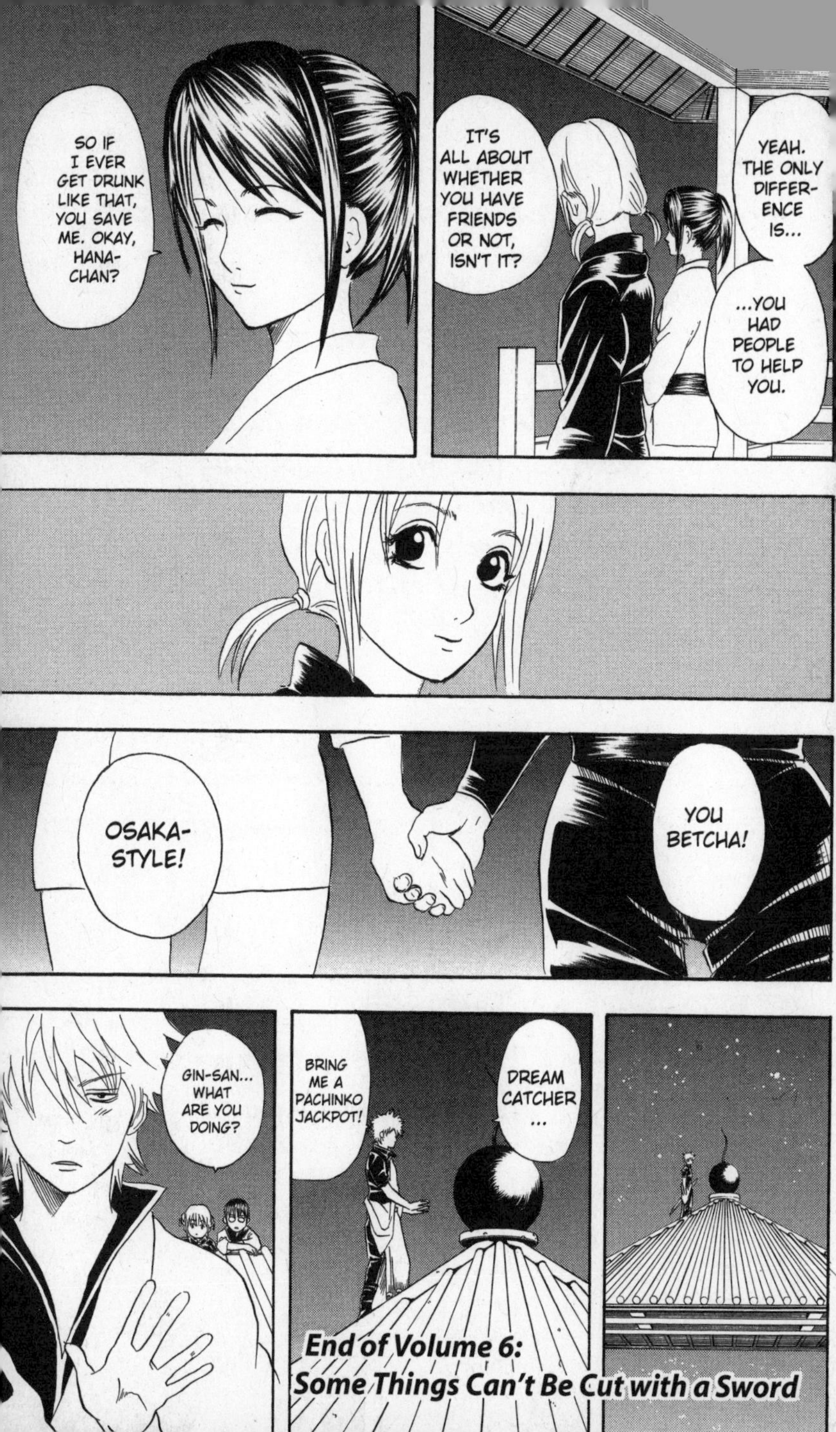
YEAH. THE ONLY DIFFER-ENCE IS...
...YOU HAD PEOPLE TO HELP YOU.
IT'S ALL ABOUT WHETHER YOU HAVE FRIENDS OR NOT, ISN'T IT?
SO IF I EVER GET DRUNK LIKE THAT, YOU SAVE ME. OKAY, HANA-CHAN?
YOU BETCHA!
OSAKA-STYLE!
DREAM CATCHER ...
BRING ME A PACHINKO JACKPOT!
GIN-SAN... WHAT ARE YOU DOING?

End of Volume 6: Some Things Can't Be Cut with a Sword

Another thing! Please don't send me letters saying you wish you'd bought the other Shinsengumi manga instead, because they hurt my feelings. Just keep those wishes to yourselves. In fact, take them to the grave with you.

This time I didn't really hang out with you readers much, but I'm still looking forward to your letters and questions, so please send them to the address below.

See you next volume!

Sayoooo-naraaaa!

Sorachi

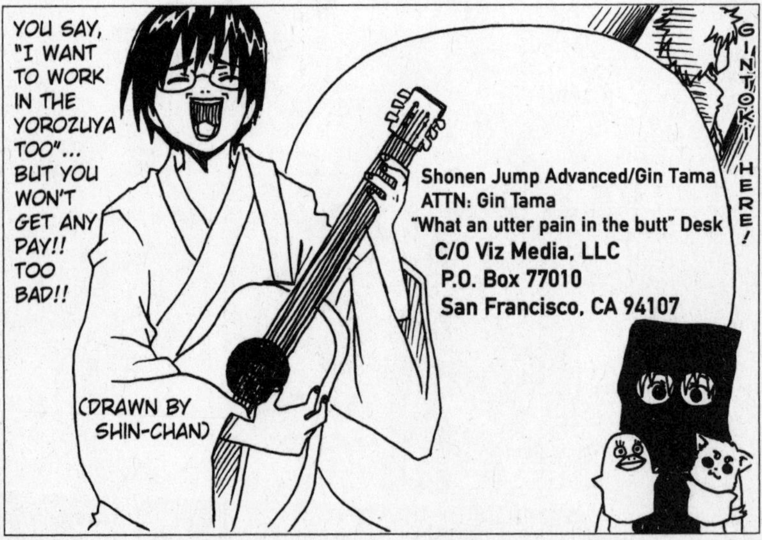

YOU SAY, "I WANT TO WORK IN THE YOROZUYA TOO"... BUT YOU WON'T GET ANY PAY!! TOO BAD!!
GINTOKI HERE!
(DRAWN BY SHIN-CHAN)

Shonen Jump Advanced/Gin Tama
ATTN: Gin Tama
"What an utter pain in the butt" Desk
C/O Viz Media, LLC
P.O. Box 77010
San Francisco, CA 94107

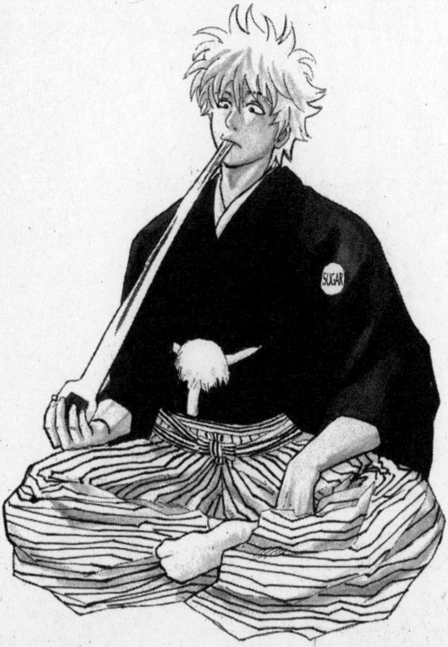
SUGAR

● Published on the cover of No. 5-6 (2005) joint issue of *Weekly Shonen JUMP*

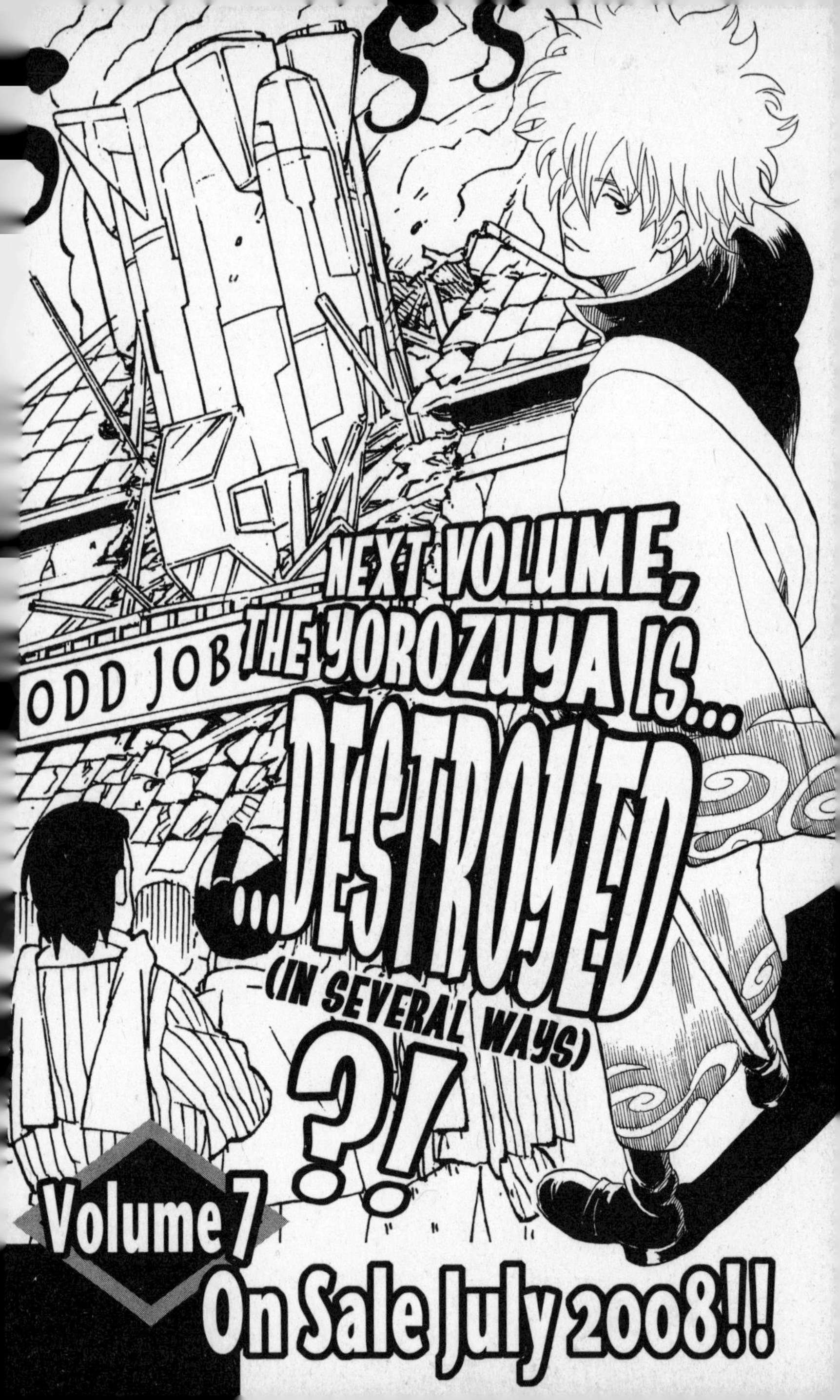

ODD JOB
NEXT VOLUME, THE YOROZUYA IS...
...DESTROYED
(IN SEVERAL WAYS)
?!
Volume 7
On Sale July 2008!!

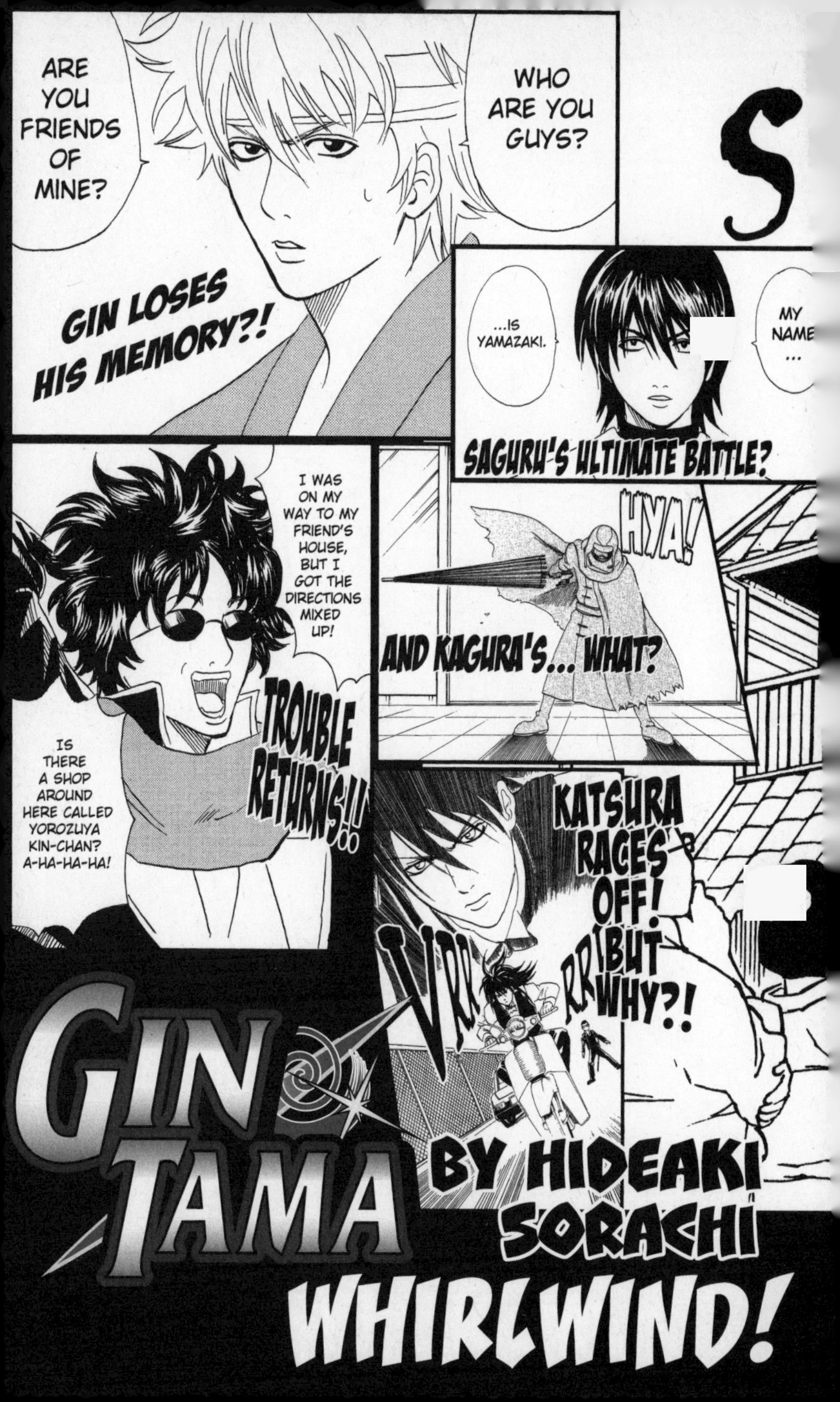
S
WHO ARE YOU GUYS?
ARE YOU FRIENDS OF MINE?
GIN LOSES HIS MEMORY?!
MY NAME...
...IS YAMAZAKI.
SAGURU'S ULTIMATE BATTLE?
HYA!
AND KAGURA'S... WHAT?
I WAS ON MY WAY TO MY FRIEND'S HOUSE, BUT I GOT THE DIRECTIONS MIXED UP!
IS THERE A SHOP AROUND HERE CALLED YOROZUYA KIN-CHAN? A-HA-HA-HA!
TROUBLE RETURNS!!
KATSURA RACES OFF! BUT WHY?!
VRRRRR
GIN TAMA
BY HIDEAKI SORACHI
WHIRLWIND!

Volume 7 Preview

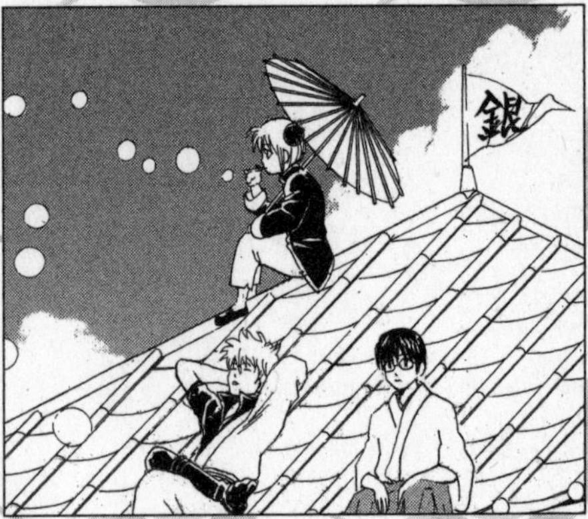

銀

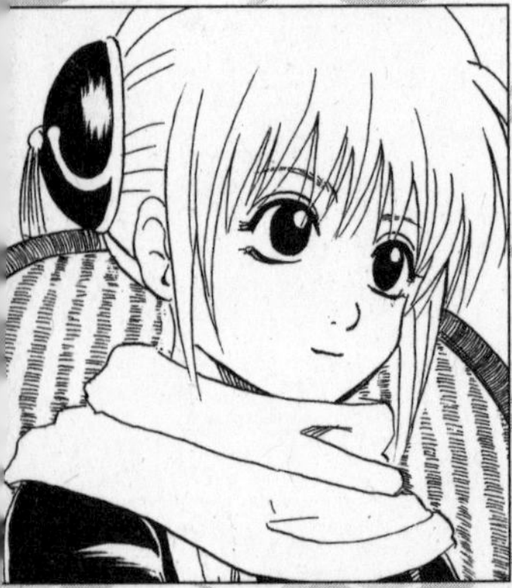

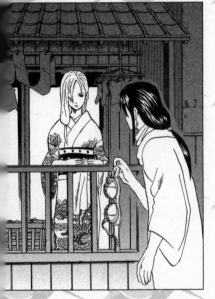

Yoruzuya Hit List
(Exploding Targets)

1. The Shinsengumi elite police and Gin (innocent bystander)
2. Chief Kondo and Gin's new workplace (during their shift)
3. Human shields named Kondo, Yamazaki, and Gin
4. The special New Year's issue of *Shonen Jump* magazine and Gin
5. Gin's apartment (more than once)
6. Fireworks and…not Gin

Plus, the secret identity of famed monster hunter Umi Bozu revealed at last!

COMING JULY 2008

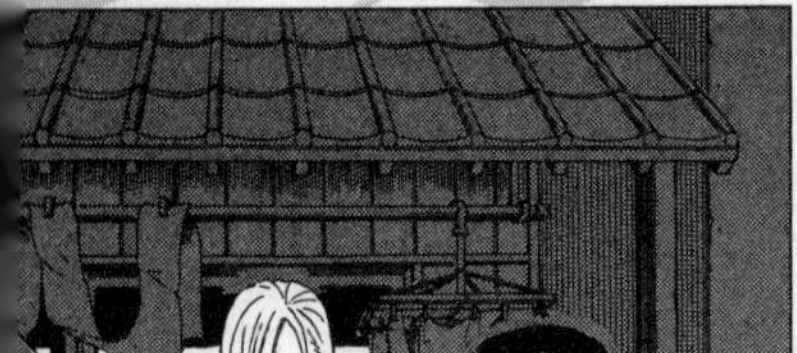

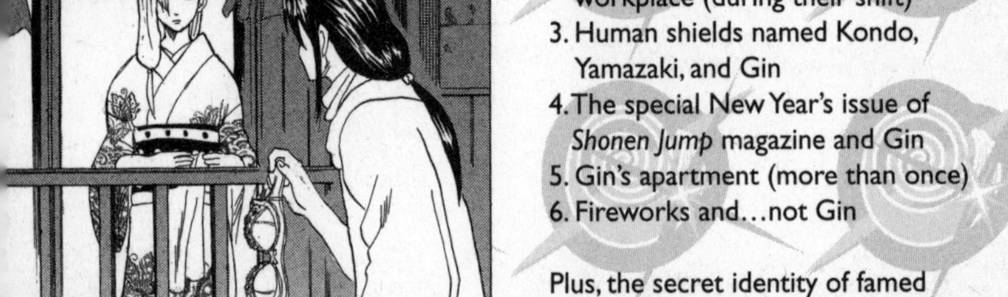

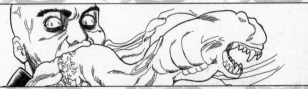

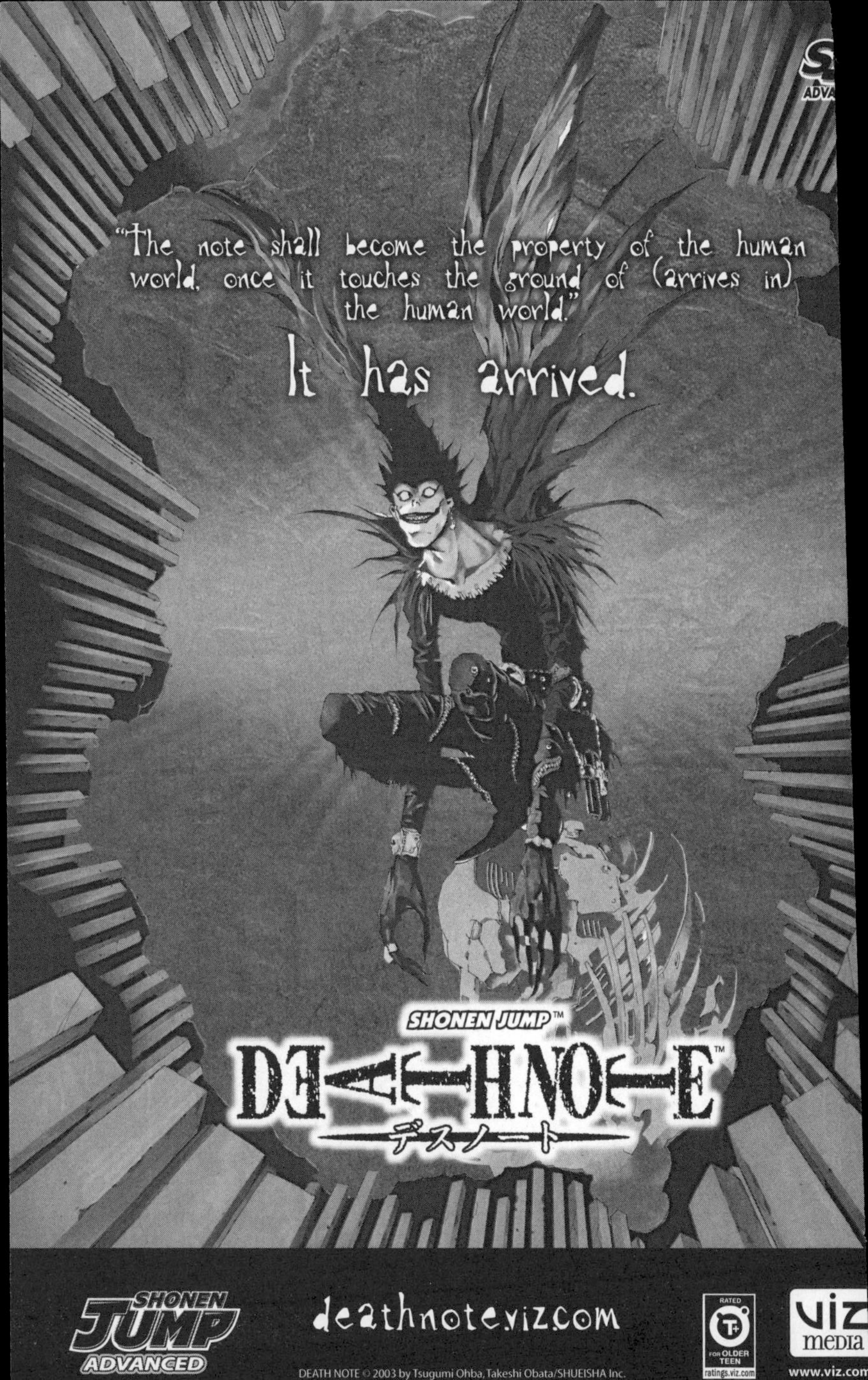
"The note shall become the property of the human world, once it touches the ground of (arrives in) the human world."
It has arrived.
SHONEN JUMP™
DEATH NOTE™
デスノート
SHONEN JUMP ADVANCED
deathnote.viz.com
RATED T+ FOR OLDER TEEN
ratings.viz.com
viz media
www.viz.com
DEATH NOTE © 2003 by Tsugumi Ohba, Takeshi Obata/SHUEISHA Inc.

SHONEN JUMP

DEATH NOTE
デスノート

"The human whose name is written in this note shall die."

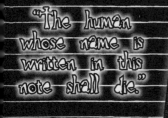

AN ORIGINAL NOVEL BASED ON THE CHARACTERS AND CONCEPTS FROM THE POPULAR MANGA SERIES

READ WHERE IT ALL BEGAN IN THE MANGA—ALL 12 VOLUMES AVAILABLE NOW

A GUIDE TO THE MANGA SERIES, COMPLETE WITH CHARACTER BIOS, STORYLINE SUMMARIES, INTERVIEWS WITH CREATORS TSUGUMI OHBA AND TAKESHI OBATA, PRODUCTION NOTES AND COMMENTARIES, AND BONUS MANGA PAGES

SHONEN JUMP
ADVANCED

ON SALE AT
deathnote.viz.com
ALSO AVAILABLE AT YOUR LOCAL BOOKSTORE AND COMIC STORE.

RATED
T+
FOR OLDER
TEEN
ratings.viz.com

VIZ
media
www.viz.com

DEATH NOTE © 2003 by Tsugumi Ohba, Takeshi Obata/SHUEISHA Inc.
DEATH NOTE - ANOTHER NOTE LOS ANGELES BB RENZOKU SATSUJIN JIKEN - © 2006 by NISIO ISIN, Tsugumi Ohba, Takeshi Obata/SHUEISHA Inc.
DEATH NOTE HOW TO READ 13 © 2006 by Tsugumi Ohba, Takeshi Obata/SHUEISHA Inc.

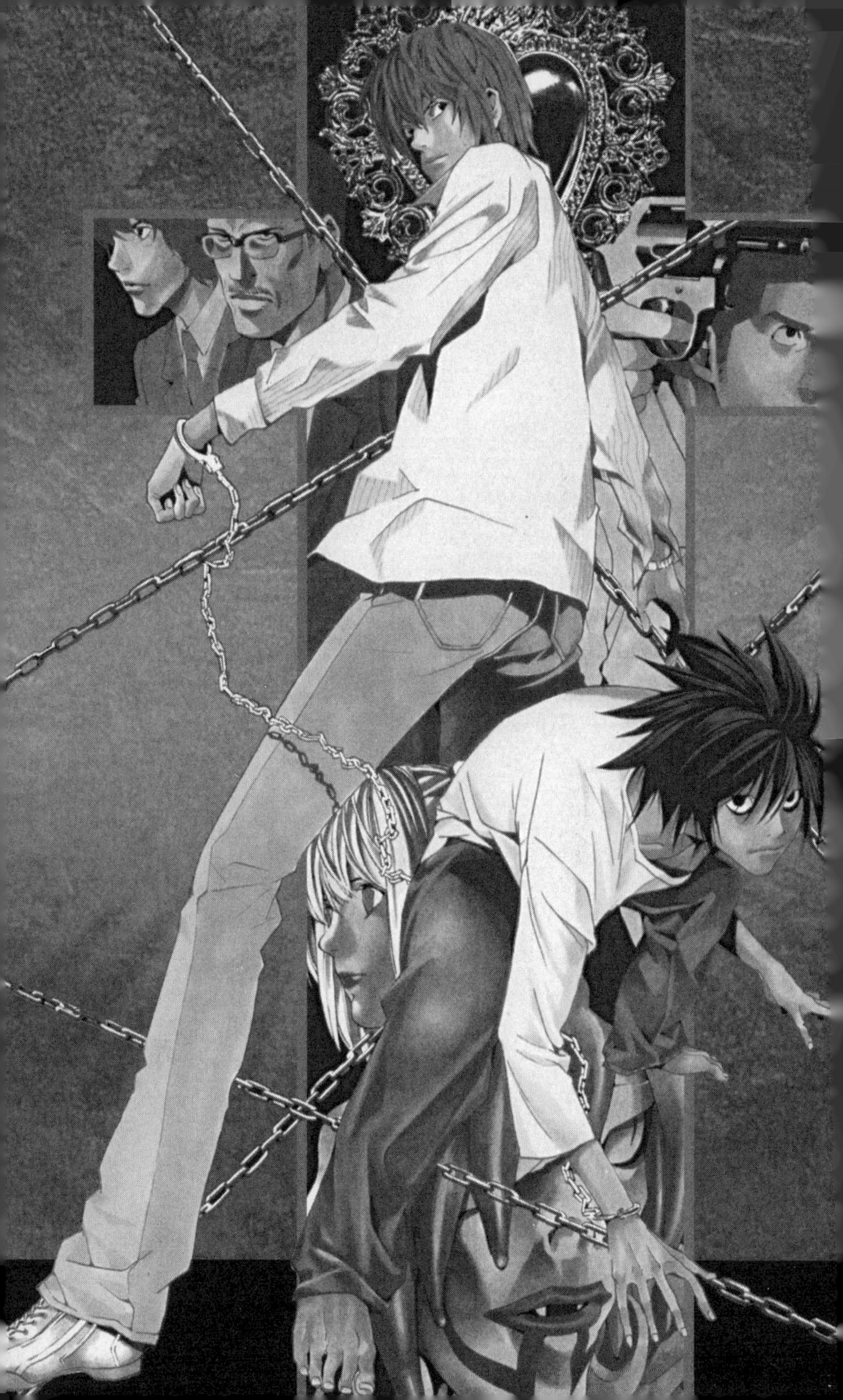

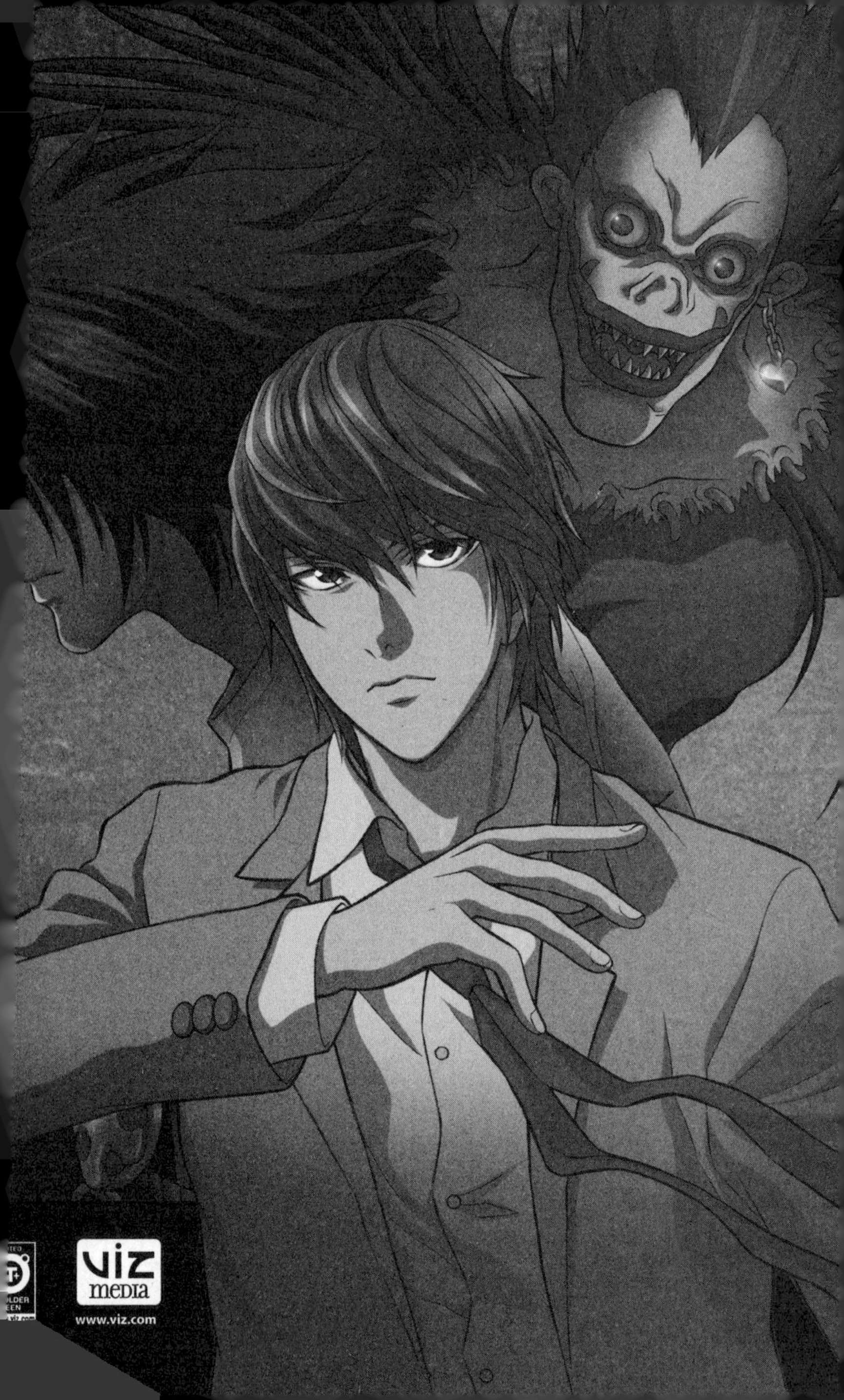
VIZ media
www.viz.com

SHONEN JUMP

DEATH NOTE
デスノート

"The human who uses this note can neither go to Heaven or Hell..."

WATCH THE FIERCE FIGHT IN ORIGINAL AND UNCUT EPISODES NOW ON DVD

COLLECTOR'S FIGURINE EDITIONS ALSO AVAILABLE— LIMITED TO 15,000

ANIME ALSO AVAILABLE FOR DOWNLOAD. FIND OUT MORE AT:
deathnote.viz.com

SHONEN JUMP HOME VIDEO

Based on the comic "DEATH NOTE" by Tsugumi Ohba, Takeshi Obata. Originally serialized in "WEEKLY SHONEN JUMP" published by Shueisha Inc. ©Tsugumi Ohba, Takeshi Obata/Shueisha. © DNDP, VAP, Shueisha, Madhouse. SHONEN JUMP™ and DEATH NOTE™ are trademarks of Shueisha, Inc. in the United States and other countries.

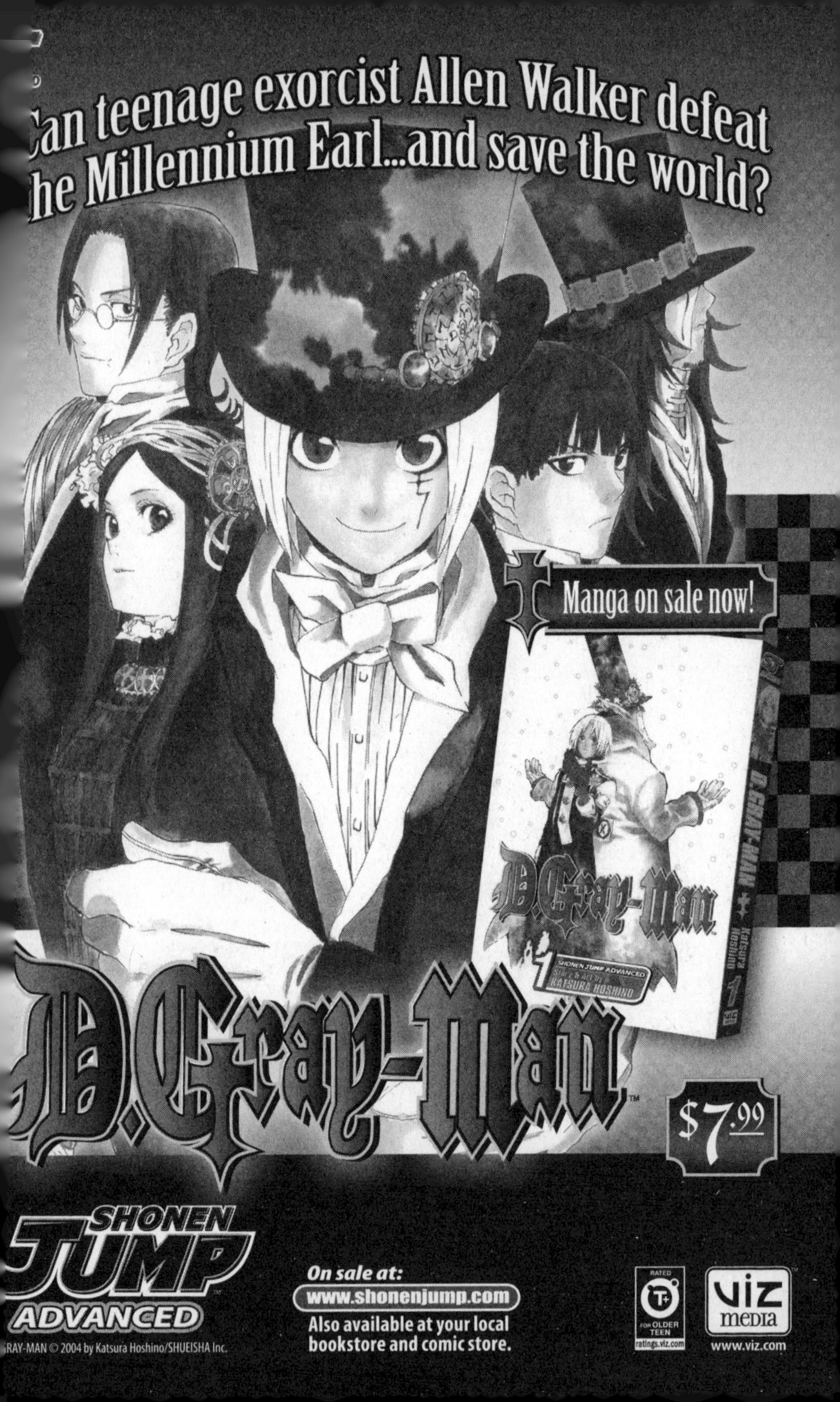

Can teenage exorcist Allen Walker defeat
the Millennium Earl...and save the world?
Manga on sale now!
D.Gray-man
SHONEN JUMP ADVANCED
Story & Art by KATSURA HOSHINO
1
D.GRAY-MAN
Katsura Hoshino
D.Gray-man™
$7.99
SHONEN JUMP ADVANCED
On sale at:
www.shonenjump.com
Also available at your local bookstore and comic store.
RATED T+ FOR OLDER TEEN
ratings.viz.com
VIZ media
www.viz.com
RAY-MAN © 2004 by Katsura Hoshino/SHUEISHA Inc.

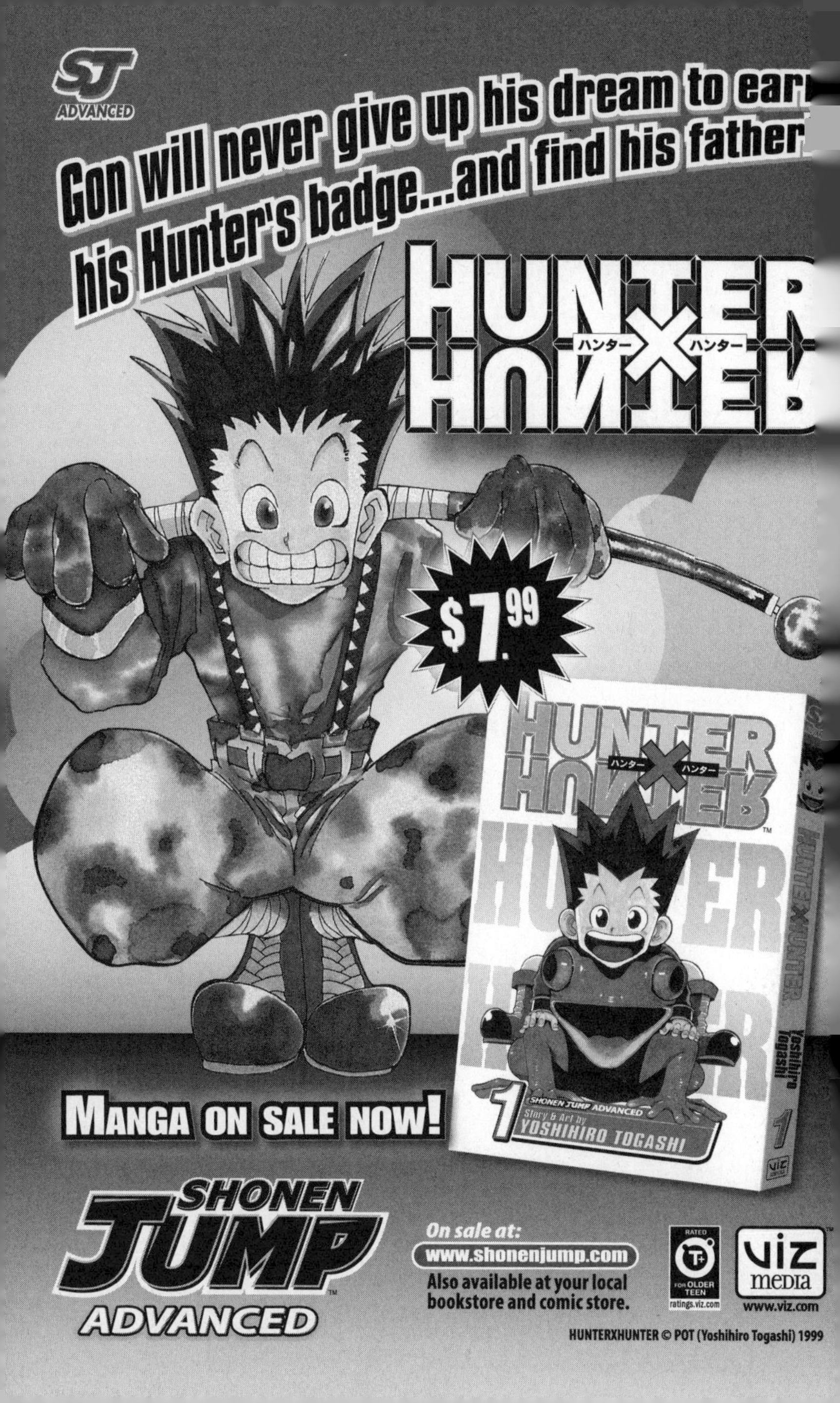

SJ ADVANCED
Gon will never give up his dream to ear
his Hunter's badge...and find his father
HUNTER × HUNTER
ハンター ハンター
$7.99
HUNTER × HUNTER
SHONEN JUMP ADVANCED
Story & Art by YOSHIHIRO TOGASHI
MANGA ON SALE NOW!
SHONEN JUMP ADVANCED
On sale at:
www.shonenjump.com
Also available at your local bookstore and comic store.
RATED T+ FOR OLDER TEEN ratings.viz.com
viz media
www.viz.com
HUNTERXHUNTER © POT (Yoshihiro Togashi) 1999

Tell us what you think about SHONEN JUMP manga!

Our survey is now available online.
Go to: www.SHONENJUMP.com/mangasurvey

Help us make our product offering better!

THE REAL ACTION STARTS IN...
SHONEN JUMP
THE WORLD'S MOST POPULAR MANGA
www.shonenjump.com

SJ ADVANCED

SJ

VIZ media

BLEACH © 2001 by Tite Kubo/SHUEISHA Inc. NARUTO © 1999 by Masashi Kishimoto/SHUEISHA Inc.
DEATH NOTE © 2003 by Tsugumi Ohba, Takeshi Obata/SHUEISHA Inc. ONE PIECE © 1997 by Eiichiro Oda/SHUEISHA Inc.

SHONEN JUMP

THE WORLD'S MOST POPULAR MANGA

12 ISSUES FOR ONLY $29.95*

THAT'S 50% OFF THE NEWSSTAND PRICE!

Each issue of SHONEN JUMP contains the coolest manga available in the U.S., anime news, and info on video & card games, toys AND more!

SUBSCRIBE TODAY and Become a Member of the ST Sub Club!

- **ENJOY** 12 HUGE action-packed issues
- **SAVE** 50% OFF the cover price
- **ACCESS** exclusive areas of www.shonenjump.com
- **RECEIVE** FREE members-only gifts

Available ONLY to Subscribers!

RATED **T** FOR TEEN
ratings.viz.com

VIZ media

www.viz.cc

3 EASY WAYS TO SUBSCRIBE!

1) Send in the subscription order form from this book OR
2) Log on to: www.shonenjump.com OR
3) Call 1-800-541-7919

*Canada price for 12 issues: $41.95 USD, including GST, HST, and QST. US/CAN orders only. Allow 6-8 weeks for delivery.
BLEACH © 2001 by Tite Kubo/SHUEISHA Inc. NARUTO © 1999 by Masashi Kishimoto/SHUEISHA Inc.
GINTAMA © 2003 by Hideaki Sorachi/SHUEISHA Inc. ONE PIECE © 1997 by Eiichiro Oda/SHUEISHA Inc.

Save **50% OFF** the cover price!

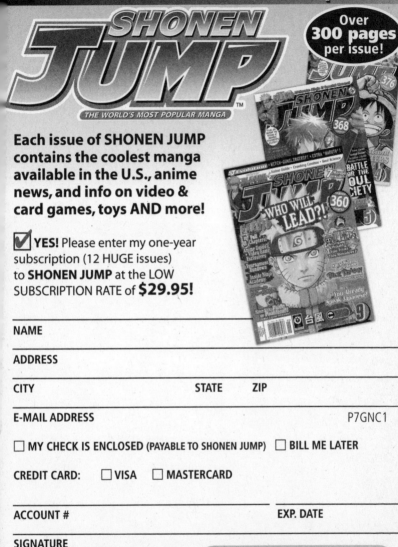

SHONEN JUMP
THE WORLD'S MOST POPULAR MANGA

Over **300 pages** per issue!

Each issue of SHONEN JUMP contains the coolest manga available in the U.S., anime news, and info on video & card games, toys AND more!

☑ **YES!** Please enter my one-year subscription (12 HUGE issues) to **SHONEN JUMP** at the LOW SUBSCRIPTION RATE of **$29.95!**

NAME

ADDRESS

CITY   STATE   ZIP

E-MAIL ADDRESS   P7GNC1

☐ MY CHECK IS ENCLOSED (PAYABLE TO SHONEN JUMP)   ☐ BILL ME LATER

CREDIT CARD: ☐ VISA   ☐ MASTERCARD

ACCOUNT #   EXP. DATE

SIGNATURE

CLIP AND MAIL TO →

SHONEN JUMP
Subscriptions Service Dept.
P.O. Box 515
Mount Morris, IL 61054-0515

Make checks payable to: **SHONEN JUMP**. Canada price for 12 issues: $41.95 USD, including GST, HST and QST. US/CAN orders only. Allow 6-8 weeks for delivery.

BLEACH © 2001 by Tite Kubo/SHUEISHA Inc. NARUTO © 1999 by Masashi Kishimoto/SHUEISHA Inc.
ONE PIECE © 1997 by Eiichiro Oda/SHUEISHA Inc.

RATED **T** FOR TEEN
ratings.viz.com